THE COMPLETE GUIDE TO
Nonprofit Corporations

Ted Nicholas

Enterprise · Dearborn
a division of Dearborn Publishing Group, Inc.

While a great deal of care has been taken to provide accurate and current information, the ideas, suggestions, general principles and conclusions presented in this text are subject to local, state and federal laws and regulations, court cases and any revisions of same. The reader is thus urged to consult legal counsel regarding any points of law—this publication should not be used as a substitute for competent legal advice.

Publisher: Kathleen A. Welton
Acquisitions Editor: Patrick J. Hogan
Associate Editor: Karen A. Christensen
Senior Project Editor: Jack L. Kiburz
Interior Design: Lucy Jenkins

Published by Enterprise • Dearborn
a division of Dearborn Publishing Group, Inc.

Printed in the United States of America

93   94   95   10   9   8   7   6   5   4   3   2   1

Library of Congress Cataloging-in-Publication Data

Nicholas, Ted, 1934–
    The complete guide to nonprofit corporations / Ted Nicholas
      p. cm.
    Includes index
    ISBN 0-79310-615-X (pbk.)
    1. Nonprofit organizations—Management.   I. Title.
  HD62.6.N53 1993
  658'.048—dc20   93-10899
                                             CIP

Books by Ted Nicholas

The Complete Book of Corporate Forms

The Complete Guide to Business Agreements

The Complete Guide to Consulting Success (coauthor, Howard Shenson)

The Complete guide to "S" Corporations

The Executive's Business Letter Book

43 Proven Ways To Raise Capital for Your Small Business

The Golden Mailbox: How To Get Rich Direct Marketing Your Product

How To Form Your Own Corporation Without a Lawyer for under $75.00

How To Get a Top Job in Tough Times (coauthor, Bethany Waller)

How To Get Your Own Trademark

Secrets of Entrepreneurial Leadership: Building Top Performance Through Trust and Teamwork

Contents

Chapter 11: A Step-by-Step Organizing Plan   115

Chapter 12: Preparing the Application for Tax Exemption   153

The History of the Nonprofit Corporation

HOW WE GOT TO WHERE WE ARE NOW

Nonprofit organizations, or their equivalent, have been with us from the very dawn of civilization. In the ancient Chinese and Egyptian civilizations of 4,000 years ago, the idea of setting aside wealth as an endowment for the support of religious and educational activities was common. This notion of charity has been an integral part of virtually all religions and cultures. throughout recorded history.

The concept of the corporation as an association of people to which the authority of the state gives formal recognition as a legal entity (a creation endowed with the same kind of rights and powers associated with a person) has existed as long as has the very idea of people joining together to accomplish common goals.

Our present-day laws of incorporation come most directly from English law. English law established the principle that a corporation is an organization of people with rights and duties separate from the rights and duties of its individual members, and that these members are not personally entitled to the assets of the corporation, nor are they liable for its debts.

English law derived in turn from the laws of ancient Rome. Even Roman law recognized distinctions between corporations according to their expressed purposes and categorized corporations as civil, ecclesiastical, law or eleemosynary (defined by Webster as relating to or supported by charity). The latter type of corporation as conceived by the early Romans was indeed the forerunner of today's nonprofit corporation.

As for the precedent of the state granting special status and privileges to nonprofit corporations, that concept, too, is well established in the history of law. The *linchpin privilege* or exemption from taxes can be readily traced to medieval days, when charitable organizations were felt to be special and thus exempted from taxes and other levies. In the United States, when Congress imposed the first federal income tax on corporations in 1894, the law included—plain as could be—an exemption for nonprofit corporations and charitable institutions. Similar exemptions for nonprofit organizations were already well established in the property tax statutes of the states by the time the federal government got around to writing its corporation tax law. The tax exemption for a variety of nonprofit corporations has remained a solid part of federal income tax law since 1894.

Under a 1950 federal tax reform act, nonprofit organizations with tax-exempt status are required to pay taxes on any income derived from what is termed *unrelated businesses*. Unrelated businesses are understood to mean commercial enterprises such as factories, stores, apartment buildings, etc., that are clearly not related to the primary purposes and goals of the nonprofit organizations that own or operate them. This is still true, even if the enterprises may serve as a source of revenue that can be used to support the organization's stated nonprofit purposes and endeavors.

However, this section of the tax code is subject to varying exceptions and interpretations. For example, is the operation of a commercial television station related or unrelated to the goals and purposes of a nonprofit university? The courts have held that the income of a commercial TV station owned by a nonprofit university is exempt from taxation, thus permitting the revenues of this business operation to go into the endowment fund of the school.

Consider the case of nonprofit, tax-exempt fraternal organizations. They may operate insurance programs, health services and other commercial business services free of income taxation as long as sales are restricted exclusively to the organization's members and the earnings are used for the organization's nonprofit goals.

The Internal Revenue Service has considered the advertising revenues derived from the publications of nonprofit organizations to be unrelated business and subject to taxation. Such magazines as *National Geographic, Smithsonian* and *Natural History* fall into this category. This particular IRS ruling has been challenged legally by at least one nonprofit publisher. The American Chemical Society has claimed that since advertisements in its publications are all of a scientific nature, they are related to the central purpose of the society. Thus, the revenue derived from this is not the result of unrelated business at all. Recently, *Ms.* magazine (which began its life as a strictly commercial, profit-making business venture) was reformulated. After following a few simple legal procedures, *Ms.* magazine is now the official publication of a duly tax-exempt, nonprofit organization—The Ms. Foundation.

Today, close to one million organizations in the United States hold tax-exempt status as nonprofit organizations. According to some sources, the entire body of public service, nonprofit, voluntary action organizations is so substantial that it is, in effect, a *third sector* of the U.S. economy. The other two sectors are the public (government) and private (business) sectors. That's not an unreasonable assumption, considering the significant fact that total annual revenues of all nonprofit organizations in the United States amount to over $500 billion. About 11 percent of all property in the United States is owned by nonprofit organizations, including, of course, churches, universities and hospitals. Some 10 percent of all service workers and about 17 percent of professional workers in the United States are employed by nonprofit organizations. All told, nonprofit organizations in this country employ about five million people, more than 5 percent of the entire U.S. work force!

It has been estimated that between one-third and one-half of all corporations existing in the United States today are nonprofit corporations. The IRS currently approves over 36,000 nonprofit organizations per year for tax-exempt status.

What does all of this mean for someone contemplating the creation of a nonprofit corporation? It means that you will *not* be sailing in uncharted waters. The type and form of organization you want to start are universally recognized and firmly established in law and historical precedent. The rights and obligations, as well as the special privileges, of nonprofit organizations are deeply rooted in the laws and traditions of civilization.

Although there are critics of this venerable concept—particularly of the special status and exemption from taxes for nonprofit corporations—they have had relatively little influence on the development of pertinent laws. Much more widely recognized and accepted is the belief that, on the whole, these organizations perform beneficial services not available from any other source. And, the privileges granted to nonprofit organizations are not only deserved but also are the legal right of any organization meeting the requirements clearly spelled out in the corporation laws of the states.

2

The Advantages of a Nonprofit Corporation

Because nonprofit organizations are presumed to be charitable in nature, the law grants them special privileges. It is the government's way of paying these organizations back for their contributions to the *general welfare*. But, as you've learned in the preceding chapter, not all nonprofit organizations are incorporated. What, then, are the advantages of forming a nonprofit corporation as opposed to alternative legal forms?

There are many benefits. Some are the same as those commonly enjoyed by *for-profit* business corporations. Others are unique to the nonprofit corporation. Perhaps the greatest advantage of all—granted exclusively to organizations with bona fide nonprofit status—is exemption from taxes at federal, state and local levels.

TAX EXEMPTION

The tax advantages enjoyed by nonprofit corporations are discussed in detail in Chapter 9. At this point, suffice it to say that if a nonprofit corporation qualifies for a federal tax exemption, little or none of its income or assets will be taxable by the federal government. In addition, once a nonprofit corporation is granted tax-exempt status by the Internal Revenue Service, it can usually expect to be exempted by state and local taxing agencies as well. In this way, the nonprofit corporation may also escape the major burden of local taxation on its real and personal property holdings as well as other state and local levies.

A word of caution: Exemption from taxation is not synonymous with non-profit status, nor does it flow automatically from an organization's incorporation as a not-for-profit agency. Once established, a nonprofit corporation must then apply to the IRS (and to separate state and local tax authorities) for recognition of tax-exempt status. Although the application process is neither complicated nor rigorous, and relatively few applicants are turned down, tax agencies, both federal and state, have been making more careful and thorough reviews of requests for tax exemption.

The primary reason for the increase in governmental attention is that the number of tax-exempt organizations has grown so much in the past decade or two that the phenomenon is considered in some quarters to be a serious threat to the tax-base stability of many political jurisdictions. Churches, hospitals, nursing homes, chambers of commerce, charities, social service agencies and the myriad other nonprofit organizations in most communities may have tax-free real estate holdings. In some cities and towns, a substantial portion of the entire lot of privately held real estate is owned by tax-exempt organizations. This means there isn't any revenue flowing into local tax coffers from this sector.

Some exempt organizations make voluntary payments for community services they utilize. Nevertheless, as corporate and individual taxes rise, those who must pay them often fault the tax-exempt sector as a prime reason for the increases. Even the tax-exempt status of churches, protected from the very beginning of the tax code, has been questioned in recent years, particularly in reference to church investments in secular properties.

One caution must be noted: The shield from taxation is not all-inclusive. The exemption does not necessarily apply to each and every dollar of income a nonprofit corporation earns. Some sources of income such as advertising space sold in publications may be subject to income tax at regular corporate rates. The same may be true of the gain from commercial enterprises similar to those of for-profit corporations—rental income from properties the corporation owns, for instance. Fortunately, if it can be demonstrated that this income is necessary to further the purposes of the nonprofit corporation, it should escape taxation, barring major revisions in the tax codes.

THE RIGHT TO SOLICIT FUNDS

Depending on the nature and purpose of the organization, the legal authority to solicit donations, gifts, bequests and other contributions from the public can be essential to its financial viability. Equal to tax exemption, this privilege can be a key to the nonprofit corporation's existence. Of course, the right to solicit is enhanced by the organization's tax-exempt status. This permits contributors to deduct their gifts from their own personal income tax liability.

In some states, the fund-raising privilege is granted automatically to a nonprofit corporation as soon as the Articles of Incorporation are filed. In other states, certain prerequisites must be met before the fund-soliciting sanction is granted. You might have to submit your corporation's proposed operating budget indicating how publicly solicited funds will be used.

Once awarded the privilege of soliciting from the public, a nonprofit corporation may have to file an annual financial report with a state or local regulatory agency. The required report may consist simply of a statement of income and expenditure of funds received from the public. In a few instances, though, a nonprofit charitable corporation's expenditure of public contributions must meet specific guidelines. One requirement might be to spend at least 25 percent of the funds for the program services outlined in the organization's charter. Another might be to spend no more than 75 percent of public contributions for administrative and fund-raising costs.

LOW POSTAGE RATES

In any incorporated enterprise, postage is a continual (and usually sizable) part of the operating budget. Qualified nonprofit corporations can use the U.S. mails at substantially lower rates than commercial firms or private individuals. To enjoy this mailing privilege, a tax-exempt nonprofit corporation need only apply to the U.S. Postal Service for a special permit. With this permit, the corporation can mail third class at 11.1 cents per letter, or, by taking maximum advantage of various discounts, as low as 5.4 cents a letter. The same kind of mailing would cost a for-profit corporation 19.8 cents per letter. An individual, of course, must pay 29 cents to mail a letter first class, which is the only rate private citizens are allowed to use for letters.

The importance of the mailing rate advantage is directly proportional to the volume of mail the nonprofit corporation generates in the course of its business. Membership solicitations are usually mailed third class. Nonprofit corporations that rely on membership income can use the mail even more extensively to service their members. So potential savings from a special mailing permit are considerable.

EXEMPTION FROM LABOR RULES

In a number of states, and under the federal government's National Labor Relations Act, nonprofit organizations are exempt from the rules and requirements of union collective bargaining. This means that the nonprofit corporation cannot be forced to engage in collective bargaining on wages and benefits with its employees, even if they should be represented by a labor union.

In some states, nonprofit corporations are also exempted from payments other employers are legally required to make. These involve state or other unemployment compensation funds. Considering that these contributions by employers usually amount to anywhere from 1.6 to 9.1 percent of payroll costs, the possible savings in the operating budget for the nonprofit corporation can be significant.

EXEMPTION FROM SPECIAL DUTIES

The Internal Revenue Code exempts certain nonprofit organizations, including those with educational and charitable purposes, from specific import and customs duties. While this may not benefit every nonprofit corporation, one whose program involves the import of artworks from overseas, for instance, would be able to escape the sometimes hefty duties imposed by U.S. Customs.

IMMUNITY FROM TORT LIABILITY

Although this privilege has been abolished in a number of states and is sharply limited in others, in more than a few states the law still provides that nonprofit charitable organizations are immune to tort liability. The immunity is limited to damages or other harm resulting from the negligence of their agents or employees. This could, of course, effectively lower insurance costs for a nonprofit organization. It is important to recognize, however, that where it exists, the immunity protects only the nonprofit corporation—not the agent or employee where negligence injures someone. So, for example, if a truck driver for a nonprofit corporation negligently causes an accident and injures a pedestrian, the nonprofit corporation may be immune from liability, but the truck driver will be fully liable for his or her negligence.

The following advantages are enjoyed by all corporations, whether they are operated for-profit or not-for-profit. These benefits are especially advantageous to nonprofit corporations because they are not available to all unincorporated nonprofit organizations.

LEGAL LIFE

A nonprofit corporation is a legal entity with a life of its own. Even though someone or some group of people must create it, the corporation subsequently exists separately and apart from those people. In effect, the corporation is an artificial person.

In the eyes of the law, a nonprofit corporation is guaranteed all the rights and powers of a natural person under the Constitution of the United States. So a nonprofit corporation may conduct whatever business it wants to in accordance with its charter. It can operate inside and outside the state in which it was incorporated. It may enter into contracts. It can own real and personal property, borrow money and secure its debts by mortgaging its property. It may hire and fire employees. It may even join an association or become a member of another corporation. It can sue and be sued in court. It can be fined but not jailed; however, its officers can be imprisoned.

LIMITED LIABILITY

As a legal entity, the nonprofit corporation is liable for debts it incurs and for court judgments against it. But the reach of its creditors and the courts is generally limited to the corporation's assets. People affiliated with the corporation—its founders, directors, officers, members and employees—are not personally liable for the corporation's debts. Their own personal assets are generally beyond the grasp of the corporation and its creditors. This is a very important and meaningful advantage of the nonprofit corporation.

The organizers and operators of an unincorporated nonprofit organization do not enjoy this protection. They are personally liable for the debts of the unincorporated nonprofit entity.

The shield against personal liability is one of the best arguments for the corporate form. However, as with any rule, there are exceptions. Foremost is that the law does not allow a person to use incorporation as a shield from liability for his or her own illegal or willfully irresponsible acts. The court will not regard the identities of the corporation and its personnel as separate in the face of evidence that any of those individuals have used the corporate entity to perpetrate or protect fraud, crime or other illegal acts. An example would be an officer who ran up debts for the corporation knowing there were not sufficient assets or operating funds to meet these obligations. Wrong- doers can't hide behind the corporate veil in such cases.

Furthermore, because the law requires that corporate bylaws designate an officer or employee of the corporation as responsible for its financial reporting and payment of taxes, government taxing agencies can hold that individual personally responsible if he or she fails to file the required financial reports or to pay taxes.

Directors and officers of a corporation have a fiduciary duty. They are expected to perform their jobs in the best interests of the corporation. If they do not, and the corporation is harmed as a consequence, a court can hold these individuals personally liable for resulting financial judgments. An example of this would be an officer who mixed personal financial affairs with those of the corporation to the detriment of the corporation.

CONTINUOUS EXISTENCE

The people involved with the nonprofit corporation may come and go, but the corporation lives on. To a far greater degree than less formally organized nonprofit organizations, the corporation has substance and permanence. For this reason alone, banks and other sources of funds usually view incorporated nonprofit organizations more favorably than unincorporated organizations, whose existence may depend on the founders or operators. If these individuals die or lose interest, their organization can cease to exist. Not so with nonprofit corporations.

At the same time, it is not true that, once incorporated, an organization is totally beyond the control of its founders and directors. Just as corporations are created, they can be dissolved. This can be done through a simple majority vote of the governing board or the general membership.

ORGANIZATIONAL FORMALITY

In any group of people, a variety of temperaments and interests is represented. It is human nature for members of the group to promote individual concerns. Incompatibility can result, especially as the group becomes larger. An unincorporated group, no matter how lofty its goals, can find itself so weakened or slowed by the necessity to rule on continual consensus that little (if anything) is accomplished.

Incorporation places the purpose and structure of an organization above the personal interests and differences of its members. With incorporation, a nonprofit group acquires a widely recognized form that carries with it a large measure of legally stipulated structure and procedure.

The corporate law of the state of incorporation will specify what structure the corporation must take. The key to that structure, as well as the answer to the problem of incompatibility, is centralized management. Corporation laws require a minimum number of directors, a certain set of officers and the like. The law will stipulate that officers bear a fiduciary responsibility to the corporation and conduct the corporation's affairs responsibly, under threat of personal liability. The law will also lay out certain procedures the corporation must follow. The procedures cover such matters as electing the corporation's board of directors and operating officers. They also provide for a constitution and bylaws as its operational framework.

The law will require the drafting and maintenance of certain documents (Articles of Incorporation, bylaws, minutes of meetings) and a set procedure for changing any of these documents. Reusable forms for several of the basic necessary forms are included in this book. In short, a nonprofit corporation must be run in an orderly and reasonably efficient manner as prescribed by universally recognized rules. The law puts the government in a position to ensure that this happens.

EMPLOYEE BENEFITS

A nonprofit corporation can establish a fringe benefits program for its employees, including directors and officers. The benefits can be as attractive as those provided by for-profit business corporations. In addition, the benefits package can be far more economical for the corporation and beneficial to the employees than any program that could be offered by unincorporated organizations.

The nonprofit corporation can establish an employee pension and retirement income plan. It can provide for sick pay and vacation pay. It may arrange for group life, accident and health insurance coverage for its officers and employees. It can elect to cover its employees' personal medical expenses that are not covered by the group insurance plans, provided that the corporation can pay all or part of the cost of the various employee benefits it sets up. It can require some contribution from the employees covered by the fringes.

FISCAL YEAR FLEXIBILITY

Corporations are not required to match their financial recordkeeping year to the calendar year. They may elect to declare any 12 consecutive months as their fiscal year. This fiscal year flexibility can be particularly advantageous to a corporation operated for-profit, as the extent of its tax liability can be affected by the timing of its tax returns.

While a tax-exempt nonprofit corporation may not be as vitally concerned with that burden, the freedom to determine its fiscal year can be advantageous. For example, a nonprofit corporation might be able to achieve some management efficiencies, with resulting savings in operating costs, by tying its financial reporting to a fiscal year that reflects the seasonal or other cyclical pattern of the corporation's income or operations.

3

Disadvantages of a
Nonprofit Corporation

You have just read about the advantages of incorporating your nonprofit organization, and you may have inferred from the generally positive tone of that chapter that there is no reason not to move ahead in your efforts to incorporate. With any decision as important and significant as creating a corporation, a bit of additional reflection on some specific cautions is in order.

Every coin has two sides. This is certainly the case with incorporation. There are some disadvantages that should be weighed against the benefits. Fortunately, the disadvantages are not as numerous as the advantages! Their importance in your planning will depend on your personal assessment of the particular circumstances of your organization.

THE COSTS OF INCORPORATING

For many people considering incorporation of a nonprofit organization, the major difference between operating as an unincorporated informal entity and existing as a nonprofit corporation comes down to a matter of dollars. The simple fact is that it can cost money to create a nonprofit corporation. On the other hand, it might cost you almost nothing except your time and effort to create an organization.

As you recall from the discussion in previous chapters, a nonprofit corporation is a legal entity given its official existence by state government. Any time the state executes such a move, some legal documentation and costs inevitably result.

The absolute minimum costs legally required need not be exorbitant. In many cases, the total can be kept to under $80, as you will discover when these costs are outlined later in this book. Nevertheless, certain fees are required by the state. This is an expense you would not have if you remained unincorporated.

The biggest costs by far are the fees of attorney and accountants hired to assist the incorporators. Engaging an attorney to advise you on the creation of a nonprofit corporation is a logical step. He or she might even prepare and file the various documents necessary. You might enlist the aid of an accountant to suggest a financial structure and strategy for your nonprofit corporation. If you use these sources of expertise, the bill for their services can easily run up to several thousand dollars. And that can be a big disadvantage by anyone's standards.

Attorneys' and accountants' fees must be added to those filing and recording fees charged by each state in order to effect incorporation. Actually, these fees levied by the state are the only costs legally required for establishing your nonprofit corporation.

The law does not require that you use an attorney or an accountant in the process of incorporating an organization. When you have finished reading this book, you will know just how to form a nonprofit corporation at a cost limited to the state-required fees. You can even avoid the cost of new necessary legal forms by using those included in Chapters 9 and 11.

Between these two cost extremes, there lies another alternative for getting your nonprofit corporation off the ground. By using the services of The Company Corporation—founded by the author to assist in low-cost incorporation previously unavailable and headquartered in Wilmington, Delaware—you can launch your corporation for less than $125.

All of this is not to say that you may never need attorneys or accountants in the planning for or incorporation of a nonprofit organization. If you can't get needed information in any other way, or you are uncertain about aspects of the incorporation procedure or specific points of corporate or tax law in a particular state, you may want to consult these professionals for help. But there is no legal requirement that you be represented by a lawyer in forming a nonprofit corporation. That is a decision you must make for yourself.

In fairness, it should be noted that if you will need the service of an attorney or an accountant to establish a nonprofit corporation, the likelihood is that you will also require the same professional services to assist you in getting an unincorporated organization off the ground. If that is the case, then the real *cost* of the advantages offered by incorporation can be as little as $120—a somewhat minimal price to pay for the package of benefits available when incorporated.

In any event, the more you learn on your own about creating a nonprofit corporation, the fewer questions you'll have that may require professional advice. And that can substantially reduce the cost of any legal help you decide to seek. A competent attorney should charge you only for the specific help or services you request in connection with the formation of a corporation.

LEGALLY REQUIRED PAPERWORK

An unincorporated nonprofit organization can be structured so informally that its operators could keep whatever records they chose on the backs of envelopes or as scribbled notes on paper napkins. Not so in a nonprofit corporation. As a legal entity, the corporation is subject to some specific recordkeeping obligations set down by the state in which it is incorporated.

Certain documents must be prepared in a specific manner and form and be filed with stipulated agencies of the state government. For instance, the Articles of Incorporation must follow a legally prescribed format, be rendered in duplicate in most cases and be filed with the state government department responsible for chartering corporations. Likewise, the nonprofit corporation is required under the law to draft a constitution or set of bylaws that outline how the organization will be run. The broad outline for this organizational plan is specified in the state law. The law will require, for instance, that a minimum number of directors be named, that certain types of officers be elected and that they meet a minimum number of times each year to conduct the corporation's affairs. Before these requirements give the appearance of being too onerous to handle conveniently, let us hasten to add that Chapter 11 will present an easy-to-follow, step-by-step guide to incorporation, including the basic forms you will need.

The first, or organizational, meeting of a nonprofit organization must be held within a prescribed period of time following its incorporation and must be run according to procedures contained in the state's corporation law. Minutes of that meeting (and other meetings) of the board of directors must be recorded and kept in the corporation's files. Chapter 13 contains the forms you will need to cover these start-up requirements.

The filing of certain reports periodically with government agencies may be required. For example, these might include an information report for the Internal Revenue Service, notices of changes of the corporation's officers and registered agent, and an annual report to be sent to the state's incorporating department. The purpose of these requirements is to ensure that the corporation conducts its affairs in a thorough, reasonably efficient and formal manner. In doing this, there is no escaping a certain amount of paperwork.

LACK OF PERSONAL CONTROL

By their very nature, the founders of organizations, whether they are drawn from business concerns or public-spirited groups, prefer to shape and control their creations. As the founder of a less formal type of organization, you should have no problem whatsoever in maintaining your control over it. After all, you alone defined the purpose of the organization and made the rules by which it would be operated. You can select whomever you choose to be a member of your group, under whatever conditions you decide.

In a nonprofit corporation, that degree of personal control may not be possible. Some states require corporations to have several directors. They, in turn, are the only people allowed by law to elect or appoint the officers who will determine corporate policy and operate the corporation on a day-to-day basis. In those states, obviously, you are legally required to share control of the corporation with other individuals. One person can effectively control a Delaware nonprofit corporation.

You might say the difference between an unincorporated organization and a corporation is similar to that between an absolute monarchy and a parliamentary government, at least in some states. In the one case, a single individual's will prevails. In the other case, decisions and direction come through a process of consensus.

A nonprofit corporation is subject to laws and regulations, including its own Articles of Incorporation and bylaws, which may allow any person who is a member of the corporation or its board to influence to one degree or another the direction of the organization—whether or not the founder is in accord. However, in a Delaware corporation the founder can control decisions, because no outside directors or officers are needed.

At the same time, the founder of a nonprofit corporation has the very same right to protect his or her interest and position within the same legal framework. The key is to exercise your influence as a founder at the beginning stage of the corporation, in the drafting of the Articles of Incorporation and bylaws. And you are not legally barred from influencing the composition of the corporation's board of directors so that it will reflect your thinking about the purpose and operation of the organization you have funded.

Consider this example. In the mid-1960s, Frankie Hewitt, a woman long interested in theater arts and culture, was dismayed that Ford's Theatre, where Abraham Lincoln was assassinated, was in a sorry state of disrepair. It was actually being used as a government storehouse. She felt the historic Washington theater should be physically restored and once again utilized for theatrical productions. Thus it would be a superb living memorial to Lincoln. Such a task would call for the raising of lots of money, as well as negotiating a "use agreement" with the government. An organization would also be needed to operate the theater and stage its productions. Obviously, that would be an impractical job for one person.

Ms. Hewitt founded a nonprofit corporation, which she called the Ford's Theatre Society. She was elected as its first president. Several years later, she became the society's executive producer. In that role, she has guided the theater to award-winning status as a cultural center.

LITTLE OPERATING FLEXIBILITY

On paper at least, a corporation often seems rigid and ponderous when it comes to changing policies. In a corporation, a majority vote by a quorum of directors is required for any policy changes not otherwise permitted by the Articles of Incorporation or bylaws. Technically, the board's decision must be formally recorded before the policy change can be implemented. This certainly appears to be a cumbersome process when contrasted with the operation of a less formal organization where one individual (or several partners) can easily and quickly decide on a change, then immediately put it into effect.

Fortunately, this disadvantage of the corporate format is more imagined than real. In practice, as long as the bylaws allow it, a vote by corporation directors can be taken by telephone, simply recorded in meeting minutes, filed in the appropriate section of the records book and then put into effect. In fact, some people wouldn't consider this legally required formality a disadvantage at all. It depends upon how you like to operate within an organizational framework. Standard forms and minutes containing nearly all of the actions of a corporation already written up are available. All you need do is fill in the blanks.

SCRUTINY BY OUTSIDERS

All types of corporations are subject to a certain amount of scrutiny by agencies of the government and, to the extent that certain corporate reports are on file as public documents, by the public. Such reports usually contain the names and addresses of directors and officers plus other information, possibly including data about the source and use of income.

Once filed by the government agencies requiring the forms from corporations, these reports are available for examination by any outsiders with a legitimate interest in the affairs of the corporation. This could make at least semi-public the kind of information you might prefer to keep confidential. This is a judgment you will have to make in relation to the values of the corporate form to your organization. Especially if it engages in raising funds from the public, a nonprofit corporation may also be subject to the scrutiny of some nongovernment agencies. The Philanthropic Advisory Service of the Council of Better Business Bureaus and the National Information Bureau are two national agencies that investigate the finances and activities of such organizations. But they have no legal authority over the groups examined. Many states do require special registration of tax-exempt nonprofit corporations that have charitable, health or educational purposes and engage in public fund-raising.

Because tax-exempt nonprofit corporations often operate enterprises that in effect compete with the activities of for-profit businesses, commercial operators who resent the competition may lobby for more government restrictions on the operations of the nonprofits. For example, magazines of nonprofit corporations, such as the *National Geographic* and *Smithsonian* magazines, compete for advertising revenues and subscribers with for-profit publications. The latter do not enjoy the same tax and postal rate advantages as the nonprofit publishers. As a result, for-profit publishers have complained to the U.S. Postal Service about the cheaper mailing rates enjoyed by some nonprofit publishers. Other business groups have urged the IRS to be more restrictive about the kinds of "business" services tax-exempt corporations are permitted to operate.

The Commission on Private Philanthropy and Public Needs filed its report in 1975 recommending a number of new laws involving nonprofit organizations. One of these recommendations asked that the federal government regulate the activities of some charitable tax-exempt nonprofit organizations. Legislation to accomplish that has been submitted to the U.S. Congress on several occasions. As of this date, no such laws have ever been enacted.

Federal tax law does prohibit the officers of certain kinds of nonprofit organizations from engaging in what is called *self-dealing*. This means arranging business transactions for a nonprofit organization in which individual officers or directors (or their outside businesses) derive special benefit. A lawyer who is president of a foundation that assigns all its legal work (at a sizable annual fee) to the law firm he owns might be accused of self-dealing. However, the law in areas like this is far from crystal clear, and an arrangement such as this one might prove to be entirely legal.

4

Basic Requirements for a Nonprofit Corporation

In this chapter you will learn about the basic legal requirements for creating a nonprofit corporation. Believe it or not, they are few and fairly simple, as you'll see in a moment. As you read on, keep in mind that the basic requirements discussed here generally apply in most states.

Depending on the state in which you wish to incorporate and on certain aspects of your particular plan, specific requirements can vary. For instance, the minimum number of incorporators required to sign the incorporating document submitted to the appropriate state agency is not the same in every state. And the requirement that you obtain the prior approval of certain state agencies interested in the nonprofit sector may depend on the particular nature of the corporation you intend to create.

The discussion that follows is not meant to cover completely the ins and outs of each requirement for incorporation. Detailed information will be presented on each of these points later in the book, where actual steps involved in creating the corporation are presented in simple, easy-to-follow chronological order.

In a later chapter, you will learn about the specific requirements for formation of a nonprofit corporation in the state of Delaware. This state's law is explained in detail because it is possible for you to incorporate your organization in Delaware regardless of where you reside or where the operating office of your corporation will be. With this understanding clearly in mind, the following are the basic requirements for establishing a nonprofit corporation.

ARRANGING FOR INCORPORATORS

As you've already learned, a nonprofit corporation cannot come into being as a *legal entity* without the efforts of real people. The law refers to these people as *incorporators*. They are the people who must sign their names to the legal document giving birth to the corporation.

Some states require a minimum of three or more incorporators. Delaware, on the other hand, permits one person to be the sole incorporator of a nonprofit corporation.

Who can these people be? What requirements must they meet personally? Ordinarily, the only prerequisites for people serving as incorporators of a nonprofit corporation are that they be legal adults (at least 18 or 21 years old, depending on the state law) and citizens of the United States. And there may be instances where U.S. citizenship is not required of all incorporators. In practical terms, the incorporators are adults who agree to involve themselves in the creation of the nonprofit organization to be incorporated.

If one individual actually originated the idea for the organization, then he or she must enlist the required number of other people to serve with him as incorporators. This person may, in truth, be the *founder* of the organization, since its creation was his or her own idea. The form and purpose of the corporation was of his or her personal design. But in a legal sense, the incorporators are all recognized as the founders.

As you recall from previous chapters, a single founder can be very influential at the beginning and throughout the life of a nonprofit corporation. The selection of the additional incorporators is the first opportunity to exercise that influence.

Most nonprofit organizations evolve from conversations among like-minded people. It should not be difficult for one person to take the lead in lining up a sufficient number of the others in a group to serve as fellow incorporators. Even if the idea for the corporation is yours alone, and you've never discussed it with another soul, the odds are good that you can interest two or more others in acting as incorporators. If you utilize the methods described in this book, the costs involved in forming the corporation will be low. So collecting a sufficient number of incorporators will not necessarily involve asking them to make a financial commitment to the organization.

SELECTING THE BOARD OF DIRECTORS

The next step is to assemble a *board of directors*, or trustees, for the organization you will incorporate. In most cases, the law will require that at least three people be named as directors at the time of incorporation. (Delaware permits a nonprofit corporation to have one director.) Again, the personal requirements for directors are quite basic. They must be adults and usually citizens of the United States, although the citizenship requirement may apply only to a majority percentage of board members.

Two factors make this task a simple one. First, people named as incorporators may also be named as directors. Thus, you do not face the necessity of recruiting additional people. Second, the directors named in the incorporating document need serve in that capacity only until the first annual meeting of the nonprofit corporation. This, of course, may come a day or two following the state's chartering of the corporation. Therefore, a director does not have to make a long-term commitment to the enterprise. At that first meeting, additional directors can be elected or an entirely new board can be selected.

DRAFTING THE ARTICLES OF INCORPORATION

Each state has a prescribed form for this document. Fortunately, the format is virtually the same in every state. Variations are few and involve minor points, such as differences in the minimum number of incorporators required, or in the name of the state agency with which the document is to be filed.

As you would expect, the format required is in the usual legal language. A specimen of a standard *Articles of Incorporation* document is included in Chapter 11. Look it over and you will see that, despite the legalese, the statements are pretty straightforward and easy to understand.

In almost every instance, the document must contain the following information:

- the name and number of the state law that applies to the incorporation of a nonprofit organization. You can obtain this information by calling your state's secretary of state. A listing of the addresses and phone numbers of each secretary of state appears in Appendix A at the end of this book.
- the name of the organization to be incorporated. Obviously, this is something you will have decided by the time you begin drafting the Articles.
- the purpose of the corporation. This is a key part of the Articles and indeed a basic requirement for the incorporation of a nonprofit organization. The statement of purpose must have both positive and negative implications. That is, in a positive sense, it must indicate what charitable, educational, social, religious or other beneficial goal of a nonprofit nature the corporation intends to achieve. The negative implication is the statement that any financial gains resulting from the corporation's activities will not be distributed as dividends or profit shares to directors, officers or members of the organization.

This statement of purpose is what separates nonprofit from for-profit corporations. It does not prevent the nonprofit corporation from engaging in activities or business operations that result in financial gain, or what would normally be called profit, as long as it is clear that those gains will be used only to further the work of the organization toward its stated goals. Nor does it prevent the directors, officers, employees and other agents of the nonprofit corporation from being paid salaries, fees, or other reasonable compensation for services they render to the corporation.

There are some standard phrases you can use to state the purpose of your nonprofit organization in accordance with the requirements of the incorporating state's nonprofit corporation law. The purpose clause in the specimen Articles of Incorporation in the back of the book, adapted to the particular goals of your organization, would be acceptable in most cases.

- the location of the corporation's main office. This is the place from which its activities will be directed and where its records will be kept. You may also have to indicate other localities where the corporation may conduct activities or simply state that it will also operate out-of-state.
- the names and home addresses of the people to be named directors, or trustees, until the first annual meeting of the corporation.
- a statement that all subscribers to the document meet whatever personal requirements are stipulated in the state's corporation law. As mentioned earlier, the usual requirements are that they be adults and U.S. citizens.
- name and address of the registered agent of the corporation. As you will learn later in this book, the registered agent is a person or agency the corporation designates for service of process. For instance, as a matter of legal form, any lawsuits filed against the corporation, as well as other legal or court papers, are presented to the registered agent. If you use The Company Corporation to incorporate your nonprofit organization, you can name it as your registered agent. Or any incorporator, director or attorney may serve as the corporation's registered agent.
- signatures and addresses of the incorporators. In some states, the signatures must be notarized; that is, a notary must attest to the fact that the signers are who they claim to be and that they affixed their signatures to the document in the presence of the notary.

This is all that is usually required in the Articles of Incorporation. However, in some states one or more of the following items may also be necessary:

- An approval statement and signature of an appropriate officer of each state government agency whose approval is required prior to incorporation of a nonprofit organization. For instance, if the corporation's purpose is charitable, a charity registration office may have to give its approval before incorporation can be completed.
- A statement that the organization presenting its Articles of Incorporation has not previously applied for incorporation in the state, or, if it has, why it was not approved. The statement will also need to reflect how the

present Articles correct any shortcomings that were the reason for rejection of the previous application.

- A statement naming the secretary of state as the corporation's agent for the service of legal process against the corporation.

FILING THE CERTIFICATE AND FEE PAYMENTS

This is the final step required to incorporate your organization. Filing simply means delivering (by mail or in person) the completed Articles of Incorporation document. This should be duly signed by the required number of incorporators, with any required approvals or affidavits attached, and returned to the state agency responsible for granting corporation charters. That may be the office of the secretary of state, State Corporation Commission or a similarly named agency. The list you'll find at the back of this book includes the name of the appropriate filing agency in each state.

Usually, you need submit only one copy of the Articles of Incorporation and attachments. Of course, you will want to have at least one more copy for your own files. And in several states, a copy must also be sent to the office of the clerk of the county in which the main office will be located. In other states, the incorporating agency will forward a copy of the document to the appropriate county clerk once it has been approved. It is this copy, incidentally, that is usually considered part of the public record and open to inspection by interested parties.

Along with the Articles of Incorporation, you must submit a filing fee required by the state. It may be a single fee or it may consist of various fees—such as a basic filing fee, a state recording fee and perhaps a filing or recording fee for the county where a copy of the document will be filed. The state's nonprofit corporation law will clearly state the amount of the fee or fees required at the time of filing the Articles of Incorporation and the manner in which the payment must be rendered.

Unlike a for-profit business corporation, a nonprofit corporation does not have to pay any taxes in connection with the filing of its Articles.

NOTICE OF ACCEPTANCE AND FILING

The state agency to which you submitted your documents and check will mail you an acknowledgment of receipt certificate. That is usually considered your evidence of the incorporation of the organization. As soon as that certificate is issued, the nonprofit corporation exists and can begin its operation.

5

General Corporation Law and Nonprofit Corporations

In most states, the various statutes governing corporations are normally grouped together and called, naturally enough, *Corporation Law* or *General Corporation Law*. These statutes define a corporation, describe how one is formed, explain how it is to be operated, lay out how it will be regulated by the state, and so forth. It is in this section of a state's coded law that you will find whatever information you need for creating any kind of corporation, including a nonprofit corporation.

For the most part, the creation of a nonprofit corporation is quite similar in every respect to the creation of a basic business or for-profit corporation. Within the state's General Corporation Law, there may be separate chapters or categories that deal with specific types of corporations, such as the nonprofit corporation and the professional corporation. In other states, these kinds of corporations may be dealt with routinely in specific paragraphs of the law concerning any and all corporations. Thus, where a section of the law relating to corporations doesn't apply to nonprofit corporations, a paragraph or two will note that exception and explain how the nonprofit corporation is to be treated.

In several states, the law relating to special types of corporations is contained in statutes entirely separate from the main body of General Corporation Law. As a rule, nonprofit corporations are considered simply a special classification or category of corporation, and the differences between the nonprofit form of corporation and the for-profit business forms—in terms of definition, creation and operation—will be clearly detailed.

All corporations are typically categorized within General Corporation Law as being one of three types:

1. ***Public corporations.*** Corporations of this kind are normally agencies and organizations established by governments of cities, states and the United States for special administrative purposes. Everyone is familiar with them. For example, a municipal district may be a *public corporation*. A public benefit corporation and a port or industrial authority are other examples.

2. ***Stock corporations.*** Generally, the ordinary business corporation established for profit would fall into this category. It is identified as a stock corporation because investors purchase and hold *stock certificates* that represent their financial interest in the ownership of the corporation. The distribution of the corporation's dividends or other revenues or assets is made according to the ownership of stock. And owners of the stock are entitled to a say in the affairs of the corporation.

3. ***Nonstock corporations.*** Charitable, fraternal, social, educational and other types of nonprofit corporations usually are *nonstock corporations*. They cannot issue stock certificates representing ownership shares of the corporation. Nonstock corporations may issue *membership certificates* that represent financial contributions to the corporation. These may resemble stock certificates, and the corporation may even call them stock certificates. Legally, however, they are only certificates of membership, even if members holding them believe they are stock certificates.

The distribution of dividends based on stock ownership is the legal test of a true stock certificate. A legally organized nonprofit corporation cannot award dividends or otherwise distribute revenue to its members—no matter what kind of certificates they might hold. If the corporation does, then, distribute such dividends or revenues, regardless of what they are called, the certificates issued by the corporation could be considered stock certificates. Then the legitimacy of the corporation's nonprofit status would be highly questionable. Most likely, it would be subject to challenge under the laws of the incorporating state.

In some states, nonstock, nonprofit corporations may be further classified under the General Corporation Law. These subcategories might include their specific identification as clubs, churches, educational organizations, co-ops, farmers' associations, savings and loan associations, and the like.

In some instances, certain kinds of nonprofit corporations may also be subject to state laws entirely separate from the General Corporation Law that controls their creation. For example, a nonprofit corporation with an educational purpose is created under the provisions of the General Corporation Law. Because its purpose is educational in nature, it may also be subject to provisions of the incorporating state's laws that pertain to the operation of schools and other educational institutions and organizations. In cases like these, the two sets of laws usually do not conflict, and the provisions of both must be adhered to by the corporation in question if they are applicable. If the state laws governing educational institutions require that all classrooms pass a state fire inspection annually, for instance, and the nonprofit corporation in question merely distributes educational material by mail and has no classrooms, then obviously that requirement has no impact on the corporation.

Delaware Corporation Law and Its Advantages for Nonprofit Corporations

Happily for anyone considering the formation of a nonprofit corporation, the legal framework for incorporation and operation of a nonprofit corporation in the state of Delaware is essentially the same as that for creation of a general business corporation. In other words, the same basic law applies to both kinds of corporations. Naturally, the differences between the for-profit and non-profit corporations are recognized in the state's General Corporation Law. It is not done in separate sections of the Code, but instead is dealt with entirely within the context of the General Corporation Law.

For example, Section 102(a)(4), the subchapter of the Delaware General Corporation Law having to do with forming corporations, covers such subjects as a corporation's authority to issue stock, the classes of stock permitted and its par value. Obviously, these provisions are not applicable to a non-stock, nonprofit corporation. So, toward the end of the section, the law states:

> The foregoing provisions of this paragraph shall not apply to corporations which are not to have authority to issue capital stock. In the case of such corporations, the fact that they are not to have authority to issue capital stock shall be stated in the certificate of incorporation. The conditions of membership of such corporations shall likewise be stated in the certificate of incorporation or the certificate may provide that the conditions of membership shall be stated in the bylaws.

This is a simple, common-sense way to deal with the creation of a nonprofit corporation without the confusion of additional sections or bodies of law. The procedure and requirements for creating a nonprofit corporation are practically the same as for a regular business corporation. The key difference is in the wording of the nonprofit corporation's *certificate of incorporation*. It is in this document that the special not-for-profit goals, and purpose, of the corporation are stated along with any other special purpose stipulations called for in the General Corporation Law, as was illustrated above.

All of this is advantageous to the creators of a nonprofit corporation in Delaware. For one thing, the incorporation procedure is well known and relatively simple to execute. Moreover, Delaware has traditionally been known as a state friendly to corporations. Indeed, the state government depends on fees from its Corporation Department as a prime source of revenue. The Department's generation of revenue, in fact, is exceeded only by that of the state's income tax.

To attract organizations to incorporate in Delaware, even if they do not intend to conduct more than a fraction of their business there, the state has historically kept its laws relevant to corporations favorable and its fees for incorporation relatively low. It is no wonder that Delaware has been called the corporation capital of the United States. Thousands of corporations—from the very largest U.S. corporate giants, to the smallest enterprises—are incorporated in Delaware. The climate for corporations, as they say, couldn't be better.

Consider these specific advantages to incorporating a nonprofit organization in the state of Delaware:

1. *There is no minimum capital requirement.* A corporation can be organized without capital at all, if the organizers wish it. Many states require that a corporation have at least $1,000 in capital in order to be incorporated.
2. *One person can hold the offices of president, treasurer, and secretary, and alone constitute the entire board of directors of a corporation in Delaware.* As you have already read, many states require at least three organizers, as well as three or more persons to serve as officers and directors of the corporation. In Delaware, you can incorporate an organization acting entirely on your own without involving anyone else. You can create a virtual one-person operation.
3. *The established body of Delaware law relevant to corporations has been tested time and again in the state's courts.* Thus, there is a high degree of predictability of the outcome of any legal proceedings in the Delaware courts that involve corporations established by the state. Delaware's Court of Chancery system is the only separate business court in the United States, and its record of pro-management decisions is long-standing.
4. *Of course, nonprofit corporations are exempt from state income taxation in Delaware.* What's more, no corporation income tax is levied on any corporations which are formed in Delaware, but don't do business in the

state. And a corporation created in Delaware is not required to do business in the state.

5. *Nonprofit corporations whose statement of purpose would qualify them for IRS tax-exempt status are exempt as well from the annual franchise or license tax on corporations in Delaware.*

6. *A person who wishes to do so can operate anonymously as the owner of a Delaware corporation.*

7. *You may form a nonprofit corporation in Delaware either by dealing directly with the appropriate state agencies, or by dealing with them through an agent of your choice—and entirely by mail.* The incorporators need never set a foot in the state. There is no requirement that a corporation formed in Delaware conduct its annual meetings in the state. They can be held anywhere its board of directors chooses to hold them.

8. *The state's Corporation Department, which is the incorporating agency in Delaware, welcomes your business, and consequently, incorporation papers filed with the department are processed very promptly.*

9. *Directors and committee members of Delaware corporations may act by unanimous written consent in lieu of formal meetings.*

10. *Nonprofit corporations may hold the stocks, bonds, or securities of for-profit corporations as well as real and personal property anywhere within and outside of the state of Delaware without limitation on the amount of these holdings.*

11. *Any corporation formed in Delaware is automatically considered to have perpetual existence unless its organizers specifically stipulate otherwise in their certificate of incorporation, or other corporation documents such as the bylaws.*

12. *The board of directors (remember, that can consist of one person) is authorized under Delaware law to make or alter the corporation's bylaws without a further vote of the membership.*

13. *Only one person is required to act as the incorporator of a nonprofit corporation in Delaware. In many states, a minimum of three incorporators is required.*

14. *Delaware is one of a very few states that permits directors and officers to be shielded from liability with respect to a breach of their duty.*

Although a nonprofit corporation formed in Delaware isn't required to conduct any business in the state, every corporation incorporated there is required to have a Delaware address, even if its headquarters are in another state. That doesn't mean the corporation must open offices in Delaware, although it may do so. A registered agent can provide the nonprofit corporation with a Delaware address. It is normal practice for the address of the Delaware registered agent retained by the corporation to constitute the legally required Delaware address for the corporation. As you will see later in this book, this is quite easy to arrange.

The Role of the Registered Agent

As you have read, with the knowledge you have gained from this book, and with the forms included, you can carry out the steps necessary to incorporate your organization, acting on your own, without a lawyer, for under $75 in several states. If you would rather not undertake the task yourself, of course, you can hire a lawyer to do it for you. But this is usually a costly step. Another alternative is to use the services of an incorporation service firm to incorporate your nonprofit organization. It will be much less costly than using a lawyer, and you can deal with these companies entirely by mail.

One leading service company is The Company Corporation, a Delaware corporation formed to serve as a registered agent for business, professional and nonprofit corporations, wherever they may be located. It can provide services required to incorporate an organization anywhere in the country, although, as you will see in a moment, it can help you incorporate in Delaware with exceptional ease and speed. The Company Corporation can also furnish at your request the fee schedule for filing a variety of corporate forms with the State of Delaware. These include, but are not limited to, the following: increases in the number of membership certificates authorized, amendments to the certificate of incorporation, dissolutions of the corporation, etc. All these services are provided by The Company Corporation at the lowest possible cost and with a minimum of time and effort required on your part.

At this point, take a minute to consider what is involved in the use of registered agent services. Registered agents are just what the name implies—individuals or companies registered with an incorporating state as the officially appointed agent of a corporation that has engaged them. They provide a legal mailing address for the purpose of receiving and forwarding all legal documents and notices directed to the corporation they represent, and they can perform other business services as well for the client corporation.

LIST OF REGISTERED AGENTS IN DELAWARE

Here is a partial list of companies in Delaware that are available to provide services to corporations, including acting as a registered agent:

The Company Corporation
201 N. Walnut Street
Wilmington, Delaware 19801
(302) 575-0440
Fax: (302) 574-1346
Initial Fee: None for filing corporate documents
Legal Fees: None

Annual Fee: $45 first calendar year; $75 second calendar year; $99 third year and thereafter annually.

Most of the companies listed below require that clients be referred to them by lawyers. Their fee schedules vary in amount.

Initial fee: $60 to $300 for filing corporate documents.
Legal fees: $300 to $3,000.
Annual fees: $75 to $250.

American Guaranty & Trust
3801 Kennett Pike
Greenville Center
Wilmington, Delaware 19807

Corporation Company of Delaware
1105 North Market Street
Wilmington, Delaware 19899

Aradel, Inc.
100 Tenth Street
506 Wilmington Trust Building
Wilmington, Delaware 19801

Corporation Guarantee & Trust
   Company
901 Market Street
722 Bank of Delaware Building
Wilmington, Delaware 19899

Capital Trust Company of
   Delaware
1105 North Market Street
Wilmington, Delaware 19899

Corporation Trust Company (The)
1105 North Market Street
Wilmington, Delaware 19899

Colonial Charter Company
1102 West Street
Wilmington, Delaware 19801

Corporate Agents, Inc.
1001 West Street
P.O. Box 1101
Wilmington, Delaware 19801

Corporation Maintenance &
   Service Company
1118 King Street
Wilmington, Delaware 19899

Delaware Charter Company
1105 North Market Street
Wilmington, Delaware 19899

Corporation Registry Company
Delaware Trust Building
900 Market Street
Wilmington, Delaware 19801

Delaware Charter Guarantee
   & Trust Company
1314 King Street
Wilmington, Delaware 19899

Corporation Service Company
1105 North Market Street
Wilmington, Delaware 19899

Delaware Corporation Agency (The)
300 Market Tower
901 Market Street
Wilmington, Delaware 19801

Corporate Development Company
1500 Harvey Road
Wilmington, Delaware 19801

Delaware Enterprises, Inc.
26 The Green
Dover, Delaware 19901

Delaware Registration Trust
   Company
900 Market Street
Wilmington, Delaware 19801

National Corporation Co.
Keith Building
Dover, Delaware 19901

Delaware Incorporating Company
901 Market Street
Wilmington, Delaware 19801

Prentice-Hall Corp. SystemInc. (The)
229 South State Street
Dover, Delaware 19901

Delaware Incorporators Trust
   Company
1105 North Market Street
Wilmington, Delaware. 19899

Registrar and Transfer Company
306 South State Street
Dover, Delaware 19901

Incorporating Services, Ltd.
26 The Green
Dover, Delaware 19901

Southern Trust Company
1300 Market Street
Beneficial Building
Wilmington, Delaware 19801

Incorporators of Delaware
48 The Green
Dover, Delaware 19901

States Charters Corporation
The Green
Dover, Delaware 19901

United States Corporation Company
306 South State Stret
Dover, Delaware 19901

By using the services of The Company Corporation, you can facilitate the entire process of incorporating your nonprofit corporation in Delaware for operation anywhere you wish. This organization can even serve as the incorporator of your corporation if you or your associates do not wish to sign the certificate of incorporation. Once incorporated, your nonprofit corporation can continue its relationship with The Company Corporation as your registered agent, and as the required Delaware mailing address.

THE COMPANY CORPORATION

Here's how a service company such as The Company Corporation, acting as your registered agent, can assist you in incorporating in Delaware:

- It will reserve the corporate name you request on the same day your request for the name is received.
- It will forward your completed certificate of incorporation to the Corporation Department of Delaware for filing.
- It will file the required copy of the certificate of incorporation in the appropriate Recorder of Deeds office.
- It will prepare checks for payment of the initial recording fees to the State of Delaware.

Following the incorporation, The Company Corporation, as your nonprofit corporation's registered agent, will perform such services as forwarding your corporation's annual report form, which you will be required to complete, to the Delaware secretary of state. The Company Corporation will receive any legal documents served on your corporation in Delaware, including those relating to lawsuits, and will forward these to the business address of your corporation. The Company Corporation will refer you to competent Delaware lawyers if legal counseling or advice is requested on any corporate matter. They will also provide a variety of other business services and materials. For instance, The Company Corporation can supply you with printed membership certificates, a corporate seal and legal forms for minutes and bylaws if you wish to order these materials. They can also supply appropriate forms for qualifying your Delaware nonprofit corporation in any other state of the United States.

The completed forms will be forwarded promptly to the Delaware Corporation Department. If, for any reason, the certificate of incorporation that you submit is not accepted by the secretary of state in Dover, Delaware, it will be returned to you by The Company Corporation. It will contain any comments made on it by the secretary of state's office, but will be without comment by The Company Corporation.

LISTING OF FEES

The only other initial costs to an organization engaging The Company Corporation as its registered agent are fees levied by the State of Delaware for the filing and processing of incorporating documents. Those fees are as follows:

- $25 for receiving, filing and indexing the certificate of incorporation.
- $15 minimum state incorporation tax.
- $10 for a certified copy of the certificate of incorporation made by the State Corporation Department for recording and filing in the county where your corporation's registered office is to be located (the office of your registered agent).
- $30 charge for the two-page certificate form in this book. (If you use a longer form, this cost can be higher, by about $9 per additional page.)

These minimum fees charged by the State of Delaware total $80. Add to that the $45 payment of the first calendar year's fee for engaging The Company Corporation as your corporation's registered agent (which also includes the handling of your incorporation documents at no additional charge). The total is $125. One check for that amount to The Company Corporation, plus the completed certificate of incorporation, and your organization can be incorporated in the state of Delaware.

Unless you want to have your certificate of incorporation drawn up personally by your own professional advisors, you can simply use the form in Chapter 11 of this book. One of the forms, marked "Sampler," has been filled in as an example of how the form is to be completed.

THE CORPORATE KIT

Forms necessary for completing your corporation's bylaws and the minutes of the first meeting are also included in this book. Although these need not be submitted to The Company Corporation or to the State of Delaware for purposes of incorporating, they must be filed in your corporation's official record book. Your nonprofit corporation can obtain a record book, as well as membership certificates and a corporate seal, from most stationery stores selling various legal forms and certificates.

As an option available to its customers—corporations using it as their registered agents—The Company Corporation provides a basic corporate kit at a one-time cost of $49.95. The kit includes:

1. A vinyl-covered record book to hold corporate records. The size is $10^{5/8}$" x $2^{1/4}$" x $11^{3/4}$" and your corporation's name will be printed on a gold-colored insert.
2. A metal corporate seal imprinted with your corporation's name, which is $1^{5/8}$" in diameter, plus a zipper pouch for storage. The seal is used to emboss various official documents of the corporation, such as membership certificates.
3. Preprinted stock certificates, minutes and bylaws forms to fit into the record book.
4. A complete set of Internal Revenue Service forms necessary in filing for tax-exempt status for a nonprofit corporation.

If you desire this optional kit in addition to the services of The Company Corporation as registered agent and for filing your incorporating documents, merely add $49.95 to the amount due for the other services and state fees. In this case, your total payment to The Company Corporation would be $174.95. Though accurate at the time this book went to press, all fees are subject to change without notice.

8

Qualification Versus Incorporation in States Other than Delaware

As you have read in the previous chapter, you can incorporate your nonprofit organization in the state of Delaware no matter where you live or where you intend to operate your corporation. As you have also read in this book, persons acting without any other assistance can incorporate a nonprofit organization in the state in which they reside and in which they wish to headquarter their corporations.

If you wish to follow the latter procedure, here is what will be involved: You will call or write to the state agency that handles the incorporation of nonprofit organizations. A list of the names and addresses of these agencies for every state is included at the end of this book in Appendix A. The incorporating agency will provide information about the appropriate state law that establishes the procedure for incorporating a nonprofit organization, a list of the fees required and instructions about how and where to obtain official forms that may be required for this purpose. Once you assemble all this information and the appropriate forms, you will type the necessary statements and covering letter, complete the forms and any other drafts of documents required, then submit your paperwork and the proper amount and form of payment to the incorporating agency. If you have prepared your materials as required in the state law, the incorporating agency should process your request for incorporation in due course and eventually return to you a certified copy of the certificate of incorporation, or similar document, for your organization.

USE OF THE REGISTERED AGENT

An alternative to this procedure that many people find attractive is to incorporate in Delaware, where the entire procedure can be completed with ease through the use of an organization such as The Company Corporation. Then, following Delaware incorporation, you may qualify, or register, the new nonprofit corporation in your home state or any other state where you intend to maintain a base of operations. Qualifying the corporation in a state is a far sight simpler than incorporating it, and the fee required for qualification will generally be minimal.

Qualification of a Delaware corporation in another state means that the corporation is officially recognized by that other state and is given authority to operate in accordance with the provisions of that state's laws governing nonprofit corporations. A Delaware corporation that has all or most of its activities in another state is supposed to qualify in that state. As to out-of-state residents who incorporate in Delaware, the secretary of state's office in Dover, Delaware, does not notify any other state as to who the new Delaware corporation directors or members are, or in what state they have their business office. And many Delaware corporations fail to register in other states. The hazard in not qualifying is usually a small fine and payment of the registration fee. Also, the unqualified Delaware corporation may not be able to use the courts of another state. You can write to the secretary of state in any state to determine its specific policies on *foreign corporations* that have not registered within that state.

FOREIGN CORPORATIONS

A corporation formed in one state and maintaining a base of operations in another is called a foreign corporation by the latter. The qualification procedure for foreign corporations in most states is usually simple and can be accomplished at any time. A Delaware registered agent can file a copy of the corporation's certificate of incorporation with any particular state or states at any time during the life of the corporation. Because each state's qualification rules and fees may change from time to time, you should check with the individual state regarding its fee schedule and regulations.

Usually, qualifying involves registering a certified copy of your Delaware certificate of incorporation, or a certificate of good standing, with the other state's corporation department. You then pay a registration fee. An annual fee may also be required to maintain the standing of your corporation in the other state.

WHEN QUALIFYING MAY NOT BE NECESSARY

Of course, you don't need to qualify your corporation in every state in which you might wish to do business, as opposed to maintaining a *base of operations*. You could qualify your corporation in every state if you wished to do so. This would be quite costly, however. Some corporations operated by people who do not reside permanently in Delaware nevertheless establish that they are legally doing business from a Delaware base because they receive and ship materials from Delaware. They also maintain a Delaware office, own property in Delaware, or transact contracts and other business in Delaware. In such cases, qualifying the corporation in any other state may not be necessary.

If you wish to incorporate your nonprofit organization in Delaware and subsequently qualify it in another state or states, you can request assistance with the qualification procedure from The Company Corporation, if you will be retaining it as your registered agent for the purpose of incorporating in Delaware. Once your organization has been incorporated by the Delaware secretary of state, The Company Corporation will supply you with the appropriate forms (and simple instructions for completing them) for qualifying your nonprofit Delaware corporation in other states that you designate. The charge for this service is nominal. The specific amount will depend on which state(s) you wish to qualify in and the nature of their particular qualification requirements and forms.

Qualification procedures differ from state to state, and the staff of The Company Corporation will determine what procedures are required in the states you designate. The staff will forward that information along with a fee schedule and the necessary forms for you to file.

9

Special-Purpose Tax Exemptions for Nonprofit Corporations

As you discovered in the earlier pages of this book, one of the most significant advantages of a nonprofit corporation is that it may be exempt from payment of taxes. This would include federal corporate income taxes, as well as Social Security taxes for which employers are normally liable, contributions to unemployment tax funds, state and local sales taxes, and income and property taxes. With federal corporate income taxes alone running up to a hefty 34 percent, an exemption from all of these taxes will amount to a hefty benefit for your nonprofit corporation.

What is the rationale behind the laws that exempt certain corporations and unincorporated organizations from taxes? It is the recognition that certain kinds of organizations serve a special and useful purpose by their very existence, that their activities result in benefits for and improvement of the general welfare of segments of society or the public at large—thus the phrase, *special-purpose tax exemptions*. By granting such organizations exemption from payment of taxes, the law allows all of their earnings to be devoted to the causes and persons they are established to benefit. Thus, tax exemptions are designed to maximize the beneficial effects produced by these organizations.

Some organizations such as churches, associations of churches, and auxiliary agencies of churches—mission societies and youth groups, for instance—are generally considered automatically tax-exempt. They are not required to request this status from the government taxing agencies. However, virtually all other kinds of organizations that fit legal definitions of eligibility for tax-exempt status due to their special benevolent purposes and goals cannot assume that status. They must ask the Internal Revenue Service to officially recognize their tax-exempt status.

The major step necessary for achieving this status is the filing of an IRS application for tax exemption. Your nonprofit corporation may also have to apply separately to state and local taxing authorities for exemptions from taxes imposed by these jurisdictions. Those steps are usually mere formalities, since state and local approval of tax exemption for the corporation is almost always based on the IRS's ruling on the organization's exemption application.

The chief legal basis for all tax exemptions is Section 501 of the Internal Revenue Code of 1954, although the tax exemption of a few types of organizations may be based on other sections of the Code, such as Section 401(a), which provides for the exemption of employee pension, profit-sharing, or stock-bonus plans.

You may be surprised to learn that, while the great bulk of nonprofit organizations are presumed to be tax-exempt in nature, there are exceptions to that premise. Also, the terms *nonprofit* and *charitable* are not interchangeable. A nonprofit organization is not necessarily charitably motivated, and, likewise, an organization that is truly charitable in nature may be a profit-making enterprise. And both kinds of organizations may be entitled to tax-exempt status from the IRS. For example, a religious and apostolic association or corporation, even if it is organized for profit, and a teachers' retirement fund association, which is operated to produce profits for its beneficiaries, are both eligible for tax exemptions.

For most kinds of organizations and nonprofit corporations, the path to tax-exempt status will be found in Section 501, and more precisely in Subsection (c), where 21 different types of organizations and corporations are defined as eligible for tax exemption. Any organization eligible for tax exemption under the provisions of Section 501(c)(3) has the added advantage, beyond the reach of all but one or two kinds of organizations in the other 20 categories, of entitling its contributors to deduct their contributions from their personal income tax liability.

IRS STANDARDS FOR EXEMPTION

For this reason, the IRS demands that corporations and organizations granted tax-exempt status under Section 501(c)(3) of the Code meet several unique standards or tests required of organizations exempted under other categories. Basically, those tests are:

1. The organization or corporation must be organized and operated exclusively for one or more of the special purposes specified in Category (3); that is, for religious, educational, charitable, scientific, or literary purposes, for testing for public safety, to foster certain national or international amateur sports competition or for the prevention of cruelty to children or animals.

2. No part of the net earnings of such a corporation will be distributed for the private benefit of shareholders or individuals.
3. Lobbying—defined as attempts to influence legislation—will not be a substantial part of the organization's activities.
4. Participation in a political campaign for or against any candidate for public office will not occur under any circumstances.

These standards must be established not only in the language of the organization's originating documents, such as the certificate of incorporation, bylaws or constitution, but also in the actual operations and activities of the organization. In the next chapter you will learn more about these special requirements and how organizations are expected to meet them.

OTHER CATEGORIES OF SECTION 501(c)

The only other categories of Section 501(c) defining organizations that are entitled to the tax deductibility advantage are Category (4) where gifts to volunteer fire departments and similar organizations may be deductible as charitable contributions, and Categories (8) and (10) in which gifts to fraternal beneficiary societies and associations and domestic fraternal societies and associations may be deductible if the contributions are to be used by those organizations for charitable purposes. Contributors may also deduct their gifts to cooperative hospital service organizations as defined in Section 501(e) and to cooperative service organizations of operating educational organizations as defined in Section 501(f).

Contributions to certain other kinds of organizations defined in Section 501(c), such as (6) business leagues, chambers of commerce, real estate boards and the like, and (21) black lung benefit trusts funded by coal mine operators, may be deducted as a business expense if the contributor can demonstrate that the donations were ordinary and necessary in the conduct of business. But they are not deductible as charitable contributions on a personal income tax return.

ORGANIZATIONS ELIGIBLE FOR TAX EXEMPTION

Here are all the types of corporations and organizations eligible for tax-exempt status, as described in Section 501 of the Revenue Code. As you study this listing, try to decide which numerical category best describes your nonprofit corporation. As you will see in Chapter 12, the category under which you seek exempt status determines which IRS form is required.

Applicable Section of IRC	Description of the Type of Organization	General Nature of Its Activities
501(c)(1)	Corporations organized under Act of Congress including Federal Credit Unions	Instrumentalities of the United States
501(c)(2)	Title-holding corporations for exempt organizations	Holding title to property of an exempt organization
501(c)(3)	Organizations that are religious, educational, charitable, scientific or literary in nature, or that are involved in testing for public safety, fostering certain national or international amateur sports competitions, or preventing cruelty to children or animals	As implied by the description of the specific class of organization
501(c)(4)	Civic leagues, social welfare organizations and local associations	Promotion of community welfare; charitable, educational or of employees' recreational functions
501(c)(5)	Labor, agricultural and horticultural organizations	Educational or instructive, the purpose being to improve conditions of work and to improve product and efficiency
501(c)(6)	Business leagues, chambers of commerce, real estate boards, etc.	Improvement of business conditions of one or more lines of business
501(c)(7)	Social and recreational clubs	Pleasure, recreation, social activities

501(c)(8)	Fraternal beneficiary societies and associations	Lodge providing for payment of life, sickness, accident or other benefits to members
501(c)(9)	Voluntary employees' beneficiary associations	Providing for payment of life, sickness, accident or other benefits to members
501(c)(10)	Domestic fraternal societies and associations	Lodge devoting its net earnings to charitable, fraternal and other specified purposes. No life, sickness or accident benefits to members
501(c)(11)	Teachers' retirement fund associations	Teachers' associations for payment of retirement benefits
501(c)(12)	Benevolent life insurance associations, mutual ditch or irrigation companies, mutual or cooperative telephone companies, etc.	Activities of a mutually beneficial nature similar to those implied by the description of the class of organization
501(c)(13)	Cemetery companies	Burials and incidental activities
501(c)(14)	State-chartered credit unions, mutual reserve funds	Loans to members
501(c)(15)	Mutual insurance companies or associations	Providing insurance to members substantially at cost

Applicable Section of IRC	Description of the Type of Organization	General Nature of Its Activities
501(c)(16)	Cooperative organizations to finance crop operations	Financing crop operations in conjunction with activities of a marketing or purchasing association
501(c)(17)	Supplemental unemployment benefit trusts	Provides for payment of supplemental unemployment compensation benefits
501(c)(18)	Employee funded pension trust (created before June 25, 1959)	Payment of benefits under a pension plan funded by employees
501(c)(19)	Post or organization of past or present members of Armed Forces	Activities implied by nature of organization
501(c)(20)	Group legal services plan organizations	Providing prepaid personal (nonbusiness) legal services for employees
501(c)(21)	Black lung benefit trust	Payment of benefits under a plan funded by coal mine operators
501(c)(22)	Withdrawal liability payment fund	Provides funds to meet liability of employer withdrawing from multi-employer pension fund
501(c)(23)	Veteran's organizations (created before 1880)	To provide insurance and other benefits to veterans
501(d)	Religious and apostolic associations	Regular business activities; communal religious community
501(e)	Cooperative hospital service organizations	Performs cooperative service for hospitals

501(f)	Cooperative service organizations of operating educational organizations	Performs collective investment services for educational organizations
521	Farmers' cooperative	Cooperative marketing associations and purchasing associations operated on a co-op basis for agricultural producers
527	Political organizations	Political parties, committees and similar organizations
528	Homeowners' associations	Homeowners' and condominium managers' associations

UNRELATED BUSINESS INCOME

Notwithstanding their tax-exempt status, all exempt organizations except U.S. instrumentalities defined in Section 501(c)(1) are liable for federal taxes on their net income from unrelated trade or business activities. A certain amount of unrelated business income is not prohibited for tax-exempt organizations, but, where it exists, Section 511 denies the benefit of exemption from taxation.

Internal Revenue Code Section 512 defines *unrelated business activities* as those that bear no direct relationship to the exempt purposes of the nonprofit corporation. For example, a workshop operated to provide jobs for handicapped people who are the beneficiaries of the corporation would certainly qualify as a related business activity. Income from this operation would not be taxed. On the other hand, if the same corporation operated luxury apartment buildings, the rent earned on them would probably be considered unrelated business income and would be subject to taxation.

Whether or not a particular trade or business activity is deemed related to the corporation's exempt purpose can often be a debatable issue. As a rule, the IRS has no choice but to accept as *related business activities* those in which all the work is performed for the corporation by volunteer workers, or a business operated for the convenience or benefit of the corporation's members, employees or beneficiaries, or a business activity involving the sale of merchandise that, for the most part, has been donated to the corporation. What the nonprofit corporation must guard against is allowing that portion of its income that is derived from business activities (that the IRS might deem unrelated) to become so substantial that the IRS might consider revoking the corporation's tax exemption altogether.

ANNUAL FINANCIAL REPORTS

The fact that exempt organizations do not have to pay taxes does not relieve them of all financial reporting obligations to taxing authorities. All the types of tax-exempt organizations defined in Section 501(c), (e), and (f) are required to file financial information returns annually with the IRS within five and a half months of the end of the organization's fiscal year. In almost every case, the form used for this purpose is either IRS Form 990, *Return of Organization Exempt from Income Tax* or Form 990 EZ, a comparable short form that can be used by organizations with gross receipts of less than $100,000 and total assets of less than $250,000 at the end of the tax year in question. In the case of private foundations, Form 990-PF is used. For Black Lung Benefit Trusts, Form 990-BL is used; for religious and apostolic associations, Form 1065.

If you have any unrelated activities, you must file Form 990-T. The first $1,000 gross income from unrelated activities is exempted from tax. If your calculations on this form show that the corporation owes taxes on this particular portion of its otherwise exempt income, the amount must be paid at the time the return is filed, or in two equal installments within five and a half months after the close of the fiscal year.

Copies of the two most commonly used returns, Form 990 (along with Schedule A and its instructions) and Form 990EZ, and the official instructions for Form 990 are included at the end of this chapter. As you can see, the forms call for the following kinds of information about your corporation's financial year.

INFORMATION TO BE REPORTED

- The sources from which its funds were derived, with amounts for each major type of source.
- The purposes for which those funds were expended.
- A separate breakdown of details on income earned from related business activities.
- Amounts that were disbursed or paid to members, officers, directors, and trustees of the corporation.
- The amount and type of depository of the corporation's reserve funds and investment funds.

- Information about the structure of the organization, such as whether or not changes have been made in the certificate of incorporation, bylaws, or other governing instruments of the corporation since the last annual report to the IRS.

On the following pages you will find examples of various tax returns pertaining to tax-exempt, nonprofit organizations.

19**91**

Department of the Treasury
Internal Revenue Service

Instructions for Form 990

Return of Organization Exempt From Income Tax

Under section 501(c) of the Internal Revenue Code (except black lung benefit trust or private foundation) or section 4947(a)(1) charitable trust

(Section references are to the Internal Revenue Code unless otherwise indicated.)

Paperwork Reduction Act Notice.—We ask for the information on this form to carry out the Internal Revenue laws of the United States. You are required to give us the information. We need it to ensure that you are complying with these laws and to allow us to figure and collect the right amount of tax.

The time needed to complete and file this form and related schedules will vary depending on individual circumstances. The estimated average times are:

Form	Recordkeeping	Learning about the law or the form	Preparing the form	Copying, assembling, and sending the form to the IRS
990	83 hr., 28 min.	14 hr., 37 min.	19 hr., 25 min.	48 min.
Sch. A (990)	43 hr., 32 min.	8 hr., 56 min.	10 hr., 2 min.	-0-

If you have comments concerning the accuracy of these time estimates or suggestions for making this form more simple, we would be happy to hear from you. You can write to both the **Internal Revenue Service,** Washington, DC 20224, Attention: IRS Reports Clearance Officer, T:FP; and the **Office of Management and Budget,** Paperwork Reduction Project (1545-0047), Washington, DC 20503. **DO NOT** send the tax form to either of these offices. Instead, see General Instruction H for information on where to file it.

General Instructions

Note: *An organization's completed Form 990 (except for the schedule of contributors) is available for public inspection as required by section 6104.*

Section 501(c)(3) organizations and section 4947(a)(1) charitable trusts not treated as a private foundation must also attach a completed Schedule A (Form 990) to their Form 990 (or Form 990EZ).

Purpose of Form.—Form 990 is used by tax-exempt organizations and nonexempt charitable trusts to provide the IRS with the information required by section 6033.

A. Who Must File Form 990.—

1. *Filing tests.*—If you do not meet any of the exceptions from filing listed in General Instruction B and your annual gross receipts are normally more than $25,000 (see General Instruction B11 below), you have a filing obligation. You can meet this obligation by filing Form 990. If, for any year, your gross receipts during the year are less than $100,000 *and* your total assets at end of year are less than $250,000, you may file **Form 990EZ,** Short Form Return of Organization Exempt From Income Tax, instead of Form 990. Even if you meet this dual test, you can always file a Form 990. However, if your gross receipts or assets are above these limits, you must file Form 990.

2. *Section 501(a), (e), (f), and (k) organizations.*—Except for those types of organizations listed in General Instruction B, an annual return on Form 990 (or Form 990EZ) is required from every organization exempt from tax under section 501(a), including foreign organizations and cooperative service organizations described in sections 501(e) and (f), and child care organizations described in section 501(k).

3. *Section 4947(a)(1) nonexempt charitable trusts.*—Any nonexempt charitable trust (described in section 4947(a)(1)) not treated as a private foundation is also required to file Form 990, or Form 990EZ, if its gross receipts are normally more than $25,000. See General Instruction C7 for information about possible relief from filing **Form 1041,** U.S. Fiduciary Income Tax Return.

4. *Exemption application pending.*—If your application for exemption is pending, check the "Application Pending" block at the top of page 1 of the return and complete the return in the normal manner.

5. *If you received a Form 990 Package.*—If you are not required to file Form 990 because your gross receipts are normally not more than $25,000 (see General Instruction B11 below), we ask that you file anyway if we sent you a Form 990 Package with a preaddressed mailing label. Attach the label to the name and address space on the return (see Specific Instructions). Check the box in item K in the area above Part I to indicate that your gross receipts are below the $25,000 filing minimum; sign the return; and send it to the Service Center for your area. You do not have to complete Parts I through IX of the return. By following this instruction, you will help us to update our records, and we will not have to contact you later asking why no return was filed. If you file a return this way, you will not be mailed a Form 990 Package in later years and need not file Form 990 (or Form 990EZ) again until your gross receipts normally exceed the $25,000 minimum, or you terminate or undergo a substantial contraction as described in the instructions for line 79.

Cat. No. 11283J

6. *Effect on contributions.*—
Organizations that are eligible to receive tax deductible contributions are listed in **Publication 78,** Cumulative List of Organizations described in Section 170(c) of the Internal Revenue Code of 1986. An organization may be removed from this listing if our records show that it is required to file Form 990 (or Form 990EZ), but it does not file a return or advise us that it is no longer required to file. However, contributions to such an organization may continue to be deductible by the general public until the IRS publishes a notice to the contrary in the Internal Revenue Bulletin.

B. Organizations Not Required To File Form 990.—(Note: *Organizations not required to file this form with the IRS may nevertheless wish to use it to satisfy state reporting requirements. For details, see General Instruction E.*)

The following types of organizations exempt from tax under section 501(a) do not have to file Form 990 (or Form 990EZ) with the IRS:

1. A church, an interchurch organization of local units of a church, a convention or association of churches, an integrated auxiliary of a church (such as a men's or women's organization, religious school, mission society, or youth group), or an internally supported, church-controlled organization (described in Rev. Proc. 86-23, 1986-1 C.B. 564).

2. A school below college level affiliated with a church or operated by a religious order.

3. A mission society sponsored by, or affiliated with, one or more churches or church denominations, if more than half of the society's activities are conducted in, or directed at persons in, foreign countries.

4. An exclusively religious activity of any religious order.

5. A state institution whose income is excluded from gross income under section 115.

6. An organization described in section 501(c)(1). Section 501(c)(1) organizations are corporations organized under an Act of Congress that are:

(a) Instrumentalities of the United States, and

(b) Exempt from Federal income taxes.

7. A private foundation exempt under section 501(c)(3) and described in section 509(a). (Required to file **Form 990-PF,** Return of Private Foundation.)

8. A black lung benefit trust described in section 501(c)(21). (Required to file **Form 990-BL,** Information and Initial Excise Tax Return for Black Lung Benefit Trusts and Certain Related Persons.)

9. A stock bonus, pension, or profit-sharing trust that qualifies under section 401. (See **Form 5500,** Annual Return/Report of Employee Benefit Plan.)

10. A religious or apostolic organization described in section 501(d). (Required to file **Form 1065,** U.S. Partnership Return of Income.)

11. An organization whose annual gross receipts are normally $25,000 or less (but see General Instruction A5).

(a) *Calculating gross receipts.*—Gross receipts are the sum of lines 1d, 2, 3, 4, 5, 6a, 7, 8a (both columns), 9a, 10a, and 11 of Part I. The organization's gross receipts are the total amount it received from all sources during its annual accounting period, without subtracting any costs or expenses.

(b) *Acting as agent.*—If a local chapter of a section 501(c)(8) fraternal organization collects insurance premiums for its parent lodge and merely sends those premiums to the parent without asserting any right to use the funds or otherwise deriving any benefit from collecting them, the local chapter should not include the premiums in its gross receipts. The parent lodge should report them instead. The same treatment applies in other situations in which one organization collects funds merely as an agent for another.

$25,000 gross receipts test.—An organization's gross receipts are considered normally to be $25,000 or less if the organization is:

(a) Up to a year old and has received, or donors have pledged to give, $37,500 or less during its first tax year;

(b) Between one and three years old and averaged $30,000 or less in gross receipts during each of its first two tax years; or

(c) Three years old or more and averaged $25,000 or less in gross receipts for the immediately preceding three tax years (including the year for which the return would be filed).

C. Forms You May Need To File or Use.—

1. Schedule A (Form 990).— Organization Exempt Under 501(c)(3) (Except Private Foundation), 501(e), 501(f), 501(k), or Section 4947(a)(1) Trust Supplementary Information. Filed **with** Form 990 (or Form 990EZ) for a section 501(c)(3) organization that is not a private foundation (including an organization described in section 501(e), 501(f), or 501(k)). Also filed **with** Form 990 (or Form 990EZ) for a section 4947(a)(1) charitable trust not treated as a private foundation. An organization is not required to file Schedule A if its gross receipts are normally $25,000 or less (see General Instruction B11).

2. Forms W-2 and W-3.—Wage and Tax Statement, and Transmittal of Income and Tax Statements.

3. Form 940.—Employer's Annual Federal Unemployment (FUTA) Tax Return.

4. Form 941.—Employer's Quarterly Federal Tax Return. Used to report social security and income taxes withheld by an employer and social security tax paid by an employer.

5. Form 990-T.—Exempt Organization Business Income Tax Return. Filed separately for organizations with gross income of $1,000 or more from business

unrelated to the organization's exempt purpose.

6. Form 990-W.—Estimated Tax on Unrelated Business Taxable Income for Tax-Exempt Organizations.

7. Form 1041.—U. S. Fiduciary Income Tax Return. Required of section 4947(a)(1) charitable trusts that also file Form 990 (or 990EZ). However, if such a trust does not have any taxable income under subtitle A of the Code, it can file either Form 990 (or 990EZ) and need not file Form 1041 to meet its section 6012 filing requirement. If this condition is met, complete question 92 of Form 990 and do not file Form 1041, but complete Form 990 in the normal manner. A section 4947(a)(1) charitable trust that normally has gross receipts of not more than $25,000 (see General Instruction B11) and has no taxable income under subtitle A must complete only the following items in the heading of Form 990:

Item

A. Fiscal year (if applicable);

B. Name and address;

C. Employer identification number;

F. Section 4947(a)(1) box; and question 92 and the signature block on page 5.

8. Form 1096.—Annual Summary and Transmittal of U.S. Information Returns.

9. Form 1099 Series.—Information returns for reporting payments such as dividends, interest, miscellaneous income (including medical and health care payments and nonemployee compensation), original issue discount, patronage dividends, real estate transactions, acquisition or abandonment of secured property, and distributions from annuities, pensions, profit-sharing and retirement plans.

10. Form 1120-POL.—U.S. Income Tax Return for Certain Political Organizations.

11. Form 1128.—Application to Adopt, Change, or Retain A Tax Year.

12. Form 2758.—Application for Extension of Time To File Certain Excise, Income, Information, and Other Returns.

13. Form 4506-A.—Request for Public Inspection or Copy of Exempt Organization Tax Form.

14. Form 4720.—Return of Certain Excise Taxes on Charities and Other Persons Under Chapters 41 and 42 of the Internal Revenue Code. Section 501(c)(3) organizations that file Form 990 (or 990EZ), as well as the managers of these organizations, use this form to report their tax on political expenditures and certain lobbying expenditures.

15. Form 5500, 5500-C/R.— Employers who maintain pension, profit-sharing, or other funded deferred compensation plans are generally required to file one of the 5500 series forms specified below. This requirement applies whether or not the plan is qualified under the Internal Revenue Code and whether or not a deduction is claimed for the current tax year.

Page 2

The forms required to be filed are:

Form 5500.—Annual Return/Report of Employee Benefit Plan. Used for each plan with 100 or more participants.

Form 5500-C/R.—Return/Report of Employee Benefit Plan. Used for each plan with fewer than 100 participants.

16. Form 5768.—Election/Revocation of Election by an Eligible Section 501(c)(3) Organization To Make Expenditures To Influence Legislation.

17. Form 8282.—Donee Information Return. Required of the donee of "charitable deduction property" who sells, exchanges, or otherwise disposes of the property within two years after receiving the property.

Also, the form is required of any successor donee who disposes of charitable deduction property within two years after the date that the donor gave the property to the original donee. (It does not matter who gave the property to the successor donee. It may have been the original donee or another successor donee.) For successor donees, the form must be filed only for any property that was transferred by the original donee after July 5, 1988.

18. Form 8300.—Report of Cash Payments Over $10,000 Received in a Trade or Business. Used to report cash amounts in excess of $10,000 that were received in a single transaction (or in two or more related transactions) in the course of a trade or business (as defined in section 162).

However, if the organization receives a charitable cash contribution in excess of $10,000, it would not be subject to the reporting requirement since the funds were not received in the course of a trade or business.

19. Form 8822.—Change of Address. Used to notify the IRS of a change in mailing address that occurs after the return is filed.

D. Publications.—

Publication 525.—Taxable and Nontaxable Income.

Publication 598.—Tax on Unrelated Business Income of Exempt Organizations.

Publication 910.—Guide to Free Tax Services.

Publication 1391.—Deductibility of Payments Made to Charities Conducting Fund-Raising Events.

These publications and forms are available free at many IRS offices or by calling **1-800-TAX-FORM** (1-800-829-3676).

E. Use of Form 990 To Satisfy State Reporting Requirements.—Some states and local government units will accept a copy of Form 990 and Schedule A (Form 990) in place of all or part of their own financial report forms. The substitution applies primarily to section 501(c)(3) organizations, but some of the other types of section 501(c) organizations are also affected.

If you intend to use Form 990 to satisfy state or local filing requirements, such as those under state charitable solicitation acts, note the following:

Determine state filing requirements.— You should consult the appropriate officials of all states and other jurisdictions in which you do business to determine their specific filing requirements. "Doing business" in a jurisdiction may include any of the following: **(a)** soliciting contributions or grants by mail or otherwise from individuals, businesses, or other charitable organizations; **(b)** conducting programs; **(c)** having employees within that jurisdiction; **(d)** maintaining a checking account; or **(e)** owning or renting property there.

Monetary tests may differ.—Some or all of the dollar limitations applicable to Form 990 when filed with IRS may not apply when using Form 990 in place of state or local report forms. Examples of IRS dollar limitations that do not meet some state requirements are the $25,000 gross receipts minimum that creates an obligation to file with IRS (see General Instruction B11) and the $30,000 minimum for listing professional fees in Part II of Schedule A (Form 990).

Additional information may be required.—State or local filing requirements may require you to attach to Form 990 one or more of the following: (a) additional financial statements, such as a complete analysis of functional expenses or a statement of changes in financial position; (b) notes to financial statements; (c) additional financial schedules; (d) a report on the financial statements by an independent accountant; and (e) answers to additional questions and other information. Each jurisdiction may require the additional material to be presented on forms they provide. The additional information does not have to be submitted with the Form 990 filed with the IRS.

Even if the Form 990 you file with the IRS is accepted by the IRS as complete, a copy of the same return filed with a state will not fully satisfy that state's filing requirement if required information is not provided, including any of the additional information discussed above, or if the state determines that the form was not completed in accordance with the applicable Form 990 instructions or supplemental state instructions. If so, you may be asked to provide the missing information or to submit an amended return.

Use of audit guides may be required.— To ensure that all organizations report similar transactions uniformly, many states require that contributions, gifts, and grants on lines 1a through 1d in Part I and functional expenses on lines 13, 14, and 15, and in Part II, be reported in accordance with the AICPA industry audit guide, *Audits of Voluntary Health and Welfare Organizations* (New York, AICPA, 1988), as supplemented by *Standards of Accounting and Financial Reporting for Voluntary Health and Welfare Organizations* (New York, National Health Council, Inc. (Washington, DC), 1988), and by

Accounting and Financial Reporting—A Guide for United Ways and Not-for-Profit Human Service Organizations (Aléxandria, Va., United Way Institute, 1989).

However, although reporting donated services and facilities as items of revenue and expense is called for in certain circumstances by the three publications named above, many states and the IRS do not permit the inclusion of those amounts in Parts I and II of Form 990. The instructions for line 82 discuss the optional reporting of donated services and facilities in Parts III and VI.

Amended returns.—If you submit supplemental information or file an amended Form 990 with the IRS, you must also furnish a copy of the information or amended return to any state with which you filed a copy of Form 990 originally to meet that state's filing requirement.

If a state requires you to file an amended Form 990 to correct conflicts with Form 990 instructions, you must also file an amended return with the IRS.

Method of accounting.—Most states require that all amounts be reported based on the accrual method of accounting. (See also Specific Instructions, page 6, item G.)

Time for filing may differ.—The time for filing Form 990 with the IRS differs from the time for filing reports with some states.

Public inspection.—The Form 990 information made available for public inspection by the IRS may differ from that made available by the states. See the cautionary note, Note (2), for line 1d.

State Registration Number.—Insert the applicable state or local jurisdiction registration or identification number in item D (in the heading on page 1) for each jurisdiction in which you file Form 990 in place of the state or local form. When filing in several jurisdictions, prepare as many copies as needed with item D blank. Then enter the applicable registration number on the copy to be filed with each jurisdiction.

F. Other Forms as Partial Substitutes for Form 990.—Except as provided below, the Internal Revenue Service will not accept any form as a substitute for one or more parts of Form 990.

1. Labor Organizations.—A labor organization that files **Form LM-2,** Labor Organization Annual Report, or the shorter **Form LM-3** with the U.S. Department of Labor (DOL) can attach a copy of the completed DOL form to Form 990 to provide some of the information required by Form 990. This substitution is not permitted if the organization files a DOL report that consolidates its financial statements with those of one or more separate subsidiary organizations.

2. Employee Benefit Plans.—An employee benefit plan may be able to substitute Form 5500 or Form 5500-C/R for part of Form 990. The substitution can be made if the organization filing Form 990 and the plan filing Form 5500 or 5500-C/R meet all the following tests:

(a) The Form 990 filer is organized under section 501(c)(9), (17), (18), or (20);

Page 3

(b) The Form 990 filer and Form 5500 filer are identical for financial reporting purposes and have identical receipts, disbursements, assets, liabilities, and equity accounts;

(c) The employee benefit plan does not include more than one section 501(c) organization, and the section 501(c) organization is not a part of more than one employee benefit plan, and

(d) The organization's accounting year and the employee plan year are the same. If they are not, you may want to change the organization's accounting year, as explained in General Instruction G, so it will coincide with the plan year.

Allowable Substitution Areas.—Whether you file Form 990 for a labor organization or for an employee plan, the areas of Form 990 for which other forms can be substituted are the same. These areas are:

Part I, lines 13 through 15 (but complete lines 16 through 21);

Part II; and

Part IV (but complete lines 59, 66, and 74, Columns (A) and (B)).

If you substitute Form LM-2 or LM-3 for any of the Form 990 Parts or line items mentioned above, you must attach a reconciliation sheet to show the relationship between the amounts on the DOL forms and the amounts on Form 990. This is particularly true of the relationship of disbursements shown on the DOL forms and the total expenses on line 17, Part I, of Form 990. You must make this reconciliation because the cash disbursements section of the DOL forms includes nonexpense items. If you substitute Form LM-2, be sure to complete its separate schedule of expenses.

G. Accounting Period Covered.—Base your return on your annual accounting period (fiscal year) if one is established. If not, base the return on the calendar year.

Your fiscal year should normally coincide with the natural operating cycle of your organization. Your fiscal year need not end on December 31 or June 30.

Use the 1991 Form 990 to report on a calendar-year 1991 accounting period or a fiscal year that began in 1991. For a group return, see General Instruction Q.

If you change your accounting period, you may also use the 1991 form as the return for a short period (less than 12 months) ending November 30, 1992, or earlier.

In general, to change your accounting period, you must file timely a return on Form 990 for the short period resulting from the change. At the top of the short period return, write *Change of Accounting Period.*

If you changed your accounting period within the 10-calendar-year period that includes the beginning of the short period, and you had a Form 990 filing requirement at any time during that 10-year period, you must also attach a Form 1128 to the short period return. See Rev. Proc. 85-58, 1985-2 C.B. 740.

H. When and Where To File.—File Form 990 by the 15th day of the 5th month after your accounting period ends.

If the organization is liquidated, dissolved, or terminated, file the return by the 15th day of the 5th month after the change.

If the return is not filed by the due date (including any extension granted), attach a statement giving your reasons for not filing timely.

If your principal office is located in—	Send your return to the Internal Revenue Service Center below—
Alabama, Arkansas, Florida, Georgia, Louisiana, Mississippi, North Carolina, South Carolina, or Tennessee	Atlanta, GA 39901
Arizona, Colorado, Kansas, New Mexico, Oklahoma, Texas, Utah, or Wyoming	Austin, TX 73301
Indiana, Kentucky, Michigan, Ohio, or West Virginia	Cincinnati, OH 45999
Alaska, California, Hawaii, Idaho, Nevada, Oregon, or Washington	Fresno, CA 93888
Connecticut, Maine, Massachusetts, New Hampshire, New York, Rhode Island, or Vermont	Holtsville, NY 00501
Illinios, Iowa, Minnesota, Missouri, Montana, Nebraska, North Dakota, South Dakota, or Wisconsin	Kansas City, MO 64999
Delaware, Maryland, New Jersey, Pennsylvania, Virginia, District of Columbia, any U.S. possession, or foreign country	Philadelphia, PA 19255

I. Extension of Time To File.—Use Form 2758 to request an extension of time to file.

J. Amended Return.—To change your return for any year, file a new return with the correct information that is complete in all respects, including required attachments. Thus, the amended return must provide all the information called for by the form and instructions, not just the new or corrected information. Write *Amended Return* at the top of the return.

You may file an amended return at any time to change or add to the information reported on a previously filed return for the same period. You must make the amended return available for public inspection for three years from the date of filing or three years from the date the original return was due, whichever is later.

Use Form 4506-A to obtain a copy of a previously filed return. You can obtain blank forms for prior years by calling the toll-free number given in General Instruction D.

K. Penalties.—

Against the organization.—Under section 6652(c), a penalty of $10 a day, not to exceed the lesser of $5,000 or 5% of the gross receipts of the organization for the year, may be charged when a return is filed late, unless you can show that the late filing was due to reasonable cause. The penalty begins on the due date for filing the Form 990. The penalty may also be charged if you file an incomplete return or furnish incorrect information. To avoid having to supply missing information later, be sure to complete all applicable line items; answer "Yes," "No," or "N/A" (not applicable) to each question on the return; make an entry (including a "-0-" when appropriate) on all *total* lines; and enter "None" or "N/A" if an entire part does not apply.

Against responsible person(s).—If you do not file a complete return or do not furnish correct information, the IRS will write to give you a fixed time to fulfill these requirements. After that period expires, the person failing to comply will be charged a penalty of $10 a day, not to exceed $5,000, unless he or she shows that not complying was due to reasonable cause. If more than one person is responsible, they are jointly and individually liable for the penalty.

There are also penalties—fines and imprisonment—for willfully not filing returns and for filing fraudulent returns and statements with IRS (sections 7203, 7206, and 7207). There are also penalties for failure to comply with public disclosure requirements as discussed in General Instruction L. States may impose additional penalties for failure to meet their separate filing requirements.

L. Public Inspection of Completed Exempt Organization Returns and Approved Exemption Applications.—
Through the IRS.—

Forms 990, 990EZ, 990-PF, and certain other completed exempt organization returns are available for public inspection and copying upon request. Approved applications for exemption from Federal income tax are also available. The IRS, however, may not disclose portions of an application relating to any trade secrets, etc., nor can the IRS disclose the schedule of contributors required by Forms 990 and 990EZ (section 6104).

A request for inspection must be in writing and must include the name and address (city and state) of the organization that filed the return or application. A request to inspect a return should indicate the type (number) of the return and the year(s) involved. The request should be sent to the District Director (Attention: Disclosure Officer) of the district in which the requester desires to inspect the return or application. If inspection at the IRS National Office is desired, the request should be sent to the Commissioner of Internal Revenue, Attention: Freedom of Information Reading Room, 1111 Constitution Avenue, N.W., Washington, DC 20224.

You can use Form 4506-A to request a copy or to inspect an exempt organization return through the IRS. There is a fee for photocopying.

Through the organization.—

(1) *Annual return.*—An organization must, during the three-year period beginning with the due date (including extensions, if any), of the Forms 990 (or 990EZ), make its return available for public inspection upon request. All parts of the return and all required schedules and attachments, other than the schedule of contributors to the organization, must be made available. Inspection must be permitted during regular business hours at the organization's principal office and at each of its regional or district offices having three or more employees.

This provision applies to any organization that files Form 990 (or 990EZ), regardless of the size of the organization and whether or not it has any paid employees.

If an organization furnishes additional information to the IRS to be made part of its return, as a result of an examination or correspondence from the Service Center processing the return, it must also make that information part of the return it provides for public inspection.

If the organization does not maintain a permanent office, it must provide a reasonable location for a requester to inspect the organization's annual returns. The organization may mail the information to a requester. However, the organization can charge for copying and postage only if the requester gives up the right to a free inspection. (Notice 88-120, 1988-2 C.B. 454)

Any person who does not comply with the public inspection requirement shall be assessed a penalty of $10 for each day that inspection was not permitted, up to a maximum of $5,000 with respect to any one return. No penalty will be imposed if the failure is due to reasonable cause. Any person who willfully fails to comply shall be subject to an additional penalty of $1,000 (sections 6652(c) and 6685).

(2) *Exemption application.*—Any section 501(c) or 501(d) organization that submitted an application for recognition of exemption to the Internal Revenue Service after July 15, 1987, must make available for public inspection a copy of its application (together with a copy of any papers submitted in support of its application) and any letter or other document issued by the Internal Revenue Service in response to the application. An organization that submitted its exemption application on or before July 15, 1987, must also comply with this requirement if it had a copy of its application on July 15, 1987. As in the case of annual returns, the copy of the application and related documents must be made available for inspection during regular business hours at the organization's principal office and at each of its regional or district offices having at least three employees.

If the organization does not maintain a permanent office, it must provide a reasonable location for the inspection of both its annual returns and exemption application. The information may be mailed. (See reference to Notice 88-120 in the discussion above for *Annual return*).

The organization need not disclose any portion of an application relating to trade secrets, etc., that would not also be disclosable by the IRS.

The penalties for failure to comply with this provision are the same as those discussed in *Annual return* above, except that the $5,000 limitation does not apply.

M. Solicitations of Nondeductible Contributions.—Any fundraising solicitation by or on behalf of any section 501(c) organization that is not eligible to receive contributions deductible as charitable contributions for Federal income tax purposes must include an express statement that contributions or gifts to it are not deductible as charitable contributions. The statement must be in a conspicuous and easily recognizable format whether the solicitation is made in written or printed form, by television or radio, or by telephone. However, this provision applies only to those organizations whose annual gross receipts are normally more than $100,000. Religious and apostolic organizations described in section 501(d), as well as political organizations (including PACs) described in section 527(e), are also required to comply with this provision.

Failure to disclose that contributions are not deductible could result in a penalty of $1,000 for each day on which a failure occurs. The maximum penalty for failures by any organization, during any calendar year, shall not exceed $10,000. In cases where the failure to make the disclosure is due to intentional disregard of the law, the $10,000 limitation does not apply and more severe penalties are applicable. No penalty will be imposed if the failure is due to reasonable cause.

N. Disclosures Regarding Certain Information and Services Furnished.—A section 501(c) organization that offers to sell or solicits money for specific information or a routine service for any individual that could be obtained by such individual from a Federal Government agency free or for a nominal charge must disclose that fact conspicuously when making such offer or solicitation. Any organization that intentionally disregards this requirement will be subject to a penalty for each day on which the offers or solicitations are made. The penalty imposed for a particular day is the greater of $1,000 or 50% of the total cost of the offers and solicitations made on that day which lacked the required disclosure.

O. Disclosures Regarding Certain Transactions and Relationships.—In their annual returns on Schedule A (Form 990), section 501(c)(3) organizations must disclose information regarding their direct or indirect transfers to, and other direct or indirect relationships with, other section 501(c) organizations (except other section 501(c)(3) organizations) or section 527 political organizations. This provision helps to prevent the diversion or expenditure of a section 501(c)(3) organization's funds for purposes not intended by section 501(c)(3). All section 501(c)(3) organizations must maintain records regarding all such

transfers, transactions and relationships. (See General Instruction K, Penalties.)

P. Erroneous Backup Withholding.—Recipients of dividend or interest payments generally must certify their correct tax identification number to the bank or other payer on **Form W-9**, Request for Taxpayer Identification Number and Certification. If the payer does not get this information, it must withhold part of the payments as "backup withholding." If your organization was subject to erroneous backup withholding because the payer did not realize you were an exempt organization and not subject to this withholding, you can claim credit on Form 990-T for the amount withheld. (See the Instructions for Form 990-T.) Claims for refund must be filed within three years after the date the original return was due; three years after the date the organization filed it; or two years after the date the tax was paid, whichever is later.

Q. Group Return.—A central, parent, or "like" organization can file a group return on Form 990 for two or more local organizations that are:

1. Affiliated with the central organization at the time its annual accounting period ends;

2. Subject to the central organization's general supervision or control;

3. Tax exempt under a group exemption letter that is still in effect; and

4. Have the same accounting period as the central organization.

If the parent organization is required to file a return itself (see General Instruction B for a list of organizations not required to file), it must file a separate return and may not be included in the group return.

Every year, each local organization must authorize the central organization in writing to include it in the group return and must declare, under penalty of perjury, that the authorization and the information it submits to be included in the group return are true and complete.

If you prepare a group Form 990, attach schedules showing: (1) the total number of local organizations included and the name, address, and employer identification number of each one; and (2) the same information for those not included. When you prepare the return, be sure not to confuse the four-digit group exemption number (GEN) in item I of the heading on page 1, with the nine-digit employer identification number in item C.

R. Organizations in Foreign Countries and U.S. Possessions.—Report amounts in U.S. dollars and state what conversion rate you use. Combine amounts from within and outside the United States and report the total for each item. All information must be given in the English language.

Specific Instructions

Completing the Heading of Form 990.—

The instructions that follow are keyed to items in the heading for Form 990.

Page 5

Item A. *Accounting Period.*—Use the 1991 Form 990 to report on a calendar year or a fiscal year accounting period that began in 1991. Show the month and day your fiscal year began in 1991 and the date the fiscal year ended. (Refer to General Instruction G.)

Item B. *Name and Address.*—If we mailed you a Form 990 Package with a preaddressed mailing label, please attach the label in the name and address space on your return. Your using the label helps us avoid errors in processing your return. If any information on the label is wrong, draw a line through that part and correct it.

Include the suite, room, or other unit number after the street address. If the Post Office does not deliver mail to the street address and the organization has a P.O. box, show the P.O. box number instead of the street address.

Item C. *Employer Identification Number.*—You should have only one Federal employer identification number. If you have more than one and have not been advised which to use, notify the Service Center for your area (from the Where To File list in General Instruction H). State what numbers you have, the name and address to which each number was assigned, and the address of your principal office. The IRS will advise you which number to use. Section 501(c)(9) organizations must use their own employer identification number and not the number of their sponsor.

Item D. *State Registration Number.*— (Refer to General Instruction E.)

Item E. *Application Pending.*—If your application for exemption is pending, check this box and complete the return.

Item F. *Type of Organization.*—If your organization is exempt under section 501(c), check the applicable box and insert within the parentheses a number that identifies your type of organization. If you are a section 4947(a)(1) charitable trust, check the applicable box, complete question 92 of Form 990, and see General Instructions C1 and C7.

Item G. *Accounting Method.*—Indicate the method of accounting used in preparing this return. Unless instructed otherwise, you should generally use the same accounting method on the return to figure revenue and expenses that you regularly use to keep the organization's books and records. To be acceptable for Form 990 reporting purposes, however, the method of accounting used must clearly reflect income.

If you prepare a Form 990 for state reporting purposes, you may file an identical return with IRS even though it does not agree with your books of account, unless how you report one or more items on the state return conflicts with the instructions for preparing Form 990 for filing with the IRS. For example, if you maintain your books on the cash receipts and disbursements method of accounting but prepare a state return based on the accrual method, you could use that return for reporting to the IRS. As another example, if a state reporting

Page 6

requirement requires you to report certain revenue, expense, or balance sheet items differently from how you normally account for them on your books, a Form 990 prepared for that state is acceptable for the IRS reporting purposes if the state reporting requirement does not conflict with the Form 990 instructions. You should keep a reconciliation of any differences between your books of account and the Form 990 you file.

Most states that accept Form 990 in place of their own forms require that all amounts be reported based on the accrual method of accounting. See General Instruction E.

Item H. *Group Return, etc.*—(Refer to General Instruction Q.)

Item I. *Group Exemption Number.*—If applicable, enter the four-digit group exemption number (GEN).

Item J. *Change of Address.*—If you changed your address since you filed your previous return, check this box.

Item K. *Gross Receipts of $25,000 or Less.*—Check this box if your gross receipts are normally not more than $25,000. However, see General Instructions A5 and B11.

Public Inspection.—All information you report on or with your Form 990, including attachments, will be available for public inspection, except the schedule of contributors required for line 1d, Part I. Please make sure your forms and attachments are clear enough to photocopy legibly.

Signature.—To make the return complete, an officer authorized to sign it must sign in the space provided. For a corporation, this officer may be the president, vice president, treasurer, assistant treasurer, chief accounting officer, or other corporate officer, such as a tax officer. A receiver, trustee, or assignee must sign any return he or she files for a corporation. For a trust, the authorized trustee(s) must sign.

If the return was prepared by an individual, firm, or corporation paid for preparing it, the paid preparer's space must also be signed. For a firm or corporation that was a paid preparer, sign in the firm's or corporation's name. If you checked the box for question 92 of the form (section 4947(a)(1) charitable trust filing Form 990 instead of Form 1041), you must also enter the paid preparer's social security number or employer identification number in the margin next to the paid preparer's space. Leave the paid preparer's space blank if the return was prepared by a regular employee of the filing organization.

Rounding Off to Whole-Dollar Amounts.—You may show money items as whole-dollar amounts. Drop any amount less than 50 cents and increase any amount from 50 through 99 cents to the next higher dollar.

Completing All Lines.—Unless you are permitted to use certain DOL forms or Form 5500 series returns as partial substitutes for Form 990 (see General Instruction F), do not leave any applicable

lines blank or attach any other forms or schedules instead of entering the required information on the appropriate line on Form 990.

Assembling Form 990.—Before filing the Form 990, assemble your package of forms and attachments in the following manner:

- Form 990
- Schedule A (Form 990)
- Attachments to Form 990
- Attachments to Schedule A (Form 990)

Attachments.—Use the schedules on the official form unless you need more space. If you use attachments, they must:

(1) Show the form number and tax year;

(2) Show the organization's name and employer identification number;

(3) Include the information required by the form;

(4) Follow the format and line sequence of the form; and

(5) Be on the same size paper as the form.

Part I—Statement of Revenue, Expenses, and Changes in Net Assets or Fund Balances.—

All organizations filing Form 990 with the IRS or any state must complete Part I. Some states that accept Form 990 in place of their own forms require additional information.

Line 1—Contributions, Gifts, Grants, and Similar Amounts Received.—On lines 1a through 1c, report amounts received as voluntary contributions; that is, payments, or the part of any payment, for which the payer (donor) does not receive full value (fair market value) from the recipient (donee) organization. (For grants, see *Grants that are equivalent to contributions,* page 7.) Report all expenses of raising contributions in column (D), Part II, and on line 15 of Part I.

Contributions can arise from special fundraising events when excess payment received for items offered.— Special fundraising activities such as dinners, door-to-door sales of merchandise, carnivals, and bingo games can produce both contributions and revenue. If a buyer, at such an event, pays more for goods or services than their retail value, report as a contribution both on line 1a and on line 9a (within parentheses) any amount paid in excess of the retail value. This usually occurs when organizations seek public support through solicitation programs that are both special fundraising events or activities and solicitations for contributions.

For example, an organization announces that anyone who contributes at least $40 to the organization can choose to receive a book worth $16 retail value. A person who gives $40, and who chooses the book, is really purchasing the book for $16 and also making a contribution of $24. The contribution of $24, which is the difference between the buyer's payment and the $16 retail value of the book, would be reported on line 1a and again on the description line of 9a (within parentheses). The revenue received ($16 retail value of the book) would be reported in the amount column on line 9a.

If a contributor gives more than $40, that person would be making a larger contribution, the difference between the book's retail value of $16 and the amount actually given. (Rev. Rul. 67-246, 1967-2 C.B. 104, explains this principle in detail. See also line 9 instructions and Publication 1391.)

The expenses relating directly to the sale of the book would be reported on line 9b. However, all other expenses of raising contributions would be reported in column (D), Part II (fundraising expense) and on line 15 of Part I.

At the time of any solicitation or payment, organizations that are eligible to receive contributions should advise patrons of the amount deductible for Federal tax purposes.

Contributions can arise from special fundraising events when items of only nominal value offered.—If an organization offers goods or services of only nominal value through a special fundraising event, report the *entire* amount received for such benefits as a contribution on line 1a (direct public support). Report all related expenses in column (D), Part II. Benefits have a nominal value when:

(1) The benefit's fair market value is not more than 2% of the payment, or $50, whichever is less; or

(2) The payment is $28.58 or more; the only benefits received are token items bearing the organization's name or symbol; and the organization's cost (as opposed to fair market value) is $5.71 or less for all benefits received by a donor during the calendar year. These two amounts are adjusted annually for inflation. (See Rev. Proc. 90-12, 1990-1 C.B. 471 and Rev. Proc. 90-64, 1990-2 C.B. 674.)

Section 501(c)(3) organizations.—Correctly dividing gross receipts from special fundraising events into revenue and contributions is especially important for a section 501(c)(3) organization that claims public support as described in section 170(b)(1)(A)(vi) or 509(a)(2). In the public support computations of these Code sections, the revenue portion of gross receipts may be: (a) excluded entirely, (b) treated as public support, or (c) if the revenue represents unrelated trade or business income, treated as nonpublic support.

Section 501(c)(3) organizations must divide gross receipts from special fundraising events into revenue and contributions according to the above instructions when preparing the Support Schedule in Part IV of Schedule A (Form 990).

The Support Schedule generally includes only the four preceding years but also includes the current year if there have

been material changes in the organization's sources of support in that year.

Section 501(c)(9), (17), (18), and (20) organizations.—These organizations provide life, sick, accident, welfare, unemployment, pension, group legal services, or similar benefits or a combination of these benefits to participants. When such an organization receives payments from participants or their employers to provide these benefits, report the payments on line 2 as program service revenue, rather than on line 1 as contributions.

Donations of services are not contributions.—In Part I, do not include the value of services donated to the organization, or items such as the free use of materials, equipment, or facilities as contributions on line 1. See the instructions for Part III and for Part VI, line 82, for the optional reporting of such amounts in Parts III and VI.

Grants that are equivalent to contributions.—Grants that encourage an organization receiving the grant to carry on programs or activities that further its exempt purposes are grants that are equivalent to contributions. Report them on line 1. The grantor may require that the programs of the grant recipient (grantee) conform to the grantor's own policies and may specify the use of the grant, such as use for the restoration of a historic building or a voter registration drive.

A grant is still equivalent to a contribution if the grant recipient provides a service or makes a product that benefits the grantor incidentally. (See examples in line 1c instructions.) However, a grant is a payment for services, and not a contribution, if the grant requires the grant recipient to provide that grantor with a specific service, facility, or product rather than to give a direct benefit primarily to the general public or to that part of the public served by the organization. In general, do not report as contributions any payments for a service, facility, or product that primarily give some economic or physical benefit to the payer.

For example, a public interest organization described in section 501(c)(4) makes a grant to another organization to conduct a nationwide survey to determine voter attitudes on issues of interest to the grantor. The grantor plans to use the results of the survey to plan its own program for the next three years. Under these circumstances, since the survey serves the grantor's direct needs and benefits the grantor more than incidentally, the grant to the organization making the survey is not a contribution. The grant recipient should not report the grant as a contribution but should report it on line 2 as program service revenue.

Treat research to develop products for the payer's use or benefit as directly serving the payer. However, generally, basic research or studies in the physical or social sciences should not be treated as serving the payer's needs.

See Regulations section 1.509(a)(3)(g) to determine if a grant is a contribution

reportable on line 1 or a revenue item reportable elsewhere on Form 990.

Noncash contributions.—To report contributions received in a form other than cash, use the market value as of the date of the contribution. For marketable securities registered and listed on a recognized securities exchange, measure market value by the average of the highest and lowest quoted selling prices (or the average between the bona fide bid and asked prices) on the contribution date. (See section 20.2031-1 of the Estate Tax Regulations for rules to determine the value of contributed stocks and bonds.) When market value cannot be readily determined, use an appraised or estimated value.

To determine the amount of any noncash contribution that is subject to an outstanding debt, subtract the debt from the property's fair market value. Record the asset at its full value and record the debt as a liability in the books of account. See also Note (1) in the instructions for line 1d.

Line 1a—Direct public support.— *Contributions, gifts, grants, and similar amounts received.*—Enter the gross amounts of contributions, gifts, grants, and bequests that the organization received directly from the public. Include amounts received from individuals, trusts, corporations, estates, and foundations. Also include contributions and grants from public charities and other exempt organizations that are neither fundraising organizations nor affiliates of the filing organization. (See the instructions for line 1b.)

Membership dues.—Report on line 1a membership dues and assessments that represent contributions from the public rather than payments for benefits received (see the instructions for line 3) or payments from affiliated organizations.

Government grants.—Report government grants on line 1c if they represent contributions, or on line 2 (and on line 93(g) of Part VII) if they represent fees for services. See line 1 and 1c instructions.

Commercial co-venture.—Report amounts contributed by a commercial co-venture on line 1a as a contribution received directly from the public. These are amounts received by an organization (donee) for allowing an outside organization to use the donee's name in a sales promotion campaign. In such a campaign, the donor advertises that it will contribute a certain dollar amount to the donee organization for each unit of a particular product or service sold or for each occurrence of a specific type.

Contributions received through special fundraising events.—Report contributions received through special fundraising events on line 1a. (See line 1 instructions above and the instructions for line 9.)

Line 1b—Indirect public support.— Enter the total contributions received indirectly from the public through solicitation campaigns conducted by federated fundraising agencies and similar fundraising organizations (such as a United

Page 7

Way organization and certain sectarian federations). These organizations normally conduct fundraising campaigns within a single metropolitan area or some part of a particular state and allocate part of the net proceeds to each participating organization on the basis of individual donors' designations and other factors.

Include on line 1b amounts contributed by other organizations closely associated with the reporting organization. This includes contributions received from a parent organization, subordinate, or another organization having the same parent. National organizations that share in fundraising campaigns conducted by their local affiliates should report the amount they receive on line 1b.

Line 1c—Government grants.—The preceding line 1 instructions, under the heading *Grants that are equivalent to contributions,* apply to this item in particular. A grant or other payment from a governmental unit represents a contribution if its primary purpose is to enable the donee to provide a service to, or maintain a facility for, the direct benefit of the public rather than to serve the direct and immediate needs of the grantor (even if the public pays part of the expense of providing the service or facility).

The following are examples of governmental grants and other payments that represent contributions:

1. Payments by a governmental unit for the construction or maintenance of library or hospital facilities open to the public;

2. Payments under government programs to nursing homes or homes for the aged in order to provide health care or other services to their residents;

3. Payments to child placement or child guidance organizations under government programs serving children in the community. The general public gets the primary and direct benefit from these payments and any benefit to the governmental unit itself would be indirect and insubstantial as compared to the public benefit.

Line 1d—Total contributions, etc.— Enter the total of amounts reported on lines 1a through 1c.

Attached schedule.—**Schedule of contributors** (not open to public inspection.) **(Caution:** See Note (2) below.)

Attach a schedule listing contributors who gave the organization, directly or indirectly, money, securities, or other property worth $5,000 or more during the year. If no one contributed the reportable minimum, you do not need to attach a schedule. Show each contributor's name and address, the total amount received, and the date received. Contributors include individuals, fiduciaries, partnerships, corporations, associations, trusts, or exempt organizations.

If an employer withholds contributions from employees' pay and periodically gives them to the organization, report only the employer's name and address and the total amount given unless you know that a particular employee gave enough to be listed separately.

In determining whether a contributor gave $5,000 or more, total that person's gifts of $1,000 or more. Do not include smaller gifts. If the contribution consists of property whose fair market value can be determined readily (such as market quotations for securities), describe the property and list its fair market value. Otherwise, estimate the property's value. See Note (1) below.

If an organization meets the terms of either of the following exceptions, some information in its schedule will vary from that described above.

Exception 1: *Organization described in section 501(c)(3) that meets the 33⅓% support test of the Regulations under section 170(b)(1)(A)(vi) (whether or not the organization is otherwise described in section 170(b)(1)(A)).*

The schedule should give the above information only for contributors whose gifts of $5,000 or over are more than 2% of the total gifts (reported on line 1d) that the organization received during the year.

Exception 2: *Organization described in section 501(c)(7), (8), (10), or (19) that received contributions or bequests for use only as described in section 170(c)(4), 2055(a)(3), or 2522(a)(3).*

The schedule should list each person whose gifts total $1,000 or more during the year. Give the donor's name, the amount given, the gift's specific purpose, and the specific use to which it was put. If an amount is set aside for a purpose described in section 170(c)(4), 2055(a)(3), or 2522(a)(3), explain how the amount is held (for instance, whether it is mingled with amounts held for other purposes). If the organization transferred the gift to another organization, name and describe the recipient and explain the relationship between the two organizations. Also show the total gifts that were $1,000 or less and were for a purpose described in section 170(c)(4), 2055(a)(3), or 2522(a)(3).

Note (1): *If you qualify to receive tax-deductible charitable contributions and you receive contributions of property (other than publicly traded securities) whose fair market value is more than $5,000, you should usually receive a partially completed* **Form 8283,** *Noncash Charitable Contributions, from the contributor. You should complete the appropriate information on Form 8283, sign it, and return it to the donor. Retain a copy for your records. See also General Instruction C17.*

Note (2): *If you file a copy of Form 990 and attachments with any state, do not include, in the attachments for the state, the schedule of contributors discussed above, unless the schedule is specifically required by the state with which you are filing the return. States that do not require the information might nevertheless make it available for public inspection along with the rest of the return.*

Lines 2 through 11.—**Note:** *Do not enter any contributions on lines 2 through 11.*

Enter all contributions on line 1. If you enter contributions on lines 2 through 11, you will be unable to complete Part VII correctly.

Line 2—Program service revenue.— Enter the total of program service revenue (exempt function income) as reported in Part VII, lines 93(a) through (g), columns (b), (d), and (e). Program services are primarily those that form the basis of an organization's exemption from tax. (For further definition, see the instructions for Part II, column (B).)

Examples.—A hospital would report on this line all of its charges for medical services (whether to be paid directly by the patients or through Medicare, Medicaid, or other third-party reimbursement), hospital parking lot fees, room charges, laboratory fees for hospital patients, and related charges for services.

Other examples of program service revenue are tuition received by a school, revenue from admissions to a concert or other performing arts event or to a museum; royalties received as author of an educational publication distributed by a commercial publisher; interest income on loans a credit union makes to its members; payments received by a section 501(c)(9) organization from participants or employers of participants for health and welfare benefits coverage; insurance premiums received by a fraternal beneficiary society; and registration fees received in connection with a meeting or convention.

Program-related investments.—Program service revenue also includes income from program-related investments. These investments are made primarily for accomplishing an exempt purpose of the investing organization rather than to produce income. Examples are scholarship loans and low interest loans to charitable organizations, indigents, or victims of a disaster. Rental income from an exempt function is another example. See line 6 instructions.

Unrelated trade or business activities.— Unrelated trade or business activities (not including any special fundraising events or activities) that generate fees for services may also be program service activities. A social club, for example, should report as program service revenue the fees it charges both members and nonmembers for the use of its tennis courts and golf course.

Sales of inventory items by hospitals, colleges, and universities.—Books and records maintained in accordance with generally accepted accounting principles for hospitals, colleges, and universities are more specialized than books and records maintained according to those accounting principles for other types of organizations that file Form 990. Accordingly, hospitals, colleges, and universities may report, as program service revenue on line 2, sales of inventory items otherwise reportable on line 10a. In that event, show the applicable cost of goods sold as program service expense on line 13 of Part I and in column (B) of Part II. All other organizations,

Page 8

however, should not report sales of inventory items on line 2.

Line 3—Membership dues and assessments.—Enter members' and affiliates' dues and assessments that are not contributions.

(a) *Dues and assessments received that compare reasonably with available benefits.*—When dues and assessments are received that compare reasonably with available membership benefits, report such dues and assessments on line 3.

(b) *Organizations that usually match dues and benefits.*—Organizations, other than those described in section 501(c)(3), generally provide benefits that have a reasonable relationship to dues. This occurs usually in organizations described in section 501(c)(5), (6), or (7), although benefits to members may be indirect. Report such dues and assessments on line 3.

(c) *Dues or assessments received that exceed the value of available membership benefits.*—Whether or not membership benefits are used, dues received by an organization, to the extent they are more than the monetary value of the membership benefits available to the dues payer, are a contribution includable on line 1a. (See Rev. Ruls. 54-565, 1954-2 C.B. 95 and 68-432, 1968-2 C.B. 104.)

(d) *Dues received primarily for the organization's support.*—If a member pays dues primarily to support the organization's activities, and not to obtain benefits of more than nominal monetary value, those dues are a contribution to the organization includable on line 1a.

Examples of membership benefits.—Examples of such benefits include subscriptions to publications, newsletters (other than one about the organization's activities only), free or reduced-rate admissions to events the organization sponsors, the use of its facilities, and discounts on articles or services that both members and nonmembers can buy. In figuring the value of membership benefits, disregard other intangible benefits, such as the right to attend meetings, vote or hold office in the organization, and the distinction of being a member of the organization.

Line 4—Interest on savings and temporary cash investments.—Enter the amount of interest income from savings and temporary cash investments reportable on line 46. So-called dividends or earnings received from mutual savings banks, etc., are actually interest and should be entered on line 4.

Line 5—Dividends and interest from securities.—Enter the amount of dividend and interest income from debt and equity securities (stocks and bonds) of the type reportable on line 54. Include amounts received from payments on securities loans, as defined in section 512(a)(5). Do not include any capital gains dividends that are reportable on line 8. See the instructions for line 2 for reporting income from program-related investments.

Line 6a—Gross rents.—Enter the gross rental income for the year from investment property reportable on line 55. Do not include rental income from an exempt function (program service). For example, an organization whose exempt purpose is to provide low-rental housing to persons with low income receives exempt function income from such rentals. Report such income on line 2 and report the related expenses in column (B) of Part II. Rental income, however, is not exempt function income when an organization rents office space, or other facilities or equipment, to *unaffiliated* exempt organizations. Report such rental income on line 6a, unless the rent charged is well below the fair rental value of the property and the purpose for charging rent at less than fair rental value was to help the organization that rented the property to carry out its own exempt purpose.

Only for purposes of completing this return, treat income from renting property to *affiliated* exempt organizations as exempt function income (program service revenue) and report it on line 2.

Line 6b—Rental expenses.—Enter the expenses paid or incurred for the income reported on line 6a. Include depreciation if it is recorded in the organization's books and records.

Line 6c—Net rental income or (loss).—Subtract line 6b from line 6a. Show any loss in parentheses.

Line 7—Other investment income.—Enter the amount of investment income not reportable on lines 4 through 6 and describe the type of income in the space provided or in an attachment. The income should be the gross amount derived from investments reportable on line 56. Include, for example, royalty income from mineral interests owned by the organization. However, do not include income from program-related investments (see the instructions for line 2). Also exclude unrealized gains and losses on investments carried at market value (see the instructions for line 20).

Lines 8a through 8d—Capital gains.—Report on lines 8a through 8c all sales of securities in column (A). Use column (B) to report sales of all other types of investments (such as real estate, royalty interests, or partnership interests) and all other capital assets (such as program-related investments and fixed assets used by the organization in its regular activities).

On line 8a, for each column, enter the total gross sales price of all involved assets. Total the cost or other basis (less depreciation), and selling expenses and enter the result on line 8b. On line 8c, enter the net gain or loss. On lines 8a and 8c, report capital gains dividends, the organization's share of capital gains and losses from a partnership, and capital gains distributions from trusts. Indicate the source on the schedule described below.

Combine the gain and/or loss figures reported on line 8c, columns (A) and (B) and report that total on line 8d. Do not include any unrealized gains or losses on securities carried at market value in the books of account. See the instructions for line 20.

For reporting sales of securities on Form 990, you may use the more convenient average cost basis method to figure the organization's gain or loss. When a security is sold, compare its sales price with the average cost basis of the particular security to determine gain or loss. However, generally, for reporting sales of securities on Form 990-T, do not use the average cost basis to determine gain or loss.

Attached schedule.—(a) *Assets other than publicly traded securities and inventory.*—Attach a schedule showing the sale or exchange of *nonpublicly* traded securities and the sale or exchange of other assets that are not inventory items. The schedule should show security transactions separately from the sale of other assets. Show for each of these assets:

(1) Date acquired and how acquired;

(2) Date sold and to whom sold;

(3) Gross sales price;

(4) Cost, other basis, or if donated, value at time acquired (state which);

(5) Expense of sale and cost of improvements made after acquisition; and

(6) If depreciable property, depreciation since acquisition.

(b) *Publicly traded securities.*—In the attached schedule, for sales of publicly traded securities through a broker, you may total the gross sales price, the cost or other basis, and the expenses of sale on all such securities sold, and report lump-sum figures in place of the detailed reporting required by the above paragraph. For preparing Form 990, publicly traded securities include common and preferred stocks, bonds (including governmental obligations), and mutual fund shares that are listed and regularly traded in an over-the-counter market or on an established exchange and for which market quotations are published or otherwise readily available.

Lines 9a through 9c—Special fundraising events and activities.—On the appropriate line, enter the gross revenue, expenses, and net income from all special fundraising events and activities, such as dinners, dances, carnivals, raffles, bingo games, other gambling activities, and door-to-door sales of merchandise. In themselves, these activities only incidentally accomplish an exempt purpose. Their sole or primary purpose is to raise funds (other than contributions) to finance the organization's exempt activities. This is done by offering goods or services that have more than a nominal value (compared to the price charged) for a payment that is more than the direct cost of those goods or services.

Characterizing any required payment as a "donation" or "contribution" on tickets or on advertising or solicitation materials does not affect how such payments should be reported on Form 990. As discussed above, the amount of the contribution is the excess of the amount paid over the value received by the payer. (See Publication 1391.)

Special fundraising events may generate both revenue and contributions.—Special fundraising events sometimes generate both contributions and revenue. When a buyer pays more than the value of the goods or services furnished, enter

(1) as gross revenue, on line 9a (in the amount column) the value of the goods or services;

(2) as a contribution, on both line 1a and line 9a (within parentheses) the amount received that exceeds the value of the goods or services given.

Report on line 9b only the expenses directly attributable to the goods or services the buyer receives from a special fundraising event. If you include an expense on line 9b, do not report it again on line 10b or in Part II.

For example, at a special fundraising event, an organization received $100 in gross receipts for goods valued at $40. The organization entered gross revenue of $40 on line 9a and entered a contribution of $60 on both line 1a and line 9a (within parentheses). The contribution was the difference between the gross revenue of $40 and the gross receipts of $100.

For further guidance regarding contributions and revenue, see line 1 and 1a instructions.

Sales of goods or services of only nominal value.—If the goods or services offered at special fundraising events have only nominal value, include all of the receipts as contributions on line 1a and all of the related expenses as fundraising expenses on line 15 and in column (D) of Part II. See line 1 instructions for a description of benefits of nominal value. These are adjusted annually for inflation.

An activity may generate only contributions.—An activity that generates only contributions, such as a solicitation campaign by mail, is not a special fundraising event and should not be reported on line 9.

Sweepstakes, raffles, and lotteries may produce revenue or contributions.—The proceeds of solicitation campaigns in which the names of contributors and other respondents are entered in a drawing for the awarding of prizes (so-called "sweepstakes" or "lotteries") are contributions and the related expenses are fundraising expenses reportable in column (D) of Part II. However, raffles and lotteries in which a payment of at least a specified minimum amount is required for each entry are special fundraising events unless the prizes awarded have only nominal value.

Attached schedule.—Attach a schedule listing the three largest special events conducted, as measured by gross receipts. Describe each of these events and indicate for each event the gross receipts; the amount of contributions included in gross receipts (see the instructions above); the gross revenue (gross receipts less contributions); the direct expenses; and the net income (gross revenue less direct expenses).

Page 10

Furnish the same information, in total figures, for all other special events held that are not among the three largest. Indicate the type and number of the events not listed individually (for example, three dances and two raffles).

An example of this schedule might appear in columnar form as follows:

Special Events:	(A)	(B)	(C)	Total
Gross Receipts	$XXX	$XXX	$XXX	$XXX
Less: Contributions	XXX	XXX	XXX	XXX
Gross Revenue	XXX	XXX	XXX	XXX
Less: Direct Expenses	XXX	XXX	XXX	XXX
Net Income or (loss)	$XXX	$XXX	$XXX	$XXX

If you use the above schedule, report the total for contributions on line 1a of Form 990 and on line 9a (within parentheses of the description line). Report the totals for gross revenue, in the amount column, on line 9a; direct expenses on line 9b; and net income or (loss) on line 9c.

Fundraising record retention.—Section 501(c) organizations that are eligible to receive tax-deductible contributions under section 170(c) of the Code must keep sample copies of their fundraising materials, such as dues statements or other fundraising solicitations, tickets, receipts, or other evidence of payments received in connection with fundraising activities. If organizations advertise their fundraising events, they must keep samples of the advertising copy. If they use radio or television to make their solicitations, they must keep samples of scripts, transcripts, or other evidence of on-air solicitations. If organizations retain outside fundraisers, they must keep samples of the fundraising materials used by the outside fundraisers. For each fundraising event, organizations must keep records to show that portion of any payment received from patrons that is not deductible; that is, the fair market value of the goods or services received by the patrons.

Lines 10a through 10c—Gross profit on sales of inventory.—Enter the gross sales (less returns and allowances), cost of goods sold, and gross profit or (loss) from the sale of all inventory items, other than those sold in special fundraising events and activities reported on line 9. Sales of inventory items, for line 10, are for those the organization either makes to sell to others or buys for resale. This does not include investments on which the organization expected to profit by appreciation and sale. Report sales of investments on line 8. On line 10, report sales revenue and the related cost of goods sold, whether the sale of the merchandise involved is an exempt function or an unrelated trade or business.

Hospitals, colleges, and universities can, however, use an optional method of reporting sales of inventory items (see line 2 instructions).

Line 11—Other revenue.—Enter the total amount from Part VII, lines 103(a) through (e), columns (b), (d), and (e). This figure represents the total income from all sources not covered by lines 1 through 10.

Examples of income includable on line 11 are interest on notes receivable not held as investments; interest on loans to officers, directors, trustees, key employees and other employees; and royalties that are not investment income or program service revenue.

Line 12—Total revenue.—Enter the total of lines 1d through 11.

Lines 13 through 15—Program services, management and general, and fundraising expenses.—

Section 4947(a)(1) charitable trusts and sections 501(c)(3) and (c)(4) organizations.—Complete Part II and then enter on lines 13 through 15 the appropriate amounts from the totals for columns (B), (C), and (D) reported on line 44, Part II.

All other organizations.—You are not required to complete lines 13 through 15.

Line 16—Payments to affiliates.—This expense classification is used to report certain types of payments to organizations "affiliated with" (closely related to) a reporting agency.

Payments to affiliated state or national organizations.—Dues payments by the local charity to its affiliated state or national (parent) organization are usually reported on line 16. Report on this line predetermined quota support and dues payments (excluding membership dues of the type described below) by local agencies to their state or national organizations for unspecified purposes; i.e., general use of funds for the national organization's own program and support services.

Purchases from affiliates.—Purchases of goods or services from affiliates are not reported on line 16 but are reported as expenses in the usual manner.

Expenses for providing goods or services to affiliates.—In addition to payments made directly to affiliated organizations, expenses incurred in providing goods or services to affiliates may be reported on line 16 if:

(1) The goods or services provided are not related to the program services conducted by the organization furnishing them (for example, when a local organization incurs expenses in the production of a solicitation film for the state or national organization); and

(2) The costs involved are not connected with the management and general or fundraising functions of the reporting organization (for example, when a local organization furnishes a copy of its mailing list to the state or national organization, the expense of preparing the copy provided may be reported on line 16, but not expenses of preparing and maintaining the local organization's master list).

Federated fundraising agencies.—These agencies (see the instructions for line 1b) should include in their own support the full amount of contributions received in connection with a solicitation campaign they conduct, even though donors designate specific agencies to receive part or all of their individual contributions.

These fundraising organizations should report the allocations to participating agencies as awards and grants (line 22) and quota support payments to their state or national organization as payments to affiliates (line 16).

Voluntary awards or grants to affiliates.— Do not report on line 16 voluntary awards or grants made by the reporting agency to its state or national organization for specified purposes. Report such awards or grants on line 22, Grants and allocations.

Membership dues paid to other organizations.—Membership dues that are paid to obtain general membership benefits, such as regular services, publications, and materials, from other organizations should be reported as "Other expenses" on line 43. This is the case, for example, if a charitable organization pays dues to a trade association comprised of otherwise unrelated members.

Attached schedule.—Attach a schedule listing the name and address of each affiliate that received payments reported on line 16. Specify the amount and purpose of the payments to each affiliate.

Note: *Properly distinguishing between payments to affiliates and awards and grants is especially important if you use Form 990 for state reporting purposes (see General Instruction E). If you use Form 990 only for reporting to IRS, payments to affiliated state or national organizations that do not represent membership dues reportable as "Other expenses" on line 43 (see instructions above) may be reported either on line 16 or line 22 and explained in the required attachment.*

Line 17—Total expenses.—Organizations using only column (A) of Part II should enter the total of line 16 and line 44 of column (A), Part II. Other organizations should enter the total of lines 13 through 16. Organizations using Form 5500, 5500-C/R, or an approved DOL form as a partial substitute for Form 990 (see General Instruction F) should enter the total expense figure from Form 5500 or 5500-C/R, or from the required reconciliation schedule if Form LM-2 or LM-3 is used.

Line 18—Excess or (deficit) for the year.—Enter the difference between lines 12 and 17. If line 17 is more than line 12, enter the difference in parentheses.

Line 19—Net assets or fund balances, beginning of year.—Enter the amount from column (A) of line 74 (or from Form 5500, 5500-C/R, or an approved DOL form if General Instruction F applies).

Line 20—Other changes in net assets or fund balances.—Attach a schedule explaining any changes in net assets or fund balances between the beginning and end of the year that are not accounted for by the amount on line 18. Amounts to report here include adjustments of earlier years' activity and unrealized gains and losses on investments carried at market value.

Line 21—Net assets or fund balances, end of year.—Enter the total of lines 18,

19, and 20. This total figure must equal the amount reported in column (B) of line 74.

Part II—Statement of Functional Expenses.—

In General.—

Column (A).—All organizations must complete column (A) unless they are using an approved DOL form or Form 5500 or 5500-C/R as a partial substitute for Form 990 in accordance with General Instruction F.

Columns (B), (C), and (D).—These columns are optional for all organizations other than section 4947(a)(1) charitable trusts and section 501(c)(3) and (c)(4) organizations. Section 4947(a)(1) charitable trusts and section 501(c)(3) and (c)(4) organizations must complete columns (B), (C), and (D).

In Part II the organization's expenses are designated by object classification (e.g., salaries, legal fees, supplies, etc.) and allocated into three functions: program services (column (B)); management and general (column (C)); and fundraising (column (D)). These functions are explained below in the instructions for the columns. Do not include in Part II any expense items you must report on lines 6b, 8b, 9b, 10b, or 16 in Part I.

For reporting to the IRS only, use the organization's normal accounting method to report total expenses in column (A) and to segregate them into functions under columns (B), (C), and (D) (but see General Instruction E and the Specific Instructions, item G, page 6.) If the accounting system does not provide for this type of segregation, a reasonable method of allocation may be used. The amounts reported should be accurate and the method of allocation documented in the organization's records.

Report in the appropriate column expenses that are directly attributable to a particular functional category. In general, allocate expenses that relate to more than one functional category. For example, allocate employees' salaries on the basis of each employee's time. For some shared expenses such as occupancy, supplies, and depreciation of office equipment, use an appropriate basis for each kind of cost. However, you should report some other shared expenses in column (C) only. The column instructions below discuss allocating expenses.

Column (A)—Total.—For column (A), total each line item of columns (B), (C), and (D) in Part II. Except for expenses you report on lines 6b, 8b, 9b, 10b, or 16 of Part I, you should use column (A) to report all expenses the organization paid or incurred.

Column (B)—Program services.— Program services are mainly those activities that the reporting organization was created to conduct and which, along with any activities commenced subsequently, form the basis of the organization's current exemption from tax. They may be self-funded or funded out of contributions, accumulated income, investment income, or any other source.

Program services can also include the organization's unrelated trade or business activities. For example, publishing a magazine is a program service even though it contains both editorials and articles that further the organization's exempt purpose and advertising, the income from which is taxable as unrelated business income.

If an organization receives a grant to do research, produce an item, or perform a service, either to meet the grantor's specific needs or to benefit the public directly, the costs incurred represent program service expenses. Do not treat these costs as fundraising expenses, even if you report the grant on line 1 as a contribution.

Column (C)—Management and general.—Use column (C) to report the organization's expenses for overall management and functioning, rather than for its direct conduct of fundraising activities or program services. Overall management usually includes the salaries and expenses of the chief officer of the organization and that officer's staff. If part of their time is spent directly supervising program services and fundraising activities, their salaries and expenses should be allocated among those functions. Other expenses to report in column (C) include those for meetings of the board of directors or similar group; committee and staff meetings (unless held in connection with specific program services or fundraising activities); general legal services; accounting, auditing, personnel, and other centralized services; investment expenses (except those relating to rental income and program-related income— report rental expenses on line 6b and program-related expenses in column (B)); general liability insurance; preparation, publication, and distribution of an annual report; and office management.

However, you should report only general expenses in column (C). Do not use this column to report costs of special meetings or other activities that relate to fundraising or specific program services.

Column (D)—Fundraising.—Fundraising expenses represent the total expenses incurred in soliciting contributions, gifts, grants, etc. Report as fundraising expenses all expenses, including allocable overhead costs, incurred in: (a) publicizing and conducting fundraising campaigns; (b) soliciting bequests and grants from foundations or other organizations, or government grants reportable on line 1c; (c) participating in federated fundraising campaigns; (d) preparing and distributing fundraising manuals, instructions, and other materials; and (e) conducting special fundraising events that generate contributions reportable on line 1a in addition to revenue reportable on line 9a. However, any expenses attributable to revenue on line 9a (that is, the direct expenses incurred in furnishing the goods or services sold) should be reported on line 9b.

Allocating indirect expenses.—Colleges, universities, hospitals, and other organizations that accumulate indirect

Page 11

expenses in various cost centers (such as the expenses of operating and maintaining the physical plant) that are reallocated to the program services and other functional areas of the organization in a single step or in multiple steps may find it easier to report these expenses in the following optional manner:

First, report the expenses of these indirect cost centers on lines 25 through 43 of the Management and general expense column in Part II, along with the expenses properly reportable in that column.

Second, allocate the total expenses for each cost center to Program services, Management and general, and Fundraising as a separate item entry on line 43, Other expenses. Enter the name of the cost center on line 43. If any of the cost center's expenses are to be allocated to the expenses listed in Part I (such as the expenses attributable to special fundraising events and activities), enter these expenses as a negative figure in columns (A) and (C). This prevents reporting the same expense in both Parts I and II. If part of the total cost center expenses are to be allocated to columns (B), Program services, and (D), Fundraising, enter these expenses as positive amounts in these columns and as single negative amounts in column (C). Do not make any entries in column (A), Total, for these offsetting entries.

The following example illustrates the above instructions. An organization reports $50,000 of actual management and general expenses and $100,000 of expenses of an indirect cost center that are allocable in part to other functions. The total of lines 25 through 43 of column (C) would be $150,000 before the allocations were made. Assume that $10,000 (of the $100,000 total expenses of the cost center) was allocable to fundraising; $70,000 to various program services; $15,000 to management and general functions; and $5,000 to special fundraising events and activities. To report this in Part II under this alternate method:

(1) Indicate the cost center, the expenses of which are being allocated, on line 43, as "Allocation of (specify) expenses";

(2) Enter a decrease of $5,000 on the same line in the Total column, representing the special fundraising event expenses already reported on line 9b in Part I;

(3) Enter $70,000 on the same line in the Program services column;

(4) Enter $10,000 on the same line in the Fundraising column; and

(5) Enter a decrease of $85,000 on the same line in the Management and general column, representing the allocations to functional areas other than management and general.

After making these allocations, the column (C) total (line 44, column (C)) would be $65,000, consisting of the $50,000 aggregate amount and the $15,000 allocation of the aggregate cost center expenses to management and general.

The above is an example of a simple one-step allocation that shows how to report the allocation in Part II. This reporting method would actually be needed more in the case of multiple step allocations in which two or more cost centers are involved. The total expenses of the first would be allocated to the other functions, including an allocation of part of these expenses to the second cost center. The expenses of the second cost center would then be allocated to other functions and any remaining cost centers to be allocated, and so on. The greater the number of these cost centers which are allocated out, the more difficult it is to preserve the identity of the object classification of the expenses of each cost center (e.g., salaries, interest, supplies, etc.). The reporting method described above avoids this problem.

Note: *The intent of the above instructions is only to facilitate reporting indirect expenses by both object classification and function. These instructions do not in any way permit the allocation to other functions of expenses that should be reported as management and general expenses.*

Line 22—Grants and allocations.— Enter the amount of awards and grants to individuals and organizations selected by the filing organization. United Way and similar fundraising organizations should include allocations to member agencies.

Report voluntary awards and grants to affiliated organizations for specific (restricted) purposes or projects also on line 22, but not required payments to affiliates reportable on line 16.

Report scholarship, fellowship, and research grants to individuals on line 22. Certain other payments to or for the benefit of individuals may be reportable on line 23 instead. See the instructions for line 23 for specific information.

Report only the amount of actual grants and awards on line 22. Report expenses incurred in selecting recipients or monitoring compliance with the terms of a grant or award on lines 25 through 43.

Attached schedule.—Attach a schedule of amounts reported on line 22. Show on the schedule: (a) each class of activity; (b) donee's name and address and the amount given; and (c) (in the case of grants to individuals) relationship of donee if related by blood, marriage, adoption, or employment (including employees' children) to any person or corporation with an interest in the organization, such as a creator, donor, director, trustee, officer, etc.

On the schedule, classify activities in more detail than in such broad terms as charitable, educational, religious, or scientific. For example, identify payments for nursing services, laboratory construction, or fellowships.

If the property's fair market value when the organization gave it is the measure of the award or grant, also show on the schedule: (a) a description of the property; (b) its book value; (c) how the book value was determined; (d) how the fair market value was determined; and (e) the date of

the gift. Record any difference between fair market value and book value in the organization's books of account.

Line 23—Specific assistance to individuals.—Enter the amount of payments to, or for the benefit of, particular clients or patients, including assistance rendered by others at the expense of the filing organization. Do not include grants to other organizations that select the person or persons to receive the assistance available through the use of the grant funds. For example, report a payment to a hospital to cover the medical expenses of a particular individual on line 23, but do not report a contribution to a hospital to provide some service to the general public or to unspecified charity patients on this line. Also, do not include scholarship, fellowship, or research grants to individuals even though selected by the grantor organization. Report these grants on line 22 instead.

Attach a schedule showing the total payments for each particular class of activity, such as food, shelter, and clothing for indigents or disaster victims; medical, dental, and hospital fees and charges; and direct cash assistance to indigents. For payments to indigent families, do not identify the individuals.

Line 24—Benefits paid to or for members.—For an organization that provides benefits to members or dependents (such as organizations exempt under section 501(c)(8), (9), or (17)), attach a schedule. Show amounts of (a) death, sickness, hospitalization, or disability benefits; (b) unemployment compensation benefits; and (c) other benefits (state their nature). Do not report the cost of employment-related benefits the organization provides its officers and employees on this line. Report those expenses on lines 27 and 28.

Line 25—Compensation of officers, directors, etc.—Enter the total compensation paid to officers, directors, and trustees for the year. In Part V give the name and compensation (if any) of each officer, director, and trustee, along with the other information requested. If no compensation was paid, enter a zero.

Each person you list should report this compensation on his or her income tax return, unless the Code specifically excludes any of the payments from income tax. See Publication 525 for more information.

You must file Form 941 to report income tax withholding and social security taxes, and you must also file Form 940 to report Federal unemployment taxes, unless the organization's exemption letter states that it is not subject to these taxes.

Line 26—Other salaries and wages.— Enter the total of employees' salaries not reported on line 25.

Line 27—Pension plan contributions.— Enter the employer's share of contributions that the organization paid to qualified and nonqualified pension plans for the year. Complete Form 5500 or 5500-C/R, as appropriate, for your plan and file as a separate return. If you have more than one plan, complete the appropriate form for each plan. File the form by the last day of the 7th month after the plan year ends. See General Instruction C15.

Line 28—Other employee benefits.— Enter the amount of your contributions to employee benefit programs (such as insurance, health, and welfare programs) that are not an incidental part of a pension plan included on line 27. Also see General Instruction C15 and the instructions for Form 5500.

Line 29—Payroll taxes.— Enter the amount of Federal, state, and local payroll taxes for the year, but only those taxes that are imposed on the organization as an employer. This includes the employer's share of Social Security and Medicare taxes, the FUTA tax, state unemployment compensation taxes, and other state and local payroll taxes. Do not include taxes withheld from employees' salaries and paid to the various governmental units (such as Federal and state income taxes and the employees' shares of Social Security and Medicare tax).

Line 30—Professional fundraising fees.— Enter the organization's fees to outside fundraisers for solicitation campaigns they conducted, or for consultation services connected with a solicitation of contributions by the organization itself.

Line 31—Accounting fees.— Enter the total accounting and auditing fees charged by outside firms and individuals who are not employees of the reporting organization.

Line 32—Legal fees.— Enter the total legal fees charged by outside firms and individuals who are not employees of the reporting organization. Do not include any penalties, fines, or judgments imposed against the organization as a result of legal proceedings. Report those expenses on line 43, Other expenses.

Line 33—Supplies.— Enter the total for office, classroom, medical, and other supplies used during the year, as determined by the organization's normal method of accounting for supplies.

Line 34—Telephone.— Enter the total telephone, telegram, and similar expenses for the year.

Line 35—Postage and shipping.— Enter the total amount of postage, parcel delivery, trucking, and other delivery expenses, including the cost of shipping materials.

Line 36—Occupancy.— Enter the total amount paid or incurred for the use of office space or other facilities, heat, light, power, and other utilities (other than those reported on line 34), outside janitorial services, mortgage interest, real estate taxes, and similar expenses. Do not include depreciation (reportable on line 42) or any salaries of your own employees (reportable on line 26).

Line 37—Equipment rental and maintenance.— Enter the cost of renting and maintaining office equipment and other equipment, except for automobile and truck expenses reportable on lines 35 and 39.

Line 38—Printing and publications.— Enter the printing and related costs of producing the reporting organization's own newsletters, leaflets, films, and other informational materials. (However, do not include any expenses, such as salaries or postage, for which a separate line is provided in Part II.) Also include the cost of any purchased publications.

Line 39—Travel.— Enter the total travel expenses, including transportation costs (fares, mileage allowances, and automobile expenses), meals and lodging, and per diem payments.

Line 40—Conferences, conventions, and meetings.— Enter the total expenses incurred by the organization in conducting meetings relating to its activities. Include such expenses as the rental of facilities, speakers' fees and expenses, and printed materials. However, do not include on this line the salaries and travel expenses of the reporting organization's own officers, directors, trustees, and employees who participate. Include the registration fees (but not travel expenses) paid for sending any of the organization's staff to conferences, meetings, or conventions conducted by other organizations.

Line 41—Interest.— Enter the total interest expense for the year, excluding any interest attributable to rental property (reported on line 6b) or any mortgage interest treated as occupancy expense on line 36.

Line 42—Depreciation, depletion, etc.— If your organization records depreciation, depletion, and similar expenses, enter the total for the year. Include any depreciation (amortization) of leasehold improvements. You are not required to use the Modified Accelerated Cost Recovery System (MACRS) to compute the depreciation you report on Form 990. If you record depreciation using MACRS, attach **Form 4562,** Depreciation and Amortization, or a schedule showing the same information required by Form 4562. If you do not use MACRS, attach a schedule showing how you computed depreciation.

You should use the same method of computing depreciation on line 42 that you use for the balance sheet, Part IV of this Form 990.

If you claim a deduction for depletion, attach a schedule explaining the deduction.

Line 43—Other expenses.— Indicate the type and amount of each significant expense for which a separate line is not provided. Report all other miscellaneous expenses as a single total. Expenses that might be reported here include: investment counseling and other professional fees not reportable on lines 30 through 32; penalties, fines, and judgments; unrelated business income taxes; and real estate taxes not attributable to rental property or reported as occupancy expenses. Attach a schedule if more space is needed.

Some states that accept Form 990 in satisfaction of their filing requirements may require that certain types of miscellaneous expenses be itemized regardless of amount. See General Instruction E.

Line 44—Total functional expenses.— Add lines 22 through 43 and enter the totals in columns (A), (B), (C), and (D). Report the column (B) total on line 13 of Part I; the column (C) total on line 14; and the column (D) total on line 15.

Part III—Statement of Program Service Accomplishments.—

Provide the information specified in the heading of Part III for each of the organization's four largest program services (as measured by total expenses incurred) or for each program service if the organization engaged in four or fewer of such activities. If part of the total expenses of any program service consists of grants and allocations reported on line 22, indicate the amount of the grants and allocations in the space provided. Section 501(c)(3) and (4) organizations and section 4947(a)(1) charitable trusts **must** show the amount of grants and allocations to others.

A program service is a major, usually ongoing objective of an organization, such as adoptions, recreation for the elderly, rehabilitation, or publication of journals or newsletters. Specify the service outputs, products, or other measures of a program service, such as clients served, days of care, therapy sessions, or publications issued. Indicate the number of outputs or products rendered, such as 4,080 counseling contacts.

If it is inappropriate to measure a quantity of output, as in a research activity, describe the objective of the activity for this time period as well as the overall longer-term goal.

You may furnish reasonable estimates for the statistical information (number of clients, patients, etc.) called for by Part III if exact figures are not readily available from your records. In that event, please indicate that the information provided is an estimate.

(a) *Donated services or facilities.—* If the organization reports, on line 82b, the value of any donated services or use of materials, equipment, or facilities it received, it can also indicate in Part III the amount received and utilized for specific program services. However, disclose the applicable amounts only on the lines for the narrative description of the appropriate program services. Do not include these amounts in the expense column in Part III.

(b) *Attached schedule.—* Attach a schedule that lists the organization's other program services and the total expenses incurred for each. For this schedule, you need not give the detailed information as required in Part III for the four largest services.

Reporting expenses optional for certain organizations.— Only section 501(c)(3) and (4) organizations and section 4947(a)(1) charitable trusts must enter the total expenses of each program service they reported in Part III. Reporting the expense totals is optional for all other organizations.

Page 13

Part IV—Balance Sheets.—

All organizations, except those that meet one of the exceptions in General Instruction F above, must complete all of Part IV and may not submit a substitute balance sheet. Failure to complete Part IV may result in penalties for filing an incomplete return. See General Instruction K. See General Instruction E for more information about completing a Form 990 to be filed with any state or local government agency.

When a schedule must be attached for any line item in Part IV, the schedule is required only for the end-of-year balance sheet figure reported in column (B). Similarly, give the end-of-year figures for any receivables or depreciable assets and the related allowance for doubtful accounts or accumulated depreciation reported within the description column.

Line 45—Cash—noninterest-bearing.— Enter the total of noninterest-bearing checking accounts, deposits in transit, change funds, petty cash funds, or any other noninterest-bearing account. Do not include advances to employees or officers or refundable deposits paid to suppliers or others.

Line 46—Savings and temporary cash investments.—Enter the total of interest-bearing checking accounts, savings and temporary cash investments, such as money market funds, commercial paper, certificates of deposit, and U.S. Treasury bills or other governmental obligations that mature in less than one year. Report the income from these investments on line 4.

Line 47—Accounts receivable.—Enter the total accounts receivable (reduced by the allowance for doubtful accounts) that arose from the sale of goods and/or the performance of services. Report claims against vendors or refundable deposits with suppliers or others here, if not significant in amount. (Otherwise, report them on line 58, Other assets.) Report any receivables due from officers, directors, trustees, or key employees on line 50. Report receivables (including loans and advances) due from other employees on line 58.

Line 48—Pledges receivable.—Enter the total pledges receivable recorded as of the beginning and end of the year, reduced by the amount of pledges estimated to be uncollectible.

Line 49—Grants receivable.—Enter the total grants receivable from governmental agencies, foundations, and other organizations as of the beginning and end of the year.

Line 50—Receivables due from officers, directors, trustees, and key employees.—Report all receivables due from officers, directors, trustees, and key employees and all secured and unsecured loans to such persons on line 50 and in an attached schedule described below. The term "key employees" refers to the chief administrative officers of an organization (such as an executive director or chancellor) but does not include the heads

of separate departments or smaller units within an organization.

Attached schedule.—

(a) *When loans should be reported separately.*—In the required schedule, report each loan separately, even if more than one loan was made to the same person or the same terms apply to all loans. Report salary advances, and other advances for the personal use and benefit of the recipient, and receivables subject to special terms or arising from nontypical transactions, as separate loans for each officer, director, etc.

(b) *When loans should be reported as a single total.*—Report receivables that are subject to the same terms and conditions (including credit limits and rate of interest) as receivables due from the general public and that arose during the normal course of the organization's operations as a single total for all the officers, directors, trustees, and key employees. Report travel advances for official business of the organization as a single total.

(c) *Schedule format.*—For each outstanding loan or other receivable that must be reported separately, the attached schedule should show the following information (preferably in columnar form):

(1) Borrower's name and title;

(2) Original amount;

(3) Balance due;

(4) Date of note;

(5) Maturity date;

(6) Repayment terms;

(7) Interest rate;

(8) Security provided by the borrower;

(9) Purpose of the loan; and

(10) Description and fair market value of the consideration furnished by the lender (for example, cash—$1,000; or 100 shares of XYZ, Inc. common stock—$9,000).

The above detail is not required for receivables or travel advances that may be reported as a single total (see instruction (b) above); however, report and identify those totals separately in the attachment.

Line 51—Other notes and loans receivable.—Enter the combined total of notes receivable and net loans receivable.

Notes receivable.—Enter the amount of all notes receivable not listed on line 50 and not acquired as investments. Attach a schedule similar to that called for in the instructions for line 50. The schedule should also identify the relationship of the borrower to any officer, director, trustee, or key employee of the organization.

Notes receivable from loans by a credit union to its members, and scholarship loans by a section 501(c)(3) organization, do not have to be itemized. Merely identify these loans as such on a schedule and indicate the total amount of such loans that are outstanding.

For a note receivable from another organization exempt under the same paragraph of section 501(c) as the filing organization, list only the name of the borrower and the balance due. For

example, a section 501(c)(3) organization would have to provide the full details of a loan to a section 501(c)(4) organization but would have to provide only the name of the borrower and the balance due on a note arising from a loan to another section 501(c)(3) organization.

Loans receivable.—Enter the gross amount of loans receivable, less the allowance for doubtful accounts, arising from the normal activities of the filing organization (such as loans by a credit union to its members or scholarship loans by a section 501(c)(3) organization). A schedule of these loans is not required.

Report loans to officers, directors, trustees, and key employees on line 50. Report loans to other employees on line 58.

Line 52—Inventories for sale or use.— Enter the amount of materials, goods, and supplies purchased or manufactured by the organization and held for future sale or use.

Line 53—Prepaid expenses and deferred charges.—Enter the amount of short-term and long-term prepayments of expenses attributable to one or more future accounting periods. Examples include prepayments of rent, insurance, and pension costs, and expenses incurred for a solicitation campaign of a future accounting period.

Line 54—Investments—securities.— Enter the book value (which may be market value) of securities held as investments. Attach a schedule that lists the securities held at the end of the year. Indicate whether the securities are listed at cost (including the value recorded at the time of receipt in the case of donated securities) or end-of-year market value. Debt securities of the U.S., state, and municipal governments, corporate stocks and bonds, and other publicly traded securities (defined in the instructions for line 8) do not have to be listed individually, except for stock holdings that represent 5% or more of the outstanding shares of stock of the same class. However, show separate totals for each type of security (U.S. Government obligations, corporate stocks, etc.). Do not include amounts reported on line 46.

Line 55—Investments—land, buildings, and equipment.—Enter the book value (cost or other basis less accumulated depreciation) of all land, buildings, and equipment held for investment purposes, such as rental properties. Attach a schedule listing these investment fixed assets held at the end of the year and showing for each item or category listed, the cost or other basis, accumulated depreciation, and book value. Report the income from these assets on line 6a.

Line 56—Investments—other.—Enter the amount of all other investment holdings not reported on line 54 or 55. Attach a schedule listing and describing each of these investments held at the end of the year. Show the book value for each and indicate whether the investment is listed at cost or end-of-year market value. Report the income from these assets on line 7. Do

Page 14

not include program-related investments (see instructions for line 58).

Line 57—Land, buildings, and equipment.—Enter the book value (cost or other basis less accumulated depreciation) of all land, buildings, and equipment owned by the organization and not held for investment. This includes any property, plant, and equipment owned and used by the organization in conducting its exempt activities. Attach a schedule listing these fixed assets held at the end of the year and showing, for each item or category listed, the cost or other basis, accumulated depreciation, and book value.

Line 58—Other assets.—List and show the book value of each category of assets not reportable on lines 45 through 57. Attach a separate schedule if more space is needed.

One type of asset reportable on line 58 is program-related investments. These are investments made primarily to accomplish some exempt purpose of the filing organization rather than to produce income.

Line 59—Total assets.—Enter the total of lines 45 through 58. The amounts on line 59 must equal the amounts on line 75 for both the beginning and end of year.

Line 60—Accounts payable and accrued expenses.—Enter the total of accounts payable to suppliers and others and accrued expenses, such as salaries payable, accrued payroll taxes, and interest payable.

Line 61—Grants payable.—Enter the unpaid portion of grants and awards that the organization has made a commitment to pay other organizations or individuals, whether or not the commitments have been communicated to the grantees.

Line 62—Support and revenue designated for future periods.—Enter the amount of contributions, governmental fees or grants, grants from foundations or other organizations, and other fees and support that contributors or grantors have designated as payable for or applicable to one or more future years, either by the terms of the gift or by the terms of the contract or other arrangement. Do not include any amounts restricted for future use by the filing organization's own governing body. Attach a schedule that describes each contribution or grant designated for one or more future periods and indicates the total amount of each item and the amount applicable to each future period.

Line 63—Loans from officers, directors, trustees, and key employees.—Enter the unpaid balance of loans received from officers, directors, trustees, and key employees (see the instructions for line 50 for definition). For loans outstanding at the end of the year, attach a schedule that provides (for each loan) the name and title of the lender and the information listed in items (2) through (10) of the instructions for line 50.

Line 64—Mortgages and other notes payable.—Enter the amount of mortgages and other notes payable at the beginning

and end of the year. Attach a schedule showing, as of the end of the year, the total amount of all mortgages payable and, for each nonmortgage note payable, the name of the lender and the other information specified in items (2) through (10) of the instructions for line 50. The schedule should also identify the relationship of the lender to any officer, director, trustee, or key employee of the organization.

Line 65—Other liabilities.—List and show the amount of each liability not reportable on lines 60 through 64. Attach a separate schedule if more space is needed.

Line 66—Total liabilities.—Enter the total of lines 60 through 65.

Lines 67 through 74—Fund Balances or Net Assets.—

(a) *Organizations using fund accounting.*—If the organization uses fund accounting, check the box above line 67 and complete lines 67 through 70 to report the various fund balances. Complete line 74 to report the sum of the fund balances and complete line 75 to report the sum of the total liabilities and fund balances.

Organizations **not** using fund accounting should see instruction **(b)** (above the line 71 instruction for completing lines 71 through 74.

Under fund accounting, an organization segregates its assets, liabilities, and net assets into separate funds according to externally imposed restrictions on the use of certain assets; similar designations by the organization's governing board; and other amounts that are unrestricted as to use. Each fund is like a separate entity in that it has a self-balancing set of accounts showing assets, liabilities, equity (fund balance), revenue, and expenses. Since these funds are actually part of a single entity, they are all included in that organization's own financial statements. Similar accounts in the various funds may or may not be consolidated in those statements according to the organization's preference and practice. *Parts I, II, IV, and VII of this form, however, require such consolidation.* Recognition of the separate funds and the net changes within the various funds during the year is accomplished by the fund balances section (lines 67 through 70) of the balance sheet.

Some states that accept Form 990 as their basic report form may require a separate statement of changes in fund balances. See General Instruction E.

Lines 67a and 67b—Current funds.—Enter the fund balances per books of the current unrestricted fund and the current restricted fund.

Line 68—Land, building, and equipment fund.—Enter the fund balance per books for the land, building, and equipment fund (plant fund).

Line 69—Endowment fund.—Enter the total of the fund balances for the permanent endowment fund and any term endowment funds. Report annuity and life income fund balances on this line if not significant in amount, or, report them on line 70. Do not include the fund balances

of any quasi-endowment funds (funds functioning as endowment) or other internally designated funds.

Line 70—Other funds.—Enter the total of the fund balances for all funds not reported on lines 67 through 69. Indicate the type of fund in the space provided or on an attachment if more than one fund is involved. On the attachment, show the beginning and end of year fund balance for each fund listed.

(b) *Organizations not using fund accounting.*—If the organization does not use fund accounting, check the box above line 71 and report account balances on lines 71 through 73. Report net assets on line 74. Also complete line 75 to report the sum of the total liabilities and net assets.

Line 71—Capital stock or trust principal.—For corporations, enter the balance per books for capital stock accounts. Show par or stated value (or for stock with no par or stated value, total amount received upon issuance) of all classes of stock issued and, as yet, uncancelled. For trusts, enter the amount in the trust principal or corpus account.

Line 72—Paid-in or capital surplus.—Enter the balance per books for all paid-in capital in excess of par or stated value for all stock issued and, as yet, uncancelled. If stockholders or others gave donations that the organization records as paid-in capital, include them here. Report any current-year donations you included on line 72 in Part I, line 1.

Line 73—Retained earnings or accumulated income.—For a corporation, enter the balance in the retained earnings or similar account, minus the cost of any corporate treasury stock. For trusts, enter the balance per books in the accumulated income or similar account.

Line 74—Total fund balances or net assets.—For organizations that use fund accounting, enter the total of lines 67 through 70. For all other organizations, enter the total of lines 71 through 73. Enter the beginning-of-the-year figure in column (A) in Part I, line 19. The end-of-year figure in column (B) must agree with the figure on line 21 of Part I.

Line 75—Total liabilities and fund balances/net assets.—Enter the total of lines 66 and 74. That amount must equal the amount for total assets reported on line 59 for both the beginning and end of the year.

Part V—List of Officers, Directors, and Trustees.—

List each of the organization's officers, directors, trustees, and other persons having responsibilities or powers similar to those of officers, directors, or trustees. List all of these persons even if they did not receive any compensation from the organization. Enter "-0-" in columns (C), (D), and (E) if none was paid. (For deferred compensation, see column (D) instructions.)

Show all forms of cash and noncash compensation received by each listed officer, etc., whether paid currently or deferred. In addition to completing Part V, you may provide an attachment describing the entire 1991 compensation package of one or more officers, directors, and trustees.

Column (C).—Enter salary, fees, bonuses, and severance payments received by each person listed. Include current year payments of amounts reported or reportable as deferred compensation in any prior year.

Column (D).—Include all forms of deferred compensation (whether or not funded; whether or not vested; and whether or not the deferred compensation plan is a qualified plan under section 401(a)) and payments to welfare benefit plans on behalf of the officers, etc. Reasonable estimates may be used if precise cost figures are not readily available.

Unless the amounts are reported in column (C), include salary and other compensation earned during the period covered by the return but not paid by the date the return was filed.

Column (E).—Enter expense allowances or reimbursements that the recipients must report as income on their separate income tax returns. Examples include amounts for which the recipient did not account to the organization or allowances that were more than the payee spent on serving the organization. Include payments made under indemnification arrangements, the value of the personal use of housing, automobiles, or other assets owned or leased by the organization (or provided for the organization's use without charge), as well as any other taxable and nontaxable fringe benefits. Refer to Publication 525 for more information.

Part VI—Other Information.—

Line 76—Change in activities.—Attach a statement explaining any significant changes in the kind of activities the organization conducts to further its exempt purpose. These new or modified activities are those not listed as current or planned in your application for recognition of exemption; or those not yet reported to IRS by a letter to your key district director or by an attachment to your return for any earlier year. Besides describing new activities or changes to current ones, also describe any major program activities that are being discontinued.

Line 77—Changes in organizing or governing documents.—Attach a conformed copy of any changes to the articles of incorporation, constitution, trust instrument, or other organizing document, or to the bylaws or other governing document.

A "conformed" copy is one that agrees with the original document and all amendments to it. If the copies are not signed, they must be accompanied by a written declaration signed by an officer authorized to sign for the organization, certifying that they are complete and accurate copies of the original documents.

Photocopies of articles of incorporation showing the certification of an appropriate state official do not have to be accompanied by such a declaration. See Rev. Proc. 68-14, 1968-1 C.B. 768, for more information. When a number of changes are made, send a copy of the entire revised organizing instrument or governing document.

Line 78—Unrelated business income.—Check "Yes" on line 78a if the organization's total gross income from all of its unrelated trades and businesses is $1,000 or more for the year. Gross income is gross receipts less the cost of goods sold. See Publication 598 for a description of unrelated business income and the Form 990-T filing requirements for section 501(c), 501(e), 501(f), and 501(k) organizations having such income. *Form 990-T is not a substitute for Form 990.* Report on Form 990 items of income and expense also reported on Form 990-T when the organization is required to file both forms. For purposes of line 78, the term "business activities" includes any income-generating activity involving the sale of goods or services or income from investments.

Note: *All tax-exempt organizations must pay estimated taxes with respect to their unrelated business income if they expect their tax liability to be $500 or more. You may use Form 990-W to compute this tax.*

Line 78c.—If you answer "Yes" to this question, complete Part IX, Information Regarding Taxable Subsidiaries.

Line 79—Liquidation, dissolution, termination, or substantial contraction.—If there was a liquidation, dissolution, termination, or substantial contraction, attach a statement explaining which took place.

For a complete liquidation of a corporation or termination of a trust, write *Final Return* at the top of the organization's Form 990. On the statement you attach, show whether the assets have been distributed and the date. Also attach a certified copy of any resolution, or plan of liquidation or termination, etc., with all amendments or supplements not already filed. In addition, attach a schedule listing: the names and addresses of all persons who received the assets distributed in liquidation or termination; the kinds of assets distributed to each one; and each asset's fair market value.

A *substantial contraction* is a partial liquidation or other major disposition of assets except transfers for full consideration or distributions from current income.

A *major disposition of assets* means any disposition for the tax year that is:

(a) At least 25% of the fair market value of the organization's net assets at the beginning of the tax year; or

(b) One of a series of related dispositions begun in earlier years that, together, add up to at least 25% of the net assets the organization had at the beginning of the tax year when the first disposition in the series was made.

Whether a major disposition of assets took place through a series of related dispositions depends on the facts in each case.

See Regulations section 1.6043-3 for special rules and exceptions.

Line 80—Relation to other organizations.—Answer "Yes" if most of the organization's governing body, officers, trustees, or membership are also officers, directors, trustees, or members of any other organization.

Disregard a coincidental overlap of membership with another organization (that is, when membership in one organization is not a condition of membership with another organization). For example, assume that a majority of the members of a section 501(c)(4) civic organization also belong to a local chamber of commerce described in section 501(c)(6). The civic organization should answer "No" on line 80 if it does not require its members to belong to the chamber of commerce.

Also disregard affiliation with any statewide or nationwide organization. Thus, the civic organization in the above example would still answer "No" on line 80 even if it belonged to a state or national federation of similar organizations. A local labor union whose members are also members of a national labor organization would answer "No" on line 80.

Line 81—Expenditures for political purposes.—A political expenditure is one intended to influence the selection, nomination, election, or appointment of anyone to a Federal, state, or local public office, or office in a political organization, or the election of Presidential or Vice Presidential electors. Whether the attempt succeeds does not matter.

An expenditure includes a payment, distribution, loan, advance, deposit, or gift of money, or anything of value. It also includes a contract, promise, or agreement to make an expenditure, whether or not legally enforceable.

(a) *All section 501(c) organizations.*—Section 501(c) organizations must file Form 1120-POL if their political expenditures and their net investment income both exceed $100 for the year.

Section 501(c) organizations that maintained separate segregated funds described in section 527(f)(3) should refer to the instructions for Form 1120-POL for filing requirements.

(b) *Section 501(c)(3) organizations.*—A section 501(c)(3) organization will lose its tax-exempt status if it engages in political activity.

A section 501(c)(3) organization must pay an excise tax for any amount paid or incurred on behalf of, or in opposition to, any candidate for public office. The organization must pay an additional excise tax if it fails to correct the expenditure timely.

A manager of a section 501(c)(3) organization who knowingly agrees to a political expenditure must pay an excise tax, unless the agreement is not willful and there is reasonable cause. A manager who does not agree to a correction of the political expenditure may have to pay an additional excise tax.

When an organization promotes a candidate for public office (or is used or controlled by a candidate or prospective candidate), amounts paid or incurred for the following purposes are political expenditures:

(1) Remuneration to the individual (a candidate or prospective candidate) for speeches or other services;

(2) Travel expenses of the individual;

(3) Expenses of conducting polls, surveys, or other studies, or preparing papers or other material for use by the individual;

(4) Expenses of advertising, publicity, and fundraising for such individual; and

(5) Any other expense that has the primary effect of promoting public recognition or otherwise primarily accruing to the benefit of the individual.

Use Form 4720 to figure and report the excise taxes.

Line 82—Donated services or facilities.— Because Form 990 is open to public inspection, you may want the return to show contributions the organization received in the form of donated services or the use of materials, equipment, or facilities at less than fair rental value. If so, and if the organization's records either show the amount and value of such items or give a clearly objective basis for an estimate, you may enter the information on line 82b. The IRS does not require any organization to keep such records. Do NOT include the value of such items in Part I or II or in the expense column in Part III. However, you may indicate the value of donated services or use of materials, equipment, or facilities in Part III in the narrative description of program services rendered. See the instructions for Part III.

Line 84a.— All organizations that qualify under section 170(c) to receive contributions that are deductible as charitable contributions for Federal income tax purposes, enter N/A.

Line 85—Section 501(c)(5) or (6) organizations.— Attempts to influence the opinion of the general public, or any segment of the general public, on legislative matters or referendums constitute grassroots lobbying. Such lobbying may be explicit, as in an advertisement that urges the public to contact legislators for the purpose of proposing, supporting, or opposing legislation. Grassroots lobbying may also be implicit in any advertisement or other communication directed at the public if the communication is an attempt to mold public opinion on a legislative matter or referendum. Any lobbying directed at the members of the organization is not grassroots lobbying. Lobbying directed at "potential" members, employees of members, or stockholders of members would be grassroots lobbying. See Regulations section 1.162-20(c) for a discussion of grassroots lobbying.

Line 86—Section 501(c)(7) organizations.— *Gross receipts test.—* A section 501(c)(7) organization may receive up to 35% of its gross receipts, including investment income, from sources outside its membership and remain tax-exempt. Part of the 35% (up to 15% of gross receipts) may be derived from public use of a social club's facilities.

For this purpose, "gross receipts" are the club's income from its usual activities. The term includes charges, admissions, membership fees, dues, assessments, investment income (such as dividends, rents, and similar receipts), and normal recurring capital gains on investments. Gross receipts do not include capital contributions (as defined in the Regulations under section 118), initiation fees, or unusual amounts of income such as income received from the club's selling its clubhouse. Although gross receipts usually do not include initiation fees, these should be included for college fraternities or sororities or other organizations that charge membership initiation fees, but not annual dues.

If the 35% and 15% limits do not affect the club's exempt status, include the income from line 86b on the club's Form 990-T.

Nondiscrimination policy.— A section 501(c)(7) organization is not exempt from income tax if any written policy statement, including the governing instrument and bylaws, allows discrimination on the basis of race, color, or religion.

However, section 501(i) allows social clubs to retain their exemption under section 501(c)(7) even though their membership is limited (in writing) to members of a particular religion if:

(1) The social club is an auxiliary of a fraternal beneficiary society that is exempt under section 501(c)(8) and limits its membership to the members of a particular religion; or

(2) The social club's membership limitation is a good-faith attempt to further the teachings or principles of that religion, and the limitation is not intended to exclude individuals of a particular race or color.

Line 87—Section 501(c)(12) organizations.— One of the requirements that an organization must meet to qualify under section 501(c)(12) is that at least 85% of its gross income consists of amounts collected from members for the sole purpose of meeting losses and expenses. For purposes of section 501(c)(12), the term "gross income" means gross receipts minus cost of goods sold.

For a mutual or cooperative electric or telephone company, "gross income" does not include amounts received or accrued as "qualified pole rentals" or from the prepayment of a loan under the Rural Electrification Act of 1936 (see section 501(c)(12)(B), (C), and (D)).

For a mutual or cooperative telephone company, "gross income" also does not include amounts received or accrued either from another telephone company for completing long distance calls to or from or between the telephone company's members, or from the sale of display listings in a directory furnished to the telephone company's members.

Line 88—Public interest law firms.— A public interest law firm exempt under section 501(c)(3) or 501(c)(4) must attach a statement that lists the cases in litigation, or that have been litigated during the year. For each case, describe the matter in dispute and explain how the litigation will benefit the public generally. See Rev. Proc. 71-39, 1971-2 C.B. 575. Also attach a report of all fees sought and recovered. See Rev. Proc. 75-13, 1975-1 C.B. 662, about acceptance of attorney's fees.

Line 89—List of states.— List each state with which you are filing a copy of this return in full or partial satisfaction of state filing requirements.

Line 92—Section 4947(a)(1) charitable trusts.— Section 4947(a)(1) charitable trusts that file Form 990 instead of Form 1041 must complete this line. The trust should include exempt-interest dividends received from a mutual fund or other regulated investment company as well as tax-exempt interest received directly.

Part VII—Analysis of Income-Producing Activities.—

An organization is exempt from income taxes only if its primary purpose is to engage in the type of activity for which it claims exemption.

An exempt organization is subject to a tax on unrelated business taxable income if such income is from a trade or business which is regularly carried on by the organization and which is not substantially related to the organization's performance of its exempt purpose or function. Generally, a tax-exempt organization with gross income of $1,000 or more for the year from an unrelated trade or business must file Form 990-T and pay any tax due.

In Part VII, show whether revenue, also reportable on lines 2 through 11 of Part I, was received from activities related to your exempt purpose or activities unrelated to your exempt purpose. Enter gross amounts unless indicated otherwise. Show also any revenue excludable from the definition of unrelated business taxable income.

The sum of amounts entered in columns (b), (d), and (e) for lines 93 through 103 of Part VII should match amounts entered for correlating lines 2 through 11 of Part I. Use the following table to verify the relationship of Part VII with Part I. Note that contributions that are reportable on lines 1a through 1d of Part I are **not** reportable in Part VII.

Amounts in Part VII on Line	Correspond to Amounts in Part I on Line
93(a) through (g)	2
94	3
95	4

Page 17

Completing Part VII.—

Column (a).—In column (a), identify any unrelated business taxable income reportable in column (b) by selecting a business code from the Codes for Unrelated Business Activity in the Instructions for Form 990-T.

Column (b).—In column (b), enter any revenue received from activities unrelated to the exempt purpose of your organization. A detailed discussion of income that constitutes unrelated business taxable income can be found in the Instructions for Form 990-T and Publication 598. If you enter an amount in column (b), then you must enter a business code in column (a).

Column (c).—In column (c), select an exclusion code, from the list on page 19 to identify any revenue excludable from unrelated business taxable income. If more than one exclusion code is applicable to a particular revenue item, select the lowest numbered exclusion code that applies. If nontaxable revenues from several sources are reportable on the same line in column (d), use the exclusion code that applies to the largest revenue source. If the list of exclusion codes does not include an item of revenue that is excludable from unrelated business taxable income, enter that item in column (e) and see the instruction for column (e).

Column (d).—For column (d), identify any revenue received that is excludable from unrelated business taxable income as defined in the Exclusion Codes list on page 19. If you enter an amount in column (d), then you must enter an exclusion code in column (c).

Column (e).—For column (e), report any revenue from activities related to your exempt purpose; that is, income received from activities that form the basis of your organization's exemption from taxation. Also report here any revenue that is excludable from gross income other than by Code section 512, 513, or 514, such as interest on state and local bonds that is excluded from tax by section 103. Explain in Part VIII how any amount you reported in column (e) related to the accomplishment of your exempt purposes.

Lines 93(a) through (f).—List the organization's revenue-producing program service activities on these lines. Program service activities are primarily those that form the basis of an organization's exemption from tax. In the appropriate columns, enter gross revenue from each program service activity and the business and exclusion codes that identify this revenue. (See the explanation of program service revenue in the instructions for Part I, line 2.)

Line 93(g).—Enter, in the appropriate columns, gross revenue from fees paid by government agencies for a service, facility, or product that benefited the government agency primarily, either economically or physically. Do not include government grants that enabled your organization to benefit the public directly and primarily. (See Part I, line 1c instructions for the distinction between government grants and fees from government agencies that are payments for services.)

Report on line 2 of Part I (program service revenue) the sum of the entries in columns (b), (d), and (e) for lines 93(a) through (g).

Lines 94 through 96.—In the appropriate columns, report the revenue received for these line items. General instructions for lines 94 through 96 are discussed in the instructions for Part I, lines 3 through 5.

Lines 97 through 98.—Report net rental income from investment property on these lines. Also report here rental income from unaffiliated exempt organizations. However, report rental income from an exempt function (program service) on line 93. Refer to the instructions for Part I, line 6. A more detailed discussion of rental income is given in the Instructions for Form 990-T and Publication 598.

Rents from real property are usually excluded in computing unrelated business taxable income, as are incidental amounts of rental income from personal property leased with real property (mixed lease). Generally, rents from personal property are incidental if they do not exceed 10% of the total rents from all leased property. In a mixed lease where the rent attributable to personal property is more than 50% of the total rent, neither rent from real or personal property is excluded from unrelated business taxable income. Nor does the exclusion apply when the real or personal property rentals depend wholly or partly on the income or profits from leased property, other than an amount based on a fixed percentage or percentage of gross receipts or sales.

The rental exclusion from unrelated business taxable income does not apply to debt-financed real property. In general, debt-financed property is any property that the organization finances by debt and holds to produce income instead of for exempt purposes. An exempt organization's income from debt-financed property is treated as unrelated business taxable income and is subject to tax in the same proportion as the property remains financed by the debt. If substantially all (85% or more) of any property is used for an organization's exempt purposes, the property is not treated as debt-financed property. The rules for debt-financed property do not apply to rents from personal property.

Lines 99 through 102.—In the appropriate columns, report the revenue received for these line items. General instructions for lines 99 through 102 are discussed in the instructions for Part I, lines 7 through 10.

Lines 103(a) through (e).—List any "Other revenue" activity. These activities are discussed in the instructions for line 11, Part I. In the appropriate columns, enter the revenue received from these activities. Select applicable business and exclusion codes. Report as "Other revenue," on line 11 of Part I, the total revenue entered in columns (b), (d), and (e) for lines 103(a) through (e).

Line 105.—Enter the total revenue reported on line 104 for columns (b), (d), and (e). The amount reported on line 105, plus the amount on line 1d of Part I, should equal the amount entered for "Total revenue" on line 12 of Part I.

Part VIII—Relationship of Activities to the Accomplishment of Exempt Purposes.—

To explain how an amount entered in Part VII, column (e) was related or exempt function income, show the line number of the amount in column (e) and give a brief description of how the activity reported in column (e) contributed importantly to the accomplishment of your exempt purposes (other than by providing funds for such purposes). Activities that generate exempt-function income are activities that form the basis of the organization's exemption from tax.

Also give the line number and an explanation for any income you entered in column (e) that is specifically excluded from gross income other than by Code sections 512, 513, or 514. If you did not enter an amount in column (e), do not complete Part VIII.

Example: M, an organization described in section 501(c)(3), operates a school for the performing arts. Admission is charged at student performances. M reported admission income in column (e) of Part VII and explained in Part VIII that performances before an audience were an essential part of the students' training and related to the exempt purpose of the organization.

Because M also reported interest from state bonds in column (e) of Part VII, M explained in Part VIII that such interest was excluded from gross income by Code section 103.

Part IX—Information Regarding Taxable Subsidiaries.—

Complete this Part if you answered "Yes" to question 78c of Part VI, Other Information.

Exclusion Codes

General Exceptions

01— Income from an activity that is not regularly carried on (section 512(a)(1))

02— Income from an activity in which labor is a material income-producing factor and substantially all (at least 85%) of the work is performed with unpaid labor (section 513(a)(1))

03— Section 501(c)(3) organization— Income from an activity carried on primarily for the convenience of the organization's members, students, patients, visitors, officers, or employees (hospital parking lot or museum cafeteria, for example) (section 513(a)(2))

04— Section 501(c)(4) local association of employees organized before 5/27/69— Income from the sale of work-related clothes or equipment and items normally sold through vending machines; food dispensing facilities; or snack bars for the convenience of association members at their usual places of employment (section 513(a)(2))

05— Income from the sale of merchandise, substantially all of which (at least 85%) was donated to the organization (section 513(a)(3))

Specific Exceptions

06— Section 501(c)(3), (4), or (5) organization conducting an agricultural or educational fair or exposition—Qualified public entertainment activity income (section 513(d)(2))

07— Section 501(c)(3), (4), (5), or (6) organization—Qualified convention and trade show activity income (section 513(d)(3))

08— Income from hospital services described in section 513(e)

09— Income from noncommercial bingo games that do not violate state or local law (section 513(f))

10— Income from games of chance conducted by an organization in North Dakota (section 311 of the Deficit Reduction Act of 1984, as amended)

11— Section 501(c)(12) organization— Qualified pole rental income (section 513(g))

12— Income from the distribution of low-cost articles in connection with the solicitation of charitable contributions (section 513(h))

13— Income from the exchange or rental of membership or donor list with an organization eligible to receive charitable contributions by a section 501(c)(3) organization; by a war veterans' organization; or an auxiliary unit or society of, or trust or foundation for, a war veterans' post or organization (section 513(h))

Modifications and Exclusions

14— Dividends, interest, or payments with respect to securities loans, and annuities excluded by section 512(b)(1)

15— Royalty income excluded by section 512(b)(2)

16— Real property rental income that does not depend on the income or profits derived by the person leasing the property and is excluded by section 512 (b)(3)

17— Rent from personal property leased with real property and incidental (10% or less) in relation to the combined income from the real and personal property (section 512(b)(3))

18— Proceeds from the sale of investments and other non-inventory property (capital gains excluded by section 512(b)(5))

19— Income (gains) from the lapse or termination of options to buy or sell securities (section 512(b)(5))

20— Income from research for the United States; its agencies or instrumentalities; or any state or political subdivision (section 512(b)(7))

21— Income from research conducted by a college, university, or hospital (section 512(b)(8))

22— Income from research conducted by an organization whose primary activity is conducting fundamental research, the results of which are freely available to the general public (section 512(b)(9))

23— Income from services provided under license issued by a Federal regulatory agency and conducted by a religious order or school operated by a religious order, but only if the trade or business has been carried on by the organization since before May 27, 1959 (section 512 (b)(15))

Foreign Organizations

24— Foreign organizations only—Income from a trade or business NOT conducted in the United States and NOT derived from United States sources (patrons) (section 512(a)(2))

Social Clubs and VEBAs

25— Section 501(c)(7), (9), (17), or (20) organization—Non-exempt function income set aside for a charitable, etc., purpose specified in section 170(c)(4) (section 512(a)(3)(B)(i))

26— Section 501(c)(7), (9), (17), or (20) organization—Proceeds from the sale of exempt function property that was or will be timely reinvested in similar property (section 512(a)(3)(D))

27— Section 501(c)(9), (17), or (20) organization—Non-exempt function income set aside for the payment of life, sick, accident, or other benefits (section 512(a)(3)(B)(ii))

Veterans' Organizations

28— Section 501(c)(19) organization— Payments for life, sick, accident, or health insurance for members or their dependents that are set aside for the payment of such insurance benefits or for a charitable, etc., purpose specified in section 170(c)(4) (section 512(a)(4))

29— Section 501(c)(19) organization— Income from an insurance set-aside (see code 28 above) that is set aside for payment of insurance benefits or for a charitable, etc., purpose specified in section 170(c)(4) (Regs. 1.512(a)-4(b)(2))

Debt-financed Income

30— Income exempt from debt-financed (section 514) provisions because at least 85% of the use of the property is for the organization's exempt purposes (**Note:** *This code is only for income from the 15% or less non-exempt purpose use.*) (section 514(b)(1)(A))

31— Gross income from mortgaged property used in research activities described in section 512(b)(7), (8), or (9) (section 514(b)(1)(C))

32— Gross income from mortgaged property used in any activity described in section 513(a)(1), (2), or (3) (section 514(b)(1)(D))

33— Income from mortgaged property (neighborhood land) acquired for exempt purpose use within ten years (section 514(b)(3))

34— Income from mortgaged property acquired by bequest or devise (applies to income received within ten years from the date of acquisition) (section 514(c)(2)(B))

35— Income from mortgaged property acquired by gift where the mortgage was placed on the property more than five years previously and the property was held by the donor for more than five years (applies to income received within ten years from the date of gift) (section 514(c)(2)(B))

36— Income from property received in return for the obligation to pay an annuity described in section 514(c)(5)

37— Income from mortgaged property that provides housing to low and moderate income persons, to the extent the mortgage is insured by the Federal Housing Administration (section 514(c)(6)) (**Note:** *In many cases, this would be exempt function income reportable in column (e). It would not be so in the case of a section 501(c)(5) or (6) organization, for example, that acquired the housing as an investment or as a charitable activity.*)

38— Income from mortgaged real property owned by: a school described in section 170(b)(1)(A)(ii); a section 509(a)(3) affiliated support organization of such a school; a section 501(c)(25) organization, or by a partnership in which any of the above organizations owns an interest if the requirements of section 514(c)(9)(B)(vi) are met (section 514(c)(9))

Special Rules

39— Section 501(c)(5) organization— Farm income used to finance the operation and maintenance of a retirement home, hospital, or similar facility operated by the organization for its members on property adjacent to the farm land (section 1951(b)(8)(B) of Public Law 94-455)

Trade or Business

40— Gross income from an unrelated activity that is regularly carried on but, in light of continuous losses sustained over a number of tax periods, cannot be regarded as being conducted with the motive to make a profit (not a trade or business)

Form **990**

Return of Organization Exempt From Income Tax

Under section 501(c) of the Internal Revenue Code (except black lung benefit trust or private foundation) or section 4947(a)(1) charitable trust

OMB No. 1545-0047

1991

This Form is Open to Public Inspection

Department of the Treasury
Internal Revenue Service

Note: You may have to use a copy of this return to satisfy state reporting requirements.

A For the calendar year 1991, or fiscal year beginning _____ , 1991, and ending _____ , 19 ___

Please use IRS label or print or type. See Specific Instructions.	**B** Name of organization	**C** Employer identification number
	Number and street (or P.O. box no. if mail is not delivered to street address) / Room/suite	**D** State registration number
	City, town, or post office, state, and ZIP code	**E** If application for exemption is pending, check here. . . . . ▶ ☐

F Check type of organization—Exempt under section ▶ ☐ 501(c)( ) (insert number),
OR ▶ ☐ section 4947(a)(1) charitable trust

G Accounting method: ☐ Cash ☐ Accrual
☐ Other (specify) ▶

H Is this a group return filed for affiliates? . . . . ☐ Yes ☐ No
If "Yes," enter the number of affiliates for which this return is filed: ▶ _____
Is this a separate return filed by a group affiliate? . . . . . ☐ Yes ☐ No

I If either answer in H is "Yes," enter four-digit group exemption number (GEN) ▶

J If address changed, check box . . . . ▶ ☐

K Check here ▶ ☐ if your gross receipts are normally not more than $25,000. You do not have to file a completed return with IRS; but if you received a Form 990 Package in the mail, you should file a return without financial data. **Some states require a completed return.**

Note: *Form 990EZ may be used by organizations with gross receipts less than $100,000 and total assets less than $250,000 at end of year.*

Section 501(c)(3) organizations and 4947(a)(1) trusts must also complete and attach Schedule A (Form 990).

Part I Statement of Revenue, Expenses, and Changes in Net Assets or Fund Balances

Revenue

1	Contributions, gifts, grants, and similar amounts received:		
a	Direct public support	1a	
b	Indirect public support	1b	
c	Government grants	1c	
d	**Total** (add lines 1a through 1c) (attach schedule—see instructions)	1d	
2	Program service revenue (from Part VII, line 93)	2	
3	Membership dues and assessments (see instructions)	3	
4	Interest on savings and temporary cash investments	4	
5	Dividends and interest from securities	5	
6a	Gross rents	6a	
b	Less: rental expenses	6b	
c	Net rental income or (loss)	6c	
7	Other investment income (describe ▶ _____)	7	
8a	Gross amount from sale of assets other than inventory		
b	Less: cost or other basis and sales expenses		
c	Gain or (loss) (attach schedule)		
d	Net gain or (loss) (combine line 8c, columns (A) and (B))	8d	
9	Special fundraising events and activities (attach schedule—see instructions):		
a	Gross revenue (not including $ _____ of contributions reported on line 1a)	9a	
b	Less: direct expenses	9b	
c	Net income	9c	
10a	Gross sales less returns and allowances	10a	
b	Less: cost of goods sold	10b	
c	Gross profit or (loss) (attach schedule)	10c	
11	Other revenue (from Part VII, line 103)	11	
12	**Total revenue** (add lines 1d, 2, 3, 4, 5, 6c, 7, 8d, 9c, 10c, and 11)	12	

Line 8a / 8b / 8c table:

	(A) Securities	(B) Other
8a		
8b		
8c		

Expenses

13	Program services (from line 44, column (B)) (see instructions)	13	
14	Management and general (from line 44, column (C)) (see instructions) . . .	14	
15	Fundraising (from line 44, column (D)) (see instructions)	15	
16	Payments to affiliates (attach schedule—see instructions)	16	
17	**Total expenses** (add lines 16 and 44, column (A))	17	

Net Assets

18	Excess or (deficit) for the year (subtract line 17 from line 12)	18	
19	Net assets or fund balances at beginning of year (from line 74, column (A)) . .	19	
20	Other changes in net assets or fund balances (attach explanation)	20	
21	Net assets or fund balances at end of year (combine lines 18, 19, and 20) . . .	21	

For Paperwork Reduction Act Notice, see page 1 of the separate instructions.   Cat. No. 11282Y   Form **990** (1991)

Part II Statement of Functional Expenses

All organizations must complete column (A). Columns (B), (C), and (D) are required for section 501(c)(3) and (c)(4) organizations and 4947(a)(1) charitable trusts but optional for others. (See instructions.)

	Do not include amounts reported on line 6b, 8b, 9b, 10b, or 16 of Part I.	(A) Total	(B) Program services	(C) Management and general	(D) Fundraising
22	Grants and allocations (attach schedule)			////	////
23	Specific assistance to individuals			////	////
24	Benefits paid to or for members			////	////
25	Compensation of officers, directors, etc.				
26	Other salaries and wages				
27	Pension plan contributions				
28	Other employee benefits				
29	Payroll taxes				
30	Professional fundraising fees		////	////	
31	Accounting fees				
32	Legal fees				
33	Supplies				
34	Telephone				
35	Postage and shipping				
36	Occupancy				
37	Equipment rental and maintenance				
38	Printing and publications				
39	Travel				
40	Conferences, conventions, and meetings				
41	Interest				
42	Depreciation, depletion, etc. (attach schedule)				
43	Other expenses (itemize): a				
b					
c					
d					
e					
f					
44	**Total functional expenses** (add lines 22 through 43) Organizations completing columns (B)-(D), carry these totals to lines 13-15				

Part III Statement of Program Service Accomplishments (See instructions.)

Describe what was achieved in carrying out your exempt purposes. Fully describe the services provided; the number of persons benefited; or other relevant information for each program title. Section 501(c)(3) and (4) organizations and section 4947(a)(1) charitable trusts must also enter the amount of grants and allocations to others.

Expenses (Required for 501(c)(3) and (4) organizations and 4947(a)(1) trusts, optional for others.)

a ....
....
....
.... (Grants and allocations $)

b ....
....
....
.... (Grants and allocations $)

c ....
....
....
.... (Grants and allocations $)

d ....
....
....
.... (Grants and allocations $)

e Other program services (attach schedule) . . . (Grants and allocations $)

f **Total** (add lines **a** through **e**) (should equal line 44, column (B)) . . . . ▶

74

Part IV   Balance Sheets

			(A) Beginning of year		**(B)** End of year
Note:	*Where required, attached schedules and amounts within the description column should be for end-of-year amounts only.*				

Assets

			(A)		(B)
45	Cash—noninterest-bearing			45	
46	Savings and temporary cash investments			46	
47a	Accounts receivable	47a			
b	Less: allowance for doubtful accounts	47b		47c	
48a	Pledges receivable	48a			
b	Less: allowance for doubtful accounts	48b		48c	
49	Grants receivable			49	
50	Receivables due from officers, directors, trustees, and key employees (attach schedule)			50	
51a	Other notes and loans receivable (attach schedule)	51a			
b	Less: allowance for doubtful accounts	51b		51c	
52	Inventories for sale or use			52	
53	Prepaid expenses and deferred charges			53	
54	Investments—securities (attach schedule)			54	
55a	Investments—land, buildings, and equipment: basis	55a			
b	Less: accumulated depreciation (attach schedule)	55b		55c	
56	Investments—other (attach schedule)			56	
57a	Land, buildings, and equipment: basis	57a			
b	Less: accumulated depreciation (attach schedule)	57b		57c	
58	Other assets (describe ▶ _____)			58	
59	**Total assets** (add lines 45 through 58) (must equal line 75)			59	

Liabilities

			(A)		(B)
60	Accounts payable and accrued expenses			60	
61	Grants payable			61	
62	Support and revenue designated for future periods (attach schedule)			62	
63	Loans from officers, directors, trustees, and key employees (attach schedule)			63	
64	Mortgages and other notes payable (attach schedule)			64	
65	Other liabilities (describe ▶ _____)			65	
66	**Total liabilities** (add lines 60 through 65)			66	

Fund Balances or Net Assets

Organizations that use fund accounting, check here ▶ ☐ and complete lines 67 through 70 and lines 74 and 75 (see instructions).

			(A)		(B)
67a	Current unrestricted fund			67a	
b	Current restricted fund			67b	
68	Land, buildings, and equipment fund			68	
69	Endowment fund			69	
70	Other funds (describe ▶ _____)			70	

Organizations that do not use fund accounting, check here ▶ ☐ and complete lines 71 through 75 (see instructions).

			(A)		(B)
71	Capital stock or trust principal			71	
72	Paid-in or capital surplus			72	
73	Retained earnings or accumulated income			73	
74	Total fund balances or net assets (add lines 67a through 70 OR lines 71 through 73: column (A) must equal line 19 and column (B) must equal line 21)			74	
75	**Total liabilities and fund balances/net assets** (add lines 66 and 74)			75	

Form 990 is available for public inspection and, for some people, serves as the primary or sole source of information about a particular organization. How the public perceives an organization in such cases may be determined by the information presented on its return. Therefore, please make sure your return is complete and accurate and fully describes your organization's programs and accomplishments.

Part V	**List of Officers, Directors, and Trustees** (List each one even if not compensated. See instructions.)				
(A) Name and address		**(B)** Title and average hours per week devoted to position	**(C)** Compensation (if not paid, enter zero)	**(D)** Contributions to employee benefit plans	**(E)** Expense account and other allowances
....					
....					
....					
....					
....					

Part VI	**Other Information**			

			Yes	**No**
76	Did you engage in any activity not previously reported to the Internal Revenue Service?	**76**		
	If "Yes," attach a detailed description of each activity.			
77	Were any changes made in the organizing or governing documents, but not reported to IRS?.	**77**		
	If "Yes," attach a conformed copy of the changes.			
78a	Did your organization have unrelated business gross income of $1,000 or more during the year covered by this return?	**78a**		
b	If "Yes," have you filed a tax return on **Form 990-T**, Exempt Organization Business Income Tax Return. for this year?	**78b**		
c	At any time during the year, did you own a 50% or greater interest in a taxable corporation or partnership? . .	**78c**		
	If "Yes," complete Part IX.			
79	Was there a liquidation, dissolution, termination, or substantial contraction during the year? (See instructions.)	**79**		
	If "Yes," attach a statement as described in the instructions.			
80a	Are you related (other than by association with a statewide or nationwide organization) through common membership, governing bodies, trustees. officers, etc., to any other exempt or nonexempt organization? (See instructions.) . .	**80a**		
b	If "Yes," enter the name of the organization ▶			
	.... and check whether it is ☐ exempt **OR** ☐ nonexempt.			
81a	Enter amount of political expenditures. direct or indirect, as described in the instructions . .	**81a**		
b	Did you file **Form 1120-POL**, U.S. Income Tax Return for Certain Political Organizations. for this year? . .	**81b**		
82a	Did you receive donated services or the use of materials, equipment. or facilities at no charge or at substantially less than fair rental value?	**82a**		
b	If "Yes," you may indicate the value of these items here. Do not include this amount as revenue in Part I or as an expense in Part II. See instructions for reporting in Part III .	**82b**		
83a	Did anyone request to see either your annual return or exemption application (or both)?	**83a**		
b	If "Yes," did you comply as described in the instructions? (See General Instruction L.)	**83b**		
84a	Did you solicit any contributions or gifts that were not tax deductible?	**84a**		
b	If "Yes," did you include with every solicitation an express statement that such contributions or gifts were not tax deductible? (See General Instruction M.)	**84b**		
85a	Section 501(c)(5) or (6) organizations.—Did you spend any amounts in attempts to influence public opinion about legislative matters or referendums? (See instructions and Regulations section 1.162-20(c).) . . .	**85a**		
b	If "Yes," enter the total amount spent for this purpose	**85b**		
86	Section 501(c)(7) organizations.—Enter:			
a	Initiation fees and capital contributions included on line 12	**86a**		
b	Gross receipts, included on line 12, for public use of club facilities (See instructions.)	**86b**		
c	Does the club's governing instrument or any written policy statement provide for discrimination against any person because of race. color, or religion? (See instructions.)	**86c**		
87	Section 501(c)(12) organizations.—Enter amount of:			
a	Gross income received from members or shareholders	**87a**		
b	Gross income received from other sources (Do not net amounts due or paid to other sources against amounts due or received from them.)	**87b**		
88	Public interest law firms.—Attach information described in the instructions.			
89	List the states with which a copy of this return is filed ▶			
90	During this tax year did you maintain any part of your accounting / tax records on a computerized system? . .	**90**		
91	The books are in care of ▶ ....Telephone no. ▶ (......)................			
	Located at ▶ .... ZIP code ▶			
92	Section 4947(a)(1) charitable trusts filing Form 990 in lieu of **Form 1041**, U.S. Fiduciary Income Tax Return, should check here ▶ ☐ and enter the amount of tax-exempt interest received or accrued during the tax year . . . ▶	**92**		

76

Part VII	**Analysis of Income-Producing Activities**

Enter gross amounts unless otherwise indicated.	Unrelated business income		Excluded by section 512, 513, or 514		(e) Related or exempt function income (See instructions.)
	(a) Business code	**(b)** Amount	**(c)** Exclusion code	**(d)** Amount	
93 Program service revenue:					
(a) _____					
(b) _____					
(c) _____					
(d) _____					
(e) _____					
(f) _____					
(g) Fees from government agencies					
94 Membership dues and assessments					
95 Interest on savings and temporary cash investments .					
96 Dividends and interest from securities . . .					
97 Net rental income or (loss) from real estate:					
(a) debt-financed property					
(b) not debt-financed property					
98 Net rental income or (loss) from personal property .					
99 Other investment income					
100 Gain or (loss) from sales of assets other than inventory					
101 Net income from special fundraising events . .					
102 Gross profit or (loss) from sales of inventory .					
103 Other revenue: (a)_____					
(b) _____					
(c) _____					
(d) _____					
(e) _____					
104 Subtotal (add columns (b), (d), and (e).) . . .					

105 TOTAL (add line 104, columns (b), (d), and (e).) . . . . ▶ _____

Note: *(Line 105 plus line 1d, Part I, should equal the amount on line 12, Part I.)*

Part VIII	**Relationship of Activities to the Accomplishment of Exempt Purposes**

Line No. ▼	Explain how each activity for which income is reported in column (e) of Part VII contributed importantly to the accomplishment of your exempt purposes (other than by providing funds for such purposes). (See instructions.)
_____	_____
_____	_____
_____	_____
_____	_____
_____	_____
_____	_____
_____	_____
_____	_____
_____	_____

Part IX	**Information Regarding Taxable Subsidiaries (Complete this Part if you answered "Yes" to question 78c.)**

Name, address, and employer identification number of corporation or partnership	Percentage of ownership interest	Nature of business activities	Total income	End-of-year assets

Please Sign Here	Under penalties of perjury, I declare that I have examined this return, including accompanying schedules and statements, and to the best of my knowledge and belief, it is true, correct, and complete. Declaration of preparer (other than officer) is based on all information of which preparer has any knowledge.
	▶ Signature of officer Date ▶ Title

Paid Preparer's Use Only	Preparer's signature ▶		Date	Check if self-employed ▶ ☐
	Firm's name (or yours if self-employed) and address ▶		ZIP code	

1991

Department of the Treasury
Internal Revenue Service

Instructions for Schedule A (Form 990)

(Section references are to the Internal Revenue Code unless otherwise noted.)

Purpose of Form.—Schedule A (Form 990) is used by section 501(c)(3), 501(e), 501(f), and 501(k) organizations and section 4947(a)(1) charitable trusts to furnish additional information not required of other types of organizations that file **Form 990,** Return of Organization Exempt From Income Tax, or **Form 990EZ,** Short Form Return of Organization Exempt From Income Tax. This additional information is required by section 6033(b) and Rev. Proc. 75-50.

For purposes of these instructions, the term "section 501(c)(3)" includes organizations exempt under sections 501(e), 501(f), and 501(k).

Changes You Should Note.—Eligible public charities that made a valid section 501(h) election to limit their lobbying expenditures must complete Part VI-A. Public charities that did not make this election must attach a classified schedule of lobbying expenses paid or incurred during the year as well as a detailed description of their lobbying activities. These nonelecting public charities, however, may complete Part VI-B instead of constructing their own lobbying expense schedule. Even if a nonelecting public charity chooses to complete the optional Part VI-B schedule, it must attach a statement describing its lobbying activities.

For 1991, completing Part VI-B is optional for nonelecting organizations. For 1992, there is a proposal to make Part VI-B a mandatory schedule for nonelecting organizations. Please send your written comments regarding this proposal to: Internal Revenue Service, Tax Forms and Publications Division, T:FP:F:CD, Room 5560, 1111 Constitution Avenue, NW, Washington, DC 20224.

General Information

A. Who must file.—If you file Form 990 (or Form 990EZ) for an organization described in section 501(c)(3), or for a nonexempt charitable trust described in section 4947(a)(1), you must complete and attach Schedule A. If you are not required to file Form 990 (or Form 990EZ), you need not file Schedule A. Do not use Schedule A if you file for a private foundation. (Private foundations file **Form 990-PF,** Return of Private Foundation, instead of Form 990.)

B. Period covered.—Your Schedule A should cover the same period as the Form 990 (or Form 990EZ) with which you file it.

C. Penalties.—Schedule A (Form 990) is an integral part of Form 990 (or Form 990EZ) for section 501(c)(3) organizations and section 4947(a)(1) charitable trusts required to file either form. Therefore, any such organization that does not submit a completed Schedule A with its Form 990 (or Form 990EZ) does not satisfy its filing requirement and may be charged a $10 a day penalty. See General Instruction K of the Form 990 (and Form 990EZ) instructions for more information about this and other penalties.

To avoid having to respond to requests for missing information, please be sure to complete all applicable line items; to answer "Yes" or "No" to each question on the return; to make an entry (including a "-0-" when appropriate) on all *total* lines; and to enter "None" or "N/A" if an entire part does not apply.

Specific Instructions

If you need more space for any part or line item, attach separate sheets on which you follow the same format and sequence as on the printed form. Show totals on the printed form. Be sure to put the organization's name and employer identification number on separate sheets and identify the part or line that the attachments support.

You may show money items as whole-dollar amounts. To do so, drop any amount less than 50 cents and increase any amount from 50 through 99 cents to the next higher dollar.

Part I

Complete Part I for the five employees with the highest annual compensation over $30,000. Do not include employees listed in Part V of Form 990 or in Part IV of Form 990EZ (List of Officers, Directors, and Trustees). Also enter in Part I the number of other employees with annual compensation over $30,000 *who are not listed in Part I.*

In columns (c) through (e), show all cash and noncash forms of compensation received by each listed

employee whether paid currently or deferred.

Column (c).—Enter salary, fees, bonuses, and severance payments received by each listed employee. Include current year payments of amounts reported or reportable as deferred compensation in any prior year.

Column (d).—Include all forms of deferred compensation (whether or not funded, whether or not vested, and whether or not the deferred compensation plan is a qualified plan under section 401(a)). Include payments to welfare benefit plans on behalf of the employee. Unless the amounts are reported in column (c), include salary and other compensation earned during the period covered by the return but not paid by the date the return was filed.

Column (e).—Enter expense allowances or reimbursements that the recipients must report as income on their separate income tax returns. Examples include amounts for which the recipient did not account to the organization or allowances that were more than the payee spent on serving the organization. Include payments made in connection with indemnification arrangements, the value of the personal use of housing, automobiles, or other assets owned or leased by the organization (or provided for the organization's use without charge), as well as any other taxable and nontaxable fringe benefits.

Part II

Complete Part II for the five highest paid independent contractors who performed personal services of a professional nature for the organization and, in return, received over $30,000 for the year from the organization. Examples of such contractors include attorneys, accountants, and doctors, whether these people perform the services as individuals or as employees of a professional service corporation. Also show the number of other independent contractors who received more than $30,000 for the year for performing such services and are not listed in Part II.

Part III

Line 1.—If you checked "Yes," you must provide the additional information

Cat. No. 11294Q

requested. Failure to do so may cause your return to be considered incomplete.

In general, a section 501(c)(3) organization may not devote a "substantial part" of its activities to attempts to influence legislation. Under the "substantial part" test, if such an organization engages in substantial lobbying activities, the organization will lose both its tax-exempt status and its ability to receive tax-deductible charitable contributions. Except for churches, certain church affiliated organizations, and private foundations, an organization that loses its section 501(c)(3) status because it failed the "substantial part" test will owe an excise tax under section 4912 on all of its lobbying expenses. Managers of the organization may also be jointly and severally liable for this tax.

As an alternative to the "substantial part" test, eligible public charities may elect the "expenditure test" of section 501(h), which generally permits higher limits for lobbying expenditures than allowed under the "substantial part" test. Additionally, electing public charities are subject to the lobbying expense definitions of section 4911, which are generally more liberal than the definitions under the "substantial part" test. Section 4911 applies only to public charities that made a valid section 501(h) election by filing **Form 5768,** Election/Revocation of Election by an Eligible Section 501(c)(3) Organization To Make Expenditures To Influence Legislation.

If the organization is an electing public charity, you must complete Part VI-A of this form.

If the organization checked "Yes," but is **not** an electing public charity, you must attach a statement giving a detailed description of the organization's lobbying activities. Also, you must attach a detailed schedule of the lobbying expenses or complete Part VI-B.

A nonelecting public charity will generally be regarded as lobbying if the organization either: (1) contacts, or urges the public to contact, members of a legislative body for the purpose of proposing, supporting, or opposing legislation; or (2) advocates the adoption or rejection of legislation.

The detailed description of lobbying activities should include **all** lobbying activities, whether expenses are incurred or not (e.g., even lobbying activities carried out by unreimbursed volunteers). For example, the activities should be included in the attached statement if an organization (either through its employees or volunteers) attempts to influence legislation in any of the following ways: sending letters or publications to government officials or legislators, meeting with or calling government officials or legislators, sending or distributing letters or

publications (including newsletters, brochures, etc.) to members or to the general public, using direct mail, placing advertisements, issuing press releases, holding news conferences, or holding rallies or demonstrations.

The schedule of lobbying expenses should include expenses paid or incurred for any lobbying activity, including, where appropriate, grants paid to another organization that lobbies. You may report your lobbying expenses in Part VI-B instead of attaching a separate expense schedule.

All charities, both electing and nonelecting, are absolutely prohibited from intervening in a political campaign for or against any candidate for an elective public office. If a charity does intervene in a political campaign, it will lose both its tax-exempt status and its ability to receive tax-deductible charitable contributions. Additionally, both the organization and its managers are subject to the tax on political expenditures under section 4955.

Line 2d.—If the only compensation or repayment relates to amounts you reported in Part V of Form 990 (or Part IV of Form 990EZ), check "Yes" and write "See Part V, Form 990" (or "See Part IV of Form 990EZ") on the dotted line to the left of the entry space.

Line 4.—*Qualify* means that organizations or individuals will use the funds you provide for charitable purposes described in sections 170(c)(1) and 170(c)(2).

Qualify also means that individual recipients belong to a charitable class and the payments are to aid them. Examples include helping the aged poor, training teachers and social workers from underdeveloped countries, and awarding scholarships to individuals.

Part IV

Definitions.—The following terms are used in more than one item in Part IV. The definitions below generally apply.

Support (boxes 10, 11, 12, Support Schedule), with certain exceptions described below, means all forms of support including (but not limited to) contributions, investment income (such as interest, rents, royalties, and dividends), and net income from unrelated business activities whether or not such activities are carried on regularly as a trade or business.

(a) *Support* does not include—

(1) Any amounts the organization receives from exercising or performing its charitable, educational, or other similar purpose or function. In general, these amounts include those from any activity which is substantially related to the furtherance of such charitable, etc., purpose or function (other than through the production of income).

Exception: Section 509(a)(2) organizations that check box 12 do include these amounts as part of their support.

(2) Any gain on the sale or exchange of property which would be considered under any section of the Code as gain from the sale or exchange of a capital asset.

(3) Contributions of services for which a deduction is not allowable.

(b) *Support from a governmental unit,* with certain exceptions described below, includes—

(1) Any amounts received from a governmental unit, including donations or contributions and amounts received in connection with a contract entered into with a governmental unit for the performance of services or in connection with a government research grant, provided these amounts are not excluded from the term *support* as amounts received from exercising or performing the organization's charitable purpose or function. An amount paid by a governmental unit to an organization is not treated as received from exercising or performing its charitable, etc., purpose or function if the payment is to enable the organization to provide a service to, or maintain a facility for, the direct benefit of the public, as for example, to maintain library facilities which are open to the public.

(2) Tax revenues levied for the organization's benefit and either paid to or expended on its behalf.

(3) The value of services or facilities (exclusive of services or facilities generally furnished, without charge, to the public) furnished by a governmental unit to the organization without charge; for example, a city pays the salaries of personnel to guard a museum, art gallery, etc., or provides the use of a building rent free. However, the term does not include the value of any exemption from Federal, state, or local tax or any similar benefit.

Indirect contributions from the general public are what the organization receives from other organizations that receive a substantial part of their support from general public contributions. An example is the organization's share of the proceeds from an annual community chest drive (such as the United Way or United Fund).

A disqualified person is:

(1) *A substantial contributor,* who is any person who gave an aggregate amount of more than $5,000, if that amount is more than 2% of the total contributions the foundation or organization received from its inception through the end of the year in which that person's contributions were received. Gifts from the contributor's spouse are treated as gifts from the contributor. Gifts are generally valued at fair market value as of the date the organization received them.

In the case of a trust. the creator of the trust is considered a substantial contributor without regard to the amount of contributions received by the trust from the creator and other persons. Any person who is a substantial contributor at any time generally remains a substantial contributor for all future periods even if later contributions by others push that person's contributions below the 2% figure discussed above.

(2) An officer, director, or trustee of the organization or any individual having powers or responsibilities similar to those of officers, directors, or trustees.

(3) An owner of more than 20% of: the voting power of a corporation, profits interest of a partnership, or beneficial interest of a trust or an unincorporated enterprise that is a substantial contributor to the organization.

(4) A family member of an individual in the first three categories. A "family member" includes only a person's spouse, ancestors, lineal descendants, and spouses of lineal descendants.

(5) A corporation, partnership, trust, or estate in which persons described in (1), (2), (3), or (4) own more than 35% of the voting power, profits interest, or beneficial interest. See section 4946(a)(1).

An organization is considered *normally* to satisfy the public support test (boxes 10, 11, and 12) for its current tax year and the tax year immediately following its current tax year if the organization satisfies the applicable support test for the 4 tax years immediately before the current tax year. If the organization has a material change (other than from unusual grants—see instructions for line 28 on page 4) in its sources of support during the current tax year, the data ordinarily required in the Support Schedule covering the years 1987 through 1990 must be submitted for the years 1987 through 1991. You must prepare and attach a 5-year schedule using the same format as provided in the Support Schedule for lines 15 through 28.

Boxes 5 through 14.—Check one box to indicate why the organization is not a private foundation. The organization's exemption letter states the reason, or your local IRS office can tell you.

Box 6.—Check box 6 for a school whose primary function is the presentation of formal instruction, and which regularly has a faculty, a curriculum, an enrolled body of students, and a place where educational activities are regularly conducted.

A private school, in addition, must have a racially nondiscriminatory policy toward its students. For more information about these requirements, see the instructions for Part V.

Box 7.—Check box 7 for an organization whose main purpose is to provide hospital or medical care. A rehabilitation institution or an outpatient clinic may qualify as a hospital, but the term does not include medical schools, medical research organizations, convalescent homes, homes for the aged, or vocational training institutions for the handicapped. Also check box 7 for a cooperative hospital service organization described in section 501(e).

Box 9.—Check box 9 for a medical research organization operated in connection with or in conjunction with a hospital. The hospital must be described in section 501(c)(3) or operated by the Federal government, a state or its political subdivision, a U.S. possession or its political subdivision, or the District of Columbia.

Medical research means studies and experiments done to increase or verify information about physical or mental diseases and disabilities and their causes, diagnosis, prevention, treatment, or control. The organization must conduct the research directly and continuously. If it primarily gives funds to other organizations (or grants and scholarships to individuals) for them to do the research, the organization is not a medical research organization.

The organization need not be an affiliate of the hospital, but there must be an understanding that they will cooperate closely and continuously in doing medical research as a joint effort.

An organization qualifies as a medical research organization if its principal purpose is medical research and it devotes more than half its assets, or spends at least 3.5% of the fair market value of its endowment, in directly conducting medical research. Either test may be met based on a computation period consisting of the immediately preceding tax year or the immediately preceding 4 tax years. If an organization does not satisfy either the assets test or the expenditure test, it may still qualify as a medical research organization based on the circumstances involved. These tests are discussed in Regulations sections 1.170A-9(c)(2)(v) and (vi). Value the organization's assets as of any day in your tax year but use the same day every year. Value the endowment at fair market value, using commonly accepted valuation methods. (See Regulations section 20.2031.)

Box 10.—Check box 10 and complete the Support Schedule (lines 15 through 28) if your organization receives and manages property for and expends funds to benefit a college or university that is owned or operated by one or more states or their political subdivisions. The school must be as described in the first paragraph of the instructions for box 6.

Expending funds to benefit a college or university includes acquiring and maintaining the campus, its buildings, and its equipment, granting scholarships and student loans, and making any other payments in connection with the normal functions of colleges and universities.

The organization must meet essentially the same public support test described below for box 11. See Rev. Rul. 82-132, 1982-2 C.B. 107.

Box 11.—Check either box 11a or 11b and complete the Support Schedule for an organization that normally receives at least 33⅓% of its support (excluding income received in exercising its charitable, etc., function) from a governmental unit; from direct or indirect contributions from the general public; or from other publicly supported (section 170(b)(1)(A)(vi)) organizations.

To determine whether the 33⅓%-of-support test is met, donor contributions are considered support from direct or indirect contributions from the general public only to the extent that the total amount received from any one donor during the 4-tax-year period is 2% or less of the organization's total support for those 4 tax years as described below:

Denominator.—Any contribution by one individual will be included in full in the total support denominator of the fraction determining the 33⅓%-of-support or the 10%-of-support limitation.

Numerator.—Only the portion of each donor's contribution that is 2% or less of the total support denominator will be included in the numerator. In applying the 2% limitation, all contributions by any person(s) related to the donor as described in section 4946(a)(1)(C) through (G) (and related regulations) will be treated as if made by the donor. The 2% limitation does not apply to support from governmental units referred to in section 170(c)(1), or to contributions from publicly supported organizations (section 170(b)(1)(A)(vi)), that check box 11a or b.

Example: For the years 1987 through 1990, the X organization received $600,000 in support from the following sources:

Investment income	$300,000
Y City (government source)	40,000
United Fund (indirect contributions from general public)	40,000
Direct contributions	220,000
Total support	$600,000

Six donors each gave more than 2% of the total support (which is $12,000). While the donors' full contributions are counted in X organization's total support, only $12,000 from each of these six donors is included in the organization's public support. The public support is figured as follows:

Page 3

Government support (Y City) $40,000

Indirect contributions from the
general public (United Fund) 40,000

Contributions from various donors,
none of whom gave over 2% of the
organization's total support 50,000

6 contributions limited to 2% of the
organization's total support
(6 × $12,000) 72,000

Public support $202,000

One-third of X organization's total support is $200,000 for years 1987 through 1990. Since the organization received more than one-third of its total support for the period from public sources, it qualifies as a publicly supported organization.

An organization that does not qualify as publicly supported under the test described above may be publicly supported on the basis of the facts in its case if it receives at least 10% of its support from the general public. If you believe your organization is publicly supported according to applicable regulations, attach a detailed statement of the facts upon which you base your conclusion.

Box 12.—Check box 12 and complete the Support Schedule (lines 15 through 28) for an organization that meets both of the following support tests (section 509(a)(2)):

(A) Normally receives more than one-third of its support in each tax year from any combination of—

(i) gifts, grants, contributions, or membership fees, and

(ii) gross receipts from admissions, sales of merchandise, performance of services, or furnishing of facilities, in an activity which is not an unrelated trade or business (within the meaning of section 513), not including such receipts from any person, or from any bureau or similar agency of a government unit (as described in section 170(c)(1)), in any tax year to the extent such receipts exceed the greater of $5,000 or 1% of the organization's support in such tax year, from persons other than disqualified persons (see Definitions, on page 2) with respect to the organization, from governmental units described in section 170(c)(1), or from organizations described in section 170(b)(1)(A) (other than in clauses (vii) and (viii)), and

(B) Normally receives not more than one-third of its support each tax year from the sum of—

(i) gross investment income (as defined in section 509(e)), and

(ii) the excess (if any) of the amount of the unrelated business taxable income (as defined in section 512) over the amount of the tax imposed by section 511.

For purposes of section 509(a)(2), determine your support solely on the cash receipts and disbursements method of accounting. For example, if a grantor makes a grant to an organization

Page 4

payable over a term of years, such grant will be includible in the support fraction of the grantee organization only when and to the extent amounts payable under the grant are received by the grantee.

Retained character of gross investment income.—When determining whether an organization meets the gross investment income test of section 509(a)(2)(B), amounts received from the following organizations retain the character of gross investment income (rather than gifts or contributions) to the extent that these organizations characterize the amounts as gross investment income:

(a) An organization that claims to be described in section 509(a)(3) because it supports a section 509(a)(2) organization; or

(b) A charitable trust, corporation, fund, or association described in section 501(c)(3) (including a charitable trust described in section 4947(a)(1)), which is required to distribute, or normally distributes, at least 25% of its adjusted net income (within the meaning of section 4942(f)) to a section 509(a)(2) organization, if the distribution normally comprises at least 5% of the distributee organization's adjusted net income.

If an organization receives an amount from a split-interest trust described in section 4947(a)(2) that is required to distribute, or normally distributes, at least 25% of its adjusted net income to a section 509(a)(2) organization, and the distribution normally comprises at least 5% of the distributee organization's adjusted net income, the amount retains the character of gross investment income if it would be characterized as gross investment income attributable to transfers in trust after May 26, 1969, if the trust were a private foundation.

All income characterized as gross investment income in the possession of the distributing organization is considered to be distributed first by the organization and keeps its character as such in the possession of the recipient.

For more details see Regulations section 1.509(a)-5, covering special rules of attribution.

If your organization received any amounts from either kind of organization above, attach a statement. Show the amounts received from each organization, including amounts, such as gifts, that are not investment income.

Box 13.—Check box 13 and complete items (a) and (b) for a supporting organization operated only for the benefit of and in connection with organizations listed above in boxes 5 through 12, or with organizations described in section 501(c) (4), (5), or (6) that meet the tests of section 509(a)(2) (described in box 12). General principles governing supporting organizations are

described in Regulations section 1.509(a)-4.

Under item 13b, "Box number from above," identify the organization supported if it is included in the list of boxes 5 through 12. For example, if your organization supported a hospital, enter "7" in item 13b.

Box 14.—Check box 14 only if the organization has received a ruling from the IRS that it is organized and operated primarily to test for public safety.

Support Schedule for Organizations Described in Sections 170(b)(1)(A)(iv) or (vi) and 509(a)(2).—Complete the Support Schedule if you checked box 10, 11, or 12.

If the organization has not existed during the whole period the schedule covers, fill in the information for the years that apply. If the organization's status is based on years not shown in the Support Schedule, attach an additional schedule for the other years.

Lines 15, 16, 17, 26, and 27.—Refer to Regulations section 1.509(a)-3:

(1) To distinguish gross receipts from gifts and contributions, grants, and gross investment income; and

(2) For the definition of membership fees and a bureau or similar agency of a governmental unit.

Line 17.—In addition to income the organization receives from performing its charitable, etc., functions, include on line 17 gross receipts from section 513(a)(1), (2), or (3) activities. These are activities in which substantially all the work is performed without compensation, or carried on by the organization primarily for the convenience of its members, or which consists of the selling of merchandise, substantially all of which has been received by the organization as gifts or contributions.

Line 28.—Unusual grants generally are substantial contributions and bequests from disinterested persons and:

(1) are attracted because of the organization's publicly supported nature,

(2) are unusual and unexpected because of the amount, and

(3) are large enough to endanger the organization's status as normally meeting the support test described in the instructions for box 10, 11, or 12.

A grant that meets these terms may be treated as an unusual grant (that is disregarded entirely in the public support computation) even if the organization receives the funds over a period of years. In your list of unusual grants, show only what the organization received during the year.

Do not treat gross investment income items as unusual grants. Instead, include all investment income in support.

See Regulations sections 1.170A-9(e)(6)(ii) and 1.509(a)-3(c)(3)

and (4) for more information about unusual grants.

Part V

All schools that checked box 6, Part IV, must complete Part V. Rev. Proc. 75-50, 1975-2 C.B. 587, gives guidelines and recordkeeping requirements for determining whether private schools that are recognized as exempt from tax have racially nondiscriminatory policies as to students.

Section 4.01 of the Rev. Proc. requires a school to include a statement in its charter, bylaws, or other governing instrument, or in a resolution of its governing body, that it has a racially nondiscriminatory policy as to students.

Section 4.02 requires every school to include a statement of its racially nondiscriminatory policy as to students in all its brochures and catalogues dealing with student admissions, programs, and scholarships. Further, every school must include a reference to its racially nondiscriminatory policy in other written advertising that it uses as a means of informing prospective students of its programs.

Section 4.03 requires a school to publicize its racially nondiscriminatory policy at least once annually during the period of its solicitation for students, or, in the absence of a solicitation program, during its registration period, unless it meets the criteria set out in section 4.03-2 of the Rev. Proc. See section 4.03-1 for examples of acceptable methods of publicizing the policy, including the use of newspapers and broadcast media. Whatever method is used, it must make the school's policy known to all segments of the general community it serves.

Section 4.03 further requires a school to be prepared to demonstrate that it has publicly denied or withdrawn any statements claimed to have been made on its behalf that are contrary to its publicity of a racially nondiscriminatory policy as to students, to the extent that the school or its principal officials were aware of such statements.

Section 4.04 requires a school to be able to show that all of its programs and facilities are operated in a racially nondiscriminatory manner.

Section 4.05 generally requires that all scholarships or other comparable benefits at any school be offered on a racially nondiscriminatory basis. However, a financial assistance program favoring members of one or more racial groups will not adversely affect exempt status if it does not significantly detract from a racially nondiscriminatory policy as to students.

Section 4.06 requires an individual authorized to take official action on behalf of a school that claims to be racially nondiscriminatory as to students

to certify annually, under penalties of perjury, that to the best of his or her knowledge and belief the school has satisfied the applicable requirements of sections 4.01 through 4.05 of the Rev. Proc. This certification is line 35 in Part V.

Part VI-A

Complete Part VI-A only for an eligible organization that elected to be subject to the lobbying expenditure limitations of section 501(h) by filing Form 5768 and for which the election was valid and in effect for its tax year beginning in 1991.

A public charity that makes a valid section 501(h) election (by filing Form 5768) may spend up to a certain percentage of its "exempt purpose expenditures" to influence legislation without incurring tax or losing its tax-exempt status. Under the "expenditure test," there are limits both upon the amount of the organization's grassroots lobbying expenditures and upon the total amount of its direct and grassroots lobbying expenditures. If the electing public charity does not meet this "expenditure test," it will owe a section 4911 excise tax on its excess lobbying expenditures. Moreover, if, over a 4-year averaging period, the organization's average annual total lobbying or grassroots lobbying expenses are more than 150% of its dollar limits, the organization will lose its exempt status.

The following terms are used throughout Part VI-A. See Regulations section 56.4911 for more specific information.

Exempt purpose expenditures.—The amount an electing public charity may spend on lobbying (without incurring tax) is a scaled percentage of the organization's exempt purpose expenditures. In general, an expenditure is an exempt purpose expenditure if it is paid or incurred by an electing public charity to accomplish the organization's exempt purpose.

In general, exempt purposes expenses are:

(1) The total amount paid or incurred for religious, charitable, scientific, literary, or educational purposes, or to foster national or international amateur sports competition (not including (except for qualified amateur sports organizations described in section 501(j)(2)) the provision of athletic facilities or equipment), or for the prevention of cruelty to children or animals,

(2) The allocable portion of administrative expenses paid or incurred for the above purposes,

(3) Amounts paid or incurred to try to influence legislation, whether or not for the purposes described in **(1)** above,

(4) Allowance for depreciation or amortization, and

(5) Fundraising expenditures, except that exempt purpose expenses do not include amounts paid to or incurred for either the organization's separate fundraising unit or other organizations, if the amounts are primarily for fundraising.

See also Regulations section 56.4911-4(c).

Lobbying expenditures.—The term "lobbying expenditures" means expenditures for the purpose of *attempting to influence legislation:*

(A) By attempting to affect the opinions of the general public, and

(B) Through communication with any member or employee of a legislative body, or with any government official or employee who may participate in the formulation of the legislation.

In determining whether an organization has spent excessive amounts on lobbying, you must know which expenditures are lobbying expenditures and which are not lobbying expenditures. An electing public charity's lobbying expenditures for a year are the sum of its expenditures during that year for: (1) direct lobbying communications ("direct lobbying expenditures") plus (2) grassroots lobbying communications ("grassroots expenditures").

(1) Direct lobbying communications.—A direct lobbying communication is any attempt to influence any legislation through communication with:

(A) Any member or employee of a legislative body, or

(B) Any government official or employee (other than a member or employee of a legislative body) who may participate in the formulation of the legislation, but only if the principal purpose of the communication is to influence legislation.

A communication with a legislator or government official will be treated as a direct lobbying communication, if, but only if, the communication:

(A) Refers to specific legislation, and

(B) Reflects a view on such legislation.

(2) Grassroots lobbying communications.—A grassroots lobbying communication is any attempt to influence any legislation through an attempt to affect the opinions of the general public or any part of the general public.

A communication is generally not a grassroots lobbying communication unless (in addition to referring to specific legislation and reflecting a view on that legislation) it encourages recipients to take action with respect to the specific legislation.

A communication encourages a recipient to take action when it: (1) states that the recipient should contact

Page 5

legislators; (2) states a legislator's address, phone number, etc.; (3) provides a petition, tear-off postcard, or similar material for the recipient to send to a legislator; or (4) specifically identifies one or more legislators who will vote on legislation as: opposing the communication's view on the legislation, being undecided about the legislation, being the recipient's representative in the legislature, or being a member of the legislative committee that will consider the legislation.

Further, a communication with the fourth type of encouragement to take action generally is grassroots lobbying only if, in addition to referring to and reflecting a view on specific legislation, it is a communication that cannot meet the "full and fair exposition" test as nonpartisan analysis, study, or research.

For purposes of section 4911, expenditures for certain communications between an organization and its members are treated more leniently than are communications to nonmembers. Expenditures for a communication that refers to, and reflects a view on, specific legislation are not lobbying expenditures if the communication satisfies the following requirements:

(1) The communication is directed only to members of the organization,

(2) The specific legislation the communication refers to, and reflects a view on, is of direct interest to the organization and its members,

(3) The communication does not directly encourage the member to engage in direct lobbying (whether individually or through the organization), and

(4) The communication does not directly encourage the member to engage in grassroots lobbying (whether individually or through the organization).

Expenditures for a communication directed only to members that refers to, and reflects a view on, specific legislation and that satisfies the requirements of paragraphs **(1)**, **(2)**, and **(4)**, but does not satisfy the requirements of paragraph **(3)** are treated as expenditures for direct lobbying.

Expenditures for a communication directed only to members that refers to, and reflects a view on, specific legislation and satisfies the requirements of paragraphs **(1)** and **(2)**, but does not satisfy the requirements of paragraph **(4)**, are treated as grassroots expenditures, whether or not the communication satisfies the requirements of paragraph **(3)**.

See Regulations section 56.4911-5 for further information.

There are special rules regarding certain paid mass media advertisements about highly publicized legislation; allocation of mixed purpose

Page 6

expenditures; certain transfers treated as lobbying expenditures and special rules regarding lobbying on referenda. ballot initiatives, and similar procedures (see Regulations sections 56.4911-2 and -3).

Legislation.—In general, the term "legislation" includes acts, bills, resolutions, or similar items. "Specific legislation" includes both legislation that has already been introduced in a legislative body and a specific legislative proposal that the organization either supports or opposes.

Exceptions to the definitions of direct lobbying communication and/or grassroots lobbying communication.—

In general, engaging in nonpartisan analysis, study, or research and making available to the general public or segment or members thereof or to governmental bodies, officials, or employees the results of such work constitute neither a direct lobbying communication nor a grassroots lobbying communication. Nonpartisan analysis, study, or research may advocate a particular position or viewpoint so long as there is a sufficiently full and fair exposition of the pertinent facts to enable the public or an individual to form an independent opinion or conclusion.

A communication that responds to a governmental body's or committee's written request for technical advice is not a direct lobbying communication.

A communication is not a direct lobbying communication if the communication is an appearance before, or communication with, any legislative body whose action might affect the organization's existence, its powers and duties, its tax-exempt status, or the deductibility of contributions to the organization, as opposed to merely affecting the scope of the organization's future activities.

Affiliated groups.—Members of an affiliated group are treated as a single organization for purposes of measuring both lobbying expenditures and permitted lobbying expenditures.

Two organizations are affiliated if one is bound by the other's decisions on legislative issues (control) or if enough representatives of one belong to the other's governing board to cause or prevent action on legislative issues (interlocking directorate). If you do not know whether your group is affiliated, ask the IRS for a ruling letter. Send the request to: Assistant Commissioner (Employee Plans and Exempt Organizations), Exempt Organizations Technical Division, E:EO, 1111 Constitution Ave., NW, Washington, DC 20224.

If the electing organization belongs to an affiliated group. complete lines 36 through 44 of column (a), Part VI-A, for the affiliated group as a whole, and

complete column (b) for the electing member of the group. The electing member must also attach a schedule showing each group member's name, address, employer identification number, and expenses. Use the format of Part VI-A, and show which members elected and which did not.

If the group has no excess amounts on either line 43 or 44, column (a), each electing member will be treated as not having excess amounts. If the group has excess amounts on line 43 or 44, column (a), each electing member will be treated as having excess amounts, and each must file **Form 4720,** Return of Certain Excise Taxes on Charities and Other Persons Under Chapters 41 and 42 of the Internal Revenue Code, and pay the tax on its proportionate share of the group's excess lobbying expenses. To find a member's proportionate share, multiply the affiliated group's total lobbying expenses (on line 43 or line 44, or both) by a fraction. The numerator is the electing member's total lobbying expenses (line 38, column (b)), and the denominator is the total lobbying expenses of all electing members of the affiliated group. Enter the proportionate share in column (b) of line 43 or line 44, or both. Include each electing member's share of the excess lobbying expenses on the schedule you attach. Any nonelecting members do not owe tax, but remain subject to the general rule, which provides that no substantial part of their activities may consist of carrying on propaganda or otherwise trying to influence legislation.

Limited control.—If two organizations are affiliated because their governing instruments provide that the decisions of one will control the other only on national legislation, apply expenses as follows:

(1) Charge the controlling organization with its own lobbying expenses and with the national legislation expenses of the affiliated organizations. Do not charge the controlling organization with other lobbying expenses (or other exempt-purpose expenses) that the affiliated organizations may have.

(2) Treat each local organization as though it were not a member of an affiliated group; that is, the local organization should account for its own expenses only. It does not include any national legislation expenses deemed to have been incurred by the controlling organization under **(1)** above.

When this type of limited control is present, each member of the affiliated group should complete column (b) only.

Group returns.—Although membership in a group affiliated for lobbying does not establish eligibility to file a group return, a group return can sometimes meet the filing requirements of more than one member of an affiliated group. (See General Instruction Q of Form 990 (or General Instruction P of Form 990EZ) to see who may file a group return.) If a central or parent organization files a group return on behalf of two or more members of the group. complete lines 36 through 44 of column (a). Part VI-A. for the affiliated group as a whole. Include the central. electing. and nonelecting members. In column (b). except on lines 43 and 44. include the amounts that apply to all electing members of the group if they are included in the group return. Also attach the schedule described above under "Affiliated groups," and show what amounts apply to each group member.

If the group return includes organizations that belong to more than one affiliated group. show the totals for all such groups in column (a). In the schedule you attach. show the amounts that apply to each affiliated group and to each group member.

If the parent organization has made the lobbying expense election, its separate return must also show in column (a) the amounts that apply to the affiliated group as a whole and, in column (b), the amounts that apply to the parent organization only. Similarly, a subordinate organization not included in the group return would also complete column (a) for the affiliated group as a whole, and column (b) for itself only.

However, if "limited control" (defined above) exists, complete only column (b) in Part VI-A of the group return for the electing members in the group. Attach a schedule to show the amounts that apply to each electing member. In the separate returns filed by the parent and by any subordinate organizations not included in the group return, complete only column (b).

Lines 36–44.—For lines 36 through 44, complete column (b) for any organization using Part VI-A, but complete column (a) only for affiliated groups.

Lines 36 through 44 are used to determine whether any of the organization's current year lobbying expenditures are subject to tax. File Form 4720 if you need to report and pay the excise tax.

Lines 45–50.—Lines 45 through 50 are used to determine if the organization exceeded lobbying expense limits during the 4-year averaging period. Any organization for which a lobbying expense election under section 501(h) was in effect for its tax year beginning in 1991 must complete columns (a) through (e) of lines 45 through 50 except in the following situations:

(1) An organization first treated as a section 501(c)(3) organization in its tax year beginning in 1991 does not have to complete any part of lines 45 through 50.

(2) An organization does not have to complete lines 45 through 50 for any

period before it is first treated as a section 501(c)(3) organization.

(3) If 1991 is the first year for which an organization's first section 501(h) election is effective. that organization is required to complete line 45. columns (a) and (e). entering the same figure in both places. The organization must then complete column (e) to determine whether the amount on line 47 is equal to or less than the lobbying ceiling amount calculated for line 46 and whether the amount on line 50 is equal to or less than the grassroots ceiling amount calculated for line 49. The organization does not satisfy both tests if either its total lobbying expenses or its grassroots lobbying expenses exceed the applicable ceiling amounts. When that occurs, all five columns must be completed and a recomputation made, unless exception **(1)** or **(2)** above applies.

(4) If 1991 is the second or third tax year for which the organization's first section 501(h) election is in effect, that organization is required to complete only the columns for the years in which the election has been in effect, entering the totals for those years in column (e). The organization must determine, for those two or three years, whether the amount entered in column (e), line 47, is equal to or less than the lobbying ceiling amount reported on line 46, and whether the amount on line 50 is equal to or less than the grassroots ceiling amount calculated for line 49. The organization does not satisfy both tests if either its total lobbying expenses or grassroots lobbying expenses exceed applicable ceiling amounts. When that occurs, all five columns must be completed and a recomputation made, unless exception **(1)** or **(2)** above applies.

If your organization is not required to complete all five columns, attach a statement explaining why. In the statement, also indicate the ending date of the tax year in which the organization made its first section 501(h) election and state whether or not that first election was revoked before the start of the organization's tax year that began in 1991.

If your organization belongs to an affiliated group, you should enter the appropriate affiliated group totals from column (a) when completing lines 45, 47, 48, and 50.

Line 45—Lobbying nontaxable amount.—For 1988–91, enter the amount from line 41 of the Schedule A (Form 990) filed for each year.

Line 47—Total lobbying expenses.—For 1988–91, enter the amount from line 38 of the Schedule A (Form 990) filed for each year.

Line 48—Grassroots nontaxable amount.—For 1988–91, enter the

amount from line 42 of the Schedule A (Form 990) filed for each year.

Line 50—Grassroots lobbying expenses.—For 1988–91, enter the amount from line 36 of the Schedule A (Form 990) filed for each year.

Part VI-B

Part VI-B provides an optional reporting format for any organization that engaged in lobbying activities in its 1991 tax year but did not make a section 501(h) lobbying expenditure election for that year by filing Form 5768. (See instructions for line 1, Part III, for information about the election and Form 5768.)

These nonelecting organizations must attach a statement giving a detailed description of their lobbying activities. They also must provide specific information about their lobbying expenses. Organizations may provide the lobbying expense information either by attaching a classified schedule of the expenses paid or incurred or by completing Part VI-B.

The Part VI-A instructions defining direct and grassroots lobbying activities by organizations that made the section 501(h) election do not apply to nonelecting organizations that complete Part VI-B or attach a separate schedule of expenses. Instead, the definitions in Regulations section 1.162-20(c) generally apply, but without regard to the rules concerning deductibility and direct interest to the organization. See also "Changes You Should Note" on page 1 of the instructions.

Part VII

Part VII is used to report direct and indirect transfers to (line 51a) and direct and indirect transactions with (line 51b) and relationships with (line 52) any other noncharitable exempt organization. A *noncharitable exempt organization* is an organization exempt under section 501(c) (that is not exempt under section 501(c)(3)), or a political organization described in section 527.

For purposes of these instructions, the section 501(c)(3) organization completing this Schedule A (Form 990) is referred to as the "reporting organization."

A noncharitable exempt organization is *related to* or *affiliated with* the reporting organization if either the two organizations share some element of common control **OR** a historic and continuing relationship exists between the two organizations. A noncharitable exempt organization is unrelated to the reporting organization if the two organizations share no element of common control **AND** a historic and continuing relationship does not exist between the two organizations.

Page 7

An *element of common control* is present when one or more of the officers, directors, or trustees of one organization are elected or appointed by the officers, directors, trustees, or members of the other. An element of common control is also present when more than 25% of the officers, directors, or trustees of one organization serve as officers, directors, or trustees of the other organization.

A *historic and continuing relationship* exists when two organizations participate in a joint effort to work in concert toward the attainment of one or more common purposes on a continuous or recurring basis rather than on the basis of one or several isolated transactions or activities. Such a relationship also exists when two organizations share facilities, equipment, or paid personnel during the year, regardless of the length of time the arrangement is in effect.

Line 51—Reporting of certain transfers and transactions.—Except as provided below, you must report on line 51 any transfer to or transaction with a noncharitable exempt organization even if the transfer or transaction constitutes the only connection with the noncharitable exempt organization.

Related organizations.—If the noncharitable exempt organization is related to or affiliated with the reporting organization, you must report all direct and indirect transfers and transactions except for contributions and grants received by the reporting organization.

Unrelated organizations.—All transfers from the reporting organization to an unrelated noncharitable exempt organization must be reported on line 51a. All transactions between the reporting organization and an unrelated noncharitable exempt organization must be shown on line 51b, unless they meet the exception in the specific instructions for that line.

Line 51a—Transfers.—Answer "Yes" to lines 51a(i) and 51a(ii) if the reporting organization made any direct or indirect transfers of any value to a noncharitable exempt organization.

A "transfer" is any transaction or arrangement whereby one organization transfers something of value (cash, other assets, services, use of property, etc.) to another organization without receiving something of more than nominal value in return. Contributions, gifts, and grants are examples of transfers.

If the only transfers between the two organizations were contributions and grants made by the noncharitable exempt organization to the reporting organization, answer "No."

Line 51b—Other transactions.—Answer "Yes" for any transaction described in lines 51b(i)-(vi), regardless of its amount, if it is with a related or affiliated organization.

Unrelated organizations.—You must answer "Yes" for any transaction between the reporting organization and an unrelated noncharitable exempt organization, regardless of its amount, if the reporting organization received less than adequate consideration. There is adequate consideration where the fair market value of the goods, other assets or services furnished by the reporting organization is not more than the fair market value of the goods, other assets or services received from the unrelated noncharitable exempt organization. The exception described below does not apply to transactions for less than adequate consideration.

You must answer "Yes" for any transaction between the reporting organization and an unrelated noncharitable exempt organization if the amount involved is more than $500. The "amount involved" is the fair market value of the goods, services, or other assets furnished by the reporting organization.

Exception: If a transaction with an unrelated noncharitable exempt organization was for adequate consideration and the amount involved was $500 or less, you need not answer "Yes" for that transaction.

Line 51b(iii).—Answer "Yes" for transactions in which the reporting organization was either the lessor or the lessee.

Line 51b(iv).—Answer "Yes" if either organization reimbursed expenses incurred by the other.

Line 51b(v).—Answer "Yes" if either organization made loans to the other or if the reporting organization guaranteed the other's loans.

Line 51b(vi).—Answer "Yes" if either organization performed services or membership or fundraising solicitations for the other.

Line 51c.—Complete line 51c regardless of whether the noncharitable exempt organization is related to or closely

affiliated with the reporting organization. For the purposes of this line, "facilities" includes office space and any other land. building, or structure whether owned or leased by, or provided free of charge to, the reporting organization or the noncharitable exempt organization.

Line 51d.—Use this schedule to describe the transfers and transactions for which you entered "Yes" on lines 51a–c above. You must describe each transfer or transaction for which you answered "Yes." You may combine all of the cash transfers (line 51a(i)) to each organization into a single entry. Otherwise, make a separate entry for each transfer or transaction.

Column (a).—For each entry, enter the line number from lines 51a–c, above. For example, if you answered "Yes" to line 51b(iii), enter "b(iii)" in column (a).

Column (d).—If you need more space than that provided, write "see attached" in column (d) and use an attached sheet for your description. If you are making more than one entry on line 51d, specify on the attached sheet which transfer or transaction you are describing.

Line 52—Reporting of certain relationships.—Enter on line 52 each noncharitable exempt organization which the reporting organization is related to, or affiliated with, as defined above. If the control factor or the historic and continuing relationship factor (or both) is present at any time during the year, you must identify the organization on line 52 even if neither factor is present at the end of the year.

Do not enter unrelated noncharitable exempt organizations on line 52 even if you report transfers to or transactions with those organizations on line 51. For example, if you reported a one-time transfer to an unrelated noncharitable exempt organization on line 51a(ii), you should not list the organization on line 52.

Column (b).—Enter the exempt category of the organization; for example, "501(c)(4)."

Column (c).—In most cases, a simple description, such as "common directors" or "auxiliary of reporting organization" will be sufficient. If you need more space, write "see attached" in column (c) and use a separate sheet to describe the relationship. If you list more than one organization on line 52, identify which organization you are describing on the attached sheet.

*U.S. Government Printing Office: 1991 — 285-138

SCHEDULE A	Organization Exempt Under 501(c)(3)	OMB No. 1545-0047
(Form 990)	(Except Private Foundation), 501(e), 501(f), 501(k), or Section 4947(a)(1) Charitable Trust Supplementary Information	1991
Department of the Treasury Internal Revenue Service	▶ Attach to Form 990 (or Form 990EZ).	

Name	Employer identification number

Part I   **Compensation of the Five Highest Paid Employees Other Than Officers, Directors, and Trustees**
(See specific instructions.) (List each one. If there are none, enter "None.")

(a) Name and address of employees paid more than $30,000	(b) Title and average hours per week devoted to position	(c) Compensation	(d) Contributions to employee benefit plans	(e) Expense account and other allowances
....				
....				
....				
....				
....				

Total number of other employees paid over $30,000 . . . . ▶

Part II   **Compensation of the Five Highest Paid Persons for Professional Services**
(See specific instructions.) (List each one. If there are none, enter "None.")

(a) Name and address of persons paid more than $30,000	(b) Type of service	(c) Compensation
....		
....		
....		
....		
....		

Total number of others receiving over $30,000 for professional services . . . . ▶

Part III   **Statements About Activities**   Yes   No

1 During the year, have you attempted to influence national, state, or local legislation, including any attempt to influence public opinion on a legislative matter or referendum? . . . . $ **1**

If "Yes," enter the total expenses paid or incurred in connection with the legislative activities. $ _____

Organizations that made an election under section 501(h) by filing Form 5768 must complete Part VI-A. For other organizations checking "Yes," attach a statement giving a detailed description of the legislative activities AND either complete Part VI-B or attach a classified schedule of the expenses paid or incurred.

2 During the year, have you, either directly or indirectly, engaged in any of the following acts with a trustee, director, principal officer, or creator of your organization, or any taxable organization or corporation with which such person is affiliated as an officer, director, trustee, majority owner, or principal beneficiary:

a Sale, exchange, or leasing of property? **2a**

b Lending of money or other extension of credit? **2b**

c Furnishing of goods, services, or facilities? **2c**

d Payment of compensation (or payment or reimbursement of expenses if more than $1,000)? **2d**

e Transfer of any part of your income or assets? **2e**

If the answer to any question is "Yes," attach a detailed statement explaining the transactions.

3 Do you make grants for scholarships, fellowships, student loans, etc.? **3**

4 Attach a statement explaining how you determine that individuals or organizations receiving grants or loans from you in furtherance of your charitable programs qualify to receive payments. (See specific instructions.)

For Paperwork Reduction Act Notice, see page 1 of the instructions to Form 990 (or Form 990EZ).   Cat. No. 11285F   **Schedule A (Form 990) 1991**

Part IV	**Reason for Non-Private Foundation Status** (See instructions for definitions.)

The organization is not a private foundation because it is (please check only **ONE** applicable box):

5 ☐ A church, convention of churches, or association of churches. Section 170(b)(1)(A)(i).

6 ☐ A school. Section 170(b)(1)(A)(ii). (Also complete Part V, page 3.)

7 ☐ A hospital or a cooperative hospital service organization. Section 170(b)(1)(A)(iii).

8 ☐ A Federal, state, or local government or governmental unit. Section 170(b)(1)(A)(v).

9 ☐ A medical research organization operated in conjunction with a hospital. Section 170(b)(1)(A)(iii). **Enter name, city, and state of hospital** ▶ ....

10 ☐ An organization operated for the benefit of a college or university owned or operated by a governmental unit. Section 170(b)(1)(A)(iv). (Also complete Support Schedule.)

11a ☐ An organization that normally receives a substantial part of its support from a governmental unit or from the general public. Section 170(b)(1)(A)(vi). (Also complete Support Schedule.)

11b ☐ A community trust. Section 170(b)(1)(A)(vi). (Also complete Support Schedule.)

12 ☐ An organization that normally receives: **(a)** no more than ⅓ of its support from gross investment income and unrelated business taxable income (less section 511 tax) from businesses acquired by the organization after June 30, 1975, and **(b)** more than ⅓ of its support from contributions, membership fees, and gross receipts from activities related to its charitable, etc., functions—subject to certain exceptions. See section 509(a)(2). (Also complete Support Schedule.)

13 ☐ An organization that is not controlled by any disqualified persons (other than foundation managers) and supports organizations described in: **(1)** boxes 5 through 12 above; or **(2)** section 501(c)(4), (5), or (6), if they meet the test of section 509(a)(2). See section 509(a)(3).

Provide the following information about the supported organizations. (See instructions for Part IV, box 13.)

(a) Name(s) of supported organization(s)	(b) Box number from above

14 ☐ An organization organized and operated to test for public safety. Section 509(a)(4). (See specific instructions.)

Support Schedule (Complete only if you checked box 10, 11, or 12 above.) Use cash method of accounting.

Calendar year (or fiscal year beginning in) ▶	(a) 1990	(b) 1989	(c) 1988	(d) 1987	(e) Total
15 Gifts, grants, and contributions received. (Do not include unusual grants. See line 28.). .					
16 Membership fees received					
17 Gross receipts from admissions, merchandise sold or services performed, or furnishing of facilities in any activity that is not a business unrelated to the organization's charitable, etc., purpose					
18 Gross income from interest, dividends, amounts received from payments on securities loans (section 512(a)(5)), rents, royalties, and unrelated business taxable income (less section 511 taxes) from businesses acquired by the organization after June 30, 1975					
19 Net income from unrelated business activities not included in line 18					
20 Tax revenues levied for your benefit and either paid to you or expended on your behalf					
21 The value of services or facilities furnished to you by a governmental unit without charge. Do not include the value of services or facilities generally furnished to the public without charge					
22 Other income. Attach schedule. Do not include gain or (loss) from sale of capital assets . .					
23 Total of lines 15 through 22.					
24 Line 23 minus line 17.					
25 Enter 1% of line 23					/////////

26 Organizations described in box 10 or 11:
  a Enter 2% of amount in column (e), line 24 . . . .
  b Attach a list (not open to public inspection) showing the name of and amount contributed by each person (other than a governmental unit or publicly supported organization) whose total gifts for 1987 through 1990 exceeded the amount shown in line 26a. Enter the sum of all excess amounts here . . . . ▶

(Continued on page 3)

Part IV　　Support Schedule (continued) **(Complete only if you checked box 10, 11, or 12 on page 2.)**

27　Organizations described in box 12, page 2:

　a　Attach a list for amounts shown on lines 15, 16, and 17, showing the name of, and total amounts received in each year from, each "disqualified person," and enter the sum of such amounts for each year:

　　(1990) .... (1989) .... (1988) .... (1987) ....

　b　Attach a list showing, for 1987 through 1990, the name and amount included in line 17 for each person (other than "disqualified persons") from whom the organization received more during that year than the larger of: **(1)** the amount on line 25 for the year; or **(2)** $5,000. Include organizations described in boxes 5 through 11 as well as individuals. Enter the sum of these excess amounts for each year:

　　(1990) .... (1989) .... (1988) .... (1987) ....

28　For an organization described in box 10, 11, or 12, page 2, that received any unusual grants during 1987 through 1990, attach a list (not open to public inspection) for each year showing the name of the contributor, the date and amount of the grant, and a brief description of the nature of the grant. Do not include these grants in line 15 above. (See specific instructions.)

Part V　　Private School Questionnaire
　　　　　　(To be completed ONLY by schools that checked box 6 in Part IV)

		Yes	No
29	Do you have a racially nondiscriminatory policy toward students by statement in your charter, bylaws, other governing instrument, or in a resolution of your governing body? **29**		
30	Do you include a statement of your racially nondiscriminatory policy toward students in all your brochures, catalogues, and other written communications with the public dealing with student admissions, programs, and scholarships? **30**		
31	Have you publicized your racially nondiscriminatory policy through newspaper or broadcast media during the period of solicitation for students, or during the registration period if you have no solicitation program, in a way that makes the policy known to all parts of the general community you serve? **31**		

　　　　If "Yes," please describe; if "No," please explain. (If you need more space, attach a separate statement.)

　　　　--
　　　　--
　　　　--

		Yes	No
32	Do you maintain the following:		
a	Records indicating the racial composition of the student body, faculty, and administrative staff? **32a**		
b	Records documenting that scholarships and other financial assistance are awarded on a racially nondiscriminatory basis? **32b**		
c	Copies of all catalogues, brochures, announcements, and other written communications to the public dealing with student admissions, programs, and scholarships? **32c**		
d	Copies of all material used by you or on your behalf to solicit contributions? **32d**		

　　　　If you answered "No" to any of the above, please explain. (If you need more space, attach a separate statement.)

　　　　--
　　　　--

		Yes	No
33	Do you discriminate by race in any way with respect to:		
a	Students' rights or privileges? **33a**		
b	Admissions policies? **33b**		
c	Employment of faculty or administrative staff? **33c**		
d	Scholarships or other financial assistance? (See instructions.). **33d**		
e	Educational policies? **33e**		
f	Use of facilities? **33f**		
g	Athletic programs? **33g**		
h	Other extracurricular activities? **33h**		

　　　　If you answered "Yes" to any of the above, please explain. (If you need more space, attach a separate statement.)

　　　　--
　　　　--

		Yes	No
34a	Do you receive any financial aid or assistance from a governmental agency? **34a**		
b	Has your right to such aid ever been revoked or suspended? **34b**		
	If you answered "Yes" to either 34a or b, please explain using an attached separate statement.		
35	Do you certify that you have complied with the applicable requirements of sections 4.01 through 4.05 of Rev. Proc. 75-50, 1975-2 C.B. 587, covering racial nondiscrimination? If "No," attach an explanation. (See instructions for Part V.) **35**		

Part VI-A	**Lobbying Expenditures by Electing Public Charities** (see instructions)

(To be completed **ONLY** by an eligible organization that filed Form 5768)

Check here ▶ **a** ☐ If the organization belongs to an affiliated group (see instructions).

Check here ▶ **b** ☐ If you checked **a** and "limited control" provisions apply (see instructions).

	Limits on Lobbying Expenses		(a) Affiliated group totals	(b) To be completed for ALL electing organizations
36	Total (grassroots) lobbying expenses to influence public opinion	36		
37	Total lobbying expenses to influence a legislative body	37		
38	Total lobbying expenses (add lines 36 and 37)	38		
39	Other exempt purpose expenses (see Part VI instructions)	39		
40	Total exempt purpose expenses (add lines 38 and 39) (see instructions)	40		
41	Lobbying nontaxable amount. Enter the smaller of $1,000,000 or the amount determined under the following table—	41		

If the amount on line 40 is— / The lobbying nontaxable amount is—

Not over $500,000 . . . . . . 20% of the amount on line 40 . . . . .

Over $500,000 but not over $1,000,000. . $100,000 plus 15% of the excess over $500,000

Over $1,000,000 but not over $1,500,000 . $175,000 plus 10% of the excess over $1,000,000

Over $1,500,000. . . . . . . $225,000 plus 5% of the excess over $1,500,000

42	Grassroots nontaxable amount (enter 25% of line 41)	42		
	(Complete lines 43 and 44. File Form 4720 if either line 36 exceeds line 42 or line 38 exceeds line 41.)			
43	Excess of line 36 over line 42	43		
44	Excess of line 38 over line 41	44		

4-Year Averaging Period Under Section 501(h)

(Some organizations that made a section 501(h) election do not have to complete all of the five columns below. See the instructions for lines 45–50 for details.)

	Calendar year (or fiscal year beginning in) ▶	(a) 1991	(b) 1990	(c) 1989	(d) 1988	(e) Total
45	Lobbying nontaxable amount (see instructions)					
46	Lobbying ceiling amount (150% of line 45(e))					
47	Total lobbying expenses (see instructions)					
48	Grassroots nontaxable amount (see instructions)					
49	Grassroots ceiling amount (150% of line 48(e))					
50	Grassroots lobbying expenses (see instructions)					

Part VI-B	**Lobbying Activity by Nonelecting Public Charities**

(For **optional** reporting by organizations that did not complete Part VI-A.)

During the year, did you attempt to influence national, state or local legislation, including any attempt to influence public opinion on a legislative matter or referendum, through the use of:	Yes	No	Amount
a Volunteers			
b Paid staff or management (include compensation in expenses reported on lines c through h)			
c Media advertisements			
d Mailings to members, legislators, or the public			
e Publications or published or broadcast statements			
f Grants to other organizations for lobbying purposes			
g Direct contact with legislators, their staffs, government officials, or a legislative body			
h Rallies, demonstrations, seminars. conventions, speeches, lectures, or any other means			
i Total lobbying expenses (add lines c through h)			

If "Yes" to any of the above, also attach a statement giving a detailed description of the activities.

Part VII	Information Regarding Transfers To and Transactions and Relationships With Noncharitable Exempt Organizations

51 Did the reporting organization directly or indirectly engage in any of the following with any other organization described in section 501(c) of the Code (other than section 501(c)(3) organizations) or in section 527, relating to political organizations?

		Yes	No
a Transfers from the reporting organization to a noncharitable exempt organization of:			
(i) Cash	**51a(i)**		
(ii) Other assets	**a(ii)**		
b Other Transactions:			
(i) Sales of assets to a noncharitable exempt organization	**b(i)**		
(ii) Purchases of assets from a noncharitable exempt organization	**b(ii)**		
(iii) Rental of facilities or equipment	**b(iii)**		
(iv) Reimbursement arrangements	**b(iv)**		
(v) Loans or loan guarantees	**b(v)**		
(vi) Performance of services or membership or fundraising solicitations	**b(vi)**		
c Sharing of facilities, equipment, mailing lists or other assets, or paid employees	**c**		

d If the answer to any of the above is "Yes," complete the following schedule. The "Amount involved" column below should always indicate the fair market value of the goods, other assets, or services given by the reporting organization. If the organization received less than fair market value in any transaction or sharing arrangement, indicate in column (d) the value of the goods, other assets, or services received.

(a) Line no.	(b) Amount involved	(c) Name of noncharitable exempt organization	(d) Description of transfers, transactions, and sharing arrangements

52a Is the organization directly or indirectly affiliated with, or related to, one or more tax-exempt organizations described in section 501(c) of the Code (other than section 501(c)(3)) or in section 527?. . . . . ☐ **Yes** ☐ **No**

b If "Yes," complete the following schedule.

(a) Name of organization	(b) Type of organization	(c) Description of relationship

★U.S.GPO:1991-0-285-137

1991

Department of the Treasury
Internal Revenue Service

Instructions for Form 990EZ

Short Form Return of Organization Exempt From Income Tax

Under section 501(c) of the Internal Revenue Code (except black lung benefit trust or private foundation) or section 4947(a)(1) charitable trust
(For organizations with gross receipts of less than $100,000 **and** total assets of less than $250,000 at end of year.)

(Section references are to the Internal Revenue Code unless otherwise indicated.)

Paperwork Reduction Act Notice.—We ask for the information on this form to carry out the Internal Revenue laws of the United States. You are required to give us the information. We need it to ensure that you are complying with these laws and to allow us to figure and collect the right amount of tax.

The time needed to complete and file this form will vary depending on individual circumstances. The estimated average times are:

Form	Recordkeeping	Learning about the law or the form	Preparing the form	Copying, assembling, and sending the form to the IRS
990EZ	26 hr., 33 min.	4 hr., 8 min.	5 hr., 41 min.	16 min.
Sch. A (990)	43 hr., 32 min.	8 hr., 56 min.	10 hr., 2 min.	-0-

If you have comments concerning the accuracy of these time estimates or suggestions for making this form more simple, we would be happy to hear from you. You can write to both the **Internal Revenue Service**, Washington, DC 20224, Attention: IRS Reports Clearance Officer, T:FP; and the **Office of Management and Budget,** Paperwork Reduction Project (1545-1150), Washington, DC 20503. **DO NOT** send the tax form to either of these offices. Instead, see General Instruction H for information on where to file it.

General Instructions

Note: *An organization's completed Form 990EZ (except for the schedule of contributors) is available for public inspection as required by section 6104. Some members of the public rely on Form 990EZ as the primary or sole source of information about a particular organization. How the public perceives an organization in such cases may be determined by the information presented on its return. Therefore, please make sure your return is complete and accurate and fully describes your organization's programs and accomplishments.*

Section 501(c)(3) organizations and section 4947(a)(1) trusts must also attach a completed Schedule A (Form 990) to their Form 990EZ (or Form 990).

Purpose of Form.—Form 990EZ, an annual information return, is a shortened version of **Form 990,** Return of Organization Exempt From Income Tax. It is designed for use by small tax-exempt organizations and nonexempt charitable trusts to provide the IRS with the information required by section 6033.

Contents

Contents

A. Who Must File.—

1. IMPORTANT NOTE: *Gross receipts and total assets requirements.*—Except for those types of organizations listed in General Instruction B, an annual return on Form 990 (or Form 990EZ) is required from every organization exempt from tax under section 501(a). This includes foreign organizations and cooperative service organizations described in sections 501(e) and (f), and child care organizations described in section 501(k).

Organizations whose annual gross receipts are normally more than $25,000 must file Form 990 (or Form 990EZ) (see General Instruction B11). An organization may file Form 990EZ, instead of Form 990, if it meets BOTH of the following requirements: its gross receipts during the year were less than $100,000 AND its total assets (line 25, column (B) of Form 990EZ) at the end of the year were less than $250,000. (See General Instruction B11(a) for calculating gross receipts.) If your organization fails to meet either of these conditions, you may not file Form 990EZ. Instead, you must file Form 990.

2. *Section 4947(a)(1) nonexempt charitable trust.*—Any nonexempt charitable trust (described in section 4947(a)(1)) not treated as a private foundation is also required to file Form 990 (or Form 990EZ) if its gross receipts are normally more than $25,000. See General Instruction A1 for Form 990EZ eligibility requirements. See General Instruction C7 for information regarding possible relief from filing **Form 1041,** U.S. Fiduciary Income Tax Return.

3. *Exemption application pending.*—If your application for exemption is pending, check the Application Pending box (item G) at the top of page 1 of the return and complete the return in the normal manner.

4. *If you received a Form 990 Package.*—If you are not required to file Form 990EZ because your gross receipts are normally not more than $25,000 (see General Instruction B11 below), we ask that you file anyway if we sent you a Form 990 Package with a preaddressed mailing label. Attach the label to the name and address space on the return (see Specific Instructions.) Check the box in item J in the area above Part I to indicate that your gross receipts are below the $25,000 filing minimum; sign the return; and send it to the Service Center for your area. You do not have to complete Parts I through V of the return. By following this instruction, you will help us to update our records, and we will not have to contact you later asking why no return was filed. If you file a return this way, you will not be mailed a Form 990 Package in later years and need not file Form 990 (or Form 990EZ) again until your gross receipts normally exceed the $25,000 minimum, or you terminate or undergo a substantial contraction as described in the instructions for line 36.

5. *Effect on contributions.*—Organizations that are eligible to receive tax-deductible contributions are listed in **Publication 78,** Cumulative List of Organizations described in Section 170(c) of the Internal Revenue Code of 1986. An organization may be removed from this listing if our records show that it is required to file Form 990 (or Form 990EZ), but it does not file a return or advise us that it is no longer required to file. However, contributions to such an organization may continue to be deductible

Cat. No. 64888C

by the general public until the IRS publishes a notice to the contrary in the Internal Revenue Bulletin.

B. Organizations Not Required To File.— (**Note:** *Organizations not required to file this form with the IRS may nevertheless wish to use it to satisfy state reporting requirements. For details, see General Instruction E.)*

The following types of organizations exempt from tax under section 501(a) do not have to file Form 990 (or Form 990EZ) with the IRS:

1. A church, an interchurch organization of local units of a church, a convention or association of churches, an integrated auxiliary of a church (such as a men's or women's organization, religious school, mission society, or youth group), or an internally supported, church-controlled organization (described in Rev. Proc. 86-23, 1986-1 C.B. 564).

2. A school below college level affiliated with a church or operated by a religious order.

3. A mission society sponsored by, or affiliated with, one or more churches or church denominations, if more than half of the society's activities are conducted in, or directed at persons in, foreign countries.

4. An exclusively religious activity of any religious order.

5. A state institution whose income is excluded from gross income under section 115.

6. An organization described in section 501(c)(1). Section 501(c)(1) organizations are corporations organized under an Act of Congress that are:

(a) Instrumentalities of the United States, and

(b) Exempt from Federal income taxes.

7. A private foundation exempt under section 501(c)(3) and described in section 509(a). (Required to file **Form 990-PF,** Return of Private Foundation.)

8. A black lung benefit trust described in section 501(c)(21). (Required to file **Form 990-BL,** Information and Initial Excise Tax Return for Black Lung Benefit Trusts and Certain Related Persons.)

9. A stock bonus, pension, or profit-sharing trust that qualifies under section 401. (See **Form 5500,** Annual Return/Report of Employee Benefit Plan.)

10. A religious or apostolic organization described in section 501(d). (Required to file **Form 1065,** U. S. Partnership Return of Income.)

11. An organization whose annual gross receipts are normally $25,000 or less is not required to file; however, see General Instruction A4.

(a) Calculating gross receipts.—The organization's gross receipts are the total amount it received from all sources during its annual accounting period, without subtracting any costs or expenses. (Gross receipts are the sum of lines 1, 2, 3, 4, 5a, 6a, 7a, and 8 of Part I. You can also calculate gross receipts by adding back

the amounts on lines 5b, 6b, and 7b to the total revenue reported on line 9.

For example: On line 9 of its Form 990EZ for 1991, Organization M reported $50,000 as total revenue. M added back the costs and expenses it had deducted on lines 5b ($2,000); 6b ($1,500); and 7b ($500) to its total revenue of $50,000 and determined that its gross receipts for the tax year were $54,000.

(b) Acting as agent.—If a local chapter of a section 501(c)(8) fraternal organization collects insurance premiums for its parent lodge and merely sends those premiums to the parent without asserting any right to use the funds or otherwise deriving any benefit from collecting them, the local chapter should not include the premiums in its gross receipts. The parent lodge should report them instead. The same treatment applies in other situations in which one organization collects funds merely as an agent for another.

(c) $25,000 gross receipts test.—An organization's gross receipts are considered normally to be $25,000 or less if the organization is:

(a) Up to a year old and has received, or donors have pledged to give, $37,500 or less during its first tax year;

(b) Between one and three years old and averaged $30,000 or less in gross receipts during each of its first two tax years; or

(c) Three years old or more and averaged $25,000 or less in gross receipts for the immediately preceding three tax years (including the year for which the return would be filed).

C. Forms You May Need To File or Use.—

1. Schedule A (Form 990).— Organization Exempt Under 501(c)(3) (Except Private Foundation), 501(e), 501(f), 501(k), or Section 4947(a)(1) Charitable Trust Supplementary Information. Filed **with** Form 990EZ for a section 501(c)(3) organization that is not a private foundation (including an organization described in section 501(e), 501(f), or 501(k)). Also filed **with** Form 990EZ for a section 4947(a)(1) charitable trust not treated as a private foundation. An organization is not required to file Schedule A if its gross receipts are normally $25,000 or less (see General Instruction B11).

2. Forms W-2 and W-3.—Wage and Tax Statement, and Transmittal of Income and Tax Statements.

3. Form 940.—Employer's Annual Federal Unemployment (FUTA) Tax Return.

4. Form 941.—Employer's Quarterly Federal Tax Return. Used to report social security and income taxes withheld by an employer and social security tax paid by an employer.

5. Form 990-T.—Exempt Organization Business Income Tax Return. Filed separately for organizations with gross income of $1,000 or more from business unrelated to the organization's exempt purpose.

6. Form 990-W.—Estimated Tax on Unrelated Business Taxable Income for Tax-Exempt Organizations.

7. Form 1041.—U. S. Fiduciary Income Tax Return. Required of section 4947(a)(1) charitable trusts that also file Form 990 (or 990EZ). However, if such a trust does not have any taxable income under Subtitle A of the Code, it can file either Form 990 (or 990EZ) and need not file Form 1041 to meet its section 6012 filing requirement. If this condition is met, check the box for question 42 on page 2 of Form 990EZ and do not file Form 1041, but complete Form 990EZ in the normal manner. A section 4947(a)(1) charitable trust that normally has gross receipts of not more than $25,000 (see General Instruction B11) and has no taxable income under Subtitle A must complete only the following items in the heading of Form 990EZ:

Item

A. Fiscal year (if applicable);

B. Name and address;

C. Employer identification number;

F. Section 4947(a)(1) box; **and** question 42 and the signature block on page 2.

8. Form 1096.—Annual Summary and Transmittal of U.S. Information Returns.

9. Form 1099 Series.—Information returns for reporting payments such as dividends, interest, miscellaneous income (including medical and health care payments and nonemployee compensation), original issue discount, patronage dividends, real estate transactions, acquisition or abandonment of secured property, and distributions from annuities, pensions, profit-sharing plans, retirement plans, etc.

10. Form 1120-POL.—U.S. Income Tax Return for Certain Political Organizations.

11. Form 1128.—Application To Adopt, Change or Retain a Tax Year.

12. Form 2758.—Application for Extension of Time To File Certain Excise, Income, Information, and Other Returns.

13. Form 4506-A.—Request for Public Inspection or Copy of Exempt Organization Tax Form.

14. Form 4720.—Return of Certain Excise Taxes on Charities and Other Persons Under Chapters 41 and 42 of the Internal Revenue Code. Section 501(c)(3) organizations that file Form 990 (or 990EZ), as well as the managers of these organizations, use this form to report their tax on political expenditures and certain lobbying expenditures.

15. Form 5500 or 5500-C/R.— Employers who maintain pension, profit-sharing, or other funded deferred compensation plans are generally required to file one of the 5500 series forms specified below. This requirement applies whether or not the plan is qualified under the Internal Revenue Code and whether or not a deduction is claimed for the current tax year.

Page 2

The forms required to be filed are:

Form 5500.—Annual Return/Report of Employee Benefit Plan. Used for each plan with 100 or more participants.

Form 5500-C/R.—Return/Report of Employee Benefit Plan. Used for each plan with fewer than 100 participants.

16. Form 5768.—Election/Revocation of Election by an Eligible Section 501(c)(3) Organization To Make Expenditures To Influence Legislation.

17. Form 8282.—Donee Information Return. Required of the donee of "charitable deduction property" who sells, exchanges, or otherwise disposes of the property within two years after receiving the property.

Also, the form is required of any successor donee who disposes of charitable deduction property within two years after the date that the donor gave the property to the original donee. (It does not matter who gave the property to the successor donee. It may have been the original donee or another successor donee.) For successor donees, the form must be filed only for any property that was transferred by the original donee after July 5, 1988.

18. Form 8300.—Report of Cash Payments Over $10,000 Received in a Trade or Business. Used to report cash amounts in excess of $10,000 that were received in a single transaction (or in two or more related transactions) in the course of a trade or business (as defined in section 162). However, if the organization receives a charitable cash contribution in excess of $10,000, it would not be subject to the reporting requirement since the funds were not received in the course of a trade or business.

19. Form 8822.—Change of Address. Used to notify the IRS of a change in mailing address that occurs after the return is filed.

D. Helpful Publications.—

Publication 525.—Taxable and Nontaxable Income.

Publication 598.—Tax on Unrelated Business Income of Exempt Organizations.

Publication 910.—Guide to Free Tax Services.

Publication 1391.—Deductibility of Payments Made to Charities Conducting Fund-Raising Events.

Publications and forms are available free at many IRS offices or by calling **1-800-TAX-FORM** (1-800-829-3676).

E. Use of Form 990EZ To Satisfy State Reporting Requirements.—Some states and local government units will accept a copy of Form 990EZ and Schedule A (Form 990) in place of all or part of their own financial report forms. The substitution applies primarily to section 501(c)(3) organizations, but some of the other types of section 501(c) organizations are also affected.

If you intend to use Form 990EZ to satisfy state or local filing requirements, such as those under state charitable solicitation acts, note the following:

Determine state filing requirements.— You should consult the appropriate officials of all states and other jurisdictions in which you do business to determine their specific filing requirements. "Doing business" in a jurisdiction may include any of the following: (a) soliciting contributions or grants by mail or otherwise from individuals, businesses, or other charitable organizations; (b) conducting programs; (c) having employees within that jurisdiction; (d) maintaining a checking account; or (e) owning or renting property there.

Monetary tests may differ.—Some or all of the dollar limitations applicable to Form 990EZ when filed with IRS may not apply when using Form 990EZ in place of state or local report forms. Examples of IRS dollar limitations that do not meet some state requirements are the $25,000 gross receipts minimum that creates an obligation to file with IRS (see General Instruction B11), and the $30,000 minimum for listing professional fees in Part II of Schedule A (Form 990).

Additional information may be required.—State or local filing requirements may require you to attach to Form 990EZ one or more of the following: (a) additional financial statements, such as a complete analysis of functional expenses or a statement of changes in financial position; (b) notes to financial statements; (c) additional financial schedules; (d) a report on the financial statements by an independent accountant; and (e) answers to additional questions and other information. Each jurisdiction may require the additional material to be presented on forms they provide. The additional information does not have to be submitted with the Form 990EZ filed with IRS.

Even if the Form 990EZ you file with IRS is accepted by IRS as complete, a copy of the same return filed with a state will not fully satisfy that state's filing requirement if required information is not provided, including any of the additional information discussed above, or if the state determines that the form was not completed in accordance with the applicable Form 990EZ instructions or supplemental state instructions. If so, you may be asked to provide the missing information or to submit an amended return.

Use of audit guides may be required.— To ensure that all organizations report similar transactions uniformly, many states require that contributions, gifts, and grants on line 1 in Part I and program service expenses in Part III be reported in accordance with the AICPA industry audit guide, *Audits of Voluntary Health and Welfare Organizations* (New York, AICPA, 1988), as supplemented by *Standards of Accounting and Financial Reporting for Voluntary Health and Welfare Organizations* (New York, National Health Council, Inc. (Washington, DC), 1988), and by *Accounting and Financial Reporting—A Guide for United Ways and Not-for-Profit Human Service Organizations* (Alexandria, Va., United Way Institute, 1989).

However, although reporting donated services and facilities as items of revenue and expense is called for in certain circumstances by the three publications named above, many states and IRS do not permit the inclusion of those amounts in Part I of Form 990EZ. The instructions in Part III(a) discuss the optional reporting of donated services and facilities.

Amended returns.—If you submit supplemental information or file an amended Form 990EZ with IRS, you must also furnish a copy of the information or amended return to any state with which you filed a copy of Form 990EZ originally to meet that state's filing requirement.

If a state requires you to file an amended Form 990EZ to correct conflicts with Form 990EZ instructions, you must also file an amended return with IRS.

Method of accounting.—Most states require that all amounts be reported based on the accrual method of accounting. See also Specific Instructions, item H.

Time for filing may differ.—The time for filing Form 990EZ with IRS differs from the time for filing reports with some states.

Public inspection.—The Form 990EZ information made available for public inspection by IRS may differ from that made available by the states. See the cautionary note for Part I, line 1, instruction D, Note (2).

State Registration Number.—Insert the applicable state or local jurisdiction registration or identification number in item D (in the heading on page 1) for each jurisdiction in which you file Form 990EZ in place of the state or local form. When filing in several jurisdictions, prepare as many copies as needed with item D blank. Then enter the applicable registration number on the copy to be filed with each jurisdiction.

F. Other Forms as Partial Substitutes for Form 990EZ.—Except as provided below, the IRS will not accept any form as a substitute for one or more parts of Form 990EZ.

(1) Labor organizations.—A labor organization that files **Form LM-2,** Labor Organization Annual Report, or the shorter **Form LM-3** with the U.S. Department of Labor (DOL) can attach a copy of the completed DOL form to provide some of the information required by Form 990EZ. This substitution is not permitted if the organization files a DOL report that consolidates its financial statements with those of one or more separate subsidiary organizations.

(2) Employee benefit plans.—An employee benefit plan may be able to substitute Form 5500, or Form 5500-C/R, for part of Form 990EZ. The substitution can be made if the organization filing Form 990EZ and the plan filing Form 5500 or 5500-C/R meet all the following tests:

(a) The Form 990EZ filer is organized under section 501(c)(9), (17), (18), or (20);

(b) The Form 990EZ filer and Form 5500 filer are identical for financial reporting purposes and have identical receipts, disbursements, assets, liabilities, and equity accounts;

Page 3

(c) The employee benefit plan does not include more than one section 501(c) organization, and the section 501(c) organization is not a part of more than one employee benefit plan; and

(d) The organization's accounting year and the employee plan year are the same. If they are not, you may want to change the organization's accounting year, as explained in General Instruction G, so it will coincide with the plan year.

Allowable substitution areas.—Whether you file Form 990EZ for a labor organization or for an employee plan, the areas of Form 990EZ for which other forms can be substituted are the same. These areas are:

Part I, lines 10 through 16 (but complete lines 17 through 21).

Part II (but complete lines 25 through 27, columns (A) and (B)).

If you substitute Form LM-2 or LM-3 for any of the Form 990EZ Parts or line items mentioned above, you must attach a reconciliation sheet to show the relationship between the amounts on the DOL forms and the amounts on Form 990EZ. This is particularly true of the relationship of disbursements shown on the DOL forms and the total expenses on line 17, Part I, of Form 990EZ. You must make this reconciliation because the cash disbursements section of the DOL forms includes nonexpense items. If you substitute Form LM-2, be sure to complete its separate schedule of expenses.

G. Accounting Period Covered.—Base your return on your annual accounting period (fiscal year) if one is established. If not, base the return on the calendar year.

Your fiscal year should normally coincide with the natural operating cycle of your organization. Your fiscal year need not end on December 31 or June 30.

Use the 1991 Form 990EZ to report on a calendar-year 1991 accounting period or a fiscal year that began in 1991.

If you change your accounting period, you may also use the 1991 form as the return for a short period (less than 12 months) ending November 30, 1992, or earlier.

In general, to change your accounting period, you must file timely a return on Form 990EZ for the short period resulting from the change. At the top of the short period return, write *Change of Accounting Period.* If you changed your accounting period within the 10-calendar-year period that includes the beginning of the short period, and you had a Form 990EZ (or Form 990) filing requirement at any time during that 10-year period, you must also attach a Form 1128 to the short period return. See Rev. Proc. 85-58, 1985-2 C.B. 740.

H. When and Where To File.—File Form 990EZ by the 15th day of the 5th month after your accounting period ends.

If the organization is liquidated, dissolved, or terminated, file the return by the 15th day of the 5th month after the change.

If the return is not filed by the due date (including any extension granted), attach a statement giving your reasons for not filing timely.

If the principal office is located in— ▼	Send your return to the Internal Revenue Service Center below ▼
Alabama, Arkansas, Florida, Georgia, Louisiana, Mississippi, North Carolina, South Carolina, Tennessee	Atlanta, GA 39901
Arizona, Colorado, Kansas, New Mexico, Oklahoma, Texas, Utah, Wyoming	Austin, TX 73301
Indiana, Kentucky, Michigan, Ohio, West Virginia	Cincinnati, OH 45999
Alaska, California, Hawaii, Idaho, Nevada, Oregon, Washington	Fresno, CA 93888
Connecticut, Maine, Massachusetts, New Hampshire, New York, Rhode Island, Vermont	Holtsville, NY 00501
Illinios, Iowa, Minnesota, Missouri, Montana, Nebraska, North Dakota, South Dakota, Wisconsin	Kansas City, MO 64999
Delaware, District of Columbia, Maryland, New Jersey, Pennsylvania, Virginia, any U.S. possession, or foreign country	Philadelphia, PA 19255

I. Extension of Time To File.—Use Form 2758 to request an extension of time to file.

J. Amended Return.—To change your return for any year, file a new return with the correct information that is complete in all respects, including required attachments. Thus, the amended return must provide all the information called for by the form and instructions, not just the new or corrected information. Write *Amended Return* at the top of the return.

You may file an amended return at any time to change or add to the information reported on a previously filed return for the same period. You must make the amended return available for public inspection for 3 years from the date of filing or 3 years from the date the original return was due, whichever is later. Use Form 4506-A to obtain a copy of a previously filed return. You can obtain blank forms for prior years by calling the toll-free number given in General Instruction D.

K. Penalties.—

Against the organization.—Under section 6652(c), a penalty of $10 a day, not to exceed the lesser of $5,000 or 5% of the gross receipts of the organization for the year, may be charged when a return is filed late, unless you can show that the late filing was due to reasonable cause. The penalty begins on the due date for filing the Form 990EZ. The penalty may also be charged if you file an incomplete return or furnish incorrect information. To avoid having to supply missing information later, be sure to complete all applicable line items; answer "Yes," "No," or "N/A" (not applicable) to each question on the return; make an entry (including a "-0-" when appropriate) on all *total* lines; and

enter "None" or "N/A" if an entire part does not apply.

Against responsible person(s).—If you do not file a complete return or do not furnish correct information, IRS will write to give you a fixed time to fulfill these requirements. After that period expires, the person failing to comply will be charged a penalty of $10 a day, not to exceed $5,000, unless he or she shows that not complying was due to reasonable cause. If more than one person is responsible, they are jointly and individually liable for the penalty.

There are also penalties—fines and imprisonment—for willfully not filing returns and for filing fraudulent returns and statements with IRS (sections 7203, 7206, and 7207). There are also penalties for failure to comply with public disclosure requirements as discussed in General Instruction L. States may impose additional penalties for failure to meet their separate filing requirements.

L. Public Inspection of Completed Exempt Organization Returns and Approved Exemption Applications.—

Through the IRS.—

Forms 990, 990EZ, 990-PF, and certain other completed exempt organization returns are available for public inspection and copying upon request. Approved applications for exemption from Federal income tax are also available. The IRS, however, may not disclose portions of an application relating to any trade secrets, etc., nor can the IRS disclose the schedule of contributors required by Forms 990 and 990EZ (section 6104).

A request for inspection must be in writing and must include the name and address (city and state) of the organization that filed the return or application. A request to inspect a return should indicate the type (number) of the return and the year(s) involved. The request should be sent to the District Director (Attention: Disclosure Officer) of the district in which the requester desires to inspect the return or application. If inspection at the IRS National Office is desired, the request should be sent to the Commissioner of Internal Revenue, Attention: Freedom of Information Reading Room, 1111 Constitution Avenue, N.W., Washington, DC 20224.

You can use Form 4506-A to request a copy or to inspect an exempt organization return. There is a fee for photocopying.

Through the Organization.—

(1) *Annual return.*—An organization must, during the three-year period beginning with the due date (including extensions, if any), of the Form 990 (or 990EZ), make its return available for public inspection upon request. All parts of the return and all required schedules and attachments, other than the schedule of contributors to the organization, must be made available. Inspection must be permitted during regular business hours at the organization's principal office and at each of its regional or district offices having

Page 4

three or more employees. This provision applies to any organization that files Form 990 (or 990EZ), regardless of the size of the organization and whether or not it has any paid employees.

If an organization furnishes additional information to IRS to be made part of its return, as a result of an examination or correspondence from the Service Center processing the return, it must also make that information part of the return it provides for public inspection.

If the organization does not maintain a permanent office, it must provide a reasonable location for a requester to inspect the organization's annual returns. The organization may mail the information to a requester. However, the organization can charge for copying and postage only if the requester gives up the right to a free inspection (Notice 88-120, 1988-2 C.B. 454).

Any person who does not comply with the public inspection requirement shall be assessed a penalty of $10 for each day that inspection was not permitted, up to a maximum of $5,000 with respect to any one return. No penalty will be imposed if the failure is due to reasonable cause. Any person who willfully fails to comply shall be subject to an additional penalty of $1,000 (sections 6652(c) and 6685).

(2) *Exemption application.*—Any section 501(c) organization that submitted an application for recognition of exemption to the Internal Revenue Service after July 15, 1987, must make available for public inspection a copy of its application (together with a copy of any papers submitted in support of its application) and any letter or other document issued by the Internal Revenue Service in response to the application. An organization that submitted its exemption application on or before July 15, 1987, must also comply with this requirement if it had a copy of its application on July 15, 1987. As in the case of annual returns, the copy of the application and related documents must be made available for inspection during regular business hours at the organization's principal office and at each of its regional or district offices having at least three employees.

If the organization does not maintain a permanent office, it must provide a reasonable location for the inspection of both its annual returns and exemption application. The information may be mailed. (See reference to Notice 88-120 in the discussion above for *Annual return.*) The organization need not disclose any portion of an application relating to trade secrets, etc., that would not also be disclosable by the IRS.

The penalties for failure to comply with this provision are the same as those discussed in *Annual return* above, except that the $5,000 limitation does not apply.

M. Disclosures Regarding Certain Information and Services Furnished.—A section 501(c) organization that offers to sell or solicits money for specific information or a routine service for any individual that could be obtained by such individual from a Federal government agency free or for a nominal charge must disclose that fact conspicuously when making such offer or solicitation. Any organization that intentionally disregards this requirement will be subject to a penalty *for each day* on which the offers or solicitations are made. The penalty imposed for a particular day is the greater of $1,000 or 50% of the total cost of the offers and solicitations made on that day which lacked the required disclosure.

N. Disclosures Regarding Certain Transactions and Relationships.—In their annual returns on Schedule A (Form 990), section 501(c)(3) organizations must disclose information regarding their direct or indirect transfers to, and other direct or indirect relationships with, other section 501(c) organizations (except other section 501(c)(3) organizations) or section 527 political organizations. This provision helps to prevent the diversion or expenditure of a section 501(c)(3) organization's funds for purposes not intended by section 501(c)(3). All section 501(c)(3) organizations must maintain records regarding all such transfers, transactions, and relationships. (See General Instruction K, Penalties.)

O. Erroneous Backup Withholding.—Recipients of dividend or interest payments generally must certify their correct tax identification number to the bank or other payer on **Form W-9,** Request for Taxpayer Identification Number and Certification. If the payer does not get this information, it must withhold part of the payments as "backup withholding." If your organization was subject to erroneous backup withholding because the payer did not realize you were an exempt organization and not subject to this withholding, you can claim credit for the amount withheld. See the Instructions for Form 990-T if you had backup withholding erroneously withheld. Claims for refund must be filed within three years after the date the original return was due; three years after the date the organization filed it; or two years after the date the tax was paid, whichever is later.

P. Group Return.—If a parent organization wants to file a group return for two or more of its subsidiaries, it must use Form 990. The parent organization cannot use Form 990EZ. See the Instructions for Form 990 for filing a group return.

Q. Organizations in Foreign Countries and U.S. Possessions.—Report amounts in U.S. dollars and state what conversion rate you use. Combine amounts from within and outside the United States and report the total for each item. All information must be given in the English language.

Specific Instructions

Completing the Heading of Form 990EZ.—

The instructions that follow are keyed to items in the heading for Form 990-EZ.

Item A. *Accounting Period.*—Use the 1991 Form 990EZ to report on a calendar year or a fiscal year accounting period that began in 1991. Show the month and day your fiscal year began in 1991 and the date the fiscal year ended. (Refer to General Instruction G.)

Item B. *Name and Address.*—If we mailed you a Form 990 Package with a preaddressed mailing label, please attach the label in the name and address space on your return. Using the label helps us avoid errors in processing your return. If any information on the label is wrong, draw a line through that part and correct it.

Include the suite, room, or other unit number after the street address. If the Post Office does not deliver mail to the street address and the organization has a P.O. box, show the P.O. box number instead of the street address.

Item C. *Employer Identification Number.*—You should have only one Federal employer identification number. If you have more than one and have not been advised which to use, notify the Service Center for your area (from the Where to File list in General Instruction H). State what numbers you have, the name and address to which each number was assigned, and the address of your principal office. The IRS will advise you which number to use. Section 501(c)(9) organizations must use their own employer identification number and not the number of their sponsor.

Item D. *State Registration Number.*—(See General Instruction E.)

Item E. *Group Exemption Number.*—If you are covered by a group exemption letter, enter the four-digit group exemption number (GEN).

Item F. *Type of Organization.*—If your organization is exempt under section 501(c), check the applicable box and insert within the parentheses a number that identifies your type of section 501(c) organization. If you are a section 4947(a)(1) trust, check the applicable box and see General Instruction C7 and question 42 of Form 990EZ.

Item G. *Application Pending.*—If your application for exemption is pending, check this box and complete the return.

Item H. *Accounting Method.*—Indicate the method of accounting used in preparing this return. Unless the specific instructions say otherwise, you should generally use the same accounting method on the return to figure revenue and expenses that you regularly use to keep the organization's books and records. To be acceptable for Form 990EZ reporting purposes, however, the method of accounting used must clearly reflect income.

If you prepare a Form 990EZ for state reporting purposes, you may file an identical return with IRS even though it does not agree with your books of account, unless how you report one or more items on the state return conflicts with the instructions for preparing Form 990EZ for filing with IRS. For example, if you maintain your books on the cash receipts and disbursements method of accounting but prepare a state return

Page 5

based on the accrual method, you could use that return for reporting to IRS. As another example, if a state reporting requirement requires you to report certain revenue, expense, or balance sheet items differently from how you normally account for them on your books, a Form 990EZ prepared for that state is acceptable for IRS reporting purposes if the state reporting requirement does not conflict with the Form 990EZ instructions. You should keep with your records a reconciliation of any differences between your books of account and the Form 990EZ you file.

Most states that accept Form 990EZ in place of their own forms require that all amounts be reported based on the accrual method of accounting. See General Instruction E.

Item I. *Change of Address.*—If you changed your address since you filed your previous return, check this box.

Item J. *Gross Receipts of $25,000 or Less.*—Check this box if your gross receipts are normally not more than $25,000. However, see General Instructions A4 and B11.

Item K. *Calculating your Gross Receipts.*—Only those organizations with gross receipts less than $100,000 and total assets less than $250,000 at the end of the year can use the Form 990EZ. If you do not meet these requirements, you must file Form 990. (See General Instruction B11.)

Public Inspection.—All information you report on or with your Form 990EZ, including attachments, will be available for public inspection, except the schedule of contributors required for line 1, Part I. Please make sure your forms and attachments are clear enough to photocopy legibly.

Signature.—To make the return complete, an officer authorized to sign it must sign in the space provided. For a corporation, this officer may be the president, vice president, treasurer, assistant treasurer, chief accounting officer, or other corporate officer, such as a tax officer. A receiver, trustee, or assignee must sign any return he or she files for a corporation. For a trust, the authorized trustee(s) must sign.

If the return was prepared by an individual, firm, or corporation paid for preparing it, the paid preparer's space must also be signed. For a firm or corporation that was a paid preparer, sign in the firm's or corporation's name. If you checked the box for question 42 on page 2 (section 4947(a)(1) charitable trust filing Form 990EZ instead of Form 1041), you must also enter the paid preparer's social security number or employer identification number in the margin next to the paid preparer's space. Leave the paid preparer's space blank if the return was prepared by a regular employee of the filing organization.

Rounding Off to Whole-Dollar Amounts.—You may show money items as whole-dollar amounts. Drop any amount less than 50 cents and increase any

amount from 50 through 99 cents to the next higher dollar.

Completing All Lines.—Unless you are permitted to use certain DOL forms or Form 5500 series returns as partial substitutes for Form 990EZ (see General Instruction F), do not leave any applicable lines blank or attach any other forms or schedules instead of entering the required information on the appropriate line on Form 990EZ.

Assembling Form 990EZ.—Before filing the Form 990EZ, assemble your package of forms and attachments in the following manner:

- Form 990EZ
- Schedule A (Form 990)
- Attachments to Form 990EZ
- Attachments to Schedule A (Form 990)

Attachments.—Use the schedules on the official form unless you need more space. If you use attachments, they must:

(1) Show the form number and tax year;

(2) Show the organization's name and employer identification number;

(3) Include the information required by the form;

(4) Follow the format and line sequence of the form; and

(5) Be on the same size paper as the form.

Part I—Statement of Revenue, Expenses, and Changes in Net Assets or Fund Balances.—

All organizations filing Form 990EZ with the IRS or any state must complete Part I. Some states that accept Form 990EZ in place of their own forms may require additional information (see General Instruction E).

Line 1.—Contributions, gifts, grants, and similar amounts received.—

A. What is included on line 1.—

Report amounts received as voluntary contributions; that is, payments, or the part of any payment, for which the payer (donor) does not receive full value (fair market value) from the recipient (donee) organization.

Enter the gross amounts of contributions, gifts, grants and bequests that the organization received from individuals, trusts, corporations, estates, affiliates, foundations, public charities, and other exempt organizations.

(a) Contributions can arise from special events when excess payment received for items offered.—Special fundraising activities such as dinners, door-to-door sales of merchandise, carnivals, and bingo games can produce both contributions and revenue. Report as a contribution on line 1 and on line 6a (within parentheses) any amount received through a special event that is greater than the value of the merchandise or services furnished by the organization to the contributor.

This situation usually occurs when organizations seek support from the public

through solicitation programs that are in part special fundraising events or activities and are in part solicitations for contributions. The primary purpose of such solicitations is to receive contributions and not to sell the merchandise at its fair market value (even though this might produce a profit).

For example, an organization announces that anyone who contributes at least $40 to the organization can choose to receive a book worth $16 retail value. A person who gives $40, and who chooses the book, is really purchasing the book for $16 and also making a contribution of $24. The contribution of $24, which is the difference between the buyer's payment and the $16 retail value of the book, would be reported on line 1 and again on the description line of 6a (within the parentheses). The revenue received ($16 retail value of the book) would be reported in the amount column on line 6a. Any expenses directly relating to the sale of the book would be reported on line 6b.

If a contributor gives more than $40, that person would be making a larger contribution, the difference between the book's retail value of $16 and the amount actually given. (See also line 6 instructions and Publication 1391.)

At the time of any solicitation or payment, organizations that are eligible to receive contributions should advise patrons of the amount deductible for Federal tax purposes.

(b) Contributions can arise from special events when items of only nominal value offered.—If an organization offers goods or services of only nominal value through a special event, report the *entire* amount received for such benefits as a contribution on line 1. Report all related expenses on lines 12 through 16.

Benefits have a nominal value when:

(1) The benefit's fair market value is not more than 2% of the payment, or $50, whichever is less; or

(2) The payment is $28.58 or more; the only benefits received are token items bearing the organization's name or symbol; and the organization's cost (as opposed to fair market value) is $5.71 or less for all benefits received by a donor during the calendar year. These amounts are adjusted annually for inflation. (See Rev. Proc. 90-12, 1990-1 C.B. 471 and Rev. Proc. 90-64, 1990-2 C.B. 674.)

(c) Section 501(c)(3) organizations.—These organizations must compute the amounts of revenue and contributions received from special events according to the above instructions when preparing their Support Schedule in Part IV of Schedule A (Form 990).

(d) Grants equivalent to contributions.—Grants made to encourage an organization receiving the grant to carry on programs or activities that further the grant recipient's exempt purposes are grants that are equivalent to contributions. Report them on line 1. The grantor may specify which of the recipient's activities the grant may be

used for, such as an adoption program or a disaster relief project.

A grant is still equivalent to a contribution if the grant recipient performs a service, or produces a work product, that benefits the grantor incidentally (but see line 1 instruction B(a) below).

(e) Contributions received through other fundraising organizations.—Contributions received indirectly from the public through solicitation campaigns conducted by federated fundraising agencies (such as United Way) are included on line 1.

(f) Contributions received from associated organizations.—Include on line 1 amounts contributed by other organizations closely associated with the reporting organization. This would include contributions received from a parent organization, subordinate, or another organization having the same parent.

(g) Contributions from a commercial co-venture.—Amounts contributed by a commercial co-venture should be included on line 1. These contributions are amounts received by the organization for allowing an outside organization or individual to use the organization's name in a sales promotion campaign.

(h) Contributions from governmental units.—A grant, or other payment from a governmental unit, represents a contribution if its primary purpose is to enable the recipient to provide a service to, or maintain a facility for, the direct benefit of the public rather than to serve the direct and immediate needs of the grantor (even if the public pays part of the expense of providing the service or facility).

(i) Contributions in the form of membership dues.—Include on line 1 membership dues and assessments to the extent they are contributions and not payments for benefits received (see line 3, instruction C(a)).

B. What is not included on line 1.—

(a) Grants that are payments for services are not contributions.—A grant is a payment for service, and not a contribution, when the terms of the grant provide the grantor with a specific service, facility, or product, rather than providing a benefit to the general public or that part of the public served by the grant recipient. The recipient organization would report such a grant as income on line 2 (program service revenue).

(b) Donations of services.—Do not include the value of services donated to the organization, or items such as the free use of materials, equipment, or facilities, as contributions on line 1. However, for the optional reporting of such amounts, see instruction (a) for Part III.

(c) Section 501(c)(9), (17), (18), and (20) organizations.—These organizations provide participants with life, sick, accident, welfare, unemployment, pension, group legal services, or similar benefits, or a combination of these benefits. When such an organization receives payments from participants, or their employers, to provide these benefits, report the payments on line 2 as program service

revenue, rather than on line 1 as contributions.

C. How to value noncash contributions.—

To report contributions received in a form other than cash, use the market value as of the date of the contribution. For marketable securities registered and listed on a recognized securities exchange, measure market value by the average of the highest and lowest quoted selling prices (or the average between the bona fide bid and asked prices) on the contribution date. When market value cannot be readily determined, use an appraised or estimated value.

To determine the amount of any noncash contribution that is subject to an outstanding debt, subtract the debt from the property's fair market value. Record the asset at its full value and record the debt as a liability in the books of account. See also line 1 instruction D, Note (1) below.

D. Schedule of contributors.—*(Not open to public inspection)* **Caution:** *See Note (2) below.*

Attached schedule.—Attach a schedule listing contributors who, during the year, gave the organization, directly or indirectly, money, securities, or other property worth $5,000 or more. If no one contributed the reportable minimum, you do not need to attach a schedule.

In the schedule, show each contributor's name and address, the total amount received, and the date received. Contributors include individuals, fiduciaries, partnerships, corporations, associations, trusts, or exempt organizations.

If an employer withholds contributions from employees' pay and periodically gives them to the organization, report only the employer's name and address and the total amount given unless you know that a particular employee gave enough to be listed separately.

In determining whether a contributor gave $5,000 or more, total that person's gifts of $1,000 or more. Do not include smaller gifts. If the contribution consists of property whose fair market value can be determined readily (such as market quotations for securities), describe the property and list its fair market value. Otherwise, estimate the property's value.

Exception: *Organization described in section 501(c)(7), (8), (10), or (19) that received contributions or bequests to be used only as described in section 170(c)(4), 2055(a)(3), or 2522(a)(3).*

If an organization meets the terms of this exception, some information in its schedule will vary from that described above.

The schedule should list each person whose gifts total $1,000 or more during the year. Give the donor's name, the amount given, the gift's specific purpose, and the specific use to which it was put. If an amount is set aside for a purpose described in section 170(c)(4), 2055(a)(3), or 2522(a)(3), explain how the amount is held (for instance, whether it is mingled with amounts held for other purposes). If

the organization transferred the gift to another organization, name and describe the recipient and explain the relationship between the two organizations. Also show the total of the gifts that were $1,000 or less and were for a purpose described in section 170(c)(4), 2055(a)(3), or 2522(a)(3).

Note (1): *If you qualify to receive tax-deductible charitable contributions and you receive contributions of property (other than publicly traded securities) whose fair market value is more than $5,000, you should usually receive a partially completed* **Form 8283,** Noncash Charitable Contributions, *from the contributor. You should complete the appropriate information on Form 8283, sign it, and return it to the donor. Retain a copy for your records. See also General Instruction C17.*

Note (2): *If you file a copy of Form 990EZ and attachments with any state, do not include, in the attachments for the state, the schedule of contributors discussed above unless the schedule is specifically required by the state with which you are filing the return. States that do not require the information might nevertheless make it available for public inspection along with the rest of the return.*

Line 2—Program service revenue.—Enter the total program service revenue (exempt function income). Program services are primarily those that form the basis of an organization's exemption from tax.

(a) Examples.—A clinic would include on line 2 all of its charges for medical services (whether to be paid directly by the patients or through Medicare, Medicaid, or other third-party reimbursement), laboratory fees, and related charges for services.

Other examples of program service revenue are tuition received by a school; revenue from admissions to a concert or other performing arts event or to a museum; royalties received as author of an educational publication distributed by a commercial publisher; payments received by a section 501(c)(9) organization from participants or employers of participants for health and welfare benefits coverage; and registration fees received in connection with a meeting or convention.

(b) Program-related investment income.—Program service revenue also includes income from program-related investments. These investments are made primarily for accomplishing an exempt purpose of the investing organization rather than to produce income. Examples are scholarship loans and low-interest loans to charitable organizations, indigents, or victims of a disaster. Rental income from an exempt function is another example. See line 4 instructions.

(c) Unrelated trade or business activities.—Unrelated trade or business activities (not including any special fundraising events or activities) that generate fees for services may also be program service activities. A social club, for example, should report as program service revenue the fees it charges both members and nonmembers for the use of its tennis courts and golf course.

Page 7

Line 3—Membership dues and assessments.—Enter members' and affiliates' dues and assessments that are not contributions.

A. What is included on line 3.—

(a) Dues and assessments received that compare reasonably with available benefits.—When dues and assessments are received that compare reasonably with available membership benefits, report such dues and assessments on line 3.

(b) Organizations that usually match dues and benefits.—Organizations, other than those described in section 501(c)(3), generally provide benefits that have a reasonable relationship to dues. This occurs usually in organizations described in sections 501(c)(5), (6), or (7), although benefits to members may be indirect. Report such dues and assessments on line 3.

B. Examples of membership benefits.—

Examples of membership benefits include subscriptions to publications; newsletters (other than one about the organization's activities only); free or reduced-rate admissions to events the organization sponsors; use of its facilities; and discounts on articles or services that both members and nonmembers can buy. In figuring the value of membership benefits, disregard such intangible benefits as the right to attend meetings, vote or hold office in the organization, and the distinction of being a member of the organization.

C. What is not included on line 3.—

(a) Dues or assessments received that exceed the value of available membership benefits.—Whether or not membership benefits are used, dues received by an organization, to the extent they exceed the monetary value of the membership benefits available to the dues payer, are a contribution includable on line 1.

(b) Dues received primarily for the organization's support.—If a member pays dues primarily to support the organization's activities, and not to obtain benefits of more than nominal monetary value, those dues are a contribution to the organization includable on line 1.

Line 4—Investment income.—

A. What is included on line 4.—

(a) Interest on savings and temporary cash investments.—Enter the amount of interest received from interest-bearing checking accounts, savings, and temporary cash investments, such as money market funds, commercial paper, certificates of deposit, and U.S. Treasury bills or other governmental obligations that mature in less than one year. So-called dividends or earnings received from mutual savings banks, etc., are actually interest and should be included on this line.

(b) Dividends and interest from securities.—Enter the amount of dividend and interest income from debt and equity securities (stocks and bonds) on this line. Include amounts received from payments

on securities loans, as defined in section 512(a)(5).

(c) Gross rents.—Include gross rental income received during the year from investment property.

Income received from renting office space, or other facilities or equipment, to unaffiliated exempt organizations should be reported on line 4 unless the rental income is exempt function income (program service) (see line 4, instruction B(b) below).

(d) Other investment income.—Include, for example, royalty income from mineral interests owned by the organization.

B. What is not included on line 4.—

(a) Capital gains dividends and unrealized gains and losses.—Do not include on this line any capital gains dividends. They are reported on line 5. Also exclude unrealized gains and losses on investments carried at market value (see instructions for line 20).

(b) Exempt function revenue (program service).—Do not include on line 4 amounts that represent income from an exempt function (program service). These amounts should be reported on line 2 as program service revenue. Expenses related to this income should be reported on lines 12 through 16.

An organization whose exempt purpose is to provide low-rental housing to persons with low income receives exempt function income from such rentals. Exempt function income also arises when an organization charges an *unaffiliated* exempt organization below-market rent for the purpose of helping that unaffiliated organization carry out its exempt purpose. The rental income received in these two instances should be reported on line 2 and not on line 4.

Only for purposes of completing Form 990EZ, treat income from renting property to *affiliated* exempt organizations as exempt function income and include such income on line 2 as program service revenue.

Lines 5a–c—Capital gains.—

A. What is included on line 5.—

Report on line 5a all sales of securities and sales of all other types of investments (such as real estate, royalty interests, or partnership interests) as well as sales of all other capital assets (such as program-related investments and fixed assets used by the organization in its regular activities).

Total the cost or other basis (less depreciation) and selling expenses and enter the result on line 5b. On line 5c, enter the net gain or loss. Report capital gains dividends, the organization's share of capital gains and losses from a partnership, and capital gains distributions from trusts on lines 5a and 5c. Indicate the source on the schedule described below.

For this return, you may use the more convenient way to figure the organization's gain or loss from sales of securities by comparing the sales price with the average-cost basis of the particular security sold. However, generally, the average-cost basis is not used to figure

the gain or loss from sales of securities reportable on Form 990-T.

B. What is not included on line 5.—

Do not include on line 5 any unrealized gains or losses on securities that are carried in the books of account at market value. (See the instructions for line 20.)

C. Attached schedule.—

(a) Assets other than publicly traded securities and inventory.—Attach a schedule showing the sale or exchange of *nonpublicly* traded securities and the sale or exchange of other assets that are not inventory items. The schedule should show security transactions separately from the sale of other assets. Show for these assets:

(1) Date acquired and how acquired;

(2) Date sold and to whom sold;

(3) Gross sales price;

(4) Cost, other basis, or if donated, value at time acquired (state which);

(5) Expense of sale and cost of improvements made after acquisition; and

(6) If depreciable property, depreciation since acquisition.

(b) Publicly traded securities.—For sales of *publicly* traded securities through a broker, you may total the gross sales price, the cost or other basis, and the expenses of sale, and report lump-sum figures in place of the detailed reporting required in the above paragraph.

For preparing Form 990EZ, publicly traded securities include common and preferred stocks, bonds (including governmental obligations), and mutual fund shares that are listed and regularly traded in an over-the-counter market or on an established exchange and for which market quotations are published or otherwise readily available.

Lines 6a–c—Special events and activities.—

On the appropriate line, enter the gross revenue, expenses, and net income from all special fundraising events and activities, such as dinners, dances, carnivals, raffles, bingo games, other gambling activities, and door-to-door sales of merchandise. In themselves, these activities only incidentally accomplish an exempt purpose. Their sole or primary purpose is to raise funds (other than contributions) to finance the organization's exempt activities.

This is done by offering goods or services that have more than a nominal value (compared to the price charged) for a payment that is more than the direct cost of those goods or services. See also line 1 instructions A(a) and (b) for further guidance in distinguishing between contributions and revenue.

Calling any required payment a "donation" or "contribution" on tickets, advertising, or solicitation materials does not change how these payments should be reported on Form 990EZ.

A. What is included on line 6.—

(a) Gross revenue/contributions.—When an organization receives payments for goods or services offered through a special event, enter—

(1) as gross revenue, on line 6a (in the amount column) the value of the goods or services.

(2) as a contribution, on both line 1 and line 6a (within the parentheses) any amount received that exceeds the value of the goods or services given.

For example, at a special event, an organization received $100 in gross receipts for goods valued at $40. The organization entered gross revenue of $40 on line 6a and entered a contribution of $60 on both line 1 and within the parentheses on line 6a. The contribution was the difference between the gross revenue of $40 and the gross receipts of $100.

(b) Raffles or lotteries.—Report as revenue, on line 6a, any amount received from raffles or lotteries that require payment of a specified minimum amount for each entry, unless the prizes awarded have only nominal value (see line 6 instruction B(a) and (b) below).

(c) Direct expenses.—Report on line 6b only the direct expenses attributable to the goods or services the buyer receives from a special event. If you include an expense on line 6b, do not report it again on line 7b.

B. What is not included on line 6.—

(a) Sales of goods or services of only nominal value.—If the goods or services offered at the special event have only nominal value, include all of the receipts as contributions on line 1 and all of the related expenses on lines 12 through 16. See line 1, instruction A(b) for a description of benefits of nominal value. These are adjusted annually for inflation.

(b) Sweepstakes, raffles, and lotteries.—Report as a contribution, on line 1, the proceeds of solicitation campaigns in which the names of contributors and other respondents are entered in a drawing for prizes.

When a minimum payment is required for each raffle or lottery entry and prizes of only nominal value are awarded, report any amount received as a contribution. Report the related expenses on lines 12 through 16.

(c) Activities that generate only contributions are not special fundraising events.—An activity that generates only contributions, such as a solicitation campaign by mail, is not a special fundraising event. Any amount received should be included on line 1 as a contribution.

C. Attached schedule.—Attach a schedule listing the three largest special events conducted, as measured by gross receipts. Describe each of these events and indicate for each event: the gross receipts; the amount of contributions included in gross receipts (see line 6, instruction A(a) above); the gross revenue

(gross receipts less contributions); the direct expenses; and the net income (gross revenue less direct expenses).

Furnish the same information, in total figures, for all other special events held that are not among the largest three. Indicate the type and number of the events not listed individually (for example, three dances and two raffles).

An example of this schedule might appear in columnar form as follows:

Special Event:	(A)	(B)	(C)	Total
Gross Receipts	$XXX	$XXX	$XXX	$XXX
Less: Contributions	XXX	XXX	XXX	XXX
Gross Revenue	XXX	XXX	XXX	XXX
Less: Direct Expenses	XXX	XXX	XXX	XXX
Net Income or (loss)	$XXX	$XXX	$XXX	$XXX

If you use this format, report the total for contributions on line 1 of Form 990EZ and on line 6a (within the parentheses of the description line). Report the totals for gross revenue, in the amount column, on line 6a; direct expenses on line 6b; and net income or (loss) on line 6c.

D. Fundraising record retention.—Section 501(c) organizations that are eligible to receive tax-deductible contributions under section 170(c) of the Code must keep sample copies of their fundraising materials, such as dues statements or other fundraising solicitations, tickets, receipts, or other evidence of payments received in connection with fundraising activities. If organizations advertise their fundraising events, they must keep samples of the advertising copy. If they use radio or television to make their solicitations, they must keep samples of scripts, transcripts, or other evidence of on-air solicitations. If organizations retain outside fundraisers, they must keep samples of the fundraising materials used by the outside fundraisers. For each fundraising event, organizations must keep records to show that portion of any payment received from patrons which is not deductible; that is, the fair market value of the goods or services received by the patrons.

Lines 7a–c—Gross sales.—

A. What is included on lines 7a–c.—

Sales of inventory.—Include on these lines the gross sales (less returns and allowances), the cost of goods sold, and the gross profit or (loss) from the sale of all inventory items, regardless of whether the sale is an exempt function or an unrelated trade or business. These inventory items are those the organization either makes to sell or buys for resale.

B. What is not included on lines 7a–c.—

(a) Sales from special events.—Do not include the sales of inventory items from special fundraising events and activities on line 7. Enter those sales on line 6.

(b) Investments.—Do not include on line 7 sales of investments on which the

organization expected to profit by appreciation and sale. Report sales of these investments on line 5.

Line 8—Other revenue.—Include on this line the total income from all sources not covered by lines 1 through 7. Examples of types of income includable on line 8 are interest on notes receivable not held as investments; interest on loans to officers, directors, trustees, key employees, and other employees; and royalties that are not investment income or program service revenue.

Line 10—Grants and similar amounts paid.—

A. What is included on line 10.—

Enter on line 10 the amount of actual grants and similar amounts paid to individuals and organizations selected by the filing organization. Include scholarship, fellowship, and research grants to individuals.

(a) Specific assistance to individuals.—Include on this line the amount of payments to, or for the benefit of, particular clients or patients, including assistance rendered by others at the expense of the filing organization.

(b) Payments, voluntary awards, or grants to affiliates.—Include on line 10 certain types of payments to organizations "affiliated with" (closely related to) a reporting agency. These include predetermined quota support and dues payments by local agencies to their state or national organizations.

Note: *If you use Form 990EZ for state reporting purposes, it is especially important to properly distinguish between payments to affiliates and awards and grants (see General Instruction E).*

B. What is not included on line 10.—

(a) Administrative expenses.—Do not include on this line expenses made in selecting recipients or monitoring compliance with the terms of a grant or award. Enter those expenses on lines 12 through 16.

(b) Purchases of goods or services from affiliates.—The cost of goods or services purchased from affiliates are not reported on line 10 but are reported as expenses on lines 12 through 16.

(c) Membership dues paid to another organization.—Membership dues that the organization pays to another organization to obtain general membership benefits, such as regular services, publications, and materials, should be reported as "Other expenses" on line 16.

C. Attached schedule.—Attach a schedule to explain the amounts reported on line 10. Show on this schedule:

(a) Each class of activity;

(b) The donee's name and address;

(c) The amount given; and

(d) The relationship of the donee (in the case of grants to individuals) if the relationship is by blood, marriage, adoption, or employment (including employees' children) to any person or

Page 9

101

corporation with an interest in the organization, such as a creator, donor, director, trustee, officer, etc.

List the name and address of each affiliate that received any payment reported on line 10. Specify both the amount and purpose of these payments.

Classify activities on this schedule in more detail than by using such broad terms as charitable, educational, religious, or scientific. For example, identify payments to affiliates; payments as nursing services; fellowships; or payments for food, shelter, or medical services for indigents or disaster victims. For payments to indigent families, do not identify the individuals.

If an organization gives property and measures an award or grant by the property's fair market value, also show on this schedule:

(a) A description of the property;

(b) The book value of the property;

(c) How you determined the book value;

(d) How you determined the fair market value; and

(e) The date of the gift.

Any difference between a property's fair market value and book value should be recorded in the organization's books of account.

Line 11—Benefits paid to or for members.—For an organization that gives benefits to members or dependents (such as organizations exempt under section 501(c)(8), (9), or (17)), enter the amounts paid for: (a) death, sickness, hospitalization, or disability benefits; (b) unemployment compensation benefits; and (c) other benefits. Do not include, on this line, the cost of employment-related benefits the organization gives its officers and employees. Report those employment-related benefits on line 12.

Line 12—Salaries, other compensation, and employee benefits.—Enter the total salaries and wages paid to all employees and the fees paid to directors and trustees. Include the total of the employer's share of the contributions the organization paid to qualified and nonqualified pension plans and the employer's share of contributions to employee benefit programs (such as insurance, health, and welfare programs) that are not an incidental part of a pension plan. Complete the Form 5500 series return/report that is appropriate for your plan.

Also include in the total the amount of Federal, state, and local payroll taxes for the year that are imposed on the organization as an employer. This includes the employer's share of Social Security and Medicare taxes, FUTA tax, state unemployment compensation tax, and other state and local payroll taxes. Taxes withheld from employees' salaries and paid over to the various governmental units (such as Federal and state income taxes and the employees' share of Social Security and Medicare taxes) are part of the employees' salaries included on line 12.

Line 13—Professional fees and other payments to independent contractors.—Enter the total amount of legal, accounting, auditing, other professional fees (such as fees for fundraising or investment services) and related expenses charged by outside firms and individuals who are not employees of the organization. Do not include any penalties, fines, or judgments imposed against the organization as a result of legal proceedings. Report and identify those expenses on line 16. Report fees paid to directors and trustees on line 12.

Line 14—Occupancy, rent, utilities, and maintenance.—Enter the total amount paid or incurred for the use of office space or other facilities, heat, light, power, and other utilities, outside janitorial services, mortgage interest, real estate taxes, and similar expenses. If your organization records depreciation on property it occupies, enter the total for the year.

Line 15—Printing, publications, postage, and shipping.—Enter the printing and related costs of producing the reporting organization's own newsletters, leaflets, films, and other informational materials. (However, do not include any expenses, such as salaries, for which a separate line is provided.) Also include the cost of any purchased publications as well as postage and shipping costs not reportable on lines 5b, 6b, or 7b.

Line 16—Other expenses.—Expenses that might be reported here include penalties, fines, and judgments; unrelated business income taxes; real estate taxes not attributable to rental property or reported as occupancy expenses; depreciation on investment property; travel and transportation costs; interest expense; and expenses for conferences, conventions and meetings.

Some states that accept Form 990EZ in satisfaction of their filing requirements may require that certain types of miscellaneous expenses be itemized. See General instruction E.

Line 18—Excess or (deficit) for the year.—Enter the difference between lines 9 and 17. If line 17 is more than line 9, enter the difference in parentheses.

Line 19—Net assets or fund balances at beginning of year.—Enter the amount from the prior year's balance sheet (or from Form 5500, 5500-C/R, or an approved DOL form if General Instruction F applies).

Line 20—Other changes in net assets or fund balances.—Attach a schedule explaining any changes in net assets or fund balances between the beginning and end of the year that are not accounted for by the amount on line 18. Amounts to report here include adjustments of earlier years' activity and unrealized gains and losses on investments carried at market value.

Part II—Balance Sheets.—

All organizations, except those that meet one of the exceptions in General Instruction F, must complete columns (A) and (B) of Part II of the return and may not submit a substitute balance sheet. Failure to complete Part II may result in penalties for filing an incomplete return. See General Instruction K.

Some states require more information. See General Instruction E for more information about completing a Form 990EZ to be filed with any state or local government agency.

Line 22—Cash, savings, and investments.—Include the total of noninterest-bearing checking accounts, deposits in transit, change funds, petty cash funds, or any other noninterest-bearing account.

Include the total of interest-bearing checking accounts, savings and temporary cash investments, such as money market funds, commercial paper, certificates of deposit, and U.S. Treasury bills or other governmental obligations that mature in less than 1 year. Report the income from these investments on line 4. Include the book value (which may be market value) of securities held as investments.

Include the amount of all other investment holdings including land and buildings held for investment.

Line 23—Land and buildings.—Enter the book value (cost or other basis less accumulated depreciation) of all land and buildings owned by the organization and not held for investment.

Line 24—Other assets.—Enter the total of other assets along with a description of those assets. Amounts to include here are (among others) receivable accounts, inventories, and prepaid expenses.

Line 25—Total assets.—Enter the amount of your total assets. If the end-of-year total assets entered in column (B) are $250,000 or more, you must file Form 990 instead of Form 990EZ.

Line 26—Total liabilities.—Enter the amount of your total liabilities along with their description.

Line 27—Net assets or fund balances.—Subtract line 26 (total liabilities) from line 25 (total assets) to determine your net assets. Enter this net asset amount on line 27.

(a) Organizations not using fund accounting.—Enter your net asset amount. The amount in column (B) should agree with the net asset amount on line 21.

(b) Organizations using fund accounting.—Under fund accounting, an organization segregates its assets, liabilities, and net assets into separate funds according to externally imposed restrictions on the use of certain assets, similar designations by the organization's governing board, and other amounts that are unrestricted as to use. Each fund is like a separate entity in that it has a self-balancing set of accounts showing assets, liabilities, equity (fund balance), revenue, and expenses. Since these funds are actually part of a single entity, they are all included in that organization's own financial statements. Similar accounts in the various funds may or may not be consolidated in those statements according to the organization's preference

Page 10

and practice. *To complete Form 990EZ, you must consolidate these funds.*

States that accept Form 990EZ as their basic report form may require a separate statement of changes in fund balances. See General Instruction E.

Part III—Statement of Program Service Accomplishments.—

Provide the information specified in the instructions above line 28 of the form for each of the organization's three largest program services (as measured by total expenses incurred) or for each program service if the organization engaged in three or fewer of such activities. The "Expenses" column must be completed by section 501(c)(3) and (4) organizations as well as section 4947(a)(1) charitable trusts. Completing the column is optional for all other filers. Report only the expenses attributable to the organization's program services described on lines 28 through 30 and in the attachment for line 31.

A program service is a major, usually ongoing objective of an organization, such as adoptions, recreation for the elderly, rehabilitation, or publication of journals or newsletters. Describe program service accomplishments through measurements such as clients served, days of care, therapy sessions, or publications issued.

If it is inappropriate to measure a quantity of output, as in a research activity, describe the objective of the activity for this time period as well as the overall longer-term goal.

You may furnish reasonable estimates for any statistical information if exact figures are not readily available from the records you normally maintain. If so, please indicate that the information provided is an estimate.

(a) Donated services.—If the organization so chooses, it may show in the narrative section of Part III the value of any donated services or use of materials, equipment, or facilities received and utilized in connection with specific program services. Do not include these amounts in the expense column in Part III.

(b) Attached schedule.—Attach a schedule that lists the organization's other program services. The detailed information required in Part III for the three largest services is not required for the services listed on this schedule.

Part IV—List of Officers, Directors, and Trustees.—

List each of the organization's officers, directors, trustees, and other persons having responsibilities or powers similar to those of officers, directors, or trustees. List all of these persons even if they did not receive any compensation from the organization. Enter "-0-" in columns (C), (D), and (E) if none was paid. (For deferred compensation, see column (D) instructions.)

Show all forms of cash and noncash compensation received by each listed officer, director, or trustee, whether paid currently or deferred. In addition to

completing Part IV, you may provide an attachment describing the entire 1991 compensation package of one or more officers, directors, and trustees.

Column (C).—Enter salary, fees, bonuses, and severance payments received by each person listed. Include current year payments of amounts reported or reportable as deferred compensation in any prior year.

Column (D).—Include all forms of deferred compensation (whether or not funded; whether or not vested; and whether or not the deferred compensation plan is a qualified plan under section 401(a)), and payments to welfare benefit plans on behalf of the officers, etc. Reasonable estimates may be used if precise cost figures are not readily available.

Unless the amounts are reported in column (C), include salary and other compensation earned during the period covered by the return but not paid by the date the return was filed.

Column (E).—Enter amounts that the recipients must report as income on their separate income tax returns. Examples include amounts for which the recipient did not account to the organization or allowances that were more than the payee spent on serving the organization. Include payments made under indemnification arrangements, the value of the personal use of housing, automobiles, or other assets owned or leased by the organization (or provided for the organization's use without charge), as well as any other taxable and nontaxable fringe benefits. Refer to Publication 525 for more information.

You must file Form 941 to report income tax withholding and social security taxes. You must also file Form 940 to report Federal unemployment tax, unless the organization's exemption letter states that it is not subject to this tax.

Part V—Other Information.—

Line 33—Change in activities.—Attach a statement explaining any significant changes in the kind of activities the organization conducts to further its exempt purpose. These new or modified activities are those not listed as current or planned in your application for recognition of exemption or those not already made known to IRS by a letter to your key district director or by an attachment to your return for any earlier year. Besides describing new activities or changes to current ones, also describe any major program activities that are being discontinued.

Line 34—Changes in organizing or governing documents.—Attach a conformed copy of any changes to the articles of incorporation, constitution, trust instrument, or other organizing document, or to the bylaws or other governing document.

A *conformed* copy is one that agrees with the original document and all amendments to it. If the copies are not signed, they must be accompanied by a written declaration signed by an officer

authorized to sign for the organization, certifying that they are complete and accurate copies of the original documents.

Photocopies of articles of incorporation showing the certification of an appropriate state official need not be accompanied by such a declaration. See Rev. Proc. 68-14, 1968-1 C.B. 768, for more information. When a number of changes are made, send a copy of the entire revised organizing instrument or governing document.

Line 35—Unrelated business income.—Check "Yes" on line 35a if the organization's total gross income from all of its unrelated trades and businesses is $1,000 or more for the year. Gross income is gross receipts less the cost of goods sold. See Publication 598 for a description of unrelated business income and the Form 990-T filing requirements. *Form 990-T is not a substitute for Form 990EZ.* Items of income and expense reported on Form 990-T must also be reported on Form 990EZ when the organization is required to file both forms. For purposes of line 35, the term "business activities" includes any income-generating activity involving the sale of goods or services or income from investments.

Note: *All tax-exempt organizations must pay estimated taxes with respect to their unrelated business income if they expect their tax liability to be $500 or more. You may use Form 990-W to compute this tax.*

Line 36—Liquidation, dissolution, termination, or substantial contraction.—If there was a liquidation, dissolution, termination, or substantial contraction, attach a statement explaining which took place.

For a complete liquidation of a corporation or termination of a trust, write *Final Return* at the top of the organization's Form 990EZ. On the statement you attach, show whether the assets have been distributed and the date. Also attach a certified copy of any resolution, or plan of liquidation or termination, etc., with all amendments or supplements not already filed. In addition, attach a schedule listing the names and addresses of all persons who received the assets distributed in liquidation or termination; the kinds of assets distributed to each one; and each asset's fair market value.

A *substantial contraction* is a partial liquidation or other major disposition of assets except transfers for full consideration or distributions from current income.

A *major disposition of assets* means any disposition for the tax year that is:

(a) At least 25% of the fair market value of the organization's net assets at the beginning of the tax year; or

(b) One of a series of related dispositions begun in earlier years that, together, add up to at least 25% of the net assets the organization had at the beginning of the tax year when the first disposition in the series was made. Whether a major disposition of assets took

Page 11

103

place through a series of related dispositions depends on the facts in each case.

See Regulations section 1.6043-3 for special rules and exceptions.

Line 37—Expenditures for political purposes.—A political expenditure is one intended to influence the selection, nomination, election, or appointment of anyone to a Federal, state, or local public office, or office in a political organization, or the election of Presidential or Vice Presidential electors. Whether the attempt succeeds does not matter.

An expenditure includes a payment, distribution, loan, advance, deposit, or gift of money, or anything of value. It also includes a contract, promise, or agreement to make an expenditure, whether or not legally enforceable.

(a) All section 501(c) organizations.—Section 501(c) organizations must file Form 1120-POL if their political expenditures and their net investment income both exceed $100 for the year.

Section 501(c) organizations that maintained separate segregated funds described in section 527(f)(3) should refer to the instructions for Form 1120-POL for filing requirements.

(b) Section 501(c)(3) organizations.—A section 501(c)(3) organization will lose its tax-exempt status if it engages in political activity.

A section 501(c)(3) organization must pay an excise tax for any amount paid or incurred on behalf of, or in opposition to, any candidate for public office. The organization must pay an additional excise tax if it fails to correct the expenditure timely.

A manager of a section 501(c)(3) organization who knowingly agrees to a political expenditure must pay an excise tax, unless the agreement is not willful and there is reasonable cause. A manager who does not agree to a correction of the political expenditure may have to pay an additional excise tax.

When an organization promotes a candidate for public office (or is used or controlled by a candidate or prospective candidate), amounts paid or incurred for the following purposes are political expenditures:

(1) Remuneration to the individual (a candidate or prospective candidate) for speeches or other services;

(2) Travel expenses of the individual;

(3) Expenses of conducting polls, surveys, or other studies, or preparing papers or other material for use by the individual;

(4) Expenses of advertising, publicity, and fundraising for such individual; and

(5) Any other expense that has the primary effect of promoting public recognition or otherwise primarily accruing to the benefit of the individual.

Use Form 4720 to figure and report the excise taxes.

Line 38—Loans to or from officers, directors, trustees, and key employees.—Enter the end-of-year unpaid balance of secured and unsecured loans made to or received from officers, directors, trustees, and key employees. For example, if the organization borrowed $1,000 from one officer and loaned $500 to another, none of which has been repaid, report $1,500 on line 38b.

The term "key employees" refers to the chief administrative officers of an organization (such as an executive director or chancellor) but does not include the heads of separate departments or smaller units within an organization.

Attached schedule.—For loans outstanding at the end of the year, attach a schedule as described below.

(a) When loans should be reported separately.—Report each loan separately, even if more than one loan was made to or received from the same person, or the same terms apply to all loans made. Salary advances and other advances for the personal use and benefit of the recipient, and receivables subject to special terms or arising from nontypical transactions, must be reported as separate loans for each officer, director, etc.

(b) When loans should be reported as a single total.—Receivables that are subject to the same terms and conditions (including credit limits and rate of interest) as receivables due from the general public and that arose during the normal course of the organization's operations may be reported as a single total for all the officers, directors, trustees, and key employees. Travel advances made in connection with official business of the organization may also be reported as a single total.

(c) Schedule format.—For each outstanding loan or other receivable that must be reported separately, the attached schedule should show the following information (preferably in columnar form):

(1) Borrower's name and title;

(2) Original amount;

(3) Balance due;

(4) Date of note;

(5) Maturity date;

(6) Repayment terms;

(7) Interest rate;

(8) Security provided by the borrower;

(9) Purpose of the loan; and

(10) Description and fair market value of the consideration furnished by the lender (for example, cash—$1,000; or 100 shares of XYZ, Inc., common stock—$9,000).

The above detail is not required for receivables or travel advances that may be reported as a single total (see instruction

(b) above); however, report and identify those totals separately in the attachment.

Line 39—Section 501(c)(7) organizations.—

(a) Gross receipts test.—A section 501(c)(7) organization may receive up to 35% of its gross receipts, including investment income, from sources outside its membership and remain tax exempt. Part of the 35% (up to 15% of gross receipts) may be derived from public use of a social club's facilities.

For this purpose, *gross receipts* are the club's income from its usual activities. The term includes charges, admissions, membership fees, dues, assessments, investment income (such as dividends, rents, and similar receipts), and normal recurring capital gains on investments. Gross receipts do not include capital contributions (as defined in the Regulations under section 118), initiation fees, or unusual amounts of income such as income received from the club's selling its clubhouse. Although gross receipts usually do not include initiation fees, these should be included for college fraternities or sororities or other organizations that charge membership initiation fees, but not annual dues.

If the 35% and 15% limits do not affect the club's exempt status, include the income from line 39b on the club's Form 990-T.

(b) Nondiscrimination policy.—A section 501(c)(7) organization is not exempt from income tax if any written policy statement, including the governing instrument and bylaws, allows discrimination on the basis of race, color, or religion.

However, section 501(i) allows social clubs to retain their exemption under section 501(c)(7) even though their membership is limited (in writing) to members of a particular religion if:

(1) The social club is an auxiliary of a fraternal beneficiary society that is exempt under section 501(c)(8) and limits its membership to the members of a particular religion; or

(2) The social club's membership limitation is a good faith attempt to further the teachings or principles of that religion, and the limitation is not intended to exclude individuals of a particular race or color.

Line 40—List of states.—List each state with which you are filing a copy of this return in full or partial satisfaction of state filing requirements.

Line 42—Section 4947(a)(1) charitable trusts.—Section 4947(a)(1) charitable trusts that file Form 990EZ instead of Form 1041 must complete this line. The trust should include exempt-interest dividends received from a mutual fund or other regulated investment company as well as tax-exempt interest received directly.

*U.S. Government Printing Office: 1991 — 285-142

Short Form

Return of Organization Exempt From Income Tax

Form **990EZ**

Under section 501(c) of the Internal Revenue Code (except black lung benefit trust or private foundation) or section 4947(a)(1) charitable trust

► For organizations with gross receipts less than $100,000 and total assets less than $250,000 at the end of the year.

You may have to use a copy of this return to satisfy state reporting requirements.

OMB No. 1545-1150

1991

This Form is Open to Public Inspection

Department of the Treasury
Internal Revenue Service

A For the calendar year 1991, or fiscal year beginning _____ , 1991, and ending _____ , 19 ___

Please use IRS label or print or type. **See Specific Instructions.**	**B** Name of organization	**C** Employer identification number
	Number and street (or P.O. box no., if mail is not delivered to street address) | Room/suite	**D** State registration number
	City, town, or post office, state, and ZIP code	**E** Enter four-digit group exemption number (GEN)

F Check type of organization—Exempt under section ► ☐ 501(c) ( ) (insert number), OR ► ☐ section 4947(a)(1) trust

G Check ► ☐ if exemption application pending.

H Accounting method: ☐ Cash ☐ Accrual ☐ Other (specify) ► _____

I Check ► ☐ if address changed.

J Check ► ☐ if your gross receipts are normally not more than $25,000. You need not file a completed return with IRS; but if you received a Form 990 Package in the mail, you should file a return without financial data. **Some states require a completed return.**

K Enter your 1991 gross receipts (**add back lines 5b, 6b, and 7b, to line 9**) . . . . ► $ _____

If $100,000 or more, you must file Form 990 instead of Form 990EZ.

Part I Statement of Revenue, Expenses, and Changes in Net Assets or Fund Balances

Revenue	**1** Contributions, gifts, grants, and similar amounts received (attach schedule—see instructions) . . .	**1**	
	2 Program service revenue	**2**	
	3 Membership dues and assessments (see instructions)	**3**	
	4 Investment income	**4**	
	5a Gross amount from sale of assets other than inventory **5a**		
	b Less: cost or other basis and sales expenses **5b**		
	c Gain or (loss) (line 5a less line 5b) (attach schedule)	**5c**	
	6 Special events and activities (attach schedule—see instructions):		
	a Gross revenue (not including $ _____ of contributions reported on line 1) **6a**		
	b Less: direct expenses **6b**		
	c Net income or (loss) (line 6a less line 6b)	**6c**	
	7a Gross sales less returns and allowances **7a**		
	b Less: cost of goods sold **7b**		
	c Gross profit or (loss) (line 7a less line 7b)	**7c**	
	8 Other revenue (describe ► _____)	**8**	
	9 **Total revenue** (add lines 1, 2, 3, 4, 5c, 6c, 7c, and 8) . . . . ►	**9**	
Expenses	**10** Grants and similar amounts paid (attach schedule)	**10**	
	11 Benefits paid to or for members	**11**	
	12 Salaries, other compensation, and employee benefits	**12**	
	13 Professional fees and other payments to independent contractors	**13**	
	14 Occupancy, rent, utilities, and maintenance	**14**	
	15 Printing, publications, postage, and shipping	**15**	
	16 Other expenses (describe ► _____)	**16**	
	17 **Total expenses** (add lines 10 through 16) . . . . ►	**17**	
Net Assets	**18** Excess or (deficit) for the year (line 9 less line 17)	**18**	
	19 Net assets or fund balances at beginning of year (from line 27, column (A)) (must agree with end-of-year figure reported on prior year's return)	**19**	
	20 Other changes in net assets or fund balances (attach explanation)	**20**	
	21 Net assets or fund balances at end of year (combine lines 18 through 20) (must agree with line 27, column (B)) . . . . ►	**21**	

Part II Balance Sheets—If Total assets on line 25, column (B) are $250,000 or more, you must file Form 990 instead of Form 990EZ.

	(A) Beginning of year		**(B)** End of year
22 Cash, savings, and investments		**22**	
23 Land and buildings		**23**	
24 Other assets (describe ► _____)		**24**	
25 **Total assets**		**25**	
26 Total liabilities (describe ► _____)		**26**	
27 **Net assets or fund balances** (column (B) must agree with line 21.)		**27**	

For Paperwork Reduction Act Notice, see page 1 of the separate instructions.   Cat. No. 10642I   Form **990EZ** (1991)

Part III	Statement of Program Service Accomplishments—(See instructions.)	Expenses
		(Required for 501(c)(3) and (4) organizations and 4947(a)(1) trusts: optional for others.)

Describe what was achieved in carrying out your exempt purposes. Fully describe the services provided, the number of persons benefited. or other relevant information for each program title.

28 ....
....
.... (Grants $)

29 ....
....
.... (Grants $)

30 ....
....
.... (Grants $)

31 Other program services (attach schedule) . . . . (Grants $)

32 **Total program service expenses** (add lines 28 through 31) . . . . ▶

| **Part IV** | List of Officers, Directors, and Trustees (List each one even if not compensated. See instructions.) |

(A) Name and address	**(B)** Title and average hours per week devoted to position	**(C)** Compensation (If not paid, enter zero.)	**(D)** Contributions to employee benefit plans	**(E)** Expense account and other allowances
....				
....				
....				
....				

Part V	Other Information—Section 501(c)(3) organizations and section 4947(a)(1) charitable trusts **must also** complete and attach Schedule A (Form 990). (See instruction C1.)	Yes	No

33 Did the organization engage in any activity not previously reported to the Internal Revenue Service? . . . .
   If "Yes," attach a detailed description of each activity.

34 Were any changes made to the organizing or governing documents but not reported to IRS? . . . .
   If "Yes," attach a conformed copy of the changes.

35 *If the organization had income from business activities, such as those reported on lines 2, 6, and 7 (among others), but NOT reported on Form 990-T, attach a statement explaining your reason for not reporting the income on Form 990-T.*

   a Did the organization have unrelated business gross income of $1,000 or more during the year covered by this return? . .

   b If "Yes," have you filed a tax return on **Form 990-T,** Exempt Organization Business Income Tax Return, for this year?

36 Was there a liquidation, dissolution, termination, or substantial contraction during the year? (See instructions.) . .
   If "Yes," attach a statement as described in the instructions.

37a Enter amount of political expenditures, direct or indirect, as described in the instructions. ▶ | 37a |

   b Did you file **Form 1120-POL,** U.S. Income Tax Return for Certain Political Organizations, for this year? . . . . .

38a Did you borrow from, or make any loans to, any officer, director, trustee, or key employee, OR were any such loans made and still unpaid at the start of the period covered by this return? . . . .

   b If "Yes," attach the schedule specified in the instructions and enter the amount involved . . | 38b |

39 *Section 501(c)(7) organizations.*—Enter:

   a Initiation fees and capital contributions included on line 9 . . . . . . | 39a |

   b Gross receipts, included on line 9, for public use of club facilities (see instructions) . . | 39b |

   c Does the club's governing instrument or any written policy statement provide for discrimination against any person because of race, color, or religion? (See instructions.) . . . .

40 List the states with which a copy of this return is filed. ▶ ....

41 The books are in care of ▶ .... Telephone no. ▶ .(   )...............
   Located at ▶ ....

42 *Section 4947(a)(1) charitable trusts filing Form 990EZ in lieu of* **Form 1041,** U.S. Fiduciary Income Tax Return.—Check here ▶ ☐
   and enter the amount of tax-exempt interest received or accrued during the tax year . . . ▶ | 42 |

Please Sign Here	Under penalties of perjury. I declare that I have examined this return, including accompanying schedules and statements, and to the best of my knowledge and belief, it is true, correct, and complete. Declaration of preparer (other than officer) is based on all information of which preparer has any knowledge.
	▶ Signature of officer ▶ Date Title

Paid Preparer's Use Only	Preparer's signature ▶		Date	Check if self-employed ▶ ☐
	Firm's name (or yours if self-employed) and address ▶		ZIP code	

Types of Nonprofit Organizations

As you have read, there are more than 20 categories of nonprofit organizations entitled to tax-exempt status under the Internal Revenue Code. The most advantageous category for an organization that hopes to attract financial support from the general public and government grants, however, is the one defined in Section 501(c)(3) of the Code:

> Corporations, and any community chest, fund or foundation, organized and operated exclusively for religious, charitable, scientific, testing for public safety, literary or educational purposes, to foster certain national or international amateur sports competition, or for the prevention of cruelty to children or animals, no part of the net earnings of which inures to the benefit of any private shareholder or individual, no substantial part of the activities of which is carrying on propaganda, or otherwise attempting to influence legislation, and which does not participate in, or intervene in (including publishing or distributing of statements), any political campaign on behalf of any candidate for public office.

In considering the tax deductibility of his/her contribution, a person thinking of giving money to tax-exempt nonprofit organizations generally has in mind the kind of organizations described in Section 501(c)(3) and commonly perceived as *charitable organizations*. Thus, it is distinctly to the financial advantage of a nonprofit corporation to qualify for a federal tax exemption under this section, which clearly can accommodate organizations that are not charitable in the strictest sense of the word.

If that is your intention for your corporation, then you must also deal with some further categorizations.

PUBLIC CHARITIES AND PRIVATE FOUNDATIONS

All organizations, incorporated and unincorporated, that gain tax-exempt status under the provisions of Section 501(c)(3), are further classified by the IRS as either public charities, private operating foundations or private foundations (often referred to as non-operating foundations). Depending on which classification it holds, a tax-exempt organization will face a limitation in the scope of the tax deductibility of contributions made to it. This is a bit confusing at first glance, and the fine-line distinctions involved may not be of concern at all to your nonprofit corporation. But you should know what the IRS is talking about here. The following explanations are simple and brief.

PUBLIC CHARITIES

The IRS defines a *public charity* as an organization that normally receives a substantial portion of its total income directly or indirectly from the general public or from the government. The key concepts of this definition are "substantial portion of income" and "general public" support.

An organization can meet the financial support test of the IRS definition if it normally receives one-third or more of its total support from government agencies and the general public, or if it receives at least one-tenth of its financial support from either or both of these sources and is also organized and operated in a way that tends to attract public or government support on a continuing basis. The public support must have a broad base; it cannot be limited to contributions from a few individuals or families.

Organizations that are considered to have the ability to attract continuing public or government support are those that receive contributions from a broad cross-section of the public, have a governing body of representatives of the community of interest served by the organization, provide facilities or services to the general public and, if a membership organization, have a wide range of members rather than a narrow or restricted group of persons.

There are other ways to qualify churches, universities, colleges, hospitals, supporting organizations of public charities, but the two mentioned are the most common. Donors of funds to nonprofit organizations classified as public charities may deduct their contributions to these groups up to an amount equal to 50 percent of their adjusted gross income in a year.

PRIVATE OPERATING FOUNDATIONS

A *private operating foundation* is an organization that lacks the broad general public support of the public charity; yet it devotes most of its earnings and assets directly to its tax-exempt purposes, as opposed to merely making grants to other organizations, which in turn use the money for tax-exempt purposes.

Contributors to private operating foundations, like those who give money to public charities, may deduct contributions in an amount equal to up to half of their adjusted gross income in a year.

PRIVATE (NONOPERATING) FOUNDATIONS

A private (nonoperating) foundation receives most of its income from investments and endowments. This income is used to make grants to other organizations with tax-exempt purposes, instead of being distributed directly by the foundation for charitable activities. In many instances, contributors to private foundations may deduct their gifts to the foundation in an amount up to only 30 percent of their adjusted gross income in a year.

As you can see, while all three types of these organizations are considered charitable and are tax-exempt, the deductibility of contributions to one type is more limited than in the case of the other two. Keep in mind that the deductibility limitations noted above for all three kinds of 501(c)(3) organizations are those applicable to individual contributors. Corporate contributors may deduct their contributions to all three types of charitable organizations up to an amount equal to 5 percent of the corporation's pretax net income in a year.

HOW TO QUALIFY

Naturally, all three types of organizations, in order to qualify for tax-exempt status under Section 501(c)(3), must demonstrate that they are diligently engaged in furthering the goals and purposes set down in their certificate of incorporation. And all three are faced with this restriction: Lobbying for or against government legislation or candidates for public office may not be a "substantial part" of their activities. That leaves the door ajar for some limited lobbying activities, of course. What the IRS allows is spelled out in a complex set of formulas. There are so many ifs and buts involved that it would not be feasible to introduce the specifics of the formulas here. The purpose of this book is to cover the essentials for you and keep them simple.

The point of this chapter is that being able to advise potential contributors that a gift to your nonprofit tax-exempt corporation can be deducted from their own personal income tax liability can enhance the appeal of your organization to contributors in general. Consequently, this may attract a larger volume of revenue to your corporation for the furtherance of its programs. This is the primary value of holding tax-exempt status under Section 501(c)(3).

At the same time, don't lose sight of the fact that meeting the criteria for 501(c)(3) categorization is not the only path to tax-exempt status. The previous chapter outlined the numerous categories available for tax exemptions. If the purpose or programs of your nonprofit corporation are such that the tax deductibility of contributions will not be critical to their successful implementation, you may choose to apply for a tax exemption under one of the other numbered categories of Section 501(c).

THE PERSONAL/PRIVATE FOUNDATION

What about a *personal nonprofit corporation*, that is, an organization created by an individual or family for the accumulation of funds and assets intended for use for charitable purposes? The precedent for this kind of organization is well established. Organizations such as the Ford Foundation, the Carnegie Foundation, the Rockefeller Brothers Fund and the Duke Endowment began in this way, although they eventually grew into mammoth nonprofit enterprises operated by boards of trustees and large staffs of administrators.

This kind of organization usually is categorized as a personal foundation. Many of them are small and are not incorporated. But many others are structured as nonprofit corporations. They may benefit a single charitable cause or project such as a local hospital or a specific college, or the foundation's benefits may be directed to a broad range of persons or institutions that are engaged in the type of endeavors that the foundation's creator wants to aid.

As you have read, if its support came from one person or family, such a foundation probably would not be considered a public charity. It could probably qualify for tax-exempt status as either a private operating foundation or a private (nonoperating) foundation as described earlier in this chapter. Which form it would take would depend on which IRS tests it chose to meet.

The history of personal foundations is clouded by episodes in which individuals created personal foundations merely as a tax dodge without any valid charitable purpose. Current tax laws contain provisions designed to prevent such practices. For instance, a tax-exempt private foundation's governing instruments—its certificate of incorporation or corporate bylaws—are expected to contain certain elements. Essentially, they must state that the operator or officers of the foundation will distribute the foundation's income in a timely manner and in such a way that it is not subject to taxes on undistributed income; that the officers not engage in any act of self-dealing or other schemes in which the foundation structure is used merely to benefit the operators financially without regard to the stated purposes on which its tax-exempt status is based.

Particularly if you have substantial funds and a favorite charity, a private foundation may be the best route for you. While you could rely on contributions to foundations set up by others, in many of them you will find that a large percentage (over 90 percent, in some cases) of the contributions goes for administrative overhead. Therefore, precious little may be going to the charitable purpose that interests you.

If you set up your own foundation through an exempt nonprofit corporation, obviously you control exactly how the funds shall be put to use.

CHOOSING AN ORGANIZATIONAL STRUCTURE FOR YOUR NONPROFIT CORPORATION

Lest you think there are no further categories, classifications and subtypes within the realm of nonprofit corporations, be advised. There is one more set of differences for you to consider. Fortunately, it is the last.

In creating a nonprofit corporation, you will have to decide at some point before incorporation whether it will be a membership or nonmembership organization. As you have read earlier, in most cases nonprofit corporations are forbidden by law from having stockholders or owners. Yet they must have the involvement of some person(s) who will determine the policies and operating procedures of the corporation. After all, corporations do not run themselves, even if they do possess the powers of individuals under the law. The people who have this distinctive relationship with the nonprofit corporation are considered its members in the eyes of the law. Both membership and nonmembership corporations have members, as you will see in a moment. Who the members are will depend on the organizational structure of the corporation.

It is solely the responsibility of the creators of a nonprofit corporation to decide which kind of organizational structure they will establish. Whether the corporation adopts a membership or nonmembership structure will have no bearing on its eligibility for tax-exempt status from the IRS under Section 501(c)(3), or any other category of the Code. Nor should it have any real effect on the ability of the corporation to attract funds and other support from the public and government. You will find both kinds of organizational structures among the most successful and very largest tax-exempt nonprofit organizations in the United States. Here is what the two types of organizational structures are all about:

MEMBERSHIP ORGANIZATIONS

The membership structure is one in which the nonprofit corporation's certificate of incorporation and bylaws provide ways for persons not involved in the creation of the corporation to become members of it. Usually their membership is acknowledged and certified by a membership certificate issued to them by the corporation. The requirements they must meet to become members can vary widely. It may be a matter of their paying dues or making a contribution to the corporation, or of their simply asking to become a member. Becoming a member gives a person the right to participate in creating and directing the corporation's policy and operation. In this way, a member of a nonprofit corporation resembles a stockholder in a for-profit stock corporation, although the membership certificate held by the nonprofit corporation member does not carry the equity value and rights that the shareholder's certificate of stock does.

The ultimate decisions about the policies and direction of the corporation are made by way of votes cast at an annual membership meeting. Under various state laws, all persons who are members of a nonprofit corporation have certain legal rights. The chief right is that of voting in the required annual membership meeting—to elect the corporation's board of directors and decide on any policy matters brought before that meeting, including amendment of the certificate of incorporation and the bylaws. Furthermore, voting members, if they are able to enlist enough support among the membership, usually are able to initiate a process that will result in the holding of a special membership meeting under certain circumstances stipulated in the corporation's bylaws.

Members of membership corporations can normally be expelled from the organization only after receiving a hearing or series of hearings, as a result of a formal determination made that there is "good cause" for their expulsion.

If you are interested in building an organization in which great numbers of people will be encouraged to participate actively in the affairs and activities of your corporation, if or you feel that granting membership is an essential part of your corporation's appeal to a broad range of potential contributors and other supporters, then you may prefer to structure the corporation as a *membership organization*. In that case, you should write into the bylaws or the certificate of incorporation a clear definition of the requirements and procedures for membership in the corporation.

NONMEMBERSHIP ORGANIZATIONS

In the absence of a specifically stated membership format as explained above, a nonprofit corporation is considered to be a *nonmembership organization*. Yet it does have "members." Legally, the board of directors of such a corporation are considered its members. The corporation has no members beyond the directors.

The board of directors in this organizational structure does not have to share its control and direction of the corporation with any other people. The annual meetings of the corporation are meetings of the board, even though the board may permit others associated with the corporation to sit in on these meetings as observers. Voting controls the corporation, and only directors may vote.

If you do not want the board of directors of your corporation to be required to share its control of the organization with any other people who choose to become members, you will want to establish a nonmembership corporation. You can indicate this in the certificate of incorporation or the bylaws (although in the absence of language establishing general membership criteria, the corporation should be considered a nonmembership organization in the eyes of the law).

You will note that the sample bylaws included in this book provide an alternative article for inclusion if you are creating a membership corporation. Without that article, the bylaws are those of a nonmembership corporation.

11

A Step-by-Step
Organizing Plan

If you have read this far, you have probably made a decision to form a nonprofit corporation, or you are very close to reaching such a decision. All that remains is to determine how you (and any other organizers you are associated with) should proceed with the mechanical steps of bringing your nonprofit organization to life as a corporate entity. That is the purpose of this chapter. It is lengthy only in that each required step in the incorporating process is described in enough detail to answer all the questions you are likely to have and to clarify as much as possible just what must be done on the path to incorporation.

STEP 1
Define the Purpose of the Corporation

This should be your first order of business, because it will be the keystone element of your nonprofit organization's corporate charter. It is the not-for-profit purpose, after all, that sets the nonprofit corporation apart from the normal business corporation when, in almost all other organization respects, the two resemble each other quite closely.

Obviously every corporation—for profit and nonprofit alike—has a purpose. The purpose of the business corporation is to earn a profit for distribution to its owners. In the case of the nonprofit corporation, however, earning profits must not be the stated motive of its organizers and administrators, even though their efforts may well result in what, on a financial balance sheet, would normally be called a profit. The earnings of the nonprofit corporation must be expressly dedicated and exclusively devoted to the support of the benevolent purpose or goal as stated in the corporation's certificate of incorporation. That *statement of purpose* in the incorporating document is essential not only for establishing the corporation's identity as a nonprofit corporation, but also for obtaining tax-exempt status under federal and state law.

As noted earlier, there would be little purpose in creating a nonprofit corporation if you did not also intend it to be tax exempt. So, in defining and drafting a statement of purpose for your corporation, you will want it to meet the requirements of both the incorporating state and the Internal Revenue Service.

STATEMENT OF PURPOSE: ELEMENTS NECESSARY FOR TAX-EXEMPT STATUS

1. The purpose as stated must be clearly within the widely acknowledged meaning of the nonprofit concept, and it must fit the specifically phrased definitions of the Internal Revenue Service as explained in IRS Publication 557.
2. The statement must not appear to indicate that the corporation will engage in activities that violate specific laws of the state (such as a statute prohibiting gambling), or that are counter to the general public welfare (such as the promotion of disrespect for law enforcement institutions).
3. The statement must not contain contradictions. For instance, one sentence describing benevolent goals of the corporation, followed by another sentence indicating that an objective of the corporation will be to earn a certain percentage of return on a variety of business operations, obviously will be contradictory.

The state incorporating agency, as well as the IRS, will review the corporation's statement of purpose for indications that it intends to carry on profit-making activities in the guise of a not-for-profit organization, or that the nonprofit form is sought solely as a device to evade taxation on individuals' private income. For this reason, it is not sufficient merely to state that the purpose of the corporation is to be a nonprofit operation. Its purpose must be described in sufficient detail for the incorporating authorities to make a positive judgment readily for themselves about the corporation's not-for-profit nature.

It need not be a wordy or lengthy statement—a short paragraph, even a few sentences, is satisfactory. Here is an example:

The corporation will have as its goal helping people to protect their person and property from crime, and by extension, making the community in which they live a safer place for all its residents. In furtherance of that goal, the corporation will help form local citizen groups to work with community law enforcement agencies in protecting their neighborhoods and generally preventing crime. The corporation will provide public groups with facts, figures and other research data about crime and crime prevention; with information on how to organize groups in their communities for this purpose and with instructions for planning and executing projects that will encourage residents of the community to be more conscious of public safety. The corporation will also publish a newsletter and other literature in the furtherance of these goals, and it will provide financial aid to community agencies, groups and programs promoting community safety and crime prevention activities.

As you will note in the sample certificate of incorporation at the end of this chapter, this statement describing the specific nature of your organization's activities and goals should be preceded by a pro forma statement indicating that this purpose and these activities fall within the provisions of the IRS Code, Section 501(c)(3).

The law presumes the declaration of the corporation's nonprofit purpose is truthful and correct unless and until proven otherwise. Unless there is ample reason for questioning a statement of purpose—for such reasons as the inclusion of contradictions or obviously illegal intentions—the statement will be accepted at face value. When the state accepts and files the certificate of incorporation of a nonprofit corporation, it not only creates a corporation, it also, in effect, confirms and approves the nonprofit nature and motive of the organization as stated in its incorporating document.

Of course, over a period of time, if the actual operation and activities of the corporation demonstrate that its statement of purpose was apparently a sham, the state can begin proceedings to revoke the corporation's charter. If there is evidence of fraudulent intent, and it is determined that the corporation is, in fact, operating as a profit-making venture for the financial benefit of its founders, backers or operators, or that its activities violate specific state laws or the public interest in general, the state can, indeed, bring charges of fraud against the organizers of the corporation.

TWO DISCLAIMERS NECESSARY IN THE CERTIFICATE OF INCORPORATION

In addition to the statement-of-purpose clause in the certificate of incorporation, the document should contain two key, related statements, or disclaimers, in separate articles.

One article consists of a promise to expend all of the corporation's available resources in furthering its benevolent goals, and a disclaimer of any intent by the corporation's members, directors or officers to earn a profit. This disclaimer should further state that the corporation will not issue or sell stock, or distribute dividends or other shares of its income or earnings to any individuals associated with the corporation.

The second article is a pledge that if the corporation is ever dissolved, all assets and funds remaining after the corporation's operating expenses have been paid will be passed on to other organizations devoted solely to benevolent purposes.

STEP 2
Decide on the Type of Corporation

Remember the discussion of types of tax-exempt nonprofit corporations in Chapter 10? Now you must decide and so indicate in your certificate of incorporation two things. First, whether your corporation will be a public charity, private operating foundation, or private (nonoperating) foundation. Second, whether it will be structured as a membership or nonmembership corporation.

Certainly, for the purpose of obtaining the most favorable type of tax exemption, the corporation should be able to qualify as a public charity under the provisions of Section 501(c)(3) of the IRS Code. Whether you choose a membership or nonmembership structure should have no bearing on the corporation's eligibility for tax-exempt status, but it will affect the operation of the corporation. And you must decide which form will be more efficient and useful in relation to the corporation's activities and goals. Keep in mind that at some point, if the board of directors of the corporation wishes to, it can change the certificate of incorporation or the bylaws to allow for a membership structure other than that which was chosen initially.

STEP 3
Organize Your Organizers

As you discovered earlier in this book, if you are incorporating in the state of Delaware, the only organizer required to create the nonprofit corporation is you. In that case, as long as you are an adult citizen of the United States, you need read no further to complete this step in the organizing of the corporation.

In some states, however, more than one person must be legally involved in the incorporation process. Those states may require the organization's incorporating document to name up to three incorporators and three directors.

In every case, persons named as incorporators may also be named as directors. So in instances other than those where one person can act alone to complete the incorporation procedure, you will be concerned with selecting up to three persons, including yourself, to serve as the organizers—incorporators and initial directors—of the nonprofit corporation.

Those who agree to join you in the effort should understand what that does and does not entail. The only legal requirements these persons must meet are: they must be adults and U.S. citizens (and there may be instances where not all of the incorporators have to be U.S. citizens). The incorporators will bear no responsibility for its operation once the nonprofit corporation gains legal existence.

Those persons named as initial directors, on the other hand, can be held legally accountable for the proper and legal operation of the corporation, for as long as they serve as directors. But at the same time, because of the very nature of a corporation, generally their personal assets are shielded from legal liability.

The directors named in the certificate of incorporation are not required to serve in that capacity beyond the first organizational meeting of the corporation. An entirely new set of directors may be elected or appointed at that meeting. But the normal procedure is for the original directors to continue in that role, at least through the first year's operation of the corporation.

Another important consideration for directors is this: If your nonprofit corporation expects to receive tax-exempt status from the IRS, its bylaws should indicate that directors of the corporation are not compensated with regular salaries, but only reasonable fees for services rendered, and for the expense of attending meetings of the board.

If the corporation will solicit and accept grants and other funds from public agencies, particularly federal government agencies, those agencies may require that the corporate bylaws contain a *conflict-of-interest statement*. Usually, that requires language to the effect that neither members of the board of directors, nor any officers of the corporation nor their close relatives may benefit individually from the receipt of funds from the corporation.

Narrowly construed, this may be interpreted to mean that directors, officers, and their relatives cannot be salaried employees of the corporation; and that the actions of the corporation cannot benefit financially the outside business or personal interest of these persons. A more tolerant interpretation of such a conflict-of-interest clause would permit any of these persons to be paid employees of the corporation. Moreover, it would not prohibit their outside business interests from benefiting from actions of the corporation so long as the potential benefits to these persons are fully disclosed by the corporation and that any director in such a position abstains from voting on matters affecting such benefits to him/her or relatives. Which interpretation of the conflict-of-interest clause is to apply will depend on the circumstances and the particular agency or agencies from which the grant or funds are sought.

If your corporation will be structured as a private foundation, you should know that, strictly in a tax sense, the IRS will identify certain persons involved in the corporation as *disqualified persons*. These are persons who have contributed more than $5,000 to the foundation, if that amount constitutes more than 2 percent of the total contributions made in the same tax year. Also, all officers, directors or trustees of the foundation, or employees having final authority for foundation actions will be disqualified. In addition, the ancestors, lineal descendants (up to and including great-grandchildren) and spouses of any of these persons will likewise be disqualified.

The owner of more than 20 percent of the total combined voting power of a corporation, the profit interests of a partnership, the beneficial interests of a trust or unincorporated enterprise (which is a substantial contributor to the foundation), or other business entities in which the person holds a 35 percent or greater ownership interest will be disqualified.

Prior tax law stated that a person once disqualified was disqualified forever. A fairly recent amendment to the tax laws provides a complicated three-part test under which disqualification can be overcome. If neither the person nor a related person has made a contribution to the foundation for ten years, was not a foundation manager during that period, and the IRS determines that the original contributions made by the person are insignificant compared to the current assets of the foundation, then the presumption of disqualification can be overcome.

If any such disqualified persons actively participate in the operation of the foundation, it will be subject to the payment of federal excise taxes, even though it may hold tax-exempt status.

Remember, this matter of disqualified persons applies only in the case of a nonprofit corporation established as a private foundation. This IRS rule is designed to prevent a tax dodge. In this way, individuals or families cannot set up a so-called charity merely to transfer all their cash and assets into its treasury, and then have the charity hire and pay salaries to all their relatives. Upon their death, the person who had established this scheme might have hoped to avoid heavy estate taxes on their assets when transferred to those relatives.

Like directors, officers, and employees of any type of corporation, those of a nonprofit corporation with tax-exempt status must avoid "self-dealing"—that is, taking actions that benefit them personally to the detriment of the corporation, its goals and its intended beneficiaries. For such dealings, directors, officers, and employees can be held personally liable by the courts, as explained in the chapter on basic requirements of nonprofit corporations.

STEP 4
Select a Name for the Corporation

Just as all of us have names to identify ourselves, so do corporations. The name you select should reflect the nature and purpose of the corporation, so that anyone encountering the name will have no difficulty figuring out what kind of corporation it is and what it stands for. In choosing a name, you will want to be sure it is not already being used by another corporation. You can ask the incorporating agency or your registered agent to check the name you have selected against its registry of corporation names.

The name you use in the certificate of incorporation will be recorded for your organization, providing no other corporation is already using it. If you want to reserve the name in advance of the filing of the incorporating document, most states will permit you to do so on request for a period of 30 days. If you discover after incorporating that an organization in another state where you want to operate is using the same name, you can change the name of your corporation or ask the other organization if it will consider changing its name.

The only restrictions that state corporation laws generally place on the selection of names for corporations are these:

- The name of the nonprofit corporation should not be misleading to the public, nor should it be one that could easily be confused with the name of another existing corporation.
- You cannot give your corporation the same name as that of another active and existing corporation. The one exception might be when that corporation plans to go out of business (or to change its name) and would give your corporation permission to use the name it is abandoning. Two organizations that plan to merge may adopt an entirely new name or retain one or the other of the existing names.

The law forbids the use of offensive or distasteful names as well as the use of any terms that are restricted to the sole and exclusive use of certain government agencies or specific kinds of other organizations. For example, a corporation cannot call itself a *labor union* unless it is actually a labor union;

the same kind of restriction applies to such words as *bank, court, insurance* and the like.

The use of a person's name (other than your own) for a corporation is generally restricted by law.

STEP 5
Establish a Headquarters Address

Wherever you incorporate your organization (whether or not you are required to list the address of the corporation's principal office in the incorporating documents), a nonprofit corporation must have one location from which its activities will be directed. This is true regardless of the number of offices the corporation will actually maintain. You may use a post office box number in conducting corporation business, but, for the official record, you should also have a street address for the principal office of the corporation. This will be in addition to the address of the corporation's registered agent, to which all legal documents and process papers are directed for forwarding to your headquarters.

In some states, the certificate of incorporation must identify at least the county, or city and state, where the corporation's principal office is located, as well as the name and address of the corporation's registered agent. However, when you complete the application for tax-exempt status for filing with the Internal Revenue Service, the corporation will be required to indicate the complete street address of its principal office. A principal office address may be that of a resident, if you intend to begin corporate operations from such an address, or it can be the address of any office space the corporation owns or rents for the purpose of housing its operations.

STEP 6
Draft the Certificate Of Incorporation

By using the forms included at the end of this chapter, you will have little or no drafting to do. Simply fill in the blanks with the appropriate information to complete the document. These forms contain all the necessary language and information required for incorporation in the state of Delaware, as well as in other states. If you will incorporate in a state other than Delaware, though, you should contact its incorporating agency for information on the form required for the incorporating document in that particular state. (See the listing of names and addresses of these state agencies in Appendix A.) As mentioned in previous chapters, some states will require certain items of information in the certificate of incorporation that are not required by Delaware and some other states.

Assuming that you incorporate your nonprofit corporation in the state of Delaware, where the process is quite straightforward and relatively simple and that you will use the form in this book, you might review the explanation given below for each section of that certificate of incorporation. By modifying the certificate in certain places, you may be able to use this same format to incorporate in states where the incorporating document is different.

If you start from scratch or re-type the incorporating document, do so on standard or legal-size white bond paper. Use the language and clause structure of the sample form wherever possible, inserting any other items required in appropriate places and in similarly styled language. Now, let's run through the sample form.

The words *nonstock* and *nonprofit* at the top left and right corners of the form clearly and instantly identify the nature of the corporation. Put the name of your corporation in the blank beneath the title of the document, in this case, the certificate of incorporation.

1. FIRST: This article establishes the name of the corporation.
2. SECOND: In Delaware, you need only indicate the name and address of the corporation's registered agent, which is assumed to be The Company Corporation in this example. In states where only the location of the corporation's principal office is required, it should be inserted in this position. In states where both the principal office location and the registered agent's address are required, both items could be included in the same article. You might add a separate numbered article for one or the other location, if necessary.
3. THIRD: In this article, place the *statement of purpose* of the corporation, as explained in STEP 1 in this chapter. It must include the phrase: "This is a nonstock, nonprofit corporation." It should be preceded by the standard "powers" clause used in the sample form. This standard phrasing merely indicates that the corporation assumes all the powers generally permitted corporations.
4. FOURTH: This phrasing establishes the nonstock structure of the corporation and indicates that the conditions of its *membership* or *nonmembership* format are detailed in the corporation's bylaws.
5. FIFTH: Indicate here the name and mailing address of the incorporator or incorporators, depending on the number required by the incorporating state. In Delaware, of course, only one incorporator is required. If you elect to use The Company Corporation as incorporator for your organization, leave this space blank when you submit this form; The Company Corporation will fill it in.

6. SIXTH: This standard clause makes clear that the authority of the incorporator(s) will end when the certificate of incorporation is filed by the state's incorporating agency. It also indicates that the persons whose names and addresses are listed will then possess control of the corporation as its directors, at least until the first meeting of the board. For incorporation purposes in Delaware, only one person need be named as director of the corporation. In other states, consult the Corporation Law to determine the number of directors that must be named in this document.

7. SEVENTH: This article is a routine elaboration of the intended structure and method of operation of the corporation. At the same time, it does not commit the corporation to specific details which are better left to the bylaws, where the rules can be more fully explained. This article does officially give the board of directors the right to make, alter, or repeal the bylaws, and to give themselves any legal powers they require (except those which the law preserves solely for the *members* of a nonprofit corporation).

8. EIGHTH: This article establishes the right of the corporation to conduct its legally required meetings and keep its financial records in any state it chooses. This procedure is permissible in Delaware. You should check the law in other states in which you might wish to incorporate, as some laws may restrict a corporation to holding its annual meetings and keeping its financial records in the incorporating state.

9. NINTH: This is an important article because it declares quite emphatically that the corporation will be operated on a nonprofit basis. This is the disclaimer mentioned in connection with the corporation's statement of purpose at the beginning of this chapter. The incorporating agency, as well as the IRS, will expect this kind of article to certify the corporation's nonprofit motive and to support its claim for tax-exempt status.

10. TENTH: This article is further evidence of the corporation's benevolent intent.

11. ELEVENTH: This standard phrasing allows the articles of the incorporating document to be changed if ever necessary, as long as the changes are accomplished according to the state law applicable at the time. It also declares that the rights of the members of the corporation do not supersede this right to make changes in the articles.

Finally, the title of the applicable state law that permits incorporation of the organization is cited, and the incorporator attests to the veracity of the document by signing and dating it. If you use the services of The Company Corporation to incorporate, leave this section blank; The Company Corporation will fill it in and provide the incorporator's signature.

STEP 7
Draft a Set of Bylaws

The bylaws of a corporation do not have to be submitted to the incorporating agency of a state in order to incorporate the organization. So, in a sense, they are not an absolutely necessary step in the incorporating process. However, since the certificate of incorporation refers to the bylaws, and it is necessary to submit the corporate bylaws to the IRS when applying for tax-exempt status, now is the best time to work on your organization's bylaws.

The bylaws of a corporation are its rule book. Whether or not they are legally mandated in a particular state, most corporations have them for their own benefit and protection. You can write whatever rules you want into a corporation's bylaws, as long as they don't violate any provisions of the incorporating state's nonprofit corporation law. In a practical sense, the more detailed and comprehensive the bylaws are, the easier it will be for the directors and officers of the corporation to guide its affairs; less will be left to chance or the whim of an individual administrator.

Another advantage of having a comprehensive set of bylaws for governing the corporation is that this identifies the corporation as a legitimate, business-like organization, especially in the eyes of the IRS. This is also true for other government agencies which monitor the activities of nonprofit organizations.

The bylaws in the sample set included at the end of this chapter cover all matters a nonprofit corporation normally deal with in conducting its affairs. You can see that by referring to these bylaws, any persons involved in the work of the corporation can understand how the organization will function. All the questions that usually come up in this regard are answered by the bylaws: Do members have a say in the affairs of the corporation? (See the articles on members and voting.) Who elects the officers? What are the powers of the directors and officers? Who can call a meeting of members of the board? Everything is covered in the bylaws.

You can adopt this set of bylaws as it is for your corporation. If you like, add new articles to cover additional matters of special concern to your particular corporation, or delete any articles that do not apply to your corporation. Remember, the directors can change and add to the corporation's bylaws at any time as long as the original bylaws outline a procedure for making such changes and additions, as Article XI of the sample set indicates. Because the IRS will expect to see them in the bylaws of tax-exempt corporations, you should be sure to include in your corporation's bylaws those items covered in Articles III and VI of the sample set.

STEP 8
Select a Registered Agent

This is a simple step. As you have already learned, any individual or firm established to act as a registered agent for corporations may be assigned as your corporation's registered agent. Lawyers are often engaged as registered agents for corporations they help to establish. A member of the board of directors or an officer of the corporation may serve as the corporation's registered agent from his/her own home or business address. As a rule, the corporation's registered agent must be located in the state in which the organization was incorporated.

It is to the address of the registered agent that all legal documents for the corporation are mailed, to be forwarded to the actual principal office of the corporation. Registered agents do not assume any financial liability for the affairs of the corporation they serve; they are merely responsible for the faithful receipt and prompt forwarding of documents to the corporation's business office.

STEP 9
Submit Your Incorporating Document

You can hand carry the incorporating document or mail it to the incorporating agency in the state in which you wish to incorporate. With your certificate of incorporation, you must also submit a cashier's check or money order for the applicable amount covering state filing and recording fees. State incorporating agencies normally do not accept personal checks from anyone except lawyers.

Properly drafted and completed, the certificate of incorporation is the only document you are required to submit. However, you may want to enclose a brief cover letter in which you note that you are submitting the document for filing and have attached the appropriate form and amount of payment to cover the incorporation costs. Especially if you mail your form, the cover letter is a good idea. Whether you submit your material by mail or in person, it is also a good idea to make photocopies of everything for your own files.

STEP 10
Apply for Tax-Exempt Status

You need not wait until your organization is incorporated to apply for and gain tax-exempt status from the Internal Revenue Service. For instructions on filing the necessary application with the IRS, see Chapter 12.

In some states, you may be required to submit an application for exemption from state corporate income and other taxes at the same time or in advance of the time you submit your certificate of incorporation for filing. Other states make their tax exemption decisions on the basis of the ruling your corporation receives from the IRS.

Whatever the case, the best time to work on your tax exemption file is now, when you are gathering the data and forms necessary to establish the corporation.

STEP 11
Your Corporation Is in Business

In a week to a month after you submit your certificate of incorporation, depending on the efficiency of the incorporating agency and on whether or not the state agencies must also review and approve the document, you should receive a certified copy of the certificate of incorporation with the filing date noted on it by the incorporating agency. In some cases, you will have first received a simple acknowledgment that your document has been received by the agency for filing.

When you have the certified copy of the certificate of incorporation in hand, your nonprofit corporation exists. It is a legal entity and can begin to function as such. Among the first priorities of the new corporation will be to hold the organizational meeting of the board of directors at which the corporation's officers will be elected and its bylaws officially adopted. The first steps involved in getting the affairs of the corporation underway are detailed in Chapter 13.

STATE FEES FOR QUALIFYING DELAWARE CORPORATION IN OTHER STATES

The following pages set out the fees charged by each state for qualifying a Delaware corporation as a foreign corporation. The qualification procedure for a foreign corporation is simple and can be carried out at any time. A

Delaware registered agent can file a copy of the certificate of incorporation with any state or group of states at any time during the life of the corporation. The Company Corporation provides this service to its customers for a service charge of $35 per state.

Qualification of a Delaware Nonprofit Corporation (One-Time Fee)

State	State Fee	State	State Fee
Alabama	$ 75	Missouri	$ 10
Alaska	65	Montana	20
Arizona	150	Nebraska	26
Arkansas	300	Nevada	35
California	55	New Hampshire	25
Colorado	10	New Jersey	100
Connecticut	20	New Mexico	10
Delaware	150	New York	135
District of Columbia	12	North Carolina	75
Florida	95	North Dakota	50
Georgia	70	Ohio	35
Hawaii	25	Oklahoma	340
Idaho	20	Oregon	40
Illinois	50	Pennsylvania	180
Indiana	26	Rhode Island	10
Iowa	25	South Carolina	40
Kansas	95	South Dakota	50
Kentucky	40	Tennessee	300
Louisiana	100	Texas	25
Maine	25	Utah	20
Maryland	50	Vermont	50
Massachusetts	300	Virginia	75
Michigan	20	Washington	30
Minnesota	35	West Virginia	10
Mississippi	125	Wisconsin	N/A
		Wyoming	10

Each state requires the applicant to provide either a certified copy of its certificate of incorporation or certificate of good standing. Both documents are available from the secretary of state's office; if you are a customer of The Company Corporation, it will obtain these documents for you. The cost of obtaining either document is $35 for each state, except for Arizona, where the charge is $70.

Minimum Annual Fee Payable to Corporation Department for Foreign and Domestic Nonprofit Corporations

State	Annual Fee	Foreign	Domestic
Alabama	Annual Permit	$5	$10
	Franchise Tax	None	None
Alaska	Annual Report	$25	$25
	Corporation Tax	None	None
Arizona	Annual Report	$30	$25
	Franchise Tax	None	None
Arkansas	Annual Report	$5	$5
	Antitrust Affidavit (must be filed)	No fee	No fee
California	Information Returns	No fee	No fee
	Annual Report	$5	$5
	Franchise Tax	None	None
Colorado	Annual Report	$5	$5
	Franchise Tax	None	None
	Annual License Fee	None	None
Connecticut	Income Tax	None	None
	License Fee	None	None
	Annual Report	$21	$21
Delaware	Franchise Tax	None	None
	Annual Report	$30	$10
D.C.	Franchise Tax	None	None
	Annual Report	$10	$10
Florida	Franchise Tax	None	None
	Annual Report	$10	$10
Georgia	Annual Report	$5	$5
	Franchise Tax	None	None
Hawaii	Annual Corp. Exhibit	$10	$10
	License Fee	None	None
Idaho	Annual Report	$1	$1
	Franchise Tax	None	None
Illinois	Annual Report	$5	$5
	Franchise Tax	None	None
Indiana	Annual Report	$15	$15
	Property Tax	None	None
Iowa	Annual Report	$5	$5
	License Fee	None	None
Kansas	Franchise Tax	None	None
	Annual Report	$5	$5
Kentucky	Annual License Fee	None	None
	Annual Verification	$5	$5

State	Annual Fee	Foreign	Domestic
Louisiana	Franchise Tax	None	None
	Annual Report	$5	$5
Maine	Annual Report	$30	$30
	Franchise Tax	None	None
Maryland	Annual Report	$40	$40
Massachusetts	Corporation Excise Tax	None	None
	Cert. of Condition		
	of Annual Report	$35	$35
Michigan	Franchise Tax	None	None
	Annual Report	$10	$10
Minnesota	Income Tax	None	None
	Annual Report	$12.50	$10
Mississippi	Franchise Tax	None	None
	Annual Report	$5	$5
Missouri	Franchise Tax	None	None
	Registration Statement	$5	$5
	Antitrust Affidavit	$5	$5
Montana	Annual Report	$5	$5
	Franchise Tax	None	None
	License Tax	None	None
Nebraska	Corp. Occupation Tax	$20	$10
Nevada	List of Officers,		
	Dir. and Agent	$20	$20
	Annual Report	$10	$10
New Hampshire	Annual Report	$30	$30
New Jersey	Annual Report	$15	$15
New Mexico	Annual Report	$5	$5
New York	Annual Report	$10	$10
North Carolina	Annual Report	$10	$10
	Franchise Tax	None	None
North Dakota	Annual Report	$10	$10
Ohio	Statement of Continued		
	Existence	$5	$5
Oklahoma	Franchise Tax	None	None
	Annual Report	$3	$3
Oregon	Annual Report	$10	$10
Pennsylvania	Annual Report	$10	$10
Rhode Island	Annual Report	$10	$10
South Carolina	Annual Report	$5	$5
South Dakota	Annual Report	$10	$10
Tennessee	Annual Report	$5	$5
Texas	Annual Report	$10	$10
Utah	Annual Report	$5	$5
Vermont	Annual Report	$10	$10

Virginia	Annual Report	$5	$5
	Annual Registration	$10	$10
Washington	Annual Report	$5	$5
West Virginia	Annual Report	$10	$10
Wisconsin	Annual Report	$15	$10

SAMPLE FORMS YOU CAN USE TO INCORPORATE YOUR ORGANIZATION

Here are a few explanatory notes about the forms found on the following pages. These forms are designed to meet the requirements for incorporating a nonprofit organization in the state of Delaware. The certificate of incorporation form assumes your use of The Company Corporation as your registered agent and that you are filing the document with the Delaware secretary of state. If this is your intention, then you may use these forms as printed, filling in the blanks with the appropriate information as indicated.

The same forms can be used in the process of incorporating your organization in many other states as well. However, in such cases, you should familiarize yourself with the incorporating state's particular requirements for the incorporating document and make any modifications to the forms that may be called for in the state's statutes. In Appendix A, you will find a list of addresses to which you can write for information about each state's nonprofit corporation law. You will also find a guide as to what the incorporating document is called in each state, the name of the office to which it must be submitted, and data on applicable state laws and fees for this procedure.

Here are examples of the differences between the incorporating document in other states and that required in the state of Delaware. In Delaware, only the name and address of your corporation's registered agent in the state of Delaware are needed in the certificate of incorporation. In some other states, that information is not required, but you must state the location—county and state, usually—of the principal office of your corporation in the incorporating document.

In Delaware, the document to be filed is called the *certificate of incorporation*, or it might be called the *articles of incorporation* or another term, such as *articles of organization*.

In Delaware, a nonprofit corporation need have only one director and one incorporator, both of whom may be the same person. In many other states, the incorporating document must include the names and addresses of at least three other persons as incorporators and directors.

Finally, in some states, the affidavit of a notary public must be affixed to the incorporating document. This statement officially establishes the identity of the persons who are filing for incorporation of the nonprofit organization. It may be typed at the bottom of the last page of the certificate of incorporation.

CERTIFICATE OF INCORPORATION

of

Associated Charities, Inc.

FIRST: The name of this corporation is *Associated Charities, Inc.*

SECOND: Its registered office in the State of *Delaware* is to be located at *201 N. Walnut Street* in the City of *Wilmington*, County of *New Castle*. The registered agent in charge thereof is The Company Corporation, and is located at the same address.

THIRD: The nature of the business and the objects and purposes proposed to be transacted, promoted and carried on, are to do any and all the things herein mentioned, as fully and to the same extent as natural persons might or could do, and in any part of the world, vis:

This is a nonstock, nonprofit corporation. The purpose of the corporation is to engage in any lawful act or activity for which nonprofit corporations may be organized under the General Corporation Law of Delaware.

Said corporation is organized exclusively for charitable, religious, educational and scientific purposes, including, for such purposes, the making of distributions to organizations that qualify as exempt organizations under Section 501(c)(3) of the Internal Revenue Code of 1954 (or the corresponding provision of any future United States Internal Revenue Law), to wit:

Providing educational material and resources for handicapped childern, regardless of the nature of the handicap, and regardless of the form in which the materials may be published, including but not limited to books, periodicals, computers, software for computers, tapes and discs.

FOURTH: The corporation shall not have any capital stock and the conditions of membership shall be stated in the Bylaws.

FIFTH: The name and mailing address of the incorporator is: *The Company Corporation, 201 N. Walnut Street, Wilmington, DE 19801.*

SIXTH: The powers of the incorporator are to terminate upon filing of the Certificate of Incorporation, and the name(s) and mailing address(es) of the persons who are to serve as director(s) until their successors are elected are as follows:

Kathy Smit, 621 North Street, Anytown, Anystate, 00000.

SEVENTH: The activities and affairs of the corporation shall be managed by a Board of Directors. The number of directors which shall constitute the whole Board shall be such as from time to time shall be fixed by, or in the manner provided in, the Bylaws, but in no case shall the number be less than one. The directors need not be members of the corporation unless so required by the Bylaws or by Statute. The Board of Directors shall be elected by the members at the annual meeting of the corporation to be held on such date as the Bylaws may provide, and shall hold office until their successors are respectively elected and qualified. The Bylaws shall specify the number of directors necessary to constitute a quorum. The Board of Directors may, by resolution or resolutions passed by a majority of the whole Board, designate one or more committees which, to the extent provided in said resolution or resolutions or in the Bylaws of the corporation, shall have and may exercise all the powers of the Board of Directors in the management of the activities and affairs of the corporation. They may further have power to authorize the seal of the corporation to be affixed to all papers which may require it; and such committee or committees shall have such name or names as may be stated in the Bylaws of the corporation or as may be determined from time to time by resolution adopted by the Board of Directors. The directors of the corporation may, if the Bylaws so provide, be classified as to term of office. The corporation may elect such officers as the Bylaws may specify, subject to the provisions of the Statute, who shall have titles and exercise such duties as the Bylaws may provide. The Board of Directors is expressly authorized to make, alter, or repeal the Bylaws of this corporation. This corporation may in its Bylaws confer powers upon its Board of Directors in addition to the foregoing, and in addition to the powers and authorities expressly conferred upon them by the Statute. This is true, provided that the Board of Directors shall not exercise any power of authority conferred herein or by Statute upon the members.

EIGHTH: Meetings of members may be held without the State of Delaware, if the Bylaws so provide. The books of the corporation may be kept (subject to any provisions contained in the Statutes) outside the State of Delaware at such place or places as may be from time to time designated by the Board of Directors.

NINTH: No part of the net earnings of the corporation shall inure to the benefit of, or be distributable to, its members, directors, officers or other private persons, except that the corporation shall be authorized and empowered to pay reasonable compensation for services rendered and to make payments and distributions in furtherance of the purposes set forth in Article Three hereof. No substantial part of the activities of the corporation shall consist of the carrying on of propaganda, or otherwise attempting to intervene in (including the publishing or distribution of statements) any of these articles. The corporation shall not carry on any other activities not permitted to be carried on (a) by a corporation exempt from federal income Tax under Section 501(c)(3) of the Internal Revenue Code of 1954 (or the corresponding provision of any future United States Internal Revenue Law) or (b) by a corporation, contributions to which are deductible under Section 170(c()2) of the Internal Revenue Code of 1954 (or the corresponding provision of any future United States Internal Revenue Law).

TENTH: Upon the dissolution of the corporation, the Board of Directors shall, after paying or making provisions for the payment of all of the liabilities of the corporation, dispose of all of the assets of the corporation exclusively for the purpose of the corporation in such manner, or to such organization or organizations and operated exclusively for charitable, educational, religious or scientific purposes as shall at the time qualify as an exempt organization under Section 501(c)(3) of the Internal Revenue Code of 1954 (or the corresponding provision of any future United States Law) as the Board of Directors shall determine. Any such assets not so disposed of shall be disposed of by the Court of Common Pleas of the county in which the principal office of the corporation is then located, exclusively for such purposes or to such organization or organizations, as said Court shall determine, which are organized and operated exclusively for such designated purposes.

ELEVENTH: The corporation reserves the right to amend, alter, change or repeal any provision contained in this Certificate of Incorporation, in the manner now or hereafter prescribed by the Statute, and all rights conferred upon members herein are granted subject to their reservation.

TWELFTH: Directors of the corporation shall not be liable to either the corporation or its members for monetary damages for a breach of fiduciary duties unless the breach involves: (1) a director's duty of loyalty to the corporation; (2) acts or omissions not in good faith or which involve intentional misconduct to a knowing violation of law; (3) a transaction from which the director derived an improper personal benefit.

I, THE UNDERSIGNED, being each of the incorporators hereinbefore named, for the purpose of forming a nonprofit corporation pursuant to *Chapter 1 of Title 8 of the Delaware Code,* do make this certificate, hereby declaring and certifying that the facts herein stated are true, and accordingly have hereunto set my hand this _____ day of _____ A.D. 19 ___ .

_____

(Signature of Incorporator)

Nonstock   Nonprofit

CERTIFICATE OF INCORPORATION

of

_____

FIRST: The name of this corporation is

SECOND: Its registered office in the State of Delaware is to be located
at   in the City of   , County of
. The registered agent in charge thereof is
at the same address.

THIRD: The nature of the business and the objects and purposes proposed
to be transacted, promoted and carried on are to do any and all the things
herein mentioned, as fully and to the same extent as natural persons might
or could do, and in any part of the world, vis:

This is a nonstock, nonprofit corporation. The purpose of the corporation is to engage in any lawful act or activity for which nonprofit corporations may be organized under the General Corporation Law of   .

Said corporation is organized exclusively for charitable, religious,
educational, and scientific purposes, including, for such purposes, the
making of distributions to organizations that qualify as exempt organizations under Section 501(c)(3) of the Internal Revenue Code of 1954 (or the
corresponding provision of any future United States Internal Revenue Law),
to wit:

FOURTH: The corporation shall not have any capital stock and the conditions of membership shall be stated in the Bylaws.

FIFTH: The name and mailing address of the incorporator is:

SIXTH: The powers of the incorporator are to terminate upon filing of the certificate of incorporation, and the name(s) and mailing address(es) of the persons who are to serve as director(s) until their successors are elected are as follows:

SEVENTH: The activities and affairs of the corporation shall be managed by a Board of Directors. The number of directors which shall constitute the whole Board shall be such as from time to time shall be fixed by, or in the manner provided in, the Bylaws, but in no case shall the number be less than one. The directors need not be members of the corporation unless so required by the Bylaws or by Statute. The Board of Directors shall be elected by the members at the annual meeting of the corporation to be held on such date as the Bylaws may provide, and shall hold office until their successors are respectively elected and qualified. The Bylaws shall specify the number of directors necessary to constitute a quorum. The Board of Directors may, by resolution or resolutions passed by a majority of the whole Board, designate one or more committees which, to the extent provided in said resolution or resolutions or in the Bylaws of the corporation, shall have and may exercise all the powers of the Board of Directors in the management of the activities and affairs of the corporation. They may further have power to authorize the seal of the corporation to be affixed to all papers which may require it; and such committee or committees shall have such name or names as may be stated in the Bylaws of the corporation or as may be determined from time to time by resolution adopted by the Board of Directors. The directors of the corporation may, if the Bylaws so provide, be classified as to term of office. The corporation may elect such officers as the Bylaws may specify, subject to the provisions of the Statute, who shall have titles and exercise such duties as the Bylaws may provide. The Board of Directors is expressly authorized to make, alter, or repeal the Bylaws of this corporation. This corporation may in its Bylaws confer powers upon its Board of Directors in addition to the foregoing, and in addition to the powers and authorities expressly conferred upon them by the Statute. This is true, provided that the Board of Directors shall not exercise any power of authority conferred herein or by Statute upon the members.

EIGHTH: Meetings of members may be held without the State of Delaware, if the Bylaws so provide. The books of the corporation may be kept (subject to any provisions contained in the Statutes) outside the State of Delaware at such place or places as may be from time to time designated by the Board of Directors.

NINTH: No part of the net earnings of the corporation shall inure to the benefit of, or be distributable to, its members, directors, officers or other private persons, except that the corporation shall be authorized and empowered to pay reasonable compensation for services rendered and to make payments and distributions in furtherance of the purposes set forth in Article Three hereof. No substantial part of the activities of the corporation shall consist of the carrying on of propaganda, or otherwise attempting to intervene in (including the publishing or distribution of statements) any of these articles. The corporation shall not carry on any other activities not permitted to be carried on (a) by a corporation exempt from Federal Income Tax under Section 501(c)(3) of the Internal Revenue Code of 1954 (or the corresponding provision of any future United States Internal Revenue Law) or (b) by a corporation, contributions to which are deductible under Section 170(c()2) of the Internal Revenue Code of 1954 (or the corresponding provision of any future United States Internal Revenue Law).

TENTH: Upon the dissolution of the corporation, the Board of Directors shall, after paying or making provisions for the payment of all of the liabilities of the corporation, dispose of all of the assets of the corporation exclusively for the purpose of the corporation in such manner, or to such organization or organizations and operated exclusively for charitable, educational, religious or scientific purposes as shall at the time qualify as an exempt organization under Section 501(c)(3) of the Internal Revenue Code of 1954 (or the corresponding provision of any future United States Law) as the Board of Directors shall determine. Any such assets not so disposed of shall be disposed of by the Court of Common Pleas of the county in which the principal office of the corporation is then located, exclusively for such purposes or to such organization or organizations, as said Court shall determine, which are organized and operated exclusively for such designated purposes.

ELEVENTH: The corporation reserves the right to amend, alter, change or repeal any provision contained in this Certificate of Incorporation, in the manner now or hereafter prescribed by the Statute, and all rights conferred upon members herein are granted subject to their reservation.

TWELFTH: Directors of the corporation shall not be liable to either the corporation or its members for monetary damages for a breach of fiduciary duties unless the breach involves: (1) a director's duty of loyalty to the corporation; (2) acts or omissions not in good faith or which involve intentional misconduct to a knowing violation of law; (3) a transaction from which the director derived an improper personal benefit.

I, THE UNDERSIGNED, being each of the incorporators hereinbefore named, for the purpose of forming a nonprofit corporation pursuant to _____ of the _____, do make this certificate, hereby declaring and certifying that the facts herein stated are true, and accordingly have hereunto set my hand this _____ day of _____ A.D. 19____.

_____

(Signature of Incorporator)

NOTARY'S AFFIDAVIT

State of   , County of   ,

THIS IS TO CERTIFY that on this date, ,   before me,

a Notary Public, personally appeared

who I am satisfied are the persons named as incorporators and executors of
the foregoing Articles of Incorporation, and who by their respective signatures in my presence have acknowledged the same as their voluntary act.

IN TESTIMONY THEREOF, I have hereunto set my hand and affixed my official
seal on the date given above.

_____

Notary Public

My commission expires: _____

BYLAWS

of

_____

ARTICLE I—OFFICES

SECTION 1. PRINCIPAL OFFICE. The principal office of the corporation shall
be in the   of   , County of
                    , State of

SECTION 2. OTHER OFFICES. The corporation may also have offices at such
other places within or without the State of   as the
Board of Directors may from time to time determine or the activities of
the corporation may require.

SECTION 3. REGISTERED OFFICE. The registered office of the corporation
shall be established and maintained at   , in
the County of   , State of

ARTICLE II—MEETING OF MEMBERS

SECTION 1. ANNUAL MEETINGS. Annual meetings of members for the election of
directors and for such other business as may be stated in the notice of
the meeting, or as many properly come before the meeting, shall be held at
such places, either within or without the State of   ,
and at such times and dates as the Board of Directors, by resolution,
shall determine and as set forth in the notice of the meeting. In the
event the Board of Directors fails to so determine the time, date and
place of the meeting, the annual meeting of members shall be held at the
principal office of the corporation on the   day of
                    at   o'clock   .M. in each year.

    If the date of the annual meeting shall fall upon a legal holiday, the
meeting shall be held on the next succeeding business day.

SECTION 2. OTHER MEETINGS. Meetings of members for any purpose other than
the election of directors may be held at such a time and place, within or

without the State of   , as shall be stated in the notice
of the meeting.

SECTION 3. VOTING. Each member entitled to vote in accordance with the
terms and provisions of the Certificate of Incorporation and these Bylaws
shall be entitled to one vote, in person or by proxy, for each membership
certificate held by such member, but no proxy shall be voted after three
years from its date unless such proxy provides for a longer period. Upon
the demand of any member, the vote for directors and upon any question before the meeting shall be by ballot. All elections for directors shall be
decided by plurality vote; all other questions shall be decided by majority vote, except as otherwise provided by the certificate of incorporation
or the laws of the State of   .

SECTION 4. MEMBERSHIP. The officer who has charge of the membership ledger
of the corporation shall at least ten days before each meeting of members
prepare a complete, alphabetically addressed, list of the members entitled
to vote at the ensuing election. Said list shall be open to the examination of any member, for a period of at least 10 days prior to the meeting,
either at a place within the city where the meeting is to be held, which
place shall be specified in the notice of the meeting, or, if not so specified, at the place where the meeting is to be held. The list shall be
available for inspection at the meeting.

SECTION 5. QUORUM. Except as otherwise required by law, by the Certificate
of Incorporation or by these Bylaws, the presence, in person or by proxy,
of a majority of the members of the corporation entitled to vote thereat
shall constitute a quorum at a meeting for the transaction of any business.

SECTION 6. SPECIAL MEETINGS. Special meetings of the members for any purpose, unless otherwise prescribed by statute or by the Certificate of Incorporation, may be called by the president and shall be called by the
president or secretary at the request in writing of a majority of the directors or members entitled to vote. Such request shall state the purpose
of the proposed meeting.

SECTION 7. NOTICE OF MEETINGS. Written notice, stating the place, date and time of the meeting, and the general nature of the business to be considered, shall be given to each member entitled to vote thereat at his address as it appears on the records of the corporation, not less than ten nor more than 50 days before the date of the meeting.

SECTION 8. BUSINESS TRANSACTED. No business other than that stated in the notice shall be transacted at any meeting without the unanimous consent of all the members entitled to vote thereat.

SECTION 9. ACTION WITHOUT MEETING. Except as otherwise provided by the Certificate of Incorporation, whenever the vote of members at a meeting thereof is required or permitted to be taken in connection with any corporate action by any provisions of the statutes or the Certificate of Incorporation or of these Bylaws, the meeting and vote of members may be dispensed with, if all the members who would have been entitled to vote upon the action if such meeting were held, shall consent in writing to such corporation action being taken.

ARTICLE III—DIRECTORS

SECTION 1. NUMBER AND TERM. The number of directors shall be , or no fewer than required by law. The directors shall be elected at the annual meeting of members and each director shall be elected to serve until his successor shall be elected and shall qualify.

SECTION 2. RESIGNATIONS. Any director, member of a committee or other officer may resign at any time. Such resignation shall be made in writing, and shall take effect at the time specified therein, and if no time be specified, at the time of its receipt by the president or secretary. The acceptance of a resignation shall not be necessary to make it effective.

SECTION 3. VACANCIES. If the office of any director, member of a committee or other officer becomes vacant, the remaining directors in office, though less than a quorum by a majority vote, may appoint any qualified person to fill such vacancy, and to hold office for the unexpired term and until his successor shall be duly chosen.

SECTION 4. REMOVAL. Any director or directors may be removed either for or without cause at any time by the affirmative vote of the holders of a majority of all the membership certificates outstanding and entitled to vote, at a special meeting of the members called for the purpose, and the vacancies thus created may be filled, at the meeting held for the purpose of removal, by the affirmative vote of a majority of the members entitled to vote.

SECTION 5. INCREASE IN NUMBER. The number of directors may be increased by amendment of these Bylaws by the affirmative vote of a majority of the directors, though less than a quorum, by the affirmative vote of a majority of the members, at the annual meeting or at a special meeting called for that purpose, and by like vote the additional directors may be chosen at such meeting to hold office until the next annual election and until their successors are elected and qualify.

SECTION 6. COMPENSATION. Directors shall not receive any stated salary for their services as directors or as members of committees, but by resolution of the Board a fixed fee and expenses of attendance may be allowed for attendance at each meeting. Nothing herein contained shall be construed to preclude any director from serving the corporation in any other capacity as an officer, agent or otherwise, and receiving compensation therefore.

SECTION 7. ACTION WITHOUT MEETING. Any action required or permitted to be taken at any meeting of the Board of Directors, or of any committee thereof, may be taken without a meeting, if prior to such action a written consent thereto is signed by all members of the Board, or of such committee as the case may be, and such written consent is filed with the minutes of proceedings of the Board or committee.

ARTICLE IV—OFFICERS

SECTION 1. OFFICERS. The officers of the corporation shall consist of a president, a treasurer, and a secretary, and shall be elected by the Board of Directors and shall hold office until their successors are elected and qualified. In addition, the Board of Directors may elect a chairman, one

146

or more vice-presidents and such assistant secretaries and assistant treasurers as it may deem proper. None of the officers of the corporation need be directors. The officers shall be elected at the first meeting of the Board of Directors after each annual meeting. More than two offices may be held by the same person, except the offices of president and secretary, unless there is only one member.

SECTION 2. OTHER OFFICERS AND AGENTS. The Board of Directors may appoint such officers and agents as it may deem advisable, who shall hold their offices for such terms and shall exercise such power and perform such duties as shall be determined from time to time by the Board of Directors.

SECTION 3. CHAIRMAN. The Chairman of the Board of Directors, if one be elected, shall preside at all meetings of the Board of Directors, and he or she shall have and perform such other duties as from time to time may be assigned to him or her by the Board of Directors.

SECTION 4. PRESIDENT. The President shall be the chief executive officer of the corporation and shall have the general powers and duties of supervision and management usually vested in the office of the president of a corporation. He or she shall preside at all meetings of the members if present thereat, and in the absence or nonelection of the Chairman of the Board of Directors, at all meetings of the Board of Directors, and shall have general supervision, direction and control of the affairs of the corporation. Except as the Board of Directors shall authorize the execution thereof in some manner, he or she shall execute bonds, mortgages, and other contracts on behalf of the corporation, and shall cause the seal to be affixed to any instrument requiring it and when so affixed the seal shall be attested by the signature of the secretary or treasurer or an assistant secretary or assistant treasurer.

SECTION 5. VICE-PRESIDENT. Each vice-president shall have such powers and shall perform such duties as shall be assigned to him by the directors.

SECTION 6. TREASURER. The treasurer shall have the custody of the corporate funds and securities and shall keep full and accurate account of receipts and disbursements in books belonging to the corporation. He shall deposit all moneys and other valuables in the name and to the credit of the corporation in such depositories as may be designated by the Board of Directors.

The treasurer shall disburse the funds of the corporation as may be ordered by the Board of Directors, or the president, taking proper vouchers for such disbursements. He or she shall render to the president and Board of Directors at the regular meetings of the Board of Directors, or whenever they may request it, an account of all his or her transactions as treasurer and of the financial condition of the corporation. If required by the Board of Directors, he or she shall give the corporation a bond for the faithful discharge of his or her duties in such amount and with such surety as the Board shall prescribe.

SECTION 7. SECRETARY. The secretary shall give, or cause to be given, notice of all meetings of members and directors, and all other notices required by law or by these Bylaws, and in case of his absence, or refusal or neglect to do so, any such notice may be given by any person thereunto directed by the president, or by the directors, or members, upon whose requisition the meeting is called as provided by these Bylaws. He or she shall record all the proceedings of the meetings of the corporation and of directors in a book to be kept for that purpose, and shall affix the seal to all instruments requiring it, when authorized by the directors or the president, and attest the same.

SECTION 8. ASSISTANT TREASURERS AND ASSISTANT SECRETARIES. Assistant treasurers and assistant secretaries, if any, shall be elected and shall have such powers and shall perform such duties as shall be assigned to them, respectively, by the directors.

(Use the following Article V only if the corporation will use a membership structure of organization.)

ARTICLE V—MEMBERSHIP

SECTION 1. CERTIFICATES OF MEMBERSHIP. Every member of the corporation shall be entitled to have a certificate, signed by, or in the name of the corporation by, the chairman or vice-chairman of the Board of Directors, or the president or a vice-president and the treasurer or an assistant treasurer, or the secretary of the corporation, certifying his or her membership in the corporation. There shall be one class of membership, and each holder of a membership certificate shall be entitled to those rights as stated in Article II in these Bylaws. No member shall be entitled to hold more than one membership certificate.

SECTION 2. LOST CERTIFICATES. New certificates of membership may be issued in the place of any certificates issued by the corporation, that are alleged to have been lost or destroyed, and the directors may, at their discretion, require the owner of the lost or destroyed certificate or his legal representative, to give the corporation a bond, in such sum as they may direct, but not exceeding any reasonable value, to indemnify the corporation against any harm on account of the alleged loss of any such new certificate.

SECTION 3. TRANSFER OF CERTIFICATES. Membership certificates shall not be transferable.

SECTION 4. MEMBERSHIP RECORD DATE. In order that the corporation may determine the members entitled to notice of or to vote at any meting of members or any adjournment thereof, or to express consent to corporate action in writing without a meeting, or entitled to receive allotment of any rights, or for the purpose of any other lawful action, the Board of Directors may fix, in advance, a record date which shall not be more than 60 nor less than 10 days before the day of such meeting, nor more than 60 days prior to any other action. A determination of members of record entitled to notice of or to vote at a meeting of members shall apply to any adjournment of the meeting; provided, however, that the Board of Directors may fix a new record date for the adjourned meeting.

ARTICLE VI—PROHIBITION OF DIVIDENDS

SECTION 1. PROHIBITION OF DIVIDENDS. No part of the net earnings of the corporation shall inure to the benefit of, or be distributable, as dividends or in any other manner, to its members, directors, officers or other private persons, except that the corporation shall be authorized and empowered to pay reasonable compensation for services rendered and to make payments and distributions in furtherance of the purpose set forth in the Certificate of Incorporation.

Further, upon the dissolution of the corporation, the Board of Directors shall, after paying or making provision for the payment of all of the liabilities of the corporation, dispose of all of the assets of the corporation exclusively for the purposes of the corporation in such manner, or to such organization or organizations organized and operated exclusively for charitable, educational, religious, or scientific purposes as shall at the time qualify as an exempt organization or organizations under Section 501(c)(3) of the Internal Revenue Code of 1954 (or the corresponding provisions of any future United States Law) as the Board of Directors shall determine. Any such assets not so disposed of shall be disposed of by the Court of Common Pleas of the County in which the principal office of the corporation is then located, exclusively for such purposes or to such organization or organizations, as said Court shall determine, which are organized and operated exclusively for such purposes.

ARTICLE VII—CORPORATE SEAL

SECTION 1. SEAL. The corporate seal shall be circular in form and shall contain the name of the corporation, the year of its creation and the words "CORPORATE SEAL _____." Said seal may be used by causing it or a facsimile thereof to be impressed or affixed or otherwise reproduced.

ARTICLE VIII—FISCAL YEAR

SECTION 1. FISCAL YEAR. The fiscal year of the corporation shall be determined by resolution of the Board of Directors.

ARTICLE IX—EXECUTION OF CORPORATION INSTRUMENTS

SECTION 1. INSTRUMENTS. All checks, drafts, or other orders for the payment of money, notes or other evidences of indebtedness issued in the name of the corporation shall be signed by officer or officers, agent or agents of the corporation, and in such manner as shall be determined from time to time by resolution of the Board of Directors.

ARTICLE X—NOTICE AND WAIVER OF NOTICE

SECTION 1. NOTICE. Whenever any notice is required by these Bylaws to be given, personal notice is not meant unless expressly stated, and any notice so required shall be deemed to be sufficient if given by depositing the same in the United States mail, postage prepaid, addressed to the person entitled thereto at his or her address as it appears on the records of the corporation, and such notice shall be deemed to have been given on the day of such mailing. Members not entitled to vote shall not be entitled to receive notice of any meetings, except as otherwise provided by statute.

SECTION 2. WAIVER OF NOTICE. Whenever any notice whatever is required to be given under the provisions of any law, or under the provisions of the Certificate of Incorporation of the corporation or these Bylaws, a waiver thereof in writing signed by the person or persons entitled to said notice, whether before or after the time stated therein, shall be deemed proper notice.

ARTICLE XI—AMENDMENTS

SECTION 1. AMENDMENTS. These Bylaws may be altered and repealed and Bylaws may be made at any annual meeting of the members or any special meeting thereof if notice thereof is contained in the notice of such special meeting, by the affirmative vote of a majority of the members entitled to vote thereat, or by the Board of Directors, at any regular meeting of the Board of Directors, or at any special meeting of the Board of Directors, if notice thereof is contained in the notice of such special meeting.

Preparing the Application for Tax Exemption

At this point, you should have completed the paperwork necessary for incorporation of your nonprofit organization. You should also have made a decision about the category under which your corporation will qualify for tax-exempt status. That done, you can proceed in assembling the IRS forms, information, and other documents needed to complete an application to the Internal Revenue Service for the appropriate tax exemption.

For the reasons explained in the previous chapters on special purpose tax exemption for nonprofit corporations, most organizations seek tax exemption as public charities under Section 501(c)(3) of the Internal Revenue Code. Therefore, the explanation, in this chapter, of the information you will need to complete your application for tax exemption is based on the filing requirements for Section 501(c)(3) organizations. This body of information is the most comprehensive required on any IRS tax-exemption form. So, if your corporation will seek tax-exempt status under another subsection of 501(c), the information you compile according to these directions should enable you to complete the forms for any other category without difficulty. The following applies only to charities and public foundations.

DEFINITIVE RULINGS

Organizations may apply for either a *definitive* or an *advance* ruling from the IRS as to their public charity or nonprofit foundation status. As the term implies, a *definitive ruling* is a final and lasting one. In order to obtain such a ruling, the organization must have been in operation for the better part of a year and be able to supply enough detailed information about its operation and activities to satisfy the IRS that the organization has met all the support tests required for classification as a tax-exempt public charity. If an organization has been able to compile a clear record of achievement of its stated charitable goals, it should certainly seek a definitive ruling. The following applies only to charities and public foundations.

ADVANCE RULINGS

Assuming you are still in the process of getting your corporation off the ground and operative, your more likely choice will be to apply for an *advance ruling* if the coporation is relying on any amount of gifts for its public charity. This is the ruling that the IRS commonly gives to nonprofit organizations that are just getting started. These have not yet established a record of sufficient length and depth to meet the requirements for a definitive ruling. An advance ruling is valid for two or three tax years. This depends on when your corporation's fiscal year ends in relation to the date on which you apply for tax exemption. During this period, your corporation will be tax-exempt and, of course, it will be expected to demonstrate by its record and activities that it is operating in such a way that it meets the IRS requirements for 501(c)(3) organizations. If that has been the case, then at the end of the advance-ruling period, the IRS will award the corporation a definitive ruling of tax-exempt status. If the record compiled by an organization over that period does not support its claim to tax exemption under Section 501(c)(3), it can be held liable, retroactively, for excise taxes on its income from investments. But contribution income during that time will not be affected.

For an advance ruling, the IRS will expect you to describe the proposed operations of your corporation in enough detail to permit them to conclude that the corporation clearly will meet the particular requirements of the Code Section under which you are seeking tax exemption. Therefore, your description of the corporation's proposed operations should include information about the activities the corporation expects to engage in; the standards, procedures and other means already adopted or planned; the sources from which it expects to derive its funds and the nature of the expenditures it intends to make in furtherance of its goals. You can make most of this information brief enough to fit on the IRS tax exemption application form.

APPLICATION FORMS

To file for tax exemption under Section 501(c)(3), you will need IRS Form 1023, *Application for Recognition of Exemption Under Section 501(c)(3) of the Internal Revenue Codes*. The same form is used to file for exemption under two other sections of the Code—Section 501(e), *Cooperative Hospital Service Organizations*, and Section 501(f), *Cooperative Service Organizations of Operating Educational Organizations, Which Perform Collective Investment Services for Educational Organizations*.

Aside from these three categories of organizations required to use Form 1023, most of the others enumerated in Section 501(c) must file Form 1024, *Application for Recognition of Exemption Under Section 501(a) or for Determination Under Section 120*. Certain kinds of organizations, such as teachers' retirement fund associations and religious and apostolic associations, are not required to submit specific application forms. Along with Form 1023, you must also file IRS Form 8718, a simple one-page document which you use to make your user fee determination request

To accompany your tax exemption application, you will also need IRS Form SS-4, *Application for Employer Identification Number,* if you have not already submitted such a request in the process of completing your incorporation paperwork. You will have to indicate your *Employer Identification Number (EIN)* or submit this form requesting one in conjunction with your tax exemption application, whether or not your corporation already has hired, or plans to hire employees.

You can obtain IRS Forms 1023, 872-C, 8718 and SS-4 from your nearest IRS office or you can use the copies of the forms included at the end of this chapter. We've also included the official instructions which contain item-by-item instructions for completing the forms.

Although Form SS-4 is quite simple and requires only enough information to establish the existence of your corporation, here is a simple tip that will save you quite a bit of time and effort. You can obtain an EIN for your organization by means of a short telephone call to the IRS. The Service has created a Tele-TIN phone number for just this purpose. The official instructions to Form SS-4 list the phone number you should call. Do not try to call your local district office—the Tele-TIN number is a different number in virtually every region. The entire call will take only a minute or two, and you'll be given your organization's EIN.

IRS PUBLICATIONS

You might also want to obtain copies of the following publications from the IRS. The first one will also come in handy as you draft the statement of purpose clause for your certificate of incorporation.

- IRS Publication 557, *Tax-Exempt Status for Your Organization*
- IRS Publication 578, *Tax Information for Private Foundations and Foundation Managers.*
- IRS Publication 598, Tax on Unrelated Business Income of Exempt Organizations

CHECKLIST FOR COMPLETING IRS FORM 1023

Study the checklist that follows. It describes all the data and materials you will need for completing the application form for tax exemption. If you get all of this information together beforehand, it will make the job go more smoothly; you will not have to scramble for data once you have started work on the application. You should note that, as on most IRS forms, the blanks on Form 1023 do not allow for a lot of elaboration. You need not write complete sentences in reply to its questions, as long as you get the key points of information across in abbreviated, shorthand style. That will be sufficient. If you need more room than the form allows, of course, you can always continue your answers on a plain sheet of paper on the top of which you have indicated the questions to which the answer refers.

1. About the Organization of the Corporation

- [ ] The name of your nonprofit corporation; the complete street address, city, and state where the principal office is located; and its EIN.
- [ ] The date of incorporation of your organization. This is the date, as indicated on your certified copy of the certificate of incorporation, when that document was officially filed by the state incorporating agency.
- [ ] Your organization's Activity Code Number. The last page of the official instructions to Form 1023 (included in this chapter) contains a chart listing Code numbers for virtually every conceivable type of exempt organization. Select one or more appropriate numbers and report them on line 7.
- [ ] An indication of whether your corporation is structured as a membership or nonmembership organization. If it is a membership organization, you must explain briefly any special qualifications for membership, what fees

are charged for membership, whether the benefits of the corporation are available only to its members, and how you intend to attract members.

☐ Identification of your corporation as one of the three classifications of 501(c)(3) organizations—public charity, private operating foundation, or private (nonoperating) foundation.

2. About the Corporation's Directors

☐ The name and telephone number of a director or other person who is authorized to be contacted by the IRS concerning the corporation's request for tax exemption. The telephone number listed may be that of the corporation's principal office.

☐ The name and, briefly, the qualifications of all the persons named as directors of the corporation in the certificate of incorporation. These do not have to be complete biographical profiles. The important thing is to show what experience or expertise each person has in the specific field in which your corporation will be involved, or in managing a business or other kind of organization. If the first organizational meeting of the board has already been held before you file your application for tax-exempt status, you should also include the names and qualifications of the officers elected at that meeting in the application. In describing the qualifications of your directors and officers, it is particularly important to note if any of them are public officials or appointees of public agencies, since one of the indications of an organization's status as a public charity is the presence of such officials on its board of directors.

☐ The application must be signed by a director of the corporation, preferably the person who is the authorized IRS contact (see line 3 of the form).

3. About the Corporation's Plans and Operations

☐ A brief but complete description of the activities your corporation will carry on in furtherance of its stated nonprofit purpose and specific goals.

☐ Information about any other organization that your corporation controls or that controls your corporation, with particular attention to the financial relationship between your corporation and that organization or organizations.

☐ A statement of the corporation's plans and intentions with respect to any lobbying activities. If the corporation will engage in some type or degree of lobbying, be sure to describe the planned activities so that it will be clear that they are within the limits allowed under Section 501(c)(3) guidelines on that subject.

4. About the Corporation's Finances

☐ Start by noting the month that the corporation's fiscal year ends.

☐ A list of the sources of financial support your corporation anticipates and an explanation of how you will solicit funds from these courses; that is, by requests for grants, public fund-raising campaigns, the operation of business activities related to the goals and purposes of your organization, investments, and/or the sale of goods or services. If any funds will come from the sale of goods or services, you should indicate what will be sold and what the corporation will charge for it, making clear that the price is reasonable. Your description of expected sources of support should indicate whether each source mentioned is a public or private source and what kind of support is involved (that is, a grant, a contribution, related business revenue and so forth). If one of the sources will be revenue from fund-raising events or other related business activities or investments, the nature of each of those kinds of income-producing activities or enterprises should be explained.

☐ Work up a financial statement current as of the date of your application for tax-exempt status. The statement should include a current balance sheet showing receipts and expenditures as well as the assets and liabilities of your corporation. The standard requirement of the IRS is a financial statement covering the current year and three previous years, or, if you haven't been in operation for a full year, a statement of proposed budget for two years. If even that is a longer period of time than your corporation has been in operation, include a statement for whatever period the corporation has been active and a copy of the corporation's proposed budget for at least the starting year's operations.

☐ A description of the nature of the expenditures the corporation intends to make. Aside from obvious expenditures for administration and general operation of the corporation and its fund-raising activities, explain what criteria will be used to select the persons, groups of persons, or organizations in whose behalf your corporation will make direct disbursements in line with its stated purpose and objectives.

ATTACHMENTS

Along with your completed application form you must also submit a number of attachments. They are:

☐ A certified copy (one with the state incorporating agency's notation of filing date on it) of the certificate of incorporation.

☐ A certified copy of the corporation's bylaws.

☐ If you have not obtained an EIN number by calling the IRS, then include a completed IRS Form SS-4, Application for Employer Identification Number. This form (or the number, if you already have one) is necessary even if your corporation does not intend to have paid employees).

☐ Copies of any literature and other materials you plan to distribute in connection with membership drives, fund-raising campaigns, fees, benefits and program services. If these items do not yet exist, you can attach outlines of such materials that your corporation proposes to use in its work.

When you have put your completed and signed application form, supporting documents, and other attachments together, mail the entire package to the District Director at the appropriate office of the Internal Revenue Service. The address can be found in the list at the end of this chapter.

Once you have submitted your application, continue normal operations of your corporation. Receipt of a ruling from the IRS on your organization's application for tax-exempt status should not take too long.

QUESTIONS FROM THE IRS

If you have not supplied all the information requested on Form 1023 and its attachments, or there are other problems or questions about your corporation's application, the IRS will call the person named on the application for an explanation. Or it may return your application with a letter explaining what is lacking and indicating a time period within which the missing information must be included in the application and the form resubmitted. The IRS will not consider the merits of any application unless and until it contains all the information required. Of course, if the IRS has to send your application back for further information or to seek explanation of the data you submitted, this will delay the processing of your request. So take care when you work on the application. Make sure it is complete and accurate when you first send it to the appropriate IRS District Director.

When the IRS has made a decision on your application, its ruling will be sent to the corporation in what is called a *ruling or determination letter.* Once you have this letter in hand, it will be your official record of tax-exempt status. Make a number of photocopies of it for your corporate files.

WHERE TO SEND YOUR APPLICATION

The instructions for Form 1023 (included in this chapter) contain a table of district offices for each region of the country. You must send your Form 1023 to the appropriate office listed in that table. Caution: These district office addresses are not the same as those used by for-profit corporations or individuals for filing purposes, so check that table for the appropriate address.

For your convenience the following forms are provided at the end of the chapter:

- Form 1023
- Form 8718
- Form 872-C
- Form SS-4

Department of the Treasury
Internal Revenue Service

Instructions for Form 1023
(Revised September 1990)

Application for Recognition of Exemption Under Section 501(c)(3) of the Internal Revenue Code

(Section references are to the Internal Revenue Code unless otherwise noted.)

Retain a copy of the completed Form 1023 in the organization's permanent records. See **General Instruction G** regarding public inspection of approved applications.

General Information

Paperwork Reduction Act Notice.—We ask for the information on this form to carry out the Internal Revenue laws of the United States. If you want to be recognized as tax exempt by IRS, you are required to give us this information. We need it to determine whether you meet the legal requirements for tax-exempt status.

The time needed to complete and file these forms will vary depending on individual circumstances. The estimated average times are:

Form	Recordkeeping	Learning about the law or the form	Preparing, and sending the form to IRS
1023 Parts I to IV	54 hrs., 17 min.	4 hrs., 53 min.	9 hrs., 34 min.
1023 Sch. A	7 hrs., 10 min.	-0- min.	7 min.
1023 Sch. B	4 hrs., 47 min.	30 min.	36 min.
1023 Sch. C	5 hrs., 1 min.	35 min.	43 min.
1023 Sch. D	4 hrs., 4 min.	42 min.	47 min.
1023 Sch. E	9 hrs., 20 min.	1 hr., 5 min.	1 hr., 17 min.
1023 Sch. F	2 hrs., 38 min.	2 hrs., 53 min.	3 hrs., 3 min.
1023 Sch. G	2 hrs., 38 min.	0 min.	21 min.
1023 Sch. H	1 hr., 55 min.	42 min.	46 min.
1023 Sch. I	3 hrs., 35 min.	-0- min.	4 min.
872-C	1 hr., 12 min.	24 min.	26 min.

If you have comments concerning the accuracy of these time estimates or suggestions for making these forms more simple, we would be happy to hear from you. You can write to both the **Internal Revenue Service,** Washington, DC 20224, Attention: IRS Reports Clearance Officer, T:FP; and the **Office of Management and Budget,** Paperwork Reduction Project (1545-0056), Washington, DC 20503. DO NOT send the tax form to either of these offices. Instead, see the instructions below for information on where to file.

General Instructions

User Fee.—The Revenue Act of 1987 requires payment of a user fee with determination letter requests submitted to the Internal Revenue Service. Form **8718,** User Fee for Exempt Organization Determination Letter Request, must be submitted with this application along with the appropriate fee as stated on Form 8718. Form 8718 may be obtained through your local IRS office or by calling the telephone number given below for obtaining forms and publications.

Helpful Information.—For additional information see **Publication 557,** Tax-Exempt Status for Your Organization; **Publication 578,** Tax Information for Private Foundations and Foundation Managers; and **Publication 598,** Tax on Unrelated Business Income of Exempt Organizations. You may also call **1-800-554-4477 (after October 1, 1990, call 1-800-829-4477);** ask for **Topics #109** and **#110** (a push-button telephone is required). For additional forms and publications, call **1-800-424-3676 (after October 1, 1990, call 1-800-829-3676).**

A. Purpose of Form

1. Completed Form 1023 required for section 501(c)(3) exemption.—Unless it meets either of the exceptions in item 2 below, or notifies the IRS that it is applying for **recognition of** section 501(c)(3) exempt status, no organization formed after October 9, 1969, will be considered tax exempt under section 501(c)(3).

An organization "notifies" IRS by filing a completed Form 1023. Form 1023 also solicits the information that IRS needs to determine if the organization is a private foundation.

2. Organizations that are not required to file Form 1023.— The following organizations will be considered tax exempt under section 501(c)(3) even if they do not file Form 1023: **(a)** Churches, their integrated auxiliaries, and conventions or associations of churches, or **(b)** Any organization which is not a private foundation (as defined in section 509(a)) and the gross receipts of which in each taxable year are normally not more than $5,000.

Even if these organizations are not required to file Form 1023 to be tax exempt, they may wish to file Form 1023 and receive a determination letter of IRS recognition of their section 501(c)(3) status in order to obtain certain incidental benefits such as: public recognition of their tax-exempt status; exemption from certain state taxes; advance assurance to donors of deductibility of contributions; exemption from certain Federal excise taxes; non-profit mailing privileges, etc.

3. Other organizations.—In applying for a determination letter, cooperative service organizations, described in section 501(e) and (f), and child care organizations, described in section 501(k), use Form 1023 and are treated as section 501(c)(3) organizations.

4. Group exemption letter.—Note: *Generally, Form 1023 is NOT used to apply for a group exemption letter. For information on how to apply for a group exemption letter, see Publication 557.*

B. What To File

1. All organizations—Pages 1 through 9, Form 1023 and additional schedules, if applicable
2. Churches—Schedule A
3. Schools—Schedule B
4. Hospitals or Medical Research—Schedule C
5. Supporting Organizations (509(a)(3))—Schedule D
6. Private Operating Foundations—Schedule E
7. Home for the Aged or Handicapped—Schedule F
8. Child Care—Schedule G
9. Scholarship Benefits or Student Aid—Schedule H
10. If your organization has taken over or will take over a "for profit" institution—Schedule I.

Attachments.—Every attachment should state that it relates to Form 1023 and identify the applicable part and line item number. The attachments should also show the organization's name, address, and employer identification number and be on 8½" × 11" paper.

In addition to the required documents and statements, you should file any additional information citing court decisions, rulings, opinions, etc., that will expedite processing of the application. Generally, attachments in the form of tape recordings are not acceptable unless accompanied by a transcript.

C. When To File

An organization formed after October 9, 1969, must file Form 1023 to be recognized as an organization described in section 501(c)(3). Generally, if an organization files its application within 15 months after the end of the month in which it was formed, and if IRS approves the application, the effective date of the organization's section 501(c)(3) status will be the date it was organized.

Generally, if an organization does not file its application (Form 1023) within 15 months after the end of the month in which it was formed, it will not qualify for exempt status during the period before the date of its application.

D. Where To File

File the completed application, and all information required, with the key district office for your principal place of business or office as listed below. As soon as possible after the complete application is received, you will be advised of IRS's determination and of the annual returns (if any) that the organization will be required to file.

161

When the principal place of business or office of the organization is in one of the districts or locations shown below ▼	Send your application to the key district listed below ▼
Anchorage, Boise, Honolulu, Laguna Niguel, Las Vegas, Los Angeles, Portland, San Jose, Seattle	Internal Revenue Service EO Application Receiving Room 5127, P.O. Box 486 Los Angeles, CA 90053-0486
Sacramento, San Francisco	Internal Revenue Service EO Application Receiving Stop SF 4446 P.O. Box 36001 San Francisco, CA 94102
Atlanta, Birmingham, Columbia, Ft. Lauderdale, Greensboro, Jackson, Jacksonville, Little Rock, Nashville, New Orleans	Internal Revenue Service EP/EO Division P.O. Box 941 Atlanta, GA 30370
Aberdeen, Chicago, Des Moines, Fargo, Helena, Milwaukee, Omaha, St. Louis, St. Paul, Springfield	Internal Revenue Service EP/EO Division 230 S. Dearborn DPN 20-5 Chicago, IL 60604
Baltimore, District of Columbia, Newark, Philadelphia, Pittsburgh, Richmond, Wilmington, any U.S. possession (except Virgin Islands) or foreign country	Internal Revenue Service EP/EO Division P.O. Box 17010 Baltimore, MD 21203
U.S. Virgin Islands	Virgin Islands Bureau of Internal Revenue Lockharts Garden No. 1A Charlotte Amalie, St. Thomas, VI 00802
Albany, Augusta, Boston, Brooklyn, Buffalo, Burlington, Hartford, Manhattan, Portsmouth, Providence	Internal Revenue Service EP/EO Division P.O. Box 1680, GPO Brooklyn, NY 11202
Cincinnati, Cleveland, Detroit, Indianapolis, Louisville, Parkersburg	Internal Revenue Service EP/EO Division P.O. Box 3159 Cincinnati, OH 45201
Albuquerque, Austin, Cheyenne, Dallas, Denver, Houston, Oklahoma City, Phoenix, Salt Lake City, Wichita	Internal Revenue Service EP/EO Division Mail Code 4950 DAL 1100 Commerce Street Dallas, TX 75242

E. Signature Requirements

An officer, a trustee who is authorized to sign, or another person authorized by a power of attorney must sign this application. Send the power of attorney with the application when you file it. **Form 2848,** Power of Attorney and Declaration of Representative, or **Form 8821,** Tax Information Authorization, may be used for this purpose.

F. Deductibility of Contributions

Deductions for charitable contributions are not allowed for any gifts or bequests made to organizations that do not qualify under section 501(c)(3). The effective date of an organization's section 501(c)(3) status determines the date that contributions to it are deductible by donors. (See General Instructions, **When To File.**)

G. Public Inspection of Form 1023

IRS Responsibilities.—If the application is approved, it and any supporting documents will be open to public inspection, as required by section 6104, in any key district office and in the Internal Revenue Service's National Office. In addition, any letter or other document issued by the IRS with regard to the application will be open to public inspection. However, information relating to a trade secret, patent, style of work or apparatus which, if released, would adversely affect the organization, or any other information which would adversely affect the national defense, will not be made available for public inspection. You must identify this information by clearly marking it "NOT SUBJECT TO PUBLIC INSPECTION" and attach a statement explaining why the organization asks that the information be withheld. If the Internal Revenue Service agrees, the information will be withheld.

Organization's Responsibilities.—The organization must make available for public inspection a copy of its approved application and supporting documents, along with any document or letter issued by the IRS. These must be available during regular business hours at the organization's principal office and at each of its regional or district offices having at least 3 paid employees. See Notice 88-120, 1988-2 C.B. 454. If any person under a duty to

comply with the inspection provisions fails to comply with these requirements, a penalty of $10 a day will be imposed for each day the failure continues.

H. Appeal Procedures

Your application will be considered by the key district office, which will either:

(1) issue a favorable determination letter;

(2) issue a proposed adverse determination letter denying the exempt status you requested; or

(3) refer the case to the National Office.

If you receive a proposed adverse determination, you will be advised of your appeal rights at that time.

I. Language and Currency Requirements

Form 1023 and attachments must be prepared in English. If the organizational document or bylaws are in any other language, an English translation must be furnished. If the organization produces or distributes foreign language publications that are submitted with the application, you may be asked to provide English translations for one or more of them during the processing of your application.

Report all financial information in U.S. dollars (state conversion rate used). Combine amounts from within and outside the United States and report the total for each item on the financial statements.

For example:

Gross Investment Income	
From U.S. sources	$4,000
From Non-U.S. sources	1,000
Amount to report on income statement	$5,000

J. Annual Information Return

If the annual information return for tax-exempt organizations becomes due while your application for recognition of exempt status is pending with IRS (including any appeal of a proposed adverse determination), you should file **Form 990,** Return of Organization Exempt From Income Tax (or **Form 990EZ,** Short Form Return of Organization Exempt From Income Tax) and **Schedule A (Form 990),** Organization Exempt Under Section 501(c)(3), or **Form 990-PF,** Return of Private Foundation, if a private foundation, and indicate that an application is pending.

K. Special Rule for Canadian Colleges and Universities

A Canadian college or university that has received a **Form T2051,** Notification of Registration, from Revenue Canada (Department of National Revenue, Taxation) and whose registration has not been revoked, does not have to complete all parts of Form 1023 that would otherwise be applicable. Such an organization must complete only Part I of Form 1023 and Schedule B (Schools, Colleges, and Universities). The organization must also attach a copy of its **Form T2050,** Application for Registration, together with all the required attachments that it submitted to Revenue Canada. If any attachments were prepared in French, an English translation must be furnished.

Other Canadian organizations seeking a determination of section 501(c)(3) status must complete Form 1023 in the same manner as U.S. organizations.

Specific Instructions

The following instructions are keyed to the line items on the application form:

Part I.—Identification of Applicant

Line 1. Full Name and Address of Organization.—Enter the organization's name exactly as it appears in its creating document including amendments. If the organization will be operating under another name, show the other name in parentheses.

Line 2. Employer Identification Number.—All organizations must have an EIN. Enter the 9-digit EIN assigned to the organization by the IRS. If the organization does **not** have an employer identification number, enter "none" and attach a completed **Form SS-4,** Application for Employer Identification Number, to the application. If the organization has previously applied for a number, attach a statement giving the date of the application and the office where it was filed.

Page 2

Line 3. Person to Contact.—Enter the name and telephone number of the person to be contacted during business hours if more information is needed. The contact person should be familiar with the organization's activities, preferably an officer, director, or authorized representative.

Line 4. Month the Annual Accounting Period Ends.—Enter the month the organization's annual accounting period ends. The accounting period is usually the 12-month period that is the organization's tax year. The organization's first tax year depends on the accounting period you choose (it could be less than 12 months).

Line 5. Date Formed.—Enter the date the organization became a legal entity. For corporations, this would be the date that the articles of incorporation were approved by the appropriate State official. For unincorporated organizations, it would be the date its constitution or articles of association was adopted.

Line 6. Activity Codes.—Select up to three of the code numbers listed on the back cover that best describe or most accurately identify the organization's purposes, activities, or type of organization. Enter the codes in the order of importance.

Line 7.—Indicate if the organization is one of the following:

501(e)   Cooperative hospital service organization;

501(f)   Cooperative service organization of operating educational organization;

501(k)   Organization providing child care.

If none of the above applies, make no entry on line 7.

Line 8.—Indicate if the organization has ever filed a Form 1023 or **Form 1024**, Application for Recognition of Exemption Under Section 501(a) or for Determination Under Section 120, with the Internal Revenue Service.

Line 9.—Indicate if the organization has ever filed Federal income tax returns as a taxable organization or filed returns as an exempt organization (e.g., Form 990, 990EZ, 990-PF, or **990-T**, Exempt Organization Business Income Tax Return).

Line 10. Type of Organization and Organizational Documents.—Submit a conformed copy of the organizing instrument. A "conformed" copy is one that agrees with the original and all amendments to it. The conformed copy may be a photocopy of the original signed and dated organizing document OR it may be a copy of the organizing document that is not signed but is accompanied by a written declaration signed by an authorized individual stating that the copy is a complete and accurate copy of the original signed and dated document.

In the case of a corporation, a copy of the certificate of incorporation, approved and dated by an appropriate State official, is sufficient by itself. If an unsigned copy of the articles of incorporation is submitted, it must be accompanied by the written declaration discussed above. Signed or unsigned copies of the articles of incorporation must be accompanied by a declaration stating that the original copy of the articles was filed with, and approved by, the State. The date filed must be specified.

In the case of an unincorporated association, the conformed copy of the constitution, articles of association, or other organizing document must indicate in the document itself, or in a written declaration, that the organization was formed by the adoption of the document by two or more persons.

In the case of a trust, a copy of the signed and dated trust instrument must be furnished.

If your organizing instrument does not contain a proper dissolution clause, and if State law does not provide for distribution of assets for one or more exempt (section 501(c)(3)) purposes upon dissolution, the organization will not qualify for exempt status. If you rely on State law, please cite the law and briefly state its provisions on an attachment. Your organizing instrument must also specify your organizational purposes and the purposes specified must be limited to one or more of those set out in section 501(c)(3).

If the organization does not have an organizing instrument, it will not qualify for exempt status. The bylaws of an organization alone are not an organizing instrument. They are merely the internal rules and regulations of the organization.

See Publication 557 for detailed instructions and for sample organizing instruments that satisfy the requirements of section 501(c)(3) and the related regulations.

Page 3

Part II.—Activities and Operational Information

Line 1.—It is important that you report all activities carried on by the organization to enable the IRS to make a proper determination of the organization's exempt status.

Line 2.—If it is anticipated that the organization's principal sources of support will increase or decrease substantially in relation to the organization's total support, attach a statement describing anticipated changes and explaining the basis for the expectation.

Line 3.—For purposes of this question, "fundraising activity" includes the solicitation of contributions and both functionally related activities and unrelated business activities. Include a description of the nature and magnitude of the activities.

Line 4a.—Furnish the mailing addresses of the organization's principal officers, directors, or trustees. Do not give the address of the organization.

Line 4b.—The annual compensation includes salary, bonus, and any other form of payment to the individual for services while employed by the organization.

Line 4c.—Public officials include anyone holding an elected position or anyone appointed to a position by an elected official.

Line 4d.—For purposes of this application, a "disqualified person" is any person who, if the applicant organization were a private foundation, is:

(1) a "substantial contributor" to the foundation (defined below);

(2) a foundation manager;

(3) an owner of more than 20% of the total combined voting power of a corporation that is a substantial contributor to the foundation;

(4) a "member of the family" of any person described in (1), (2), or (3) above;

(5) a corporation, partnership, or trust in which persons described in (1), (2), (3), or (4) above, hold more than 35% of the combined voting power, the profits interest, or the beneficial interests; and

(6) any other private foundation that is effectively controlled by the same persons who control the first-mentioned private foundation or any other private foundation substantially all of whose contributions were made by the same contributors.

A substantial contributor is any person who gave a total of more than $5,000 to the organization, and those contributions are more than 2% of all the contributions and bequests received by the organization from the date it was created up to the end of the year the contributions by the substantial contributor were received. A creator of a trust is treated as a substantial contributor regardless of the amount contributed by that person or others.

See Publication 578 for more information on "disqualified persons."

Line 5.—If your organization controls or is controlled by another exempt organization or a taxable organization, answer "Yes." Examples of special relationships would be: common officers and the sharing of office space or employees.

Line 6.—If the organization conducts any financial transactions (either receiving funds or paying out funds), or non-financial activities with an exempt organization (other than 501(c)(3) organizations), or with a political organization, answer "Yes," and explain.

Line 7.—If the organization must report its income and expense activity to any other organization (tax-exempt or taxable entity), answer "Yes."

Line 8.—Examples of assets used to perform an exempt function are: land, building, equipment, and publications. Do not include cash or property producing investment income. If you have no assets used in performing the organization's exempt function, answer "N/A."

Line 9a.—Answer "Yes," if the organization is managed by another exempt organization, a taxable organization, or an individual.

Line 9b.—If the organization leases property from anyone or leases any of its property to anyone, answer "Yes."

Line 10.—A membership organization for purposes of this question refers to an organization that is composed of individuals or organizations who:

(1) share in the common goal for which the organization was created;

(2) actively participate in achieving the organization's purposes; and

(3) pay dues.

Line 11.—Examples of benefits, products, and services would be: meals to homeless people, home for the aged, museum open to the public, and a symphony orchestra giving public performances.

Line 12.—An organization is attempting to influence legislation if it contacts or urges the public to contact members of a legislative body, or if it advocates the adoption or rejection of legislation.

If you answer "Yes," you may want to file **Form 5768,** Election/Revocation of Election by an Eligible Section 501(c)(3) Organization to Make Expenditures to Influence Legislation.

Line 13.—An organization is intervening in a political campaign if it promotes or opposes the candidacy or prospective candidacy of an individual for public office.

Part III.—Technical Requirements

Line 1.—If you check "Yes," proceed to question 7. If you check "No," proceed to question 2.

Line 2.—If you fit one of the exceptions, do not answer questions 3 through 6. Proceed to question 7.

Line 3.—Relief from the 15-month filing requirement may be granted under certain circumstances. (See the instructions for Line 4 below.)

Line 4.—The reasons for late filing should be specific to your particular organization and situation. Revenue Procedure 79-63, 1979-2 C.B. 578 lists the factors that will be taken into consideration by the Service in determining whether good cause exists for granting an extension of time to file the application. (Also see Publication 557.) To address these factors, your response on line 4 should provide the following information:

(1) Whether or not you consulted an attorney or accountant knowledgeable in tax matters or communicated with a responsible Internal Revenue Service employee (before or after the organization was created) to ascertain the organization's Federal filing requirements and, if so, the names and occupations or titles of the persons contacted, the approximate dates, and the substance of the information obtained;

(2) How and when you learned about the 15-month deadline for filing Form 1023;

(3) Whether any significant intervening circumstances beyond your control prevented you from submitting the application timely or within a reasonable period of time after you learned of the requirement to file the application within the 15-month period; and

(4) Any other information that you believe may establish good cause for not filing timely or otherwise justify granting the relief sought.

Line 5.—If you answer "No," you may receive an adverse letter limiting the effective date of your exempt status, if:

(1) You are not filing this application within 15 months from the end of the month you were formed;

(2) You do not satisfy any of the exceptions listed in Line 2 of Part III; or

(3) You do not wish to request relief in Line 3, Part III.

Line 6.—The organization may still be able to qualify for exemption under section 501(c)(4) for the period preceding the effective date of its exemption as a section 501(c)(3) organization. If the organization is qualified under section 501(c)(4) and page 1 of Form 1024 is filed as directed, the organization will not be liable for income tax returns as a taxable entity. Contributions to section 501(c)(4) organizations are generally not deductible by donors as charitable contributions.

Line 7.—Private foundations are subject to various requirements, restrictions, and excise taxes under Chapter 42 of the Internal Revenue Code that do not apply to public charities. Also, contributions to private foundations may receive less favorable treatment than contributions to public charities. (See Publication 578.) Therefore, it is usually to an organization's advantage to show that it qualifies as a public charity rather than as a private foundation if its activities or sources of support permit it to do so. Unless an organization meets one of the exceptions below, it is a private foundation. In general, an organization is **not** a private foundation if it is:

(1) a church, school, hospital, or governmental unit;

(2) a medical research organization operated in conjunction with a hospital;

(3) an organization operated for the benefit of a college or university that is owned or operated by a governmental unit;

(4) an organization that normally receives a substantial part of its support in the form of contributions from a governmental unit or from the general public as provided in section 170(b)(1)(A)(vi);

(5) an organization that normally receives not more than one-third of its support from gross investment income and more than one-third of its support from contributions, membership fees, and gross receipts related to its exempt functions (subject to certain exceptions) as provided in section 509(a)(2);

(6) an organization operated solely for the benefit of, and in connection with, one or more organizations described above (or for the benefit of one or more of the organizations described in section 501(c)(4), (5), or (6) of the Code and also described in (5) above), but not controlled by disqualified persons other than foundation managers, as provided in section 509(a)(3); or

(7) an organization organized and operated to test for public safety as provided in section 509(a)(4).

Line 8.—Basis for Private Operating Foundation status: (Complete this question **only** if you answered "Yes" to question 7.)

A "private operating foundation" is a private foundation that spends substantially all of its adjusted net income or its minimum investment return, whichever is less, directly for the active conduct of the activities constituting the purpose or function for which it is organized and operated. The foundation must satisfy the income test and one of the three supplemental tests: **(1)** the assets test; **(2)** the endowment test; or **(3)** the support test. (For additional information, see Publication 578.)

Line 9.—Basis for Non-Private Foundation status: Check the box that shows why you are not a private foundation.

Box (a). A church or convention or association of churches.

Box (b). A school.—See the definition in the instructions for Schedule B.

Box (c). A hospital or medical research organization.—See the instructions for Schedule C.

Box (d). A governmental unit.—This category includes a State, a possession of the United States, or a political subdivision of any of the foregoing, or the United States, or the District of Columbia.

Box (e). Organizations operated in connection with or solely for organizations described in (a) through (d) or (g), (h), and (i).—The organization must be organized and operated for the benefit of, to perform the functions of, or to carry out the purposes of one or more specified organizations described in section 509(a)(1) or (2). It must be operated, supervised, or controlled by or in connection with one or more of the organizations described in the instructions for boxes **(a)** through **(d)** or **(g), (h),** and **(i).** It must not be controlled directly or indirectly by disqualified persons (other than foundation managers or organizations described in section 509(a)(1) or (2)). To show whether the organization satisfies these tests, complete Schedule D.

Box (f). An organization testing for public safety.—An organization in this category is one that tests products to determine their acceptability for use by the general public. It does not include any organization testing for the benefit of a manufacturer as an operation or control in the manufacture of its product.

Box (g). Organization for the benefit of a college or university owned and operated by a governmental unit.—The organization must be organized and operated exclusively for the benefit of a college or university that is an educational organization within the meaning of section 170(b)(1)(A)(ii) and is an agency or instrumentality of a State or political subdivision of a State; is owned or operated by a State or political subdivision of a State; or is owned or operated by an agency or instrumentality of one or more States or political subdivisions. The organization must also normally receive a substantial part of its support from the United States or any State or political subdivision of a State, or from direct or indirect contributions from the general public or from a combination of these sources. An organization described in

Page 4

164

section 170(b)(1)(A)(iv) will be subject to the same publicly supported rules that are applicable to 170(b)(1)(A)(vi) organizations described in box (h) below.

Box (h). Organization receiving support from a governmental unit or from the general public.—The organization must receive a substantial part of its support from the United States or any State or political subdivision, or from direct or indirect contributions from the general public or from a combination of these sources. The organization may satisfy the support requirement in either of two ways. It will be treated as publicly supported if the support it normally receives from the above-described governmental units and the general public equals at least one-third of its total support. It will also be treated as publicly supported if the support it normally receives from governmental or public sources equals at least 10% of total support and the organization is set up to attract new and additional public or governmental support on a continuous basis. If the organization's governmental and public support is at least 10%, but not over one-third of its total support, questions 1 through 13 of Part II will apply to determine both the organization's claim of exemption and whether it is publicly supported. Preparers should exercise care to assure that those questions are answered in detail.

Box (i). Organization described in section 509(a)(2).—The organization must satisfy the support test under section 509(a)(2)(A) and the gross investment income test under section 509(a)(2)(B). To satisfy the support test, the organization must normally receive more than one-third of its support from: **(a)** gifts, grants, contributions, or membership fees, and **(b)** gross receipts from admissions, sales of merchandise, performance of services, or furnishing of facilities, in an activity which is not an unrelated trade or business (subject to certain limitations discussed below). This one-third of support must be from organizations described in section 509(a)(1), governmental sources, or persons other than disqualified persons. In computing gross receipts from admissions, sales of merchandise, performance of services, or furnishing of facilities in an activity that is not an unrelated trade or business, the gross receipts from any one person or from any bureau or similar agency of a governmental unit are includible only to the extent they do not exceed the greater of $5,000 or 1% of the organization's total support. To satisfy the gross investment income test, the organization must not receive more than one-third of its support from gross investment income.

Box (j).—If you believe the organization meets the public support test of section 170(b)(1)(A)(vi) or 509(a)(2) but are uncertain as to which public support test it satisfies, check box (j). By checking this box, you are claiming that the organization is not a private foundation and are agreeing to let the IRS compute the public support of your organization and determine the correct foundation status.

Line 10.—To receive a definitive (final) ruling under sections 170(b)(1)(A)(vi) and 509(a)(1) or under section 509(a)(2), an organization must have completed a tax year consisting of at least 8 months. Organizations that checked box (h), (i), or (j) on line 9 that do not satisfy the 8-month requirement must request an advance ruling covering its first 5 tax years instead of a definitive ruling.

An organization that satisfies the 8-month requirement has two options:

(1) It may request a definitive ruling. In this event, the organization's qualification under sections 170(b)(1)(A)(vi) and 509(a)(1) or under section 509(a)(2) will be based on the support that the organization has received to date; or

(2) It may request an advance ruling. If the Internal Revenue Service issues the advance ruling, the organization's public support computation will be based on the support it receives during its first 5 tax years. An organization should consider this option if it has not received significant public support during its first tax year or during its first and second tax years, but it reasonably expects to receive such support by the end of its fifth tax year. An organization that receives an advance ruling is treated, during the 5-year advance ruling period, as a public charity (rather than a private foundation) for certain purposes, including those relating to the deductibility of contributions by the general public.

Line 11.—For definition of an unusual grant, see instructions for Part IV-A, line 12.

Line 12.—Answer this question only if you checked box (g) or (h) in question 9.

Line 13.—Answer this question only if you checked box (i) in question 9 and are requesting a definitive ruling in question 10.

Line 14.—Answer "Yes" or "No" on each line. If "Yes," you must complete the appropriate Schedule. Each Schedule is included in this application package with accompanying instructions. For a brief definition of each type of organization, see the appropriate Schedule.

Part IV.—Financial Data

The Statement of Revenue and Expenses must be completed **for the current year and each of the 3 years immediately before it** *(or the years the organization has existed, if less than 4). Any applicant that has existed for less than 1 year must give financial data for the current year and proposed budgets for the following 2 years.* We may request financial data for more than 4 years if necessary. All financial information for the current year must cover the period ending within 60 days of the date of application. Prepare the balance sheet as of the last day of the current year period covered by the Statement of Revenue and Expenses. Prepare the statements using the method of accounting the organization uses in keeping its books and records. If the organization uses a method other than the cash receipts and disbursements method, attach a statement explaining the method used.

A. Revenue and Expenses

Line 1.—Do not include amounts received from the general public or a governmental unit for the exercise or performance of the organization's exempt functions. However, payments made by a governmental unit to enable the organization to provide a service to the general public should be included. Also, do not include unusual grants. (For an explanation of unusual grants, see instructions for line 12 below.)

Line 2.—Include amounts received from members for the basic purpose of providing support to the organization. Do not include payments to purchase admissions, merchandise, services, or use of facilities.

Line 3.—Include on this line the income received from dividends, interest, payments received on securities loans, rents, and royalties.

Line 4.—Enter the organization's net income from any activities that are regularly carried on and not related to the organization's exempt purposes. Examples of such income include fees from the commercial testing of products; income from renting office equipment or other personal property; and income from the sale of advertising in an exempt organization periodical. See Publication 598 for information about unrelated business income and activities.

Line 5.—Enter the amount collected by the local tax authority from the general public that has been allocated for your organization.

Line 6.—To report the value of services and/or facilities furnished by a governmental unit, use the fair market value at the time the service/facility was furnished to your organization. Do not include any other donated services or facilities in Part IV.

Line 7.—Enter the total income from all sources that is not reported on lines 1 through 6, or lines 9, 11, and 12. Attach a schedule that lists each type of revenue source and the amount derived from each.

Line 9.—Include income generated by the organization's exempt function activities (charitable, educational, etc.) and by its nontaxable fundraising events (excluding any contributions received). Examples of such income include the income derived by a symphony orchestra from the sale of tickets to its performances; and raffles, bingo, or other fundraising-event income that would not be taxable as unrelated business income because the income-producing activities were not regularly carried on or because they were conducted with substantially all (at least 85%) volunteer labor.

Line 11.—Attach a schedule that shows a description of each asset, the name of the person to whom sold, and the amount received. In the case of publicly traded securities sold through a broker, the name of the purchaser is not required.

Line 12.—Unusual grants generally consist of substantial contributions and bequests from disinterested persons that:

(1) are attracted by reason of the publicly supported nature of the organization;

(2) are unusual and unexpected as to the amount; and

(3) would, by reason of their size, adversely affect the status of the organization as normally meeting the support test of section 170(b)(1)(A)(vi) or section 509(a)(2), as the case may be.

If the organization is awarded an unusual grant and the terms of the granting instrument provide that the organization will receive the funds over a period of years, the amount received by the organization each year under the grant may be excluded. See the regulations under sections 170 and 509.

Line 14.—Fundraising expenses represent the total expenses incurred in soliciting contributions, gifts, grants, etc.

Line 15.—Attach a schedule showing the name of the recipient, a brief description of the purposes or conditions of payment, and the amount paid. The following example shows the format and amount of detail required for this schedule:

Recipient	Purpose	Amount
Museum of Natural History	General operating budget	$9,000
State University	Books for needy students	4,500
Richard Roe	Educational scholarship	2,200

Line 16.—Attach a schedule showing the name of each recipient, a brief description of the purposes or condition of payment, and amount paid. Do not include any amounts that are on line 15. The schedule should be similar to the schedule shown in the line 15 instructions above.

Line 17.—Attach a schedule that shows the name of the person compensated; the office or position; the average amount of time devoted to business per week, month, etc.; and the amount of annual compensation. The following example shows the format and amount of detail required:

Name	Position	Time devoted	Annual salary
Philip Poe	President and general manager	16 hrs. per wk.	$7,500

Line 18.—Enter the total of employees' salaries not reported on line 17.

Line 19.—Enter the total interest expense for the year, excluding mortgage interest treated as occupancy expense on line 20.

Line 20.—Enter the amount paid for the use of office space or other facilities, heat, light, power, and other utilities, outside janitorial services, mortgage interest, real estate taxes, and similar expenses.

Line 21.—If your organization records depreciation, depletion, and similar expenses, enter the total.

Line 22.—Attach a schedule listing the type and amount of each **significant** expense for which a separate line is not provided. Report other miscellaneous expenses as a single total if not substantial in amount.

B. Balance Sheet

Line 1.—Enter the total cash in checking and savings accounts, temporary cash investments (money market funds, CDs, treasury bills or other obligations that mature in less than 1 year), change funds, and petty cash funds.

Line 2.—Enter the total accounts receivable that arose from the sale of goods and/or performance of services.

Line 3.—Enter the amount of materials, goods, and supplies purchased or manufactured by the organization and held to be sold or used in some future period.

Line 4.—Attach a schedule that shows the name of the borrower, a brief description of the obligation, the rate of return on the principal indebtedness, the due date, and the amount due. The following example shows the format and amount of detail required:

Name of borrower	Description of obligation	Rate of return	Due date	Amount
Hope Soap Corporation	Debenture bond (no senior issue outstanding)	10%	Jan. 1999	$ 7,500
Big Spool Company	Collateral note secured by company's fleet of 20 delivery trucks	12%	Jan. 1998	62,000

Line 5.—Attach a schedule listing the organization's corporate stock holdings. For stock of closely held corporations, the statement should show the name of the corporation, a brief summary of the corporation's capital structure, the number of shares held and their value as carried on the organization's books. If such valuation does not reflect current fair market value, also include fair market value. For stock traded on an organized exchange or in substantial quantities over the counter, the statement should show the name of the corporation, a description of the stock and the principal exchange on which it is traded, the number of shares held, and their value as carried on the organization's books. The following example shows the format and the amount of detail required:

Name of corporation	Capital structure (or exchange on which traded)	Shares	Book amount	Fair market value
Little Spool Corporation	100 shares nonvoting preferred issued and outstanding, no par value; 50 shares common issued and outstanding, no par value.			
	Preferred shares:	50	$20,000	$24,000
	Common shares:	10	25,000	30,000
Flintlock Corporation	Class A common N.Y.S.E.	20	3,000	3,500

Line 6.—Report each loan separately, even if more than one loan was made to the same person. Attach a schedule that shows the borrower's name, purpose of loan, repayment terms, interest rate, and original amount of loan.

Line 7.—Enter the book value of securities held of the U.S., State, or municipal government. Also enter the book value of buildings and equipment held for investment purposes. Attach a schedule identifying and reporting the book value of each.

Line 8.—Enter the book value of buildings and equipment **not** held for investment. This would include plant and equipment used by the organization in conducting its exempt activities. Attach a schedule listing these assets held at the end of the current tax-year period and the cost or other basis.

Line 9.—Enter the book value of land **not** held for investment.

Line 10.—Enter the book value of each category of assets not reported on lines 1 through 9. Attach a schedule listing each.

Line 12.—Enter the total of accounts payable to suppliers and others, such as: salaries payable, accrued payroll taxes, and interest payable.

Line 13.—Enter the unpaid portion of grants and contributions that the organization has made a commitment to pay other organizations or individuals.

Line 14.—Enter the total of mortgages and other notes payable at the end of the current tax-year period. Attach a schedule that shows each item separately and the lender's name, purpose of loan, repayment terms, interest rate, and original amount.

Line 15.—Enter the amount of each liability not reported on lines 12 through 14. Attach a separate schedule.

Line 17.—Under fund accounting, an organization segregates its assets, liabilities, and net assets into separate funds according to restrictions on the use of certain assets. Each fund is like a separate entity in that it has a self-balancing set of accounts showing assets, liabilities, equity (fund balance), income, and expenses. If the organization does not use fund accounting, report only the "net assets" account balances, such as: capital stock, paid-in capital, and retained earnings or accumulated income.

Procedural Checklist

Make sure your application is complete.

If you do not complete all applicable parts of the application or do not provide all required attachments, we may return the incomplete application to you for resubmission with the missing information or attachments. This will delay the processing of your application and may delay the effective date of your exempt status. You may also incur additional user fees.

Have you . . .

_____ Attached **Form 8718** (User Fee for Exempt Organization Determination Letter Request) along with the appropriate fee?

_____ Located the correct **key district office** for the mailing of your application? (See "Where To File" on page 1 under General Instructions.) Do **not** file the application with your local Internal Revenue Service Center.

_____ Completed Parts I through IV and any other Schedules that apply to the organization?

_____ Shown your **employer identification number**?
a. If your organization has one, write it in the space provided.
b. If you are a newly formed organization and do not have an employer identification number, attach a completed Form SS-4 if you have not already applied for one.

_____ Described your organization's **specific activities** as directed in Part II, question 1 of the application?

_____ Included a **conformed copy** of the complete organizing instrument? (See Part I, question 10 instructions.)

_____ Had the application signed by one of the following:
a. An officer or trustee who is authorized to sign (e.g., President, Treasurer); or
b. A person authorized by a power of attorney (submit Form 2848, 8821, or other power of attorney)?

_____ Enclosed **financial statements** (Part IV)?
a. Current year (must include period up to within 60 days of the date the application is filed) and 3 preceding years.
b. Detailed breakdown of revenue and expenses (no lump sums).
c. If the organization has been in existence less than one year, you must also submit proposed budgets for 2 years showing the amounts and types of receipts and expenditures anticipated.

Note: _During the technical review of a completed application by the Employee Plans/Exempt Organization's Division in the key district or by Exempt Organizations Technical Division in the National Office, it may be necessary to contact you for more specific or additional information._

Do not send this checklist with your application.

Page 7

Activity Code Numbers of Exempt Organizations (select up to three codes which best describe or most accurately identify your purposes, activities operations or type of organization and enter in block 6, page 1, of the application. Enter first the code which most accurately identifies you.)

Code

Religious Activities

- 001 Church, synagogue, etc.
- 002 Association or convention of churches
- 003 Religious order
- 004 Church auxiliary
- 005 Mission
- 006 Missionary activities
- 007 Evangelism
- 008 Religious publishing activities
- ---- Bookstore (use 918)
- ---- Genealogical activities (use 094)
- 029 Other religious activities

Schools, Colleges and Related Activities

- 030 School, college, trade school, etc.
- 031 Special school for the blind, handicapped, etc.
- 032 Nursery school
- ---- Day care center (use 574)
- 033 Faculty group
- 034 Alumni association or group
- 035 Parent or parent-teachers association
- 036 Fraternity or sorority
- ---- Key club (use 323)
- 037 Other student society or group
- 038 School or college athletic association
- 039 Scholarships for children of employees
- 040 Scholarships (other)
- 041 Student loans
- 042 Student housing activities
- 043 Other student aid
- 044 Student exchange with foreign country
- 045 Student operated business
- ---- Financial support of schools, colleges, etc. (use 602)
- ---- Achievement prizes or awards (use 914)
- ---- Student bookstore (use 918)
- ---- Student travel (use 299)
- ---- Scientific research (see Scientific Research Activities)
- 046 Private school
- 059 Other school related activities

Cultural, Historical or Other Educational Activities

- 060 Musuem, zoo, planetarium, etc.
- 061 Library
- 062 Historical site, records or reenactment
- 063 Monument
- 064 Commemorative event (centennial, festival, pageant, etc.)
- 065 Fair
- 088 Community theatrical group
- 089 Singing society or group
- 090 Cultural performances
- 091 Art exhibit
- 092 Literary activities
- 093 Cultural exchanges with foreign country
- 094 Genealogical activities
- ---- Achievement prizes or awards (use 914)
- ---- Gifts or grants to individuals (use 561)
- ---- Financial support of cultural organizations (use 602)
- 119 Other cultural or historical activities

Other Instruction and Training Activities

- 120 Publishing activities
- 121 Radio or television broadcasting
- 122 Producing films
- 123 Discussion groups, forums, panels, lectures, etc.
- 124 Study and research (non-scientific)
- 125 Giving information or opinion (see also Advocacy)
- 126 Apprentice training
- ---- Travel tours (use 299)
- 149 Other instruction and training

Health Services and Related Activities

- 150 Hospital
- 151 Hospital auxiliary
- 152 Nursing or convalescent home
- 153 Care and housing for the aged (see also 382)
- 154 Health clinic
- 155 Rural medical facility
- 156 Blood bank
- 157 Cooperative hospital service organization
- 158 Rescue and emergency service
- 159 Nurses register or bureau
- 160 Aid to the handicapped (see also 031)
- 161 Scientific research (diseases)
- 162 Other medical research
- 163 Health insurance (medical, dental, optical, etc.)
- 164 Prepared group health plan
- 165 Community health planning
- 166 Mental health care
- 167 Group medical practice association
- 168 In-faculty group practice association
- 169 Hospital pharmacy, parking facility, food services, etc.
- 179 Other health services

Scientific Research Activities

- 180 Contract or sponsored scientific research for industry
- 181 Scientific research for government
- ---- Scientific research (diseases) (use 161)
- 199 Other scientific research activities

Business and Professional Organizations

- 200 Business promotion (chamber of commerce, business league, etc.)
- 201 Real estate association
- 202 Board of trade
- 203 Regulating business
- 204 Promotion of fair business practices
- 205 Professional association
- 206 Professional association auxiliary
- 207 Industry trade shows
- 208 Convention displays
- ---- Testing products for public safety (use 905)
- 209 Research, development and testing
- 210 Professional athletic league
- ---- Attracting new industry (use 403)
- ---- Publishing activities (use 120)
- ---- Insurance or other benefits for members (see Employee or Membership Benefit Organizations)
- 211 Underwriting municipal insurance
- 212 Assigned risk insurance activities
- 213 Tourist bureau
- 229 Other business or professional group

Farming and Related Activities

- 230 Farming
- 231 Farm bureau
- 232 Agricultural group
- 233 Horticultural group
- 234 Farmers cooperative marketing or purchasing
- 235 Financing crop operations
- ---- FFA, FHA, 4-H club, etc. (use 322)
- ---- Fair (use 065)
- 236 Dairy herd improvement association
- 237 Breeders association
- 249 Other farming and related activities

Mutual Organizations

- 250 Mutual ditch, irrigation, telephone, electric company or like organization
- 251 Credit union
- 252 Reserve funds or insurance for domestic building and loan association, cooperative bank, or mutual savings bank
- 253 Mutual insurance company
- 254 Corporation organized under an Act of Congress (see also 904)
- ---- Farmers cooperative marketing or purchasing (use 234)
- ---- Cooperative hospital service organization (use 157)
- 259 Other mutual organization

Employee or Membership Benefit Organizations

- 260 Fraternal beneficiary society, order, or association
- 261 Improvement of conditions of workers
- 262 Association of municipal employees
- 263 Association of employees
- 264 Employee or member welfare association
- 265 Sick, accident, death, or similar benefits
- 266 Strike benefits
- 267 Unemployment benefits
- 268 Pension or retirement benefits
- 269 Vacation benefits
- 279 Other services or benefits to members or employees

Sports, Athletic, Recreational and Social Activities

- 280 Country club
- 281 Hobby club
- 282 Dinner club
- 283 Variety club
- 284 Dog club
- 285 Women's club
- ---- Garden club (use 356)
- 286 Hunting or fishing club
- 287 Swimming or tennis club
- 288 Other sports club
- ---- Boys Club, Little League, etc. (use 321)
- 296 Community center
- 297 Community recreational facilities (park, playground, etc.)
- 298 Training in sports
- 299 Travel tours
- 300 Amateur athletic association
- ---- School or college athletic association (use 038)
- 301 Fundraising athletic or sports event
- 317 Other sports or athletic activities
- 318 Other recreational activities
- 319 Other social activities

Youth Activities

- 320 Boy Scouts, Girl Scouts, etc.
- 321 Boys Club, Little League, etc.
- 322 FFA, FHA, 4-H club, etc.
- 323 Key club
- 324 YMCA, YWCA, YMHA, etc.
- 325 Camp
- 326 Care and housing of children (orphanage, etc.)
- 327 Prevention of cruelty to children
- 328 Combat juvenile delinquency
- 349 Other youth organization or activities

Conservation, Environmental and Beautification Activities

- 350 Preservation of natural resources (conservation)
- 351 Combating or preventing pollution (air, water, etc.)
- 352 Land acquisition for preservation
- 353 Soil or water conservation
- 354 Preservation of scenic beauty
- ---- Litigation (see Litigation and Legal Aid Activities)
- ---- Combat community deterioration (use 402)
- 355 Wildlife sanctuary or refuge
- 356 Garden club
- 379 Other conservation, environmental or beautification activities

Housing Activities

- 380 Low-income housing
- 381 Low and moderate income housing
- 382 Housing for the aged (see also 153)
- ---- Nursing or convalescent home (use 152)
- ---- Student housing (use 042)
- ---- Orphanage (use 326)
- 398 Instruction and guidance on housing
- 399 Other housing activities

Inner City or Community Activities

- 400 Area development, redevelopment or renewal
- ---- Housing (see Housing Activities)
- 401 Homeowners association
- 402 Other activity aimed at combating community deterioration
- 403 Attracting new industry or retaining industry in an area
- 404 Community promotion
- ---- Community recreational facility (use 297)
- ---- Community center (use 296)
- 405 Loans or grants for minority businesses
- ---- Job training, counseling, or assistance (use 566)
- ---- Day care center (use 574)
- ---- Referral service (social agencies) (use 569)
- ---- Legal aid to indigents (use 462)
- 406 Crime prevention
- 407 Voluntary firemen's organization or auxiliary
- ---- Rescue squad (use 158)
- 408 Community service organization
- 429 Other inner city or community benefit activities

Civil Rights Activities

- 430 Defense of human and civil rights
- 431 Elimination of prejudice and discrimination (race, religion, sex, national origin, etc.)
- 432 Lessen neighborhood tensions
- 449 Other civil rights activities

Litigation and Legal Aid Activities

- 460 Public interest litigation activities
- 461 Other litigation or support of litigation
- 462 Legal aid to indigents
- 463 Providing bail
- 465 Plan under IRC section 120

Legislative and Political Activities

- 480 Propose, support, or oppose legislation
- 481 Voter information on issues or candidates
- 482 Voter education (mechanics of registering, voting, etc.)
- 483 Support, oppose, or rate political candidates
- 484 Provide facilities or services for political campaign activities
- 509 Other legislative and political activities

Advocacy

Attempt to influence public opinion concerning:

- 510 Firearms control
- 511 Selective Service System
- 512 National defense policy
- 513 Weapons systems
- 514 Government spending
- 515 Taxes or tax exemption
- 516 Separation of church and state
- 517 Government aid to parochial schools
- 518 U.S. foreign policy
- 519 U.S. military involvement
- 520 Pacifism and peace
- 521 Economic-political system of U.S.
- 522 Anti-communism
- 523 Right to work
- 524 Zoning or rezoning
- 525 Location of highway or transportation system
- 526 Rights of criminal defendants
- 527 Capital punishment
- 528 Stricter law enforcement
- 529 Ecology or conservation
- 530 Protection of consumer interests
- 531 Medical care service
- 532 Welfare system
- 533 Urban renewal
- 534 Busing students to achieve racial balance
- 535 Racial integration
- 536 Use of intoxicating bevarage
- 537 Use of drugs or narcotics
- 538 Use of tobacco
- 539 Prohibition of erotica
- 540 Sex education in public schools
- 541 Population control
- 542 Birth control methods
- 543 Legalized abortion
- 559 Other matters

Other Activities Directed to Individuals

- 560 Supplying money, goods or services to the poor
- 561 Gifts or grants to individuals (other than scholarships)
- ---- Scholarships for children of employees (use 039)
- ---- Scholarships (other) (use 040)
- ---- Student loans (use 041)
- 562 Other loans to individuals
- 563 Marriage counseling
- 564 Family planning
- 565 Credit counseling and assistance
- 566 Job training, counseling, or assistance
- 567 Draft counseling
- 568 Vocational counseling
- 569 Referral service (social agencies)
- 572 Rehabilitating convicts or ex-convicts
- 573 Rehabilitating alcoholics, drug abusers, compulsive gamblers, etc.
- 574 Day care center
- 575 Services for the aged (see also 153 and 382)
- ---- Training of or aid to the handicapped (see 031 and 160)

Activities Directed to Other Organizations

- 600 Community Chest, United Way, etc.
- 601 Booster club
- 602 Gifts, grants, or loans to other organizations
- 603 Non-financial services or facilities to other organizations

Other Purposes and Activities

- 900 Cemetery or burial activities
- 901 Perpetual care fund (cemetery, columbarium, etc.)
- 902 Emergency or disaster aid fund
- 903 Community trust or component
- 904 Government instrumentality or agency (see also 254)
- 905 Testing products for public safety
- 906 Consumer interest group
- 907 Veterans activities
- 908 Patriotic activities
- 909 4947(a)(1) trust
- 910 Domestic organization with activities outside U.S.
- 911 Foreign organization
- 912 Title holding corporation
- 913 Prevention of cruelty to animals
- 914 Achievement prizes or awards
- 915 Erection or maintenance of public building or works
- 916 Cafeteria, restaurant, snack bar, food services, etc.
- 917 Thrift shop, retail outlet, etc.
- 918 Book, gift or supply store
- 919 Advertising
- 920 Association of employees
- 921 Loans or credit reporting
- 922 Endowment fund or financial services
- 923 Indians (tribes, cultures, etc.)
- 924 Traffic or tariff bureau
- 925 Section 501(c)(1) with 50% deductibility
- 926 Government instrumentality other than section 501(c)
- 927 Fundraising
- 928 4947(a)(2) trust
- 930 Prepaid legal services plan exempt under IRC section 501(c)(20)
- 931 Withdrawal liability payment fund
- 990 Section 501(k) child care organization

Form **1023**

(Rev. September 1990)

Department of the Treasury
Internal Revenue Service

Application for Recognition of Exemption
Under Section 501(c)(3) of the Internal Revenue Code

OMB No. 1545-0056

If exempt status is approved, this application will be open for public inspection.

Read the instructions for each Part carefully.
A User Fee must be attached to this application.

If the required information and appropriate documents are not submitted along with Form 8718 (with payment of the appropriate user fee), the application may be returned to you.

Part I   Identification of Applicant

1a Full name of organization (as shown in organizing document)

2 Employer identification number **(If none, see instructions.)**

1b c/o Name (if applicable)

3 Name and telephone number of person to be contacted if additional information is needed

1c Address (number, street, and room or suite no.)

(   )

1d City or town, state, and ZIP code

4 Month the annual accounting period ends

5 Date incorporated or formed

6 Activity codes (See instructions.)

7 Check here if applying under section:
a ☐ 501(e)   b ☐ 501(f)   c ☐ 501(k)

8 Did the organization previously apply for recognition of exemption under this Code section or under any other section of the Code? . . . . ☐ Yes   ☐ No
If "Yes," attach an explanation.

9 Has the organization filed Federal income tax returns or exempt organization information returns? . . . . . ☐ Yes   ☐ No
If "Yes," state the form numbers, years filed, and Internal Revenue office where filed.

10 Check the box for your type of organization. BE SURE TO ATTACH A COMPLETE COPY OF THE CORRESPONDING DOCUMENTS TO THE APPLICATION BEFORE MAILING.

a ☐ Corporation— Attach a copy of your Articles of Incorporation, (including amendments and restatements) showing approval by the appropriate State official; also include a copy of your bylaws.

b ☐ Trust— Attach a copy of your Trust Indenture or Agreement, including all appropriate signatures and dates.

c ☐ Association— Attach a copy of your Articles of Association, Constitution, or other creating document, with a declaration (see instructions) or other evidence the organization was formed by adoption of the document by more than one person; also include a copy of your bylaws.

If you are a corporation or an unincorporated association that has not yet adopted bylaws, check here . . . . ▶ ☐

I declare under the penalties of perjury that I am authorized to sign this application on behalf of the above organization and that I have examined this application, including the accompanying schedules and attachments, and to the best of my knowledge it is true, correct, and complete.

Please Sign Here ▶

_____   _____   _____
(Signature)   (Title or authority of signer)   (Date)

For Paperwork Reduction Act Notice, see page 1 of the instructions.

Complete the Procedural Checklist (page 7 of the instructions) prior to filing.

169

Part II   **Activities and Operational Information**

1   Provide a detailed narrative description of all the activities of the organization—past, present, and planned. **Do not merely refer to or repeat the language in your organizational document.** Describe each activity separately in the order of importance. Each description should include, as a minimum, the following: **(a)** a detailed description of the activity including its purpose; **(b)** when the activity was or will be initiated; and **(c)** where and by whom the activity will be conducted.

2   What are or will be the organization's sources of financial support? List in order of size.

3   Describe the organization's fundraising program, both actual and planned, and explain to what extent it has been put into effect. Include details of fundraising activities such as selective mailings, formation of fundraising committees, use of volunteers or professional fundraisers, etc. Attach representative copies of solicitations for financial support.

Part II	**Activities and Operational Information** (Continued)

4   Give the following information about the organization's governing body:

a Names, addresses, and titles of officers, directors, trustees, etc.	**b** Annual Compensation

c   Do any of the above persons serve as members of the governing body by reason of being public officials or being appointed by public officials? . . . . ☐ **Yes**   ☐ **No**
If "Yes," name those persons and explain the basis of their selection or appointment.

d   Are any members of the organization's governing body "disqualified persons" with respect to the organization (other than by reason of being a member of the governing body) or do any of the members have either a business or family relationship with "disqualified persons"? (See the specific instructions for line 4d.) . . . . ☐ **Yes**   ☐ **No**
If "Yes," explain.

5   Does the organization control or is it controlled by any other organization? . . . . ☐ **Yes**   ☐ **No**
Is the organization the outgrowth of (or successor to) another organization, or does it have a special relationship with another organization by reason of interlocking directorates or other factors? . . . . ☐ **Yes**   ☐ **No**
If either of these questions is answered "Yes," explain.

6   Does or will the organization directly or indirectly engage in any of the following transactions with any political organization or other exempt organization (other than 501(c)(3) organizations): **(a)** grants; **(b)** purchases or sales of assets; **(c)** rental of facilities or equipment; **(d)** loans or loan guarantees; **(e)** reimbursement arrangements; **(f)** performance of services, membership, or fundraising solicitations; or **(g)** sharing of facilities, equipment, mailing lists or other assets, or paid employees? . . . . ☐ **Yes**   ☐ **No**
If "Yes," explain fully and identify the other organizations involved.

7   Is the organization financially accountable to any other organization? . . . . ☐ **Yes**   ☐ **No**
If "Yes," explain and identify the other organization. Include details concerning accountability or attach copies of reports if any have been submitted.

Part II   **Activities and Operational Information** *(Continued)*

4   Give the following information about the organization's governing body:

a   Names, addresses, and titles of officers, directors, trustees, etc.

b Annual Compensation

c   Do any of the above persons serve as members of the governing body by reason of being public officials or being appointed by public officials? . . . .   ☐ **Yes**   ☐ **No**

If "Yes," name those persons and explain the basis of their selection or appointment.

d   Are any members of the organization's governing body "disqualified persons" with respect to the organization (other than by reason of being a member of the governing body) or do any of the members have either a business or family relationship with "disqualified persons"? (See the specific instructions for line 4d.) . . . .   ☐ **Yes**   ☐ **No**

If "Yes," explain.

5   Does the organization control or is it controlled by any other organization? . . . .   ☐ **Yes**   ☐ **No**

Is the organization the outgrowth of (or successor to) another organization, or does it have a special relationship with another organization by reason of interlocking directorates or other factors? . . . .   ☐ **Yes**   ☐ **No**

If either of these questions is answered "Yes," explain.

6   Does or will the organization directly or indirectly engage in any of the following transactions with any political organization or other exempt organization (other than 501(c)(3) organizations): **(a)** grants; **(b)** purchases or sales of assets; **(c)** rental of facilities or equipment; **(d)** loans or loan guarantees; **(e)** reimbursement arrangements; **(f)** performance of services, membership, or fundraising solicitations; or **(g)** sharing of facilities, equipment, mailing lists or other assets, or paid employees? . . . .   ☐ **Yes**   ☐ **No**

If "Yes," explain fully and identify the other organizations involved.

7   Is the organization financially accountable to any other organization? . . . .   ☐ **Yes**   ☐ **No**

If "Yes," explain and identify the other organization. Include details concerning accountability or attach copies of reports if any have been submitted.

172

Part III	**Technical Requirements**

1   Are you filing Form 1023 within 15 months from the end of the month in which you were created or formed?   ☐ **Yes**   ☐ **No**
If you answer "Yes," do not answer questions 2 through 6.

2   If one of the exceptions to the 15-month filing requirement shown below applies, check the appropriate box and proceed to question 7.

Exceptions—You are not required to file an exemption application within 15 months if the organization:

☐ **(a)** Is a church, interchurch organization, local unit of a church, a convention or association of churches, or an integrated auxiliary of a church;

☐ **(b)** Is not a private foundation and normally has gross receipts of not more than $5,000 in each tax year; or,

☐ **(c)** Is a subordinate organization covered by a group exemption letter, but only if the parent or supervisory organization timely submitted a notice covering the subordinate.

3   If you do not meet any of the exceptions in question 2, do you wish to request relief from the 15-month filing requirement? . . . .   ☐ **Yes**   ☐ **No**

4   If you answer "Yes" to question 3, please give your reasons for not filing this application within 15 months from the end of the month in which your organization was created or formed. (**See the Instructions before completing this item.**)

5   If you answer "No" to both questions 1 and 3 and do not meet any of the exceptions in question 2, your qualification as a section 501(c)(3) organization can be recognized only from the date this application is filed with your key District Director. Therefore, do you want us to consider your application as a request for recognition of exemption as a section 501(c)(3) organization from the date the application is received and not retroactively to the date you were formed? . . . .   ☐ **Yes**   ☐ **No**

6   If you answer "Yes" to question 5 above and wish to request recognition of section 501(c)(4) status for the period beginning with the date you were formed and ending with the date your Form 1023 application was received (the effective date of your section 501(c)(3) status), check here ▶ ☐ and attach a completed page 1 of Form 1024 to this application.

Part III **Technical Requirements** *(Continued)*

7 Is the organization a private foundation?
   ☐ **Yes** (Answer question 8.)
   ☐ **No**   (Answer question 9 and proceed as instructed.)

8 If you answer "Yes" to question 7, do you claim to be a private operating foundation?
   ☐ **Yes** (Complete Schedule E)
   ☐ **No**

   After answering this question, go to Part IV.

9 If you answer "No" to question 7, indicate the public charity classification you are requesting by checking the box below that most appropriately applies:

   THE ORGANIZATION IS NOT A PRIVATE FOUNDATION BECAUSE IT QUALIFIES:

   (a) ☐ As a church or a convention or association of churches
   (CHURCHES MUST COMPLETE SCHEDULE A).
   Sections 509(a)(1) and 170(b)(1)(A)(i)

   (b) ☐ As a school (MUST COMPLETE SCHEDULE B).
   Sections 509(a)(1) and 170(b)(1)(A)(ii)

   (c) ☐ As a hospital or a cooperative hospital service organization, or a medical research organization operated in conjunction with a hospital (MUST COMPLETE SCHEDULE C).
   Sections 509(a)(1) and 170(b)(1)(A)(iii)

   (d) ☐ As a governmental unit described in section 170(c)(1).
   Sections 509(a)(1) and 170(b)(1)(A)(v)

   (e) ☐ As being operated solely for the benefit of, or in connection with, one or more of the organizations described in (a) through (d), (g), (h), or (i) (MUST COMPLETE SCHEDULE D).
   Section 509(a)(3)

   (f) ☐ As being organized and operated exclusively for testing for public safety.
   Section 509(a)(4)

   (g) ☐ As being operated for the benefit of a college or university that is owned or operated by a governmental unit.
   Sections 509(a)(1) and 170(b)(1)(A)(iv)

   (h) ☐ As receiving a substantial part of its support in the form of contributions from publicly supported organizations, from a governmental unit, or from the general public.
   Sections 509(a)(1) and 170(b)(1)(A)(vi)

   (i) ☐ As normally receiving not more than one-third of its support from gross investment income and more than one-third of its support from contributions, membership fees, and gross receipts from activities related to its exempt functions (subject to certain exceptions).
   Section 509(a)(2)

   (j) ☐ We are a publicly supported organization but are not sure whether we meet the public support test of block (h) or block (i). We would like the Internal Revenue Service to decide the proper classification.
   Sections 509(a)(1) and 170(b)(1)(A)(vi) or Section 509(a)(2)

   If you checked one of the boxes (a) through (f) in question 9, go to question 14.
   If you checked box (g) in question 9, go to questions 11 and 12.
   If you checked box (h), (i), or (j), go to question 10.

Part III	Technical Requirements *(Continued)*

10 If you checked box (h), (i), or (j) in question 9, have you completed a tax year of at least 8 months?

    ☐ Yes—Indicate whether you are requesting:

        ☐ A definitive ruling (Answer questions 11 through 14.)

        ☐ An advance ruling (Answer questions 11 and 14 and attach 2 Forms 872-C completed and signed.)

    ☐ No—**You must request an advance ruling by completing and signing 2 Forms 872-C and attaching them to your application.**

11 If the organization received any unusual grants during any of the tax years shown in Part IV-A, attach a list for each year showing the name of the contributor; the date and the amount of the grant; and a brief description of the nature of the grant.

12 If you are requesting a definitive ruling under section 170(b)(1)(A)(iv) or (vi), check here ▶ ☐ and:

    a Enter 2% of line 8, column (e) of Part IV-A _____

    b Attach a list showing the name and amount contributed by each person (other than a governmental unit or "publicly supported" organization) whose total gifts, grants, contributions, etc., were more than the amount you entered on line **12a** above.

13 If you are requesting a definitive ruling under section 509(a)(2), check here ▶ ☐ and:

    a For each of the years included on lines 1, 2, and 9 of Part IV-A, attach a list showing the name of and amount received from each "disqualified person."

    b For each of the years included on line 9 of Part IV-A, attach a list showing the name of and amount received from each payer (other than a "disqualified person") whose payments to the organization were more than $5,000. For this purpose, "payer" includes, but is not limited to, any organization described in sections 170(b)(1)(A)(i) through (vi) and any governmental agency or bureau.

14 Indicate if your organization is one of the following. If so, complete the required schedule. (Submit only those schedules that apply to your organization. **Do not submit blank schedules.**)

	Yes	No	If "Yes," complete Schedule:
Is the organization a church?			A
Is the organization, or any part of it, a school?			B
Is the organization, or any part of it, a hospital or medical research organization?			C
Is the organization a section 509(a)(3) supporting organization?			D
Is the organization an operating foundation?			E
Is the organization, or any part of it, a home for the aged or handicapped?			F
Is the organization, or any part of it, a child care organization?			G
Does the organization provide or administer any scholarship benefits, student aid, etc.?			H
Has the organization taken over, or will it take over, the facilities of a "for profit" institution?			I

Part IV   **Financial Data**

Complete the financial statements for the current year and for each of the 3 years immediately before it. If in existence less than 4 years, complete the statements for each year in existence. **If in existence less than 1 year, also provide proposed budgets for the 2 years following the current year.**

A.—Statement of Revenue and Expenses

		Current tax year	3 prior tax years or proposed budget for 2 years			
		(a) From _____ to	**(b)** 19	**(c)** 19	**(d)** 19	**(e)** TOTAL
Revenue	1 Gifts, grants, and contributions received (not including unusual grants—see instructions)					
	2 Membership fees received					
	3 Gross investment income (see instructions for definition)					
	4 Net income from organization's unrelated business activities not included on line 3					
	5 Tax revenues levied for and either paid to or spent on behalf of the organization					
	6 Value of services or facilities furnished by a governmental unit to the organization without charge (not including the value of services or facilities generally furnished the public without charge)					
	7 Other income (not including gain or loss from sale of capital assets) (attach schedule)					
	8 **Total** (add lines 1 through 7)					
	9 Gross receipts from admissions, sales of merchandise or services, or furnishing of facilities in any activity that is not an unrelated business within the meaning of section 513					
	10 **Total** (add lines 8 and 9)					
	11 Gain or loss from sale of capital assets (attach schedule)					
	12 Unusual grants					
	13 **Total** revenue (add lines 10 through 12)					
Expenses	14 Fundraising expenses					
	15 Contributions, gifts, grants, and similar amounts paid (attach schedule)					
	16 Disbursements to or for benefit of members (attach schedule)					
	17 Compensation of officers, directors, and trustees (attach schedule)					
	18 Other salaries and wages					
	19 Interest					
	20 Occupancy (rent, utilities, etc.)					
	21 Depreciation and depletion					
	22 Other (attach schedule)					
	23 **Total** expenses (add lines 14 through 22)					
	24 Excess of revenue over expenses (line 13 minus line 23)					

176

Part IV	**Financial Data** *(Continued)*

B.—Balance Sheet (at the end of the period shown)		Current tax year
		Date ....

Assets

1	Cash	**1**	
2	Accounts receivable, net	**2**	
3	Inventories	**3**	
4	Bonds and notes receivable (attach schedule)	**4**	
5	Corporate stocks (attach schedule)	**5**	
6	Mortgage loans (attach schedule)	**6**	
7	Other investments (attach schedule)	**7**	
8	Depreciable and depletable assets (attach schedule)	**8**	
9	Land	**9**	
10	Other assets (attach schedule)	**10**	
11	**Total assets** (add lines 1 through 10)	**11**	

Liabilities

12	Accounts payable	**12**	
13	Contributions, gifts, grants, etc., payable	**13**	
14	Mortgages and notes payable (attach schedule)	**14**	
15	Other liabilities (attach schedule)	**15**	
16	**Total liabilities** (add lines 12 through 15)	**16**	

Fund Balances or Net Assets

17	Total fund balances or net assets	**17**	
18	**Total liabilities and fund balances or net assets** (add line 16 and line 17)	**18**	

If there has been any substantial change in any aspect of your financial activities since the end of the period shown above, check
the box and attach a detailed explanation . . . . ▶ ☐

177

Schedule A.—Churches

1   Provide a brief history of the development of the organization, including the reasons for its formation.

2   Does the organization have a written creed or statement of faith? . . . . ☐ Yes   ☐ No
    If "Yes," attach a copy.

3   Does the organization require prospective members to renounce other religious beliefs or their membership in other churches or religious orders to become members? . . . . ☐ Yes   ☐ No

4   Does the organization have a formal code of doctrine and discipline for its members? . . . . ☐ Yes   ☐ No
    If "Yes," describe.

5   Describe your form of worship and attach a schedule of your worship services.

6   Are your services open to the public? . . . . ☐ Yes   ☐ No
    If "Yes," describe how you publicize your services and explain your criteria for admittance.

7   Explain how you attract new members.

8   (a) How many active members are currently enrolled in your church?

    (b) What is the average attendance at your worship services?

9   In addition to your worship services, what other religious services (such as baptisms, weddings, funerals, etc.) do you conduct?

Schedule A.—Churches *(Continued)*

10 Does the organization have a school for the religious instruction of the young? . ☐ **Yes**   ☐ **No**

11 Were your current deacons, minister, and pastor formally ordained after a prescribed course of study? . . . . ☐ **Yes**   ☐ **No**

12 Describe your religious hierarchy or ecclesiastical government.

13 Does your organization have an established place of worship? . . . . ☐ **Yes**   ☐ **No**

If "Yes," provide the name and address of the owner or lessor of the property and the address and a description of the facility.

If you have no regular place of worship, state where your services are held and how the site is selected.

14 Does (or will) the organization license or otherwise ordain ministers (or their equivalent) or issue church charters? . . . . ☐ **Yes**   ☐ **No**

If "Yes," describe in detail the requirements and qualifications needed to be so licensed, ordained, or chartered.

15 Did the organization pay a fee for a church charter? . . . . ☐ **Yes**   ☐ **No**

If "Yes," state the name and address of the organization to which the fee was paid, attach a copy of the charter, and describe the circumstances surrounding the chartering.

16 Show how many hours a week your minister/pastor and officers each devote to church work and the amount of compensation paid each of them. If your minister or pastor is otherwise employed, indicate by whom employed, the nature of the employment, and the hours devoted to that employment.

Schedule A.—Churches *(Continued)*

17 Will any funds or property of your organization be used by any officer, director, employee, minister, or pastor for his or her personal needs or convenience? . . . . ☐ **Yes**   ☐ **No**

If "Yes," describe the nature and circumstances of such use.

18 List any officers, directors, or trustees related by blood or marriage.

19 Give the name of anyone who has assigned income to you or made substantial contributions of money or other property. Specify the amounts involved.

Instructions

Although a church, its integrated auxiliaries, or a convention or association of churches is not required to file Form 1023 to be exempt from Federal income tax or to receive tax deductible contributions, such an organization may find it advantageous to obtain recognition of exemption. In this event, you should submit information showing that your organization is a church, synagogue, association or convention of churches, religious order or religious organization that is an integral part of a church, and that it is carrying out the functions of a church.

In determining whether an admittedly religious organization is also a church, the Internal Revenue Service does not accept any and every assertion that such an organization is a church. Because beliefs and practices vary so widely, there is no single definition of the word "church" for tax purposes. The Internal Revenue Service considers the facts and circumstances of each organization applying for church status.

The Internal Revenue Service maintains two basic guidelines in determining that an organization meets the religious purposes test:

(a)   that the particular religious beliefs of the organization are truly and sincerely held, and

(b)   that the practices and rituals associated with the organization's religious beliefs or creed are not illegal or contrary to clearly defined public policy.

In order for the Internal Revenue Service to properly evaluate your organization's activities and religious purposes, it is important that all questions in this Schedule are answered accurately.

The information submitted with this Schedule will be a determining factor in granting the "church" status requested by your organization. In completing the Schedule, the following points should be considered:

(a)   The organization's activities in furtherance of its beliefs must be exclusively religious,

(b)   An organization will not qualify for exemption if it has a substantial nonexempt purpose of serving the private interests of its founder or the founder's family.

Schedule B.—Schools, Colleges, and Universities

1   Does, or will, the organization normally have: **(a)** a regularly scheduled curriculum, **(b)** a regular faculty of qualified teachers, **(c)** a regularly enrolled body of students, and **(d)** facilities where its educational activities are regularly carried on? . . . . ☐ **Yes**   ☐ **No**

   If "No," do not complete the rest of this Schedule.

2   Is the organization an instrumentality of a State or political subdivision of a State? . . . . ☐ **Yes**   ☐ **No**

   If "Yes," document this in Part II and do not complete items 3 through 10 of this Schedule. (See instructions for Schedule B.)

3   Does or will the organization (or any department or division within it) discriminate in any way on the basis of race with respect to:

a   Admissions? . . . . ☐ **Yes**   ☐ **No**

b   Use of facilities or exercise of student privileges? . . . . ☐ **Yes**   ☐ **No**

c   Faculty or administrative staff? . . . . ☐ **Yes**   ☐ **No**

d   Scholarship or loan programs? . . . . ☐ **Yes**   ☐ **No**

   If "Yes" for any of the above, explain.

4   Does the organization include a statement in its charter, bylaws, or other governing instrument, or in a resolution of its governing body, that it has a racially nondiscriminatory policy as to students? . . . . . . ☐ **Yes**   ☐ **No**

   Attach whatever corporate resolutions or other official statements the organization has made on this subject.

5a   Has the organization made its racially nondiscriminatory policies known in a manner that brings the policies to the attention of all segments of the general community that it serves? . . . . ☐ **Yes**   ☐ **No**

   If "Yes," describe how these policies have been publicized and how often relevant notices or announcements have been made. If no newspaper or broadcast media notices have been used, explain.

b   If applicable, attach clippings of any relevant newspaper notices or advertising, or copies of tapes or scripts used for media broadcasts. Also attach copies of brochures and catalogues dealing with student admissions, programs, and scholarships, as well as representative copies of all written advertising used as a means of informing prospective students of your programs.

6   Attach a numerical schedule showing the racial composition, as of the current academic year, and projected as far as may be feasible for the next academic year, of: **(a)** the student body, and **(b)** the faculty and administrative staff.

7   Attach a list showing the amount of any scholarship and loan funds awarded to students enrolled and the racial composition of the students who have received the awards.

8a   Attach a list of the organization's incorporators, founders, board members, and donors of land or buildings, whether individuals or organizations.

b   State whether any of the organizations listed in **8a** have as an objective the maintenance of segregated public or private school education, and, if so, whether any of the individuals listed in **8a** are officers or active members of such organizations.

9a   Indicate the public school district and county in which the organization is located.

b   Was the organization formed or substantially expanded at the time of public school desegregation in the above district or county? . . . . ☐ **Yes**   ☐ **No**

10   Has the organization ever been determined by a State or Federal administrative agency or judicial body to be racially discriminatory? . . . . ☐ **Yes**   ☐ **No**

   If "Yes," attach a detailed explanation identifying the parties to the suit, the forum in which the case was heard, the cause of action, the holding in the case, and the citations (if any) for the case. Also describe in detail what changes in your operation, if any, have occurred since then.

For more information, see back of Schedule B.

Instructions

A "school" is an organization that has the primary function of presenting formal instruction, normally maintains a regular faculty and curriculum, normally has a regularly enrolled body of students, and has a place where its educational activities are carried on. The term generally corresponds to the definition of an "educational organization" in section 170(b)(1)(A)(ii). Thus, the term includes primary, secondary, preparatory and high schools, and colleges and universities. The term does not include organizations engaged in both educational and non-educational activities unless the latter are merely incidental to the educational activities. A school for handicapped children would be included within the term, but an organization merely providing handicapped children with custodial care would not.

For purposes of this Schedule, "Sunday schools" that are conducted by a church would not be included in the term "schools," but separately organized schools (such as parochial schools, universities, and similar institutions) would be included in the term.

A private school that otherwise meets the requirements of section 501(c)(3) as an educational institution will not qualify for exemption under section 501(a) unless it has a racially nondiscriminatory policy as to students. This policy means that the school admits students of any race to all the rights, privileges, programs, and activities generally accorded or made available to students at that school, and that the school does not discriminate on the basis of race in the administration of its educational policies, admissions policies, scholarship and loan programs, and athletic, or other school-administered programs. The Internal Revenue Service considers discrimination on the basis of race to include discrimination on the basis of color and national or ethnic origin. A policy of a school that favors racial minority groups in admissions, facilities, programs, and financial assistance will not constitute discrimination on the basis of race when the purpose and effect is to promote the establishment and maintenance of that school's racially nondiscriminatory policy as to students. See Rev. Proc. 75-50, 1975-2 C.B. 587, for guidelines and recordkeeping requirements for determining whether private schools that are applying for recognition of exemption have racially nondiscriminatory policies as to students.

Line 2.—An instrumentality of a State or political subdivision of a State may qualify under section 501(c)(3) if it is organized as a separate entity from the governmental unit that created it and if it otherwise meets the organizational and operational tests of section 501(c)(3). (See Rev. Rul. 60-384, 1960-2 C.B. 172.) Any such organization that is a school is not a private school and, therefore, is not subject to the provisions of Rev. Proc. 75-50.

Schools that incorrectly answer "Yes" to line 2 will be contacted to furnish the information called for by lines 3 through 10 in order to establish that they meet the requirements for exemption. To prevent delay in the processing of your application, be sure to answer line 2 correctly and complete lines 3 through 10 if applicable.

Schedule C.—Hospitals and Medical Research Organizations

☐　Check here if you are claiming to be a hospital; complete the questions in Section I of this Schedule; and write "N/A" in Section II.

☐　Check here if you are claiming to be a medical research organization operated in conjunction with a hospital; complete the questions in Section II of this Schedule; and write "N/A" in Section I.

Section I　Hospitals

1a How many doctors are on the hospital's courtesy staff? . . . . _____

b Are all the doctors in the community eligible for staff privileges? . . . . ☐ Yes　☐ No
If "No," give the reasons why and explain how the courtesy staff is selected.

2a Does the hospital maintain a full-time emergency room? . . . . ☐ Yes　☐ No

b What is the hospital's policy on administering emergency services to persons without apparent means to pay?

c Does the hospital have any arrangements with police, fire, and voluntary ambulance services for the delivery or admission of emergency cases? . . . . ☐ Yes　☐ No
Explain.

3a Does or will the hospital require a deposit from persons covered by Medicare or Medicaid in its admission practices? . . . . ☐ Yes　☐ No
If "Yes," explain.

b Does the same deposit requirement apply to all other patients? . . . . ☐ Yes　☐ No
If "No," explain.

4 Does or will the hospital provide for a portion of its services and facilities to be used for charity patients? . . . ☐ Yes　☐ No
Explain your policy regarding charity cases. Include data on the hospital's past experience in admitting charity patients and arrangements it may have with municipal or government agencies for absorbing the cost of such care.

5 Does or will the hospital carry on a formal program of medical training and research? . . . . ☐ Yes　☐ No
If "Yes," describe.

6 Does the hospital provide office space to physicians carrying on a medical practice? . . . . ☐ Yes　☐ No
If "Yes," attach a list setting forth the name of each physician, the amount of space provided, the annual rent, the expiration date of the current lease and whether the terms of the lease represent fair market value.

Section II　Medical Research Organizations

1 Name the hospitals with which you have a relationship and describe the relationship.

2 Attach a schedule describing your present and proposed (indicate which) medical research activities; show the nature of the activities, and the amount of money that has been or will be spent in carrying them out. (Making grants to other organizations is not direct conduct of medical research.)

3 Attach a statement of assets showing the fair market value of your assets and the portion of the assets directly devoted to medical research.

For more information, see back of Schedule C.

183

Additional Information

Hospitals.—To be entitled to status as a "hospital," an organization must have, as its principal purpose or function, the providing of medical or hospital care or medical education or research. "Medical care" includes the treatment of any physical or mental disability or condition, the cost of which may be taken as a deduction under section 213, whether the treatment is performed on an inpatient or outpatient basis. Thus, a rehabilitation institution, outpatient clinic, or community mental health or drug treatment center may be a hospital if its principal function is providing the above described services. On the other hand, a convalescent home or a home for children or the aged would not be a hospital. Similarly, an institution whose principal purpose or function is to train handicapped individuals to pursue some vocation would not be a hospital. Moreover, a medical education or medical research institution is not a hospital, unless it is also actively engaged in providing medical or hospital care to patients on its premises or in its facilities on an inpatient or outpatient basis.

Cooperative Hospital Service Organizations.—Cooperative hospital service organizations (section 501(e)) should not complete Schedule C.

Medical Research Organizations.—To qualify as a medical research organization, the principal function of the organization must be the direct, continuous and active conduct of medical research in conjunction with a hospital that is described in section 501(c)(3), a Federal hospital, or an instrumentality of a governmental unit referred to in section 170(c)(1). For purposes of section 170(b)(1)(A)(iii) only, the organization must be set up to use the funds it receives in the active conduct of medical research by January 1 of the fifth calendar year after receipt. The arrangement it has with donors to assure use of the funds within the five-year period must be legally enforceable. As used here, "medical research" means investigations, experiments and studies to discover, develop, or verify knowledge relating to the causes, diagnosis, treatment, prevention, or control of the physical or mental diseases and impairments of man. For further information, see Regulations section 1.170A-9(c)(2).

Schedule D.—Section 509(a)(3) Supporting Organization

1a Organizations supported by the applicant organization: Name and address of supported organization	**b** Has the supported organization received a ruling or determination letter that it is not a private foundation by reason of section 509(a)(1) or (2)?	
--	☐ **Yes**	☐ **No**
--	☐ **Yes**	☐ **No**
--	☐ **Yes**	☐ **No**
--	☐ **Yes**	☐ **No**
--	☐ **Yes**	☐ **No**

c If "No" for any of the organizations listed in 1a, explain.

2 Does the organization you support have tax-exempt status under section 501(c)(4), 501(c)(5), or 501(c)(6)? . ☐ **Yes** ☐ **No**
If "Yes," attach: **(a)** a copy of its ruling or determination letter, and **(b)** an analysis of its revenue for the current year and the preceding three years. (Provide the financial data using the formats in Part IV-A (lines 1–13) and Part III (questions 11, 12, and 13).)

3 Does your governing document indicate that the majority of your governing board is elected or appointed by the supported organizations? . . . . ☐ **Yes** ☐ **No**
If "Yes," skip to question 9.
If "No," you must answer questions 4 through 9.

4 Does your governing document indicate the common supervision or control that you and the supported organizations share? . . . . ☐ **Yes** ☐ **No**
If "Yes," give the article and paragraph numbers. If "No," explain.

5 To what extent do the supported organizations have a significant voice in your investment policies, in the making and timing of grants, and in otherwise directing the use of your income or assets?

6 Does the mentioning of the supported organizations in your governing instrument make you a trust that the supported organizations can enforce under state law and compel to make an accounting? . . . . ☐ **Yes** ☐ **No**
If "Yes," explain.

7a What percentage of your income do you pay to each supported organization?

b What is the total annual income of each supported organization?

c How much do you contribute annually to each supported organization?

For more information, see back of Schedule D.

Schedule D.—Section 509(a)(3) Supporting Organization *(Continued)*

8   To what extent do you conduct activities that would otherwise be carried on by the supported organizations? Explain why these activities would otherwise be carried on by the supported organizations.

9   Is the applicant organization controlled directly or indirectly by one or more "disqualified persons" (other than one who is a disqualified person solely because he or she is a manager) or by an organization which is not described in section 509(a)(1) or (2)?   . . . .   ☐ **Yes**   ☐ **No**

If "Yes," explain.

Instructions

For an explanation of the types of organizations defined in section 509(a)(3) as being excluded from the definition of a private foundation, see Publication 557, Chapter 3.

Line 1.—List each organization that is supported by your organization and indicate in item 1b if the supported organization has received a letter recognizing exempt status as a section 501(c)(3) public charity as defined in section 509(a)(1) or 509(a)(2).

If you answer "No" in 1b to any of the listed organizations, please explain in 1c.

Line 3.—Your governing document may be articles of incorporation, articles of association, constitution, trust indenture, or trust agreement.

Line 9.—For a definition of a "disqualified person," see specific instructions for Part II, line 4d, on page 3 of the application's instructions.

Schedule E.—Private Operating Foundation

		Most recent tax year
	Income Test	
1a	Adjusted net income, as defined in Regulations section 53.4942(a)-2(d)	**1a**	
b	Minimum investment return, as defined in Regulations section 53.4942(a)-2(c)	**1b**	
2	Qualifying distributions:	
a	Amounts (including administrative expenses) paid directly for the active conduct of the activities for which organized and operated under section 501(c)(3) (attach schedule)	**2a**	
b	Amounts paid to acquire assets to be used (or held for use) directly in carrying out purposes described in section 170(c)(1) or 170(c)(2)(B) (attach schedule)	**2b**	
c	Amounts set aside for specific projects that are for purposes described in section 170(c)(1) or 170(c)(2)(B) (attach schedule)	**2c**	
d	**Total** qualifying distributions (add lines 2a, b, and c)	**2d**	
3	Percentages:	
a	Percentage of qualifying distributions to adjusted net income (divide line 2d by line 1a)	**3a**	%
b	Percentage of qualifying distributions to minimum investment return (divide line 2d by line 1b) . . . . (Percentage must be at least 85% for 3a or 3b)	**3b**	%
	Assets Test	
4	Value of organization's assets used in activities that directly carry out the exempt purposes. Do not include assets held merely for investment or production of income (attach schedule)	**4**	
5	Value of any stock of a corporation that is controlled by applicant organization and carries out its exempt purposes (attach statement describing corporation)	**5**	
6	Value of all qualifying assets (add lines 4 and 5)	**6**	
7	Value of applicant organization's total assets	**7**	
8	Percentage of qualifying assets to total assets (divide line 6 by line 7—percentage must exceed 65%) . .	**8**	%
	Endowment Test	
9	Value of assets not used (or held for use) directly in carrying out exempt purposes:	
a	Monthly average of investment securities at fair market value	**9a**	
b	Monthly average of cash balances	**9b**	
c	Fair market value of all other investment property (attach schedule)	**9c**	
d	**Total** (add lines 9a, b, and c)	**9d**	
10	Acquisition indebtedness related to line 9 items (attach schedule)	**10**	
11	Balance (subtract line 10 from line 9d)	**11**	
12	Multiply line 11 by 3⅓% (⅔ of the percentage for the minimum investment return computation under section 4942(e)). Line 2d above must equal or exceed the result of this computation	**12**	
	Support Test	
13	Applicant organization's support as defined in section 509(d)	**13**	
14	Gross investment income as defined in section 509(e)	**14**	
15	Support for purposes of section 4942(j)(3)(B)(iii) (subtract line 14 from line 13)	**15**	
16	Support received from the general public, 5 or more exempt organizations, or a combination of these sources (attach schedule)	**16**	
17	For persons (other than exempt organizations) contributing more than 1% of line 15, enter the total amounts that are more than 1% of line 15	**17**	
18	Subtract line 17 from line 16	**18**	
19	Percentage of total support (divide line 18 by line 15—must be at least 85%)	**19**	%
20	Does line 16 include support from an exempt organization that is more than 25% of the amount of line 15? .	☐ Yes ☐ No
21	Newly created organizations with less than one year's experience: Attach a statement explaining how the organization is planning to satisfy the requirements of section 4942(j)(3) for the income test and one of the supplemental tests during its first year's operation. Include a description of plans and arrangements, press clippings, public announcements, solicitations for funds, etc.	
22	Does the amount entered on line 2a include any grants that you made?	☐ Yes ☐ No
	If "Yes," attach a statement explaining how those grants satisfy the criteria for "significant involvement" grants described in section 53.4942(b)-1(b)(2) of the regulations.	

For more information, see back of Schedule E.

Instructions

If the organization claims to be an operating foundation described in section 4942(j)(3) and—

(a) bases its claim to private operating foundation status on normal and regular operations over a period of years; or

(b) is newly created, set up as a private operating foundation, and has at least one year's experience;

provide the information under the income test and under one of the three supplemental tests (assets, endowment, or support). If the organization does not have at least one year's experience, provide the information called for on line 21. If the organization's private operating foundation status depends on its normal and regular operations as described in (a) above, attach a schedule similar to the one shown on the front of this schedule showing the data in tabular form for the three years preceding the most recent tax year. (See Regulations section 53.4942(b)-1 for additional information before completing the "Income Test" section of this schedule.) Organizations claiming section 4942(j)(5) status must satisfy the income test and the endowment test.

A "private operating foundation" described in section 4942(j)(3) is a private foundation that spends substantially all of the lesser of its adjusted net income (as defined below) or its minimum investment return directly for the active conduct of the activities constituting the purpose or function for which it is organized and operated. The foundation must satisfy the income test under section 4942(j)(3)(A), as modified by Regulations section 53.4942(b)-1, and one of the following three supplemental tests: **(1)** the assets test under section 4942(j)(3)(B)(i); **(2)** the endowment test under section 4942(j)(3)(B)(ii); or **(3)** the support test under section 4942(j)(3)(B)(iii).

Certain long-term care facilities described in section 4942(j)(5) are treated as private operating foundations for purposes of section 4942 only.

"Adjusted net income" is the excess of gross income for the tax year over the sum of deductions determined with the modifications described below. Items of gross income from any unrelated trade or business and the deductions directly connected with the unrelated trade or business will be taken into account in computing the organization's adjusted net income:

Income modifications (adjustments to gross income).—

(1) Section 103 (relating to interest on certain governmental obligations) does not apply. Thus, interest that otherwise would have been excluded should be included in gross income.

(2) Except as provided in (3) below, capital gains and losses are taken into account only to the extent of the net short-term gain. Long-term gains and losses will be disregarded.

(3) The gross amount received from the sale or disposition of certain property should be included in gross income to the extent that the acquisition of the property constituted a qualifying distribution under section 4942(g)(1)(B).

(4) Repayments of prior qualifying distributions (as defined in section 4942(g)(1)(A)) will constitute items of gross income.

(5) Any amount set aside under section 4942(g)(2) that is "not necessary for the purposes for which it was set aside" will constitute an item of gross income.

Deduction modifications (adjustments to deductions).—

(1) Expenses for the general operation of the organization according to its charitable purposes (as contrasted with expenses for the production or collection of income and management, conservation, or maintenance of income producing property) should not be taken as deductions. If only a portion of the property is used for production of income subject to section 4942 and the remainder is used for general charitable purposes, the expenses connected with that property should be divided according to those purposes and only expenses related to the income producing portion will be allowed as a deduction.

(2) Charitable contributions, deductible under section 170 or 642(c), should not be taken into account as deductions for adjusted net income.

(3) The net operating loss deduction prescribed under section 172 should not be taken into account as a deduction for adjusted net income.

(4) The special deductions for corporations (such as the dividends-received deduction) allowed under sections 241 through 250 should not be taken into account as deductions for adjusted net income.

(5) Depreciation and depletion should be determined in the same manner as under section 4940(c)(3)(B).

Section 265 (relating to the expenses and interest connected with tax-exempt interest) should not be taken into account.

You may find it easier to figure adjusted net income by completing Column (c), Part 1, Form 990-PF, according to the instructions for that form.

An organization that has been held to be a private operating foundation will continue to be such an organization only if it meets the income test and either the assets, endowment, or support test in later years. See Regulations section 53.4942(b) for additional information. No additional request for ruling will be necessary or appropriate for an organization to maintain its status as a private operating foundation. However, data related to the above tests must be submitted with the organization's annual information return, Form 990-PF.

Schedule F.—Homes for the Aged or Handicapped

1 What are the requirements for admission to residency? Explain fully and attach promotional literature and application forms.

2 Does or will the home charge an entrance or founder's fee? . . . . ☐ **Yes**   ☐ **No**
If "Yes," explain and specify the amount charged.

3 What periodic fees or maintenance charges are or will be required of its residents?

4a What established policy does the home have concerning residents who become unable to pay their regular charges?

b What arrangements does the home have or will it make with local and Federal welfare units, sponsoring organizations, or others to absorb all or part of the cost of maintaining those residents?

5 What arrangements does or will the home have to provide for the health needs of its residents?

6 In what way are the home's residential facilities designed to meet some combination of the physical, emotional, recreational, social, religious, and similar needs of the aged or handicapped?

7 Provide a description of the home's facilities and specify both the residential capacity of the home and the current number of residents.

8 Attach a sample copy of the contract or agreement the organization makes with or requires of its residents.

For more information, see back of Schedule F.

Instructions

Line 1.— Provide the criteria for admission to the home and submit brochures, pamphlets, or other printed material used to inform the public about the home's admissions policy.

Line 2.— Indicate whether the fee charged is an entrance fee or a monthly charge, etc. Also, if the fee is an entrance fee, is it payable in a lump sum or on an installment basis? If there is no fee, indicate "N/A."

Line 4.— Indicate the organization's policy regarding residents who are unable to pay. Also, indicate whether the organization is subsidized for all or part of the cost of maintaining those residents who are unable to pay.

Line 5.— Indicate whether the organization provides health care to the residents, either directly or indirectly, through some continuing arrangement with other organizations, facilities, or health personnel. If no health care is provided, indicate "N/A."

Schedule G.—Child Care Organizations

1 Is the organization's primary activity the providing of care for children away from their homes? . . . . □ **Yes** □ **No**

2 How many children is the organization authorized to care for by the State (or local governmental unit), and what was the average attendance during the past 6 months, or the number of months the organization has been in existence if less than 6 months?

3 How many children are currently cared for by the organization?

4 Is substantially all (at least 85%) of the care provided for the purpose of enabling parents to be gainfully employed or to seek employment? . . . . □ **Yes** □ **No**

5 Are the services provided available to the general public? . . . . □ **Yes** □ **No**
If "No," explain.

6 Indicate the category, or categories, of parents whose children are eligible for your child-care services (check as many as apply):

□ low income parents

□ any working parents (or parents looking for work)

□ anyone with the ability to pay

□ other (explain)

Instructions

Line 5.— If your services are not available to the general public, indicate the particular group or groups that may utilize your services.

REMINDER—If this organization claims to operate a school, then it must also fill out Schedule B.

Schedule H.—Organizations Providing Scholarship Benefits, Student Aid, Etc., to Individuals

1a Describe the nature and the amount of the scholarship benefit, student aid, etc., including the terms and conditions governing its use, whether a gift or a loan, and how the availability of the scholarship is publicized. If the organization has established or will establish several categories of scholarship benefits, identify each kind of benefit and explain how the organization determines the recipients for each category. Attach a sample copy of any application the organization requires individuals to complete to be considered for scholarship grants, loans, or similar benefits. (Private foundations that make grants for travel, study, or other similar purposes are required to obtain advance approval of scholarship procedures. See Regulations sections 53.4945-4(c) and (d).)

b If you want this application considered as a request for approval of grant procedures in the event we determine that you are a private foundation, check here . . . . ▶ ☐

c If you checked the box in 1b above, indicate the sections for which you wish to be considered.

☐ 4945(g)(1) ☐ 4945(g)(2) ☐ 4945(g)(3)

2 What limitations or restrictions are there on the class of individuals who are eligible recipients? Specifically explain whether there are, or will be, any restrictions or limitations in the selection procedures based upon race or the employment status of the prospective recipient or any relative of the prospective recipient. Also indicate the approximate number of eligible individuals.

3 Indicate the number of grants you anticipate making annually . . . . ▶

4 If you base your selections in any way on the employment status of the applicant or any relative of the applicant, indicate whether there is or has been any direct or indirect relationship between the members of the selection committee and the employer. Also indicate whether relatives of the members of the selection committee are possible recipients or have been recipients.

5 Describe any procedures you have for supervising grants (such as obtaining reports or transcripts) that you award, and any procedures you have for taking action if the terms of the grant are violated.

For more information, see back of Schedule H.

192

Additional Information

Private foundations that make grants to individuals for travel, study, or other similar purposes are required to obtain advance approval of their grant procedures from the Internal Revenue Service. Such grants that are awarded under selection procedures that have not been approved by the Internal Revenue Service are subject to a 10% excise tax under section 4945. (See Regulations sections 53.4945-4(c) and (d).)

If you are requesting advance approval of your grant procedures, the following sections apply to line 1c:

4945(g)(1)— The grant constitutes a scholarship or fellowship grant that meets the provisions of section 117(a) prior to its amendment by the Tax Reform Act of 1986 and is to be used for study at an educational organization (school) described in section 170(b)(1)(A)(ii).

4945(g)(2)— The grant constitutes a prize or award that is subject to the provisions of section 74(b), if the recipient of such a prize or award is selected from the general public.

4945(g)(3)— The purpose of the grant is to achieve a specific objective, produce a report or other similar product, or improve or enhance a literary, artistic, musical, scientific, teaching, or other similar capacity, skill, or talent of the grantee.

Schedule I.—Successors to "For Profit" Institutions

1 What was the name of the predecessor organization and the nature of its activities?

2 Who were the owners or principal stockholders of the predecessor organization? (If more space is needed, attach schedule.)

Name and address	Share or interest
....	
....	
....	
....	
....	

3 Describe the business or family relationship between the owners or principal stockholders and principal employees of the predecessor organization and the officers, directors, and principal employees of the applicant organization.

4a Attach a copy of the agreement of sale or other contract that sets forth the terms and conditions of sale of the predecessor organization or of its assets to the applicant organization.

b Attach an appraisal by an independent qualified expert showing the fair market value at the time of sale of the facilities or property interest sold.

5 Has any property or equipment formerly used by the predecessor organization been rented to the applicant organization or will any such property be rented? . . . . ☐ **Yes**　☐ **No**
　If "Yes," explain and attach copies of all leases and contracts.

6 Is the organization leasing or will it lease or otherwise make available any space or equipment to the owners, principal stockholders, or principal employees of the predecessor organization? . . . . ☐ **Yes**　☐ **No**
　If "Yes," explain and attach a list of these tenants and a copy of the lease for each such tenant.

7 Were any new operating policies initiated as a result of the transfer of assets from a profit-making organization to a nonprofit organization? . . . . ☐ **Yes**　☐ **No**
　If "Yes," explain.

Additional Information

　A "for profit" institution for purposes of this Schedule includes any organization in which a person may have a proprietary or partnership interest, hold corporate stock, or otherwise exercise an ownership interest. The institution need not have operated for the purpose of making a profit.

Form 8718

(Rev. October 1990)

Department of the Treasury
Internal Revenue Service

User Fee for Exempt Organization Determination Letter Request

▶ Attach this form to determination letter application.
(Form 8718 is NOT a determination letter application)

For IRS Use Only

Control number _____

Amount paid _____

User fee screener

1 Name of organization

2	Type of request (check only one box and include a check or money order made payable to Internal Revenue Service for the amount of the indicated fee):	**Fee**

a ☐ Initial request for an exempt organization determination letter (do NOT use for a pension plan determination letter) by an organization whose annual gross receipts have not exceeded (or are not expected to exceed) $10,000, averaged over the preceding four taxable years, or new organizations which anticipate annual gross receipts averaging not more than $10,000 during their first four years. If you check this box you must complete the income certification below . . . . **$ 150**

Certification

I hereby certify that the annual gross receipts of .... have not
(enter name of organization)

exceeded (or are not expected to exceed) $10,000, averaged over the preceding four (or the first four) years of

operation.

Signature ▶ .... Title ....

b ☐ Initial request for an exempt organization determination letter (do NOT use for a pension plan determination letter) by an organization whose annual gross receipts have exceeded (or are expected to exceed) $10,000, averaged over the preceding four taxable years, or a new organization which anticipates annual gross receipts averaging more than $10,000 during their first four years . . . . **$ 375**

c ☐ Private foundation which has completed a section 507 termination and which seeks a determination letter that it is now a public charity . . . . **$ 200**

d ☐ Group exemption letters . . . . **$ 500**

Instructions

The Omnibus Budget Reconciliation Act of 1990 requires payment of a user fee for determination letter requests submitted to the Internal Revenue Service. The fee must accompany each request submitted to a key district office.

The fee for each type of request for an exempt organization determination letter is listed in item 2 of this form. Check the block that describes the type of request you are submitting, and attach this form to the front of your request form along with a check or money order for the amount indicated. Make the check or money order payable to the Internal Revenue Service.

Determination letter requests received with no payment or with an insufficient payment will be returned to the applicant for submission of the proper fee. To avoid delays in receiving a determination letter,

be sure that your application is sent to the applicable address shown below. These addresses supersede the addresses listed in Publication 557 and all application forms.

If entity is in this IRS District ▼	Send fee and request for determination letter to this address ▼
Albany, Augusta, Boston, Brooklyn, Buffalo, Burlington, Hartford, Manhattan, Portsmouth, Providence	Internal Revenue Service EP/EO Division P. O. Box 1680, GPO Brooklyn, NY 11202
Baltimore, District of Columbia, Pittsburgh, Richmond, Newark, Philadelphia, Wilmington, any U.S. possession or foreign country	Internal Revenue Service EP/EO Division P. O. Box 17010 Baltimore, MD 21203
Cincinnati, Cleveland, Detroit, Indianapolis, Louisville, Parkersburg	Internal Revenue Service EP/EO Division P. O. Box 3159 Cincinnati, OH 45201
Albuquerque, Austin, Cheyenne, Dallas, Denver, Houston, Oklahoma City, Phoenix, Salt Lake City, Wichita	Internal Revenue Service EP/EO Division Mail Code 4950 DAL 1100 Commerce Street Dallas, TX 75242
Atlanta, Birmingham, Columbia, Ft. Lauderdale, Greensboro, Jackson, Jacksonville, Little Rock, Nashville, New Orleans	Internal Revenue Service EP/EO Division P.O. Box 941 Atlanta, GA 30370
Anchorage, Boise, Las Vegas, Los Angeles, Honolulu, Portland, Laguna Niguel, San Jose, Seattle	Internal Revenue Service EO Application Receiving Room 5127, P. O. Box 486 Los Angeles, CA 90053-0486
Sacramento, San Francisco	Internal Revenue Service EO Application Receiving Stop SF 4446 P. O. Box 36001 San Francisco, CA 94102
Aberdeen, Chicago, Des Moines, Fargo, Helena, Milwaukee, Omaha, St. Louis, St. Paul, Springfield	Internal Revenue Service EP/EO Division 230 S. Dearborn DPN 20-5 Chicago, IL 60604

Attach Check or Money Order Here

★ U.S.GPO:1990-0-282-002/40012

Form **8718** (Rev. 10-90)

You must complete this form and attach it to your application if you checked box (h), (i), or (j) of Part III, question 9, and you have not completed a tax year of at least 8 months.

For example: If you incorporated May 15 and your year ends December 31, you have completed a tax year of only 7½ months. Therefore, Form 872-C must be completed.

(a) Enter the name of the organization. This must be entered exactly as it is written in the organizing document. Do not use abbreviations unless the organizing document does.

(b) Enter the current address.

(c) Enter ending date of first tax year.

For example:

(a) If you were formed on June 15 and you have chosen December 31, as your year end, enter December 31, 19 ....

(b) If you were formed June 15 and have chosen June 30 as your year end, enter June 30, 19......... In this example your first tax year consists of only 15 days.

(d) The form must be signed by an authorized officer or trustee, generally the President or Treasurer.

(e) Enter the date that the form was signed.

DO NOT MAKE ANY OTHER ENTRIES.

196

Consent Fixing Period of Limitation Upon Assessment of Tax Under Section 4940 of the Internal Revenue Code

(See instructions on reverse side.)

OMB No. 1545-0056

To be used with Form 1023. Submit in duplicate.

Under section 6501(c)(4) of the Internal Revenue Code, and as part of a request filed with Form 1023 that the organization named below be treated as a publicly supported organization under section 170(b)(1)(A)(vi) or section 509(a)(2) during an advance ruling period,

----
(Exact legal name of organization as shown in organizing document)

(Number, street, city or town, state, and ZIP code)

} and the

**District Director of
Internal Revenue, or
Assistant Commissioner
(Employee Plans and
Exempt Organizations)**

Consent and agree that the period for assessing tax (imposed under section 4940 of the Code) for any of the 5 tax years in the advance ruling period will extend 8 years, 4 months, and 15 days beyond the end of the first tax year.

However, if a notice of deficiency in tax for any of these years is sent to the organization before the period expires, the time for making an assessment will be further extended by the number of days the assessment is prohibited, plus 60 days.

Ending date of first tax year ....
(Month, day, and year)

Name of organization (as shown in organizing document)	Date
Officer or trustee having authority to sign	
Signature ▶	

For IRS use only

District Director or Assistant Commissioner (Employee Plans and Exempt Organizations)	Date

By ▶

For Paperwork Reduction Act Notice, see page 1 of the Form 1023 Instructions.

Form **SS-4**
(Rev. April 1991)
Department of the Treasury
Internal Revenue Service

Application for Employer Identification Number

(For use by employers and others. Please read the attached instructions before completing this form.)

EIN

OMB No. 1545-0003
Expires 4-30-94

Please type or print clearly.

1 Name of applicant (True legal name) (See instructions.)

2 Trade name of business, if different from name in line 1

3 Executor, trustee, "care of" name

4a Mailing address (street address) (room, apt., or suite no.)

5a Address of business (See instructions.)

4b City, state, and ZIP code

5b City, state, and ZIP code

6 County and state where principal business is located

7 Name of principal officer, grantor, or general partner (See instructions.) ▶

8a Type of entity (Check only one box.) (See instructions.)
☐ Individual SSN _____
☐ REMIC
☐ State/local government
☐ Other nonprofit organization (specify) _____
☐ Other (specify) ▶ _____

☐ Estate
☐ Plan administrator SSN _____
☐ Other corporation (specify) _____
☐ Personal service corp.
☐ National guard
☐ Federal government/military
☐ Church or church controlled organization
If nonprofit organization enter GEN (if applicable) _____

☐ Trust
☐ Partnership
☐ Farmers' cooperative

8b If a corporation, give name of foreign country (if applicable) or state in the U.S. where incorporated ▶

Foreign country

State

9 Reason for applying (Check only one box.)
☐ Started new business
☐ Hired employees
☐ Created a pension plan (specify type) ▶ _____
☐ Banking purpose (specify) ▶
☐ Changed type of organization (specify) ▶ _____
☐ Purchased going business
☐ Created a trust (specify) ▶ _____
☐ Other (specify) ▶

10 Date business started or acquired (Mo., day, year) (See instructions.)

11 Enter closing month of accounting year. (See instructions.)

12 First date wages or annuities were paid or will be paid (Mo., day, year). **Note:** *If applicant is a withholding agent, enter date income will first be paid to nonresident alien. (Mo., day, year)* . . . . ▶

13 Enter highest number of employees expected in the next 12 months. **Note:** *If the applicant does not expect to have any employees during the period, enter "0."* . . . . ▶

Nonagricultural	Agricultural	Household

14 Principal activity (See instructions.) ▶

15 Is the principal business activity manufacturing? . . . . ☐ **Yes** ☐ **No**
If "Yes," principal product and raw material used ▶

16 To whom are most of the products or services sold? Please check the appropriate box.
☐ Public (retail)   ☐ Other (specify) ▶
☐ Business (wholesale)
☐ N/A

17a Has the applicant ever applied for an identification number for this or any other business? . . . . ☐ **Yes** ☐ **No**
Note: *If "Yes," please complete lines 17b and 17c.*

17b If you checked the "Yes" box in line 17a, give applicant's true name and trade name, if different than name shown on prior application.

True name ▶

Trade name ▶

17c Enter approximate date, city, and state where the application was filed and the previous employer identification number if known.

Approximate date when filed (Mo., day, year) | City and state where filed

Previous EIN

Under penalties of perjury, I declare that I have examined this application, and to the best of my knowledge and belief, it is true, correct, and complete

Telephone number (include area code)

Name and title (Please type or print clearly.) ▶

Signature ▶

Date ▶

Note: *Do not write below this line.   For official use only.*

Please leave blank ▶	Geo.	Ind.	Class	Size	Reason for applying

For Paperwork Reduction Act Notice, see attached instructions.

Cat. No. 16055N

Form **SS-4** (Rev. 4-91)

199

General Instructions

(Section references are to the Internal Revenue Code unless otherwise noted.)

Paperwork Reduction Act Notice.—We ask for the information on this form to carry out the Internal Revenue laws of the United States. You are required to give us this information. We need it to ensure that you are complying with these laws and to allow us to figure and collect the right amount of tax.

The time needed to complete and file this form will vary depending on individual circumstances. The estimated average time is:

Recordkeeping.	7 min.
Learning about the law or the form	21 min.
Preparing the form	42 min.
Copying, assembling, and sending the form to IRS	20 min.

If you have comments concerning the accuracy of these time estimates or suggestions for making this form more simple, we would be happy to hear from you. You can write to both the **Internal Revenue Service,** Washington, DC 20224, Attention: IRS Reports Clearance Officer, T:FP; and the **Office of Management and Budget,** Paperwork Reduction Project (1545-0003), Washington, DC 20503. **DO NOT** send the tax form to either of these offices. Instead, see **Where To Apply.**

Purpose.—Use Form SS-4 to apply for an employer identification number (EIN). The information you provide on this form will establish your filing requirements.

Who Must File.—You must file this form if you have not obtained an EIN before and

● You pay wages to one or more employees.

● You are required to have an EIN to use on any return, statement, or other document, even if you are not an employer.

● You are required to withhold taxes on income, other than wages, paid to a nonresident alien (individual, corporation, partnership, etc.). For example, individuals who file **Form 1042,** Annual Withholding Tax Return for U.S. Source Income of Foreign Persons, to report alimony paid to nonresident aliens must have EINs.

Individuals who file **Schedule C,** Profit or Loss From Business, or **Schedule F,** Profit or Loss From Farming, of **Form 1040,** U.S. Individual Income Tax Return, must use EINs if they have a Keogh plan or are required to file excise, employment, or alcohol, tobacco, or firearms returns.

The following must use EINs even if they do not have any employees:

● Trusts, except an IRA trust, unless the IRA trust is required to file **Form 990-T,** Exempt Organization Business Income Tax Return, to report unrelated business taxable income or is filing Form 990-T to obtain a refund of the credit from a regulated investment company.

● Estates

● Partnerships

● REMICS (real estate mortgage investment conduits)

● Corporations

● Nonprofit organizations (churches, clubs, etc.)

● Farmers' cooperatives

● Plan administrators

*New Business.—*If you become the new owner of an existing business, **DO NOT** use the EIN of the former owner. If you already have an EIN, use that number. If you do not have an EIN, apply for one on this form. If you become the "owner" of a corporation by acquiring its stock, use the corporation's EIN.

If you already have an EIN, you may need to get a new one if either the organization or ownership of your business changes. If you incorporate a sole proprietorship or form a partnership, you must get a new EIN. However, **DO NOT** apply for a new EIN if you change only the name of your business.

File Only One Form SS-4.—File only one Form SS-4, regardless of the number of businesses operated or trade names under which a business operates. However, each corporation in an affiliated group must file a separate application.

If you do not have an EIN by the time a return is due, write "Applied for" and the date you applied in the space shown for the number. **DO NOT** show your social security number as an EIN on returns.

If you do not have an EIN by the time a tax deposit is due, send your payment to the Internal Revenue service center for your filing area. (See **Where To Apply** below.) Make your check or money order payable to Internal Revenue Service and show your name (as shown on Form SS-4), address, kind of tax, period covered, and date you applied for an EIN.

For more information about EINs, see **Pub. 583,** Taxpayers Starting a Business.

How To Apply.—You can apply for an EIN either by mail or by telephone. You can get an EIN immediately by calling the Tele-TIN phone number for the service center for your state, or you can send the completed Form SS-4 directly to the service center to receive your EIN in the mail.

*Application by Tele-TIN.—*The Tele-TIN program is designed to assign EINs by telephone. Under this program, you can receive your EIN over the telephone and use it immediately to file a return or make a payment.

To receive an EIN by phone, complete Form SS-4, then call the Tele-TIN phone number listed for your state under **Where To Apply.** The person making the call must be authorized to sign the form (see **Signature block** on page 3).

An IRS representative will use the information from the Form SS-4 to establish your account and assign you an EIN. Write the number you are given on the upper right-hand corner of the form, sign and date it, and promptly mail it to the Tele-TIN Unit at the service center address for your state.

*Application by mail.—*Complete Form SS-4 at least 4 to 5 weeks before you will need an EIN. Sign and date the application and mail it to the service center address for your state. You will receive your EIN in the mail in approximately 4 weeks.

Note: *The Tele-TIN phone numbers listed below will involve a long-distance charge to callers outside of the local calling area, and should only be used to apply for an EIN. Use 1-800-829-1040 to ask about an application by mail.*

Where To Apply.—

If your principal business, office or agency, or legal residence in the case of an individual, is located in:	Call the Tele-TIN phone number shown or file with the Internal Revenue service center at:
Florida, Georgia, South Carolina	Atlanta, GA 39901 (404) 455-2360
New Jersey, New York City and counties of Nassau, Rockland, Suffolk, and Westchester	Holtsville, NY 00501 (516) 447-4955
New York (all other counties), Connecticut, Maine, Massachusetts, New Hampshire, Rhode Island, Vermont	Andover, MA 05501 (508) 474-9717
Illinois, Iowa, Minnesota, Missouri, Wisconsin	Kansas City, MO 64999 (816) 926-5999
Delaware, District of Columbia, Maryland, Pennsylvania, Virginia	Philadelphia, PA 19255 (215) 961-3980
Indiana, Kentucky, Michigan, Ohio, West Virginia	Cincinnati, OH 45999 (606) 292-5467
Kansas, New Mexico, Oklahoma, Texas	Austin, TX 73301 (512) 462-7845
Alaska, Arizona, California (counties of Alpine, Amador, Butte, Calaveras, Colusa, Contra Costa, Del Norte, El Dorado, Glenn, Humboldt, Lake, Lassen, Marin, Mendocino, Modoc, Napa, Nevada, Placer, Plumas, Sacramento, San Joaquin, Shasta, Sierra, Siskiyou, Solano, Sonoma, Sutter, Tehama, Trinity, Yolo, and Yuba), Colorado, Idaho, Montana, Nebraska, Nevada, North Dakota, Oregon, South Dakota, Utah, Washington, Wyoming	Ogden, UT 84201 (801) 625-7645
California (all other counties), Hawaii	Fresno, CA 93888 (209) 456-5900
Alabama, Arkansas, Louisiana, Mississippi, North Carolina, Tennessee	Memphis, TN 37501 (901) 365-5970

If you have no legal residence, principal place of business, or principal office or agency in any Internal Revenue District, file your form with the Internal Revenue Service Center, Philadelphia, PA 19255 or call (215) 961-3980.

Specific Instructions

The instructions that follow are for those items that are not self-explanatory. Enter N/A (nonapplicable) on the lines that do not apply.

Line 1.—Enter the legal name of the entity applying for the EIN.

*Individuals.—*Enter the first name, middle initial, and last name.

*Trusts.—*Enter the name of the trust.

*Estate of a decedent.—*Enter the name of the estate.

*Partnerships.—*Enter the legal name of the partnership as it appears in the partnership agreement.

*Corporations.—*Enter the corporate name as set forth in the corporation charter or other legal document creating it.

*Plan administrators.—*Enter the name of the plan administrator. A plan administrator who already has an EIN should use that number.

Line 2.—Enter the trade name of the business if different from the legal name.

Note: *Use the full legal name entered on line 1 on all tax returns to be filed for the entity. However, if a trade name is entered on line 2, use only the name on line 1 or the name on line 2 consistently when filing tax returns.*

Line 3.—Trusts enter the name of the trustee. Estates enter the name of the executor, administrator, or other fiduciary. If the entity applying has a designated person to receive tax information, enter that person's name as the "care of" person. Print or type the first name, middle initial, and last name.

Lines 5a and 5b.—If the physical location of the business is different from the mailing address (lines 4a and 4b), enter the address of the physical location on lines 5a and 5b.

Line 7.—Enter the first name, middle initial, and last name of a principal officer if the business is a corporation; of a general partner if a partnership; and of a grantor if a trust.

Line 8a.—Check the box that best describes the type of entity that is applying for the EIN. If not specifically mentioned, check the "other" box and enter the type of entity. Do not enter N/A.

Individual.—Check this box if the individual files Schedule C or F (Form 1040) and has a Keogh plan or is required to file excise, employment, or alcohol, tobacco, or firearms returns. If this box is checked, enter the individual's SSN (social security number) in the space provided.

Plan administrator.—The term plan administrator means the person or group of persons specified as the administrator by the instrument under which the plan is operated. If the plan administrator is an individual, enter the plan administrator's SSN in the space provided.

New withholding agent.—If you are a new withholding agent required to file Form 1042, check the "other" box and enter in the space provided "new withholding agent."

REMICs.—Check this box if the entity is a real estate mortgage investment conduit (REMIC). A REMIC is any entity

1. To which an election to be treated as a REMIC applies for the tax year and all prior tax years,

2. In which all of the interests are regular interests or residual interests,

3. Which has one class of residual interests (and all distributions, if any, with respect to such interests are pro rata),

4. In which as of the close of the 3rd month beginning after the startup date and at all times thereafter, substantially all of its assets consist of qualified mortgages and permitted investments,

5. Which has a tax year that is a calendar year, and

6. With respect to which there are reasonable arrangements designed to ensure that: (a) residual interests are not held by disqualified organizations (as defined in section 860E(e)(5)), and (b) information necessary for the application of section 860E(e) will be made available.

For more information about REMICs see the Instructions for **Form 1066**, U. S. Real Estate Mortgage Investment Conduit Income Tax Return.

Personal service corporations.—Check this box if the entity is a personal service corporation. An entity is a personal service corporation for a tax year only if

1. The entity is a C corporation for the tax year.

2. The principal activity of the entity during the testing period (as defined in Temporary Regulations section 1.441-4T(f)) for the tax year is the performance of personal service.

3. During the testing period for the tax year, such services are substantially performed by employee-owners.

4. The employee-owners own 10 percent of the fair market value of the outstanding stock in the entity on the last day of the testing period for the tax year.

For more information about personal service corporations, see the instructions to **Form 1120**, U.S. Corporation Income Tax Return, and Temporary Regulations section 1.441-4T.

Other corporations.—This box is for any corporation other than a personal service corporation. If you check this box, enter the type of corporation (such as insurance company) in the space provided.

Other nonprofit organizations.—Check this box if the nonprofit organization is other than a church or church-controlled organization and specify the type of nonprofit organization (for example, an educational organization.)

Group exemption number (GEN).—If the applicant is a nonprofit organization that is a subordinate organization to be included in a group exemption letter under Revenue Procedure 80-27, 1980-1 C.B. 677, enter the GEN in the space provided. If you do not know the GEN, contact the parent organization for it. GEN is a four-digit number. Do not confuse it with the nine-digit EIN.

Line 9.—Check only one box. Do not enter N/A.

Started new business.—Check this box if you are starting a new business that requires an EIN. If you check this box, enter the type of business being started. **DO NOT** apply if you already have an EIN and are only adding another place of business.

Changed type of organization.—Check this box if the business is changing its type of organization, for example, if the business was a sole proprietorship and has been incorporated or has become a partnership. If you check this box, specify in the space provided the type of change made, for example, "from sole proprietorship to partnership."

Purchased going business.—Check this box if you acquired a business through purchase. Do not use the former owner's EIN. If you already have an EIN, use that number.

Hired employees.—Check this box if the existing business is requesting an EIN because it has hired or is hiring employees and is therefore required to file employment tax return for which an EIN is required. **DO NOT** apply if you already have an EIN and are only hiring employees.

Created a trust.—Check this box if you created a trust, and enter the type of trust created.

Created a pension plan.—Check this box if you have created a pension plan and need this number for reporting purposes. Also, enter the type of plan created.

Banking purpose.—Check this box if you are requesting an EIN for banking purpose only and enter the banking purpose (for example, checking, loan, etc.).

Other (specify).—Check this box if you are requesting an EIN for any reason other than those for which there are checkboxes and enter the reason.

Line 10.—If you are starting a new business, enter the starting date of the business. If the business you acquired is already operating, enter the date you acquired the business. Trusts should enter the date the trust was legally created. Estates should enter the date of death of the decedent whose name appears on line 1.

Line 11.—Enter the last month of your accounting year or tax year. An accounting year or tax year is usually 12 consecutive months. It may be a calendar year or a fiscal year (including a period of 52 or 53 weeks). A calendar year is 12 consecutive months ending on December 31. A fiscal year is either 12 consecutive months ending on the last day of any month other than December or a 52-53 week year. For more information

on accounting periods, see **Pub. 538**, Accounting Periods and Methods.

Individuals.—Your tax year generally will be a calendar year.

Partnerships.—Partnerships generally should conform to the tax year of either (1) its majority partners; (2) its principal partners; (3) the tax year that results in the least aggregate deferral of income (see Temporary Regulations section 1.706-1T); or (4) some other tax year, if (a) a business purpose is established for the fiscal year, or (b) the fiscal year is a "grandfather" year, or (c) an election is made under section 444 to have a fiscal year. (See the Instructions for **Form 1065**, U.S. Partnership Return of Income, for more information.)

REMICs.—Remics must have a calendar year as their tax year.

Personal service corporations.—A personal service corporation generally must adopt a calendar year unless:

1. It can establish to the satisfaction of the Commissioner that there is a business purpose for having a different tax year, or

2. It elects under section 444 to have a tax year other than a calendar year.

Line 12.—If the business has or will have employees, enter on this line the date on which the business began or will begin to pay wages to the employees. If the business does not have any plans to have employees, enter N/A on this line.

New withholding agent.—Enter the date you began or will begin to pay income to a nonresident alien. This also applies to individuals who are required to file Form 1042 to report alimony paid to a nonresident alien.

Line 14.—Generally, enter the exact type of business being operated (for example, advertising agency, farm, labor union, real estate agency, steam laundry, rental of coin-operated vending machine, investment club, etc.).

Governmental.—Enter the type of organization (state, county, school district, or municipality, etc.)

Nonprofit organization (other than governmental).—Enter whether organized for religious, educational, or humane purposes, and the principal activity (for example, religious organization—hospital, charitable).

Mining and quarrying.—Specify the process and the principal product (for example, mining bituminous coal, contract drilling for oil, quarrying dimension stone, etc.).

Contract construction.—Specify whether general contracting or special trade contracting. Also, show the type of work normally performed (for example, general contractor for residential buildings, electrical subcontractor, etc.).

Trade.—Specify the type of sales and the principal line of goods sold (for example, wholesale dairy products, manufacturer's representative for mining machinery, retail hardware, etc.).

Manufacturing.—Specify the type of establishment operated (for example, sawmill, vegetable cannery, etc.).

Signature block.—The application must be signed by: (1) the individual, if the person is an individual, (2) the president, vice president, or other principal officer, if the person is a corporation, (3) a responsible and duly authorized member or officer having knowledge of its affairs, if the person is a partnership or other unincorporated organization, or (4) the fiduciary, if the person is a trust or estate.

☀ U.S.GPO:1992-0-312-699/60110

13

After Incorporation: Getting Under Way

So your nonprofit organization has now been incorporated. It is time to activate the corporation, and to lend a steadying hand as it takes those first steps of its new legal life.

In the discussion that follows, we will not attempt to present a complete course in sound business management of your corporation. Most people who are serious enough about a nonprofit endeavor to have been involved in the steps necessary to incorporate it will have some knowledge of how the organization will work once that is done. You may have operated other kinds of organizations in the past. Or, if you have been an officer of an unincorporated association, club, or similar organization, you should have a fairly good idea of the operations of a nonprofit corporation.

If you feel you need some basic business management instruction, search out a school that offers such courses or take a look at books available on this subject in the business section of your library. Of course, as the activities of your nonprofit corporation expand, they can become more complex. Eventually, you may want to seek help and advice from professional advisers. But at the start, getting your corporation off to a good start will not be that difficult.

Your basic guide to running the nonprofit corporation will be the corporation's bylaws, which you have had a hand in creating. In a previous chapter, you have learned how to put a set of bylaws together and have had a chance to study the sample set included in this book. They are fairly comprehensive. Most corporations use this kind of bylaws structure as a basic operational guide. Of course, if there are aspects of your corporation's activities not covered by the sample set of bylaws, you can simply add new sections or articles to establish procedures for dealing with additional matters.

What we will do here is to present a checklist of actions your corporation should take soon after its certificate of incorporation has been approved and filed by the incorporating state. Once your board of directors has completed all the actions in this checklist, you will discover that your nonprofit corporation will be proceeding steadily along.

THE CHECKLIST

☐ **The first order of business for the corporation is to obtain an official corporate record book, a corporate seal, and a supply of membership certificates** (if it will be a membership corporation, as defined in Chapter 9). You can purchase all of these items in a stationery store supplying business and legal forms. Costs will vary, of course, depending on stores and locations, but the total amount should not be prohibitive.

As you have already read, you can order all of these items from The Company Corporation at the time you engage the company as a registered agent and submit your certificate of incorporation for filing in Delaware. If ordered from The Company Corporation, the record book, seal, and other materials will arrive at the same time you receive the certified copy of the approved and filed certificate of incorporation.

☐ **The next order of business is to hold the first organizational meeting of your corporation's board of directors.**

This meeting will launch the legal operation of the corporation. There is a standard procedure to be followed in this first meeting; certain items of business must be taken up at this time. Minutes of the meeting, as well as some other forms resulting from the meeting, must be filed in the record book following the meeting.

Forms for use in conducting your first meeting are included at the end of this chapter. Indeed, you can use the "Minutes" form as outlined for conducting the meeting.

In the paragraphs below, we will walk you through the procedure for organizing and holding the first meeting of the directors.

1. As the chief organizer of the corporation, you must call any and all of the other persons named as directors in the certificate of incorporation and ask them to come to the first meeting of the board at a place and time you have set. Of course, if you incorporated the organization in the state of Delaware and are the only person named as incorporator or director, you need not involve any other persons in the first meeting. You should,

nevertheless, run through the meeting procedure by yourself and file the documents indicated.

2. All persons named as directors should attend the first meeting. There must be a sufficient number of directors in attendance to constitute a quorum, as defined in the bylaws you have drafted; otherwise, you cannot legally proceed.

3. Before you begin the meeting, ask all directors to sign a document called *Waiver of Notice of the First Meeting of the Board of Directors*. You will find a copy of this form at the end of the chapter. By signing this document, the directors are saying, for the legal record, "We waive the requirement in the bylaws that calls for a specific procedure and advance notice of the time and place of board meetings, and we agree to hold this first meeting of the board at this time and place and to transact any and all business necessary." The form should indicate the date, time, and place of the first meeting.

Now the meeting can actually begin. The best way to proceed is to follow the order of the agenda in the printed form called *Minutes of the First Meeting of the Board of Directors*, which will also be found at the end of this chapter. If you are the sole director, use the alternative form called *Organizational Minutes of the Sole Director*. These forms will also save you the time and trouble of having to write up minutes of the first meeting. All you need do is fill in the blanks on the forms with the appropriate information as you proceed. If you like, you may add details of any other action taken or discussion held during the meeting. The forms cover the minimum agenda requirements for a first meeting. Nothing more is necessary, but you are certainly not prohibited from including any number of other matters in the meeting agenda.

Subsequent meetings of the board and the membership should be conducted using *Roberts Rules of Order* as a guide for parliamentary procedure, and full minutes of all meetings should be made by the corporation secretary for filing in the record book. The first order of business at all meetings after the first one should be the presentation and reading of the minutes of the previous meeting for approval of the board or membership, and filing.

To return to the first meeting, look over the *minutes* form. The business to be conducted in this meeting will include the following matters in this order:

1. The organizer of the meeting calls it to order.
2. The group assembled then elects a temporary chairman to preside over the meeting, and a temporary secretary to keep the minutes.
3. The temporary secretary then reads aloud the certified copy of the certificate of incorporation you have received from the state in which the organization has been incorporated. Also read is the letter from the Internal Revenue Service ruling that the corporation has tax-exempt status, if you have already applied for and received that determination

letter. If you haven't yet applied for tax-exempt status, make it a priority matter for the president or the board.

4. The next order of business is the election of the officers of the corporation: a president, vice-president, secretary and treasurer. The election is conducted just as it would be in a club or association such as the PTA. A person or persons are nominated for office; someone must second the nominations, then the board members vote on the candidates. Once elected, these officers immediately assume their respective offices in the place of the temporary chairman and secretary, who, in fact, may be the very same person.

5. The group may elect, or in effect, re-elect the members of the board of directors. However, if there are to be no changes in the make-up of the board from the names listed in the certificate of incorporation, you need not go through the motion of an election at this meeting. The certificate of incorporation states that the directors named will serve until such time as new directors are elected and installed.

6. Next, the secretary or the president should present and read aloud the bylaws proposed for the corporation, which you and the other organizers have drafted. The board should discuss any changes or additions to the bylaws. If any are to be made, this should be done before voting to approve and adopt the bylaws. When they are ready for approval, a director should make a motion to that effect. After it is seconded, the board should vote to adopt the bylaws.

That is all you actually need to do at the first meeting in order to satisfy the requirements of state corporation law. If there is no more business to take up, a motion can be made to adjourn the meeting. The minutes of the meeting, waiver of notice form, and the bylaws can then be filed in the record book.

Before adjourning the meeting, however, you may want to consider one or all of the following items of business for a vote by the Board and inclusion in the minutes of the meeting:

- Passing a resolution that establishes for the record, the location of the principal office of the corporation for transaction of business, if that has not already been indicated in the certificate of incorporation.
- Establishing where the bank account for the corporation will be opened and maintained.
- Determining the amount of compensation, if any, that will be paid to the officers of the corporation and the fees, if any, to be paid to directors for their meeting attendance and other services they may render the corporation.

☐ **If the corporation has been set up as a membership-type organization, the board should adopt an official form for the membership certificates that will be used to identify persons who become**

members of the corporation. The names and addresses of the original members, including the directors and officers, if they are to be voting members, should be recorded for entry into the record book.

After the first meeting of the directors, the corporation will be launched. The officers elected at that meeting are now in charge of running the corporation on a day-to-day basis without further consultation with the board of directors. among the first matters of business the officers should attend to are these:

☐ **Apply for a nonprofit organization mailing permit from the U.S. Postal Service.** As discussed earlier in this book, nonprofit organizations are entitled to use the U.S. mails at a much lower rate than are individuals and for-profit corporations. For example, the rate for the first two ounces under a nonprofit mailing permit is considerably lower than the Third Class Bulk rate.

To get such a permit, you must complete a Postal Service application form and submit it to the Postal Service along with copies of the corporation's certificate of incorporation, bylaws, IRS tax exemption determination letter, and an initial fee of $75. Your local postmaster can supply the forms you will need. Within a relatively short period of time, you should receive a nonprofit mailing rate permit number and an imprint of it issued from your local post office. For subsequent years the corporation must pay an annual fee of $75 which will be due each year the permit is in effect. The corporation can then mail all letters and parcels at the special low nonprofit organization rates, as long as the permit imprint appears on each envelope or package cover with the appropriate postage.

☐ **Register the corporation with any state or local government agencies that require registration of nonprofit tax-exempt organizations within their jurisdiction.** An example of such an agency is a local Charities Registration Bureau.

☐ **Obtain any local or state government licenses or permits that a corporation must have to conduct certain business in its location.** For instance, you may have to obtain a local building occupation permit for your offices.

☐ **Obtain and file any other forms necessary for the establishment of normal business operations, such as those for tax and Social Security withholding for employees of the corporation.** Also check into such matters as obtaining insurance and other services the corporation will need.

A WORD ABOUT THE FORMS THAT FOLLOW

In this chapter, there are references to a number of forms that you will need to complete the organization and begin the operation of your newly incorporated nonprofit corporation. They are: *Minutes of the First Meeting Waiver of Notice of the First Meeting of the Board of Directors,* and the *Organizational Minutes of the Sole Director.*

These forms are designed for your personal use. To complete the organizational procedures outlined in this chapter, all you need to do is follow the format of these forms and fill in the blanks on them with the appropriate information as you proceed. Feel free to add details of other actions taken up in your organizational meeting, either on the form itself or on an attached sheet. When you have completed the forms, and they contain the required signatures of officers and directors, they should be placed in your organization's corporate record book. The forms are intended to become part of the permanent corporate records of your nonprofit corporation.

WAIVER OF NOTICE OF THE FIRST MEETING OF

THE BOARD OF DIRECTORS OF

_____

We, the undersigned, being all the directors of the above corporation, hereby agree and consent that the first meeting of the board to be held on the date and at the time and place stated below for the purpose of elect- ing officers and the transaction thereat of all such other business as may lawfully come before said meeting and hereby waive all notice of the meet- ing and of any adjournment thereof.

    Place of meeting:

    Date of meeting:

    Time of meeting:

                                               _____

                                               Director

                                               _____

                                               Director

                                               _____

                                               Director

    Dated: ; 19

MINUTES OF THE FIRST MEETING OF

THE BOARD OF DIRECTORS OF

_____

The first meeting of directors was held at

on the   day of   19   at   o'clock

    .M.

The following were present:

being a quorum and all the directors of the corporation.

One of the directors called the meeting to order. Upon motion duly

made, seconded and carried,   was duly elected chair-

man of the meeting and   was duly elected secretary

thereof. They accepted their respective offices and proceeded with the dis-

charge of their duties.

A written waiver of notice of this meeting signed by the directors was

submitted, read by the secretary, and ordered appended to these minutes.

The secretary then presented and read to the meeting a certified copy of

the certificate of incorporation of the corporation which was filed by the

Secretary of State of   on   19   ,

and a copy of a determination letter from the Internal Revenue Service con-

firming the corporation's tax-exempt status under Section 501(c)(3) of the

Internal Revenue Code. Upon motion duly made, seconded and carried, these

documents were accepted and the secretary was directed to append them to

these minutes for inclusion in the official records of the corporation.

The chairman stated that the election of officers was then in order.

The following were duly nominated and, a vote having been taken, were

unanimously elected officers of the corporation to serve for one year and

until their successors are elected and qualified:

President:

Vice-President:

Secretary:

Treasurer:

The president and secretary thereupon assumed their respective offices in place and in stead of the temporary chairman and the temporary secretary. The secretary presented and read to the meeting the proposed bylaws regulating the conduct of the affairs of the corporation. Upon motion duly made, seconded and carried, they were adopted and in all respects ratified, confirmed and approved, and the secretary was directed to insert them in the official records of the corporation.

There being no further business before the meeting, the same was, on motion, duly adjourned.

Date: ,19   .

_____
Secretary

_____
President

ORGANIZATIONAL MINUTES OF THE SOLE DIRECTOR OF

_____

The undersigned, being the sole director of the corporation, organized under the General Corporation Law of Delaware, took the following action to organize the corporation and in furtherance of its purposes and objectives on the date and at the place set forth below:

A certified copy of the certificate of incorporation filed in the office of the Secretary of State on   , 19   and recorded in the office of the Recorder of the County of   on

     , 19   was appended to these minutes.

The office of the corporation was fixed at

in the City of   and State of

Bylaws regulating the conduct of the affairs of the corporation were adopted and appended to these minutes for inclusion in the official records of the corporation.

The following were (was) appointed officers of the corporation to serve for one year and until their successors are appointed or elected and qualified:

President:

Vice-President:

Secretary:

Treasurer:

Each officer thereupon assumed the duties of his office.

There being no further business before the meeting, the same was adjourned.

Dated: , 19

_____

President

APPENDIX A

Where To Get Information on Nonprofit Corporation Laws and Forms in Every State

ALABAMA

Office of the Secretary of State
Corporations Division
East Montgomery, AL 36106
205-242-5324

ALASKA

Commissioner of Commerce
333 Willoughby Avenue
Floor 9
Juneau, AK 99811-0800
907-465-2530

ARIZONA

Arizona Corporation Commission
1200 West Washington Street
Room 102
Phoenix, AZ 85005
602-542-3026

ARKANSAS

Secretary of State
Corporation Department
Room 058
Fifth & Woodlawn Streets
Little Rock, AR 72201
501-682-7200

CALIFORNIA

Secretary of State
Corporation Department
1230 J Street
Sacramento, CA 95814
916-445-0620

COLORADO

Secretary of State
Corporations Section
1650 Broadway
Suite 200
Denver, CO 80202
303-894-2251

CONNECTICUT

Secretary of State
Commercial Recording
30 Trinity Street
Hartford, CT 06106
203-566-2211

DELAWARE

Department of State
Division of Corporations
John G. Townsend Building
Dover, DE 19901
302-739-3073

DISTRICT OF COLUMBIA

Superintendent of Corporations
Department of Consumer &
     Regulatory Affairs
Business Regulation Administration
Corporations Division
614 H Street, N.W.
Room 407
Washington, DC 20001
202-727-7278

FLORIDA

Secretary of State
Corporate Records Bureau
Division of Corporations
409 East Gaines Street
Tallahassee, FL 32399
904-488-3680

GEORGIA

Secretary of State
Corporations Department
#2 Martin Luther King, Jr. Dr., S.E.
Suite 315
West Tower
Atlanta, GA 30334
404-656-2881

HAWAII

Department of Commerce &
    Consumer Affairs
Business Regulation Division
1010 Richards Street
Honolulu, HI 96810
808-548-6111

IDAHO

Secretary of State
Corporation Department
State House
Room 203
Boise, ID 83720
208-334-2300

ILLINOIS

Secretary of State
Department of Business Services
330 Centennial Building
Springfield, IL 62756
217-782-7808

INDIANA

Secretary of State
Corporations Division
Room 155
State Capitol Building

Washington & Capital Sts.
Indianapolis, IN 46204
317-232-6576

IOWA

Secretary of State
Corporation Division
Hoover Building
2nd Floor South
East 14th & Walnut Sts.
Des Moines, IA 50319
515-281-5204

KANSAS

Secretary of State
Corporation Department
Capitol Building
Second Floor
10th St. & Jackson Ave.
Topeka, KS 66612
913-296-2236

KENTUCKY

Secretary of State
Corporation Division
State Capitol Building
Room 154
Frankfort, KY 40602-0718
502-564-3490

LOUISIANA

Secretary of State
Corporations Division
3851 Essen Lane
Baton Rouge, LA 70809
504-925-4704

MAINE

Secretary of State
Corporation Department
State House
Station 101
Augusta, ME
207-289-4180

MARYLAND

State Department of Assessments &
   Taxation
301 West Preston Street
Baltimore, MD 21201
800-962-7010

MASSACHUSETTS

Secretary of the Commonwealth
Corporations Divisions
One Ashburton Place
17th Floor
Boston, MA 02108
617-727-2800

MICHIGAN

Department of Commerce
Corporation Division
Corporation & Securities Bureau
6546 Mercantile Way
Lansing, MI 48910
517-334-6206

MINNESOTA

Secretary of State
Business Services Division
State Office Building
Room 180
100 Constitution Avenue
St. Paul, MN 55155
612-296-2803

MISSISSIPPI

Secretary of State
Corporation Department
401 Mississippi Street
Heber Ladner Building
Jackson, MS 339201
601-359-1350

MISSOURI

Secretary of State
Business Services Department
Missouri State Information Center
600 West Main Street
P.O. Box 778

Jefferson City, MO 65102
314-751-4936

MONTANA

Secretary of State
Business Services Bureau
State Capitol
Room 25
Montana St. & 6th Ave.
Helena, MT 59620
406-444-2034

NEBRASKA

Secretary of State
Corporation Department
Capitol Building
16th Street
Lincoln, NE 68509
402-471-4079

NEVADA

Secretary of State
Corporation Department
Capitol Complex
Carson Street
Carson City, NV
702-687-5203

NEW HAMPSHIRE

Secretary of State
Corporation Division
State House
Room 204
107 North Main Street
Concord, NH 03301
603-271-3244

NEW JERSEY

Secretary of State
State House
125 West State Street
Trenton, NJ 08625
609-984-1900

NEW MEXICO

State Corporation Division
Corporation and Franchise Tax
    Departments
Capital Complex
Pera Building
Room 411
Santa Fe, NM 87504-1269
505-827-4504

NEW YORK

Department of State
Division of Corporations and State
    Records
162 Washington Avenue
Albany, NY 12231
518-474-6200

NORTH CAROLINA

Secretary of State
Corporations Division
Legislative Office Building
300 N. Salisbury Street
Raleigh, NC 27640
919-733-3166

NORTH DAKOTA

Secretary of State
Division of Corporations
State Capitol Building
600 East Boulevard Avenue
Bismarck, ND 58505-0500
701-224-4284

OHIO

Secretary of State
Corporation Department
State Office Tower
14th Floor
30 East Broad Street
Columbus, OH 43266-0418
614-466-3910

OKLAHOMA

Secretary of State
Corporation Department
Room 101
State Capitol Building
Oklahoma City, OK 73105
405-521-3911

OREGON

Secretary of State
Corporation Division
158 12th Street, N.E.
Salem, OR 97310
503-378-4383

PENNSYLVANIA

Department of State
Corporation Bureau
308 North Office Building
Harrisburg, PA 17120-0029
717-787-1997

PUERTO RICO

Department of State
Corporation Division
P.O. Box 3271
San Juan, PR 00904
809-722-2121

RHODE ISLAND

Secretary of State
Corporation Division
100 North Main Street
Providence, RI 02903
401-277-3040

SOUTH CAROLINA

Secretary of State
Corporation Department
Wade Hampton Office Building
P.O. Box 11350
Columbia, SC 29214
803-737-4705

SOUTH DAKOTA

Secretary of State
Corporation Department
State Capitol Building
Second floor
500 E. Capitol Avenue
Pierre, SD 57501
605-773-3537

TENNESSEE

Department of State
Division of Services
Suite 1800
James K. Polk Building
Nashville, TN 37243-0306
615-741-2816

TEXAS

Secretary of State
Corporations Section
1019 Brazos
Room 105
Austin, TX 78701
512-463-5555

UTAH

Department of Commerce
Division of Corporations and
   Commercial Code
160 East 300 South
P.O. Box 45801
Salt Lake City, UT 84145-0801
801-530-4849

VERMONT

Secretary of State
Corporations/UCC Division
109 State Street
Montpelier, VT 05609-1104
802-828-1110

VIRGINIA

State Corporation Division
Jefferson Building

1st Floor
1220 Bank Street
Richmond, VA 23219
804-786-3672

WASHINGTON

Secretary of State
Corporations Division
Second Floor
505 East Union (PM-21)
Olympia, WA 98504
206-753-7120

WEST VIRGINIA

Secretary of State
Corporations/UCC Division
Capitol Building
Room W-139
Charleston, WV 25328
304-348-2501

WISCONSIN

Secretary of State
Corporations Division
30 West Mifflin Street
9th Floor
Madison, WI 53703
608-266-3590

WYOMING

Secretary of State
Corporation & UCC Department
110 Capitol Building
24th St. & Capitol Ave.
Cheyenne, WY 82002-0020
307-777-7311

APPENDIX B

Text of Internal Revenue Code Sections 501, 521, 527 and 528

Sec. 501. Exemption from tax on corporations, certain trusts, etc.

(a) Exemption from taxation.

An organization described in subsection (c) or (d) or section 401(a) shall be exempt from taxation under this subtitle unless such exemption is denied under section 502 or 503.

(b) Tax on unrelated business income and certain other activities.

An organization exempt from taxation under subsection (a) shall be subject to tax to the extent provided in parts II, III, and VI of this subchapter, but (notwithstanding parts II, III, and VI of this subchapter) shall be considered an organization exempt from income taxes for the purpose of any law which refers to organizations exempt from income taxes.

(c) List of exempt organizations.

The following organizations are referred to in subsection (a):

(1) Any corporation organized under Act of Congress which is an instrumentality of the United States but only if such corporation—
(A) is exempt from Federal income taxes—
(i) under such Act as amended and supplemented before July 18, 1984, or
(ii) under this title without regard to any provision of law which is not contained in this title and which is not contained in a revenue Act, or

(B) is described in subsection (1)

(2) Corporations organized for the exclusive purpose of holding title to property, collecting income therefrom, and turning over the entire

amount thereof, less expenses, to an organization which itself is exempt under this section.

(3) Corporations, and any community chest, fund, or foundation, organized and operated exclusively for religious, charitable, scientific, testing for public safety, literary, or educational purposes, or to foster national or international amateur sports competition (but only if no part of its activities involve the provision of athletic facilities or equipment), or for the prevention of cruelty to children or animals, no part of the net earnings of which inures to the benefit of any private shareholder or individual, no substantial part of the activities of which is carrying on propaganda, or otherwise attempting, to influence legislation (except as otherwise provided in subsection (h)), and which does not participate in, or intervene in (including the publishing or distributing of statements), any political campaign on behalf of (or in opposition to) any candidate for public office.

(4) Civic leagues or organizations not organized for profit but operated exclusively for the promotion of social welfare, or local associations of employees, the membership of which is limited to the employees of a designated person or persons in a particular municipality, and the net earnings of which are devoted exclusively to charitable, educational, or recreational purposes.

(5) Labor, agricultural, or horticultural organizations.

(6) Business leagues, chambers of commerce, real-estate boards, boards of trade, or professional football leagues (whether or not administering a pension fund for football players), not organized for profit and no part of the net earnings of which inures to the benefit of any private shareholder or individual.

(7) Clubs organized for pleasure, recreation, and other non-profitable purposes, substantially all of the activities of which are for such purposes and no part of the net earnings of which inures to the benefit of any private shareholder.

(8) Fraternal beneficiary societies, orders, or associations—

(A) operating under the lodge system or for the exclusive benefit of the members of a fraternity itself operating under the lodge system, and

(B) providing for the payment of life, sick, accident, or other benefits to the members of such society, order, or association or their dependents.

(9) Voluntary employees' beneficiary associations providing for the payment of life, sick, accident, or other benefits to the members of such association or their dependents or designated beneficiaries, if no part of the net earnings of such association inures (other than through such payments) to the benefit of any private shareholder or individual.

(10) Domestic fraternal societies, orders, or associations, operating under the lodge system—

    (A) the net earnings of which are devoted exclusively to religious, charitable, scientific, literary, educational, and fraternal purposes, and

    (B) which do not provide for the payment of life, sick, accident, or other benefits.

(11) Teachers' retirement fund associations of a purely local character, if—

    (A) no part of their net earnings inures (other than through payment of retirement benefits) to the benefit of any private shareholder or individual, and

    (B) the income consists solely of amounts received from public taxation, amounts received from assessments on the teaching salaries of members, and income in respect of investments.

(12) (A) Benevolent life insurance associations of a purely local character, mutual ditch or irrigation companies, mutual or cooperative telephone companies, or like organizations; but only if 85 percent or more of the income consists of amounts collected from members for the sole purpose of meeting losses and expenses.

    (B) In the case of a mutual or cooperative telephone company, subparagraph (A) shall be applied without taking into account any income received or accrued—

        (i)   from a nonmember telephone company for the performance of communication services which involve members of the mutual or cooperative telephone company,

        (ii) from qualified pole rentals,

        (iii) from the sale of display listings in a directory furnished to the members of the mutual or cooperative telephone company, or

        (iv) from the prepayment of a loan under section 306A, 306B, or 311 of the Rural Electrification Act of 1936 (as in effect on January 1, 1987).

    (C) In the case of a mutual or cooperative electric company, subparagraph (A) shall be applied without taking into account any income received or accrued—

        (i)   from qualified pole rentals, or

        (ii) from the prepayment of a loan under section 306A, 306B, or 311 of the Rural Electrification Act of 1936 (as in effect on January 1, 1987).

    (D) For purposes of this paragraph, the term "qualified pole rental" means any rental of a pole (or other structure used to support wires) if such pole (or other structure)—

        (i)   is used by the telephone or electric company to support one or more wires which are used by such company in providing telephone or electric services to its members, and

(ii) is used pursuant to the rental to support one or more wires (in addition to the wires described in clause (i)) for use in connection with the transmission by wire of electricity or of telephone or other communications.

For purposes of the preceding sentence, the term "rental" includes any sale of the right to use the pole (or other structure).

(13) Cemetery companies owned and operated exclusively for the benefit of their members or which are not operated for profit; and any corporation chartered solely for the purpose of the disposal of bodies by burial or cremation which is not permitted by its charter to engage in any business not necessarily incident to that purpose and no part of the net earnings of which inures to the benefit of any private shareholder or individual.

(14) (A) Credit unions without capital stock organized and operated for mutual purposes and without profit.

(B) Corporations or associations without capital stock organized before September 1, 1957, and operated for mutual purposes and without profit for the purpose of providing reserve funds for, and insurance of shares or deposits in—

(i) domestic building and loan associations,

(ii) cooperative banks without capital stock organized and operated for mutual purposes and without profit,

(iii) mutual savings banks not having capital stock represented by shares, or

(iv) mutual savings banks described in section 591(b)[.]

(C) Corporations or associations organized before September 1, 1957, and operated for mutual purposes and without profit for the purpose of providing reserve funds for associations or banks described in clause (i), (ii), or (iii) of subparagraph (B); but only if 85 percent or more of the income is attributable to providing such reserve funds and to investments. This subparagraph shall not apply to any corporation or association entitled to exemption under subparagraph (B).

(15) (A) Insurance companies or associations other than life (including interinsurers and reciprocal underwriters) if the net written premiums (or, if greater, direct written premiums) for the taxable year do not exceed $350,000.

(B) For purposes of subparagraph (A), in determining whether any company or association is described in subparagraph (A), such company or association shall be treated as receiving during the taxable year amounts described in subparagraph (A) which are received during such year by all other companies or associations which are members of the same controlled group as the insurance company or association for which the determination is being made.

(C) For purposes of subparagraph (B), the term "controlled group" has the meaning given such term by section 831(b)(2)(B)(ii).

(16) Corporations organized by an association subject to part IV of this subchapter or members thereof, for the purpose of financing the ordinary crop operations of such members or other producers, and operated in conjunction with such association. Exemption shall not be denied any such corporation because it has capital stock, if the dividend rate of such stock is fixed at not to exceed the legal rate of interest in the State of incorporation or 8 percent per annum, whichever is greater, on the value of the consideration for which the stock was issued, and if substantially all such stock (other than nonvoting preferred stock, the owners of which are not entitled or permitted to participate, directly or indirectly, in the profits of the corporation, on dissolution or otherwise, beyond the fixed dividends) is owned by such association, or members thereof; nor shall exemption be denied any such corporation because there is accumulated and maintained by it a reserve required by State law or a reasonable reserve for any necessary purpose.

(17) (A) A trust or trusts forming part of a plan providing for the payment of supplemental unemployment compensation benefits, if—

(i) under the plan, it is impossible, at any time prior to the satisfaction of all liabilities, with respect to employees under the plan, for any part of the corpus or income to be (within the taxable year or thereafter) used for, or diverted to, any purpose other than the providing of supplemental unemployment compensation benefits,

(ii) such benefits are payable to employees under a classification which is set forth in the plan and which is found by the Secretary not to be discriminatory in favor of employees who are highly compensated employees (within the meaning of section 414(q)), and

(iii) such benefits do not discriminate in favor of employees who are highly compensated employees (within the meaning of section 414(q)). A plan shall not be considered discriminatory within the meaning of this clause merely because the benefits received under the plan bear a uniform relationship to the total compensation, or the basic or regular rate of compensation, of the employees covered by the plan.

(B) In determining whether a plan meets the requirements of subparagraph (A), any benefits provided under any other plan shall not be taken into consideration, except that a plan shall not be considered discriminatory—

(i) merely because the benefits under the plan which are first determined in a nondiscriminatory manner within the meaning of subparagraph (A) are then reduced by any sick, accident, or unemployment compensation benefits received under State or Federal law (or reduced by a portion of such benefits if determined in a nondiscriminatory manner), or

(ii) merely because the plan provides only for employees who are not eligible to receive sick, accident, or unemployment compensation benefits under State or Federal law the same benefits (or a portion of such benefits if determined in a nondiscriminatory manner) which such employees would receive under such laws if such employees were eligible for such benefits, or

(iii) merely because the plan provides only for employees who are not eligible under another plan (which meets the requirements of subparagraph (A)) of supplemental unemployment compensation benefits provided wholly by the employer the same benefits (or a portion of such benefits if determined in a nondiscriminatory manner) which such employees would receive under such other plan if such employees were eligible under such other plan, but only if the employees eligible under both plans would make a classification which would be nondiscriminatory within the meaning of subparagraph (A).

(C) A plan shall be considered to meet the requirements of subparagraph (A) during the whole of any year of the plan if on one day in each quarter it satisfies such requirements.

(D) The term "supplemental unemployment compensation benefits" means only—

(i) benefits which are paid to an employee because of his involuntary separation from the employment of the employer (whether or not such separation is temporary) resulting directly from a reduction in force, the discontinuance of a plant or operation, or other similar conditions, and

(ii) sick and accident benefits subordinate to the benefits described in clause (i).

(E) Exemption shall not be denied under subsection (a) to any organization entitled to such exemption as an association described in paragraph (9) of this subsection merely because such organization provides for the payment of supplemental unemployment benefits (as defined in subparagraph (D)(i)).

(18) A trust or trusts created before June 25, 1959, forming part of a plan providing for the payment of benefits under a pension plan funded only by contributions of employees, if—

(A) under the plan, it is impossible, at any time prior to the satisfaction of all liabilities with respect to employees under the plan, for any part of the corpus or income to be (within the taxable year or thereafter) used for, or diverted to, any purpose other than the providing of benefits under the plan,

(B) such benefits are payable to employees under a classification which is set forth in the plan and which is found by the Secretary not to be discriminatory in favor of employees who are highly compensated employees (within the meaning of section 414(q)),

(C) such benefits do not discriminate in favor of employees who are highly compensated employees (within the meaning of section 414(q)). A plan shall not be considered discriminatory within the meaning of this subparagraph merely because the benefits received under the plan bear a uniform relationship to the total compensation, or the basic or regular rate of compensation, of the employees covered by the plan, and

(D) in the case of a plan under which an employee may designate certain contributions as deductible—

(i) such contributions do not exceed the amount with respect to which a deduction is allowable under section 219(b)(3),

(ii) requirements similar to the requirements of section 401(k)(3)(A)(ii) are met with respect to such elective contributions,

(iii) such contributions are treated as elective deferrals for purposes of section 402(g) (other than paragraph (4) thereof), and

(iv) the requirements of section 401(a)(30) are met.

For purposes of subparagraph (D)(ii), rules similar to the rules of section 401(k)(8) shall apply. For purposes of section 4979, any excess contribution under clause (ii) shall be treated as an excess contribution under a cash or deferred arrangement.

(19) A post or organization of past or present members of the Armed Forces of the United States, or an auxiliary unit or society of, or a trust or foundation for, any such post or organization—

(A) organized in the United States or any of its possessions,

(B) at least 75 percent of the members of which are past or present members of the Armed Forces of the United States and substantially all of the other members of which are individuals who are cadets or are spouses, widows, or widowers of past or present members of the Armed Forces of the United States or of cadets, and

(C) no part of the net earnings of which inures to the benefit of any private shareholder or individual.

(20) an organization or trust created or organized in the United States, the exclusive function of which is to form part of a qualified group legal services plan or plans, within the meaning of section 120. An organization or trust which receives contributions because of section 120(c)(5)(C) shall not be prevented from qualifying as an organization described in this paragraph merely because it provides legal services or indemnification against the cost of legal services unassociated with a qualified group legal services plan.

(21) (A) A trust or trusts established in writing, created or organized in the United States, and contributed to by any person (except an insurance company) if—

(i) the purpose of such trust or trusts is exclusively—

(I) to satisfy, in whole or in part, the liability of such person for, or with respect to, claims for compensation for disability or death due to pneumoconiosis under Black Lung Acts,

(II) to pay premiums for insurance exclusively covering such liability,

(III) to pay administrative and other incidental expenses of such trust in connection with the operation of the trust and the processing of claims against such person under Black Lung Acts, and

(IV) to pay accident or health benefits for retired miners and their spouses and dependents (including administrative and other incidental expenses of such trust in connection therewith) or premiums for insurance exclusively covering such benefits; and

(ii) no part of the assets of the trust may be used for, or diverted to, any purpose other than—

(I) the purposes described in clause (i),

(II) investment (but only to the extent that the trustee determines that a portion of the assets is not currently needed for the purposes described in clause (i)) in qualified investments, or

(III) payment into the Black Lung Disability Trust Fund established under section 9501, or into the general fund of the United States Treasury (other than in satisfaction of any tax or other civil or criminal liability of the person who established or contributed to the trust).

(B) No deduction shall be allowed under this chapter for any payment described in subparagraph (A)(i)(IV) from such trust.

(C) Payments described in subparagraph (A)(i)(IV) may be made from such trust during a taxable year only to the extent that the aggregate amount of such payments during such taxable year does not exceed the lesser of—

(i) the excess (if any) (as of the close of the preceding taxable year) of—

(I) the fair market value of the assets of the trust, over

(II) 110 percent of the present value of the liability described in subparagraph (A)(i)(I) of such person, or

(ii) the excess (if any) of—

(I) the sum of a similar excess determined as of the close of the last taxable year ending before the date of the enactment of this subparagraph plus earnings thereon as of the close of the taxable year preceding the taxable year involved, over

(II) the aggregate payments described in subparagraph (A)(i)(IV) made from the trust during all taxable years beginning after the date of the enactment of this subparagraph.

The determinations under the preceding sentence shall be made by an independent actuary using actuarial methods and assumptions (not inconsistent with the regulations prescribed under section 192(c)(1)(A)) each of which is reasonable and which are reasonable in the aggregate.

(D) For purposes of this paragraph:
　　　　(i)　The term "Black Lung Acts" means part C of title IV of the Federal Mine Safety and Health Act of 1977, and any State law providing compensation for disability or death due to that pneumoconiosis.
　　　　(ii)　The term "qualified investments" means—
　　　　　　(I)　public debt securities of the United States,
　　　　　　(II)　obligations of a State or local government which are not in default as to principal or interest, and
　　　　　　(III) time or demand deposits in a bank (as defined in section 581) or an insured credit union (within the meaning of section 101(6) of the Federal Credit Union Act, 12 U.S.C. 1752(6)) located in the United States.
　　　　(iii)　The term "miner" has the same meaning as such term has when used in section 402(d) of the Black Lung Benefits Act (30 U.S.C. 902(d)).
　　　　(iv)　The term "incidental expenses" includes legal, accounting, actuarial, and trustee expenses.
　　(22) A trust created or organized in the United States and established in writing by the plan sponsors of multiemployer plans if—
　　　　(A) the purpose of such trust is exclusively—
　　　　　　(i)　to pay any amount described in section 4223(c) or (h) of the Employee Retirement Income Security Act of 1974, and
　　　　　　(ii)　to pay reasonable and necessary administrative expenses in connection with the establishment and operation of the trust and the processing of claims against the trust,
　　　　(B) no part of the assets of the trust may be used for, or diverted to, any purpose other than—
　　　　　　(i)　the purposes described in subparagraph (A), or
　　　　　　(ii)　the investment in securities, obligations, or time or demand deposits described in clause (ii) of paragraph (21)(B),
　　　　(C) such trust meets the requirements of paragraphs (2), (3), and (4) of section 4223(b), 4223(h), or, if applicable, section 4223(c) of the Employee Retirement Income Security Act of 1974, and
　　　　(D) the trust instrument provides that, on dissolution of the trust, assets of the trust may not be paid other than to plans which have participated in the plan or, in the case of a trust established under section 4223(h) of such Act, to plans with respect to which employers have participated in the fund.
　　(23) Any association organized before 1880 more than 75 percent of the members of which are present or past members of the Armed

Forces and a principal purpose of which is to provide insurance and other benefits to veterans or their dependents.

(24) A trust described in section 4049 of the Employee Retirement Income Security Act of 1974 (as in effect on the date of the enactment of the Single-Employer Pension Plan Amendments Act of 1986).

(25) (A) Any corporation or trust which—

(i) has no more than 35 shareholders or beneficiaries,

(ii) has only 1 class of stock or beneficial interest, and

(iii) is organized for the exclusive purposes of—

(I) acquiring real property and holding title to, and collecting income from, such property, and

(II) remitting the entire amount of income from such property (less expenses) to 1 or more organizations described in subparagraph (C) which are shareholders of such corporation or beneficiaries of such trust.

For purposes of clause (iii), the term "real property" shall not include any interest as a tenant in common (or similar interest) and shall not include any indirect interest.

(B) A corporation or trust shall be described in subparagraph (A) without regard to whether the corporation or trust is organized by 1 or more organizations described in subparagraph (C).

(C) An organization is described in this subparagraph if such organization is—

(i) a qualified pension, profit sharing, or stock bonus plan that meets the requirements of section 401(a),

(ii) a governmental plan (within the meaning of section 414(d)),

(iii) the United States, any State or political subdivision thereof, or any agency or instrumentality of any of the foregoing, or

(iv) any organization described in paragraph (3).

(D) A corporation or trust shall in no event be treated as described in subparagraph (A) unless such corporation or trust permits its shareholders or beneficiaries—

(i) to dismiss the corporation's or trust's investment adviser, following reasonable notice, upon a vote of the shareholders or beneficiaries holding a majority of interest in the corporation or trust, and

(ii) to terminate their interest in the corporation or trust by either, or both, of the following alternatives, as determined by the corporation or trust:

(I) by selling or exchanging their stock in the corporation or interest in the trust (subject to any Federal or State securities law) to any organization described in subparagraph (C) so long as the sale or exchange does not increase the number of shareholders or beneficiaries in such corporation or trust above 35, or

(II) by having their stock or interest redeemed by the corporation or trust after the shareholder or beneficiary has provided 90 days, notice to such corporation or trust.

(E)(i) For purposes of this title—

(I) a corporation which is a qualified subsidiary shall not be treated as a separate corporation, and

(II) all assets, liabilities, and items of income, deduction, and credit of a qualified subsidiary shall be treated as assets, liabilities, and such items (as the case may be) of the corporation or trust described in subparagraph (A).

(ii) For purposes of this subparagraph, the term "qualified subsidiary" means any corporation if, at all times during the period such corporation was in existence, 100 percent of the stock of such corporation is held by the corporation or trust described in subparagraph (A).

(iii) For purposes of this subtitle, if any corporation which was a qualified subsidiary ceases to meet the requirements of clause (ii), such corporation shall be treated as a new corporation acquiring all of its assets (and assuming all of its liabilities) immediately before such cessation from the corporation or trust described in subparagraph (A) in exchange for its stock.

(F) For purposes of subparagraph (A), the term "real property" includes any personal property which is leased under, or in connection with, a lease of real property, but only if the rent attributable to such personal property (determined under the rules of section 856(d)(1)) for the taxable year does not exceed 15 percent of the total rent for the taxable year attributable to both the real and personal property leased under, or in connection with, such lease.

(d) Religious and apostolic organizations.

The following organizations are referred to in subsection (a): Religious or apostolic associations or corporations, if such associations or corporations have a common treasury or community treasury, even if such associations or corporations engage in business for the common benefit of the members, but only if the members thereof include (at the time of filing their returns) in their gross income their entire pro rata shares, whether distributed or not, of the taxable income of the association or corporation for such year. Any amount so included in the gross income of a member shall be treated as a dividend received.

(e) Cooperative hospital service organizations.

For purposes of this title, an organization shall be treated as an organization organized and operated exclusively for charitable purposes, if—

(1)   such organization is organized and operated solely—

(A) to perform, on a centralized basis, one or more of the following services which, if performed on its own behalf by a hospital which is an organization described in subsection (c)(3) and exempt from taxation under subsection (a), would constitute activities in exercising or performing the purpose or function constituting the basis for its exemption: data processing, purchasing (including the purchasing of insurance on a group basis), warehousing, billing and collection, food, clinical, industrial engineering, laboratory, printing, communications, record center, and personnel (including selection, testing, training, and education of personnel) services; and

(B) to perform such services solely for two or more hospitals each of which is—

(i)   an organization described in subsection (c)(3) which is exempt from taxation under subsection (a),

(ii)   a constituent part of an organization described in subsection (c)(3) which is exempt from taxation under subsection (a) and which, if organized and operated as a separate entity, would constitute an organization described in subsection (c)(3), or

(iii) owned and operated by the United States, a State, the District of Columbia, or a possession of the United States, or a political subdivision or an agency or instrumentality of any of the foregoing;

(2)   such organization is organized and operated on a cooperative basis and allocates or pays, within 8 1/2 months after the close of its taxable year, all net earnings to patrons on the basis of services performed for them; and

(3)   if such organization has capital stock, all of such stock outstanding is owned by its patrons.

For purposes of this title, any organization which, by reason of the preceding sentence, is an organization described in subsection (c)(3) and exempt from taxation under subsection (a), shall be treated as a hospital and as an organization referred to in section 170(b)(1)(A)(iii).

(f) Cooperative service organizations of operating educational organizations.

For purposes of this title, if an organization is—

(1)   organized and operated solely to hold, commingle, and collectively invest and reinvest (including arranging for and supervising the performance by independent contractors of investment services related thereto) in stocks and securities, the moneys contributed thereto by each of the members of such organization, and to collect income therefrom and turn over the entire amount thereof, less expenses, to such members,

(2) organized and controlled by one or more such members, and

(3) comprised solely of members that are organizations described in clause (ii) or (iv) of section 170(b)(1)(A)—

(A) which are exempt from taxation under subsection (a), or

(B) the income of which is excluded from taxation under section 115(a),

then such organization shall be treated as an organization organized and operated exclusively for charitable purposes.

(g) Definition of agricultural.

For purposes of subsection (c)(5), the term "agricultural" includes the art or science of cultivating land, harvesting crops or aquatic resources, or raising livestock.

(h) Expenditures by public charities to influence legislation.

(1) General rule. In the case of an organization to which this subsection applies, exemption from taxation under subsection (a) shall be denied because a substantial part of the activities of such organization consists of carrying on propaganda, or otherwise attempting, to influence legislation, but only if such organization normally—

(A) makes lobbying expenditures in excess of the lobbying ceiling amount for such organization for each taxable year, or

(B) makes grass roots expenditures in excess of the grass roots ceiling amount for such organization for each taxable year.

(2) Definitions. For purposes of this subsection—

(A) Lobbying expenditures. The term "lobbying expenditures" means expenditures for the purpose of influencing legislation (as defined in section 4911(d)).

(B) Lobbying ceiling amount. The lobbying ceiling amount for any organization for any taxable year is 150 percent of the lobbying nontaxable amount for such organization for such taxable year, determined under section 4911.

(C) Grass roots expenditures. The term "grass roots expenditures" means expenditures for the purpose of influencing legislation (as defined in section 4911(d) without regard to paragraph (1)(B) thereof).

(D) Grass roots ceiling amount. The grass roots ceiling amount for any organization for any taxable year is 150 percent of the grass roots nontaxable amount for such organization for such taxable year, determined under section 4911.

(3) Organizations to which this subsection applies. This subsection shall apply to any organization which has elected (in such manner and at such time as the Secretary may prescribe) to have the provisions of this subsection apply to such organization and which, for the taxable year

which includes the date the election is made, is described in subsection (c)(3) and—

      (A) is described in paragraph (4), and

      (B) is not a disqualified organization under paragraph (5).

    (4) Organizations permitted to elect to have this subsection apply. An organization is described in this paragraph if it is described in—

      (A) section 170(b)(1)(A)(ii) (relating to educational institutions),

      (B) section 170(b)(1)(A)(iii) (relating to hospitals and medical research organizations),

      (C) section 170(b)(1)(A)(iv) (relating to organizations supporting government schools),

      (D) section 170(b)(1)(A)(vi) (relating to organizations publicly supported by charitable contributions),

      (E) section 509(a)(2) (relating to organizations publicly supported by admissions, sales, etc.), or

      (F) section 509(a)(3) (relating to organizations supporting certain types of public charities) except that for purposes of this subparagraph, section 509(a)(3) shall be applied without regard to the last sentence of section 509(a).

    (5) Disqualified organizations. For purposes of paragraph (3) an organization is a disqualified organization if it is—

      (A) described in section 170(b)(1)(A)(i) (relating to churches),

      (B) an integrated auxiliary of a church or of a convention or association of churches, or

      (C) a member of an affiliated group of organizations (within the meaning of section 4911(f)(2)) if one or more members of such group is described in subparagraph (A) or (B).

    (6) Years for which election is effective. An election by an organization under this subsection shall be effective for all taxable years of such organization which—

      (A) end after the date the election is made, and

      (B) begin before the date the election is revoked by such organization (under regulations prescribed by the Secretary).

    (7) No effect on certain organizations. With respect to any organization for a taxable year for which—

      (A) such organization is a disqualified organization (within the meaning of paragraph (5)), or

      (B) an election under this subsection is not in effect for such organization,

nothing in this subsection or in section 4911 shall be construed to affect the interpretation of the phrase, "no substantial part of the activities of which is carrying on propaganda, or otherwise attempting, to influence legislation," under subsection (c)(3).

(8) Affiliated organizations. For rules regarding affiliated organizations, see section 4911(f).

(i) Prohibition of discrimination by certain social clubs.

Notwithstanding subsection (a), an organization which is described in subsection (c)(7) shall not be exempt from taxation under subsection (a) for any taxable year if, at any time during such taxable year, the charter, by-laws, or other governing instrument, of such organization or any written policy statement of such organization contains a provision which provides for discrimination against any person on the basis of race, color, or religion. The preceding sentence to the extent it relates to discrimination on the basis of religion shall not apply to—

(1) an auxiliary of a fraternal beneficiary society if such society—

(A) is described in subsection (c)(8) and exempt from tax under subsection (a), and

(B) limits its membership to the members of a particular religion, or

(2) a club which in good faith limits its membership to the members of a particular religion in order to further the teachings or principles of that religion, and not to exclude individuals of a particular race or color.

(j) Special rules for certain amateur sports organizations.

(1) In general. In the case of a qualified amateur sports organization—

(A) the requirement of subsection (c)(3) that no part of its activities involve the provision of athletic facilities or equipment shall not apply, and

(B) such organization shall not fail to meet the requirements of subsection (c)(3) merely because its membership is local or regional in nature.

(2) Qualified amateur sports organization defined. For purposes of this subsection, the term "qualified amateur sports organization" means any organization organized and operated exclusively to foster national or international amateur sports competition if such organization is also organized and operated primarily to conduct national or international competition in sports or to support and develop amateur athletes for national or international competition in sports.

(k) Treatment of certain organizations providing child care.

For purposes of subsection (c)(3) of this section and sections 170(c)(2), 2055(a)(2), and 2522(a)(2), the term "educational purposes" includes the providing of care of children away from their homes if—

      (1) substantially all of the care provided by the organization is for purposes of enabling individuals to be gainfully employed, and

      (2) the services provided by the organization are available to the general public.

      (l) Government corporations exempt under subsection (c)(1).

For purposes of subsection (c)(1), the following organizations are described in this subsection:

      (1) The Central Liquidity Facility established under title III of the Federal Credit Union Act (12 U.S.C. 1795 et seq.).

      (2) The Resolution Trust Corporation established under section 21A of the Federal Home Loan Bank Act.

      (3) The Resolution Funding Corporation established under section 21B of the Federal Home Loan Bank Act.

Sec. 521. Exemption of farmers' cooperatives from tax.

(a) Exemption from tax.

A farmers' cooperative organization described in subsection (b)(1) shall be exempt from taxation under this subtitle except as otherwise provided in part I of subchapter T (sec. 1381 and following). Notwithstanding part I of subchapter T (sec. 1381 and following), such an organization shall be considered an organization exempt from income taxes for purposes of any law which refers to organizations exempt from income taxes.

(b) Applicable rules.
(1) Exempt farmers' cooperatives. The farmers' cooperatives exempt from taxation to the extent provided in subsection (a) are farmers', fruit growers', or like associations organized and operated on a cooperative basis (A) for the purpose of marketing the products of members or other producers, and turning back to them the proceeds of sales, less the necessary marketing expenses, on the basis of either the quantity or the value of the products furnished by them, or (B) for the purpose of purchasing supplies and equipment for the use of members or other persons, and turning over such supplies and equipment to them at actual cost, plus necessary expenses.
(2) Organizations having capital stock. Exemption shall not be denied any such association because it has capital stock, if the dividend rate of such stock is fixed at not to exceed the legal rate of interest in the State of incorporation or 8 percent per annum, whichever is greater, on the value of the consideration for which the stock was issued, and if substantially all such stock (other than nonvoting preferred stock, the owners of which are not entitled or permitted to participate, directly or indirectly, in the profits of the association, upon dissolution or otherwise, beyond the fixed dividends) is owned by producers who market their products or purchase their supplies and equipment through the association.
(3) Organizations maintaining reserve. Exemption shall not be denied any such association because there is accumulated and maintained by it a reserve required by State law or a reasonable reserve for any necessary purpose.
(4) Transactions with nonmembers. Exemption shall not be denied any such association which markets the products of nonmembers in an amount the value of which does not exceed the value of the products marketed for members, or which purchases supplies and equipment for nonmembers in an amount the value of which does not exceed the value of the supplies and equipment purchased for members, provided the value of the purchases made for persons who are neither members nor producers does not exceed 15 percent of the value of all its purchases.

(5) Business for the United States. Business done for the United States or any of its agencies shall be disregarded in determining the right to exemption under this section.

(6) Netting of losses. Exemption shall not be denied any such association because such association computes its net earnings for purposes of determining any amount available for distribution to patrons in the manner described in paragraph (1) of section 1388(j).

Sec. 527. Political organizations.

(a) General rule.

A political organization shall be subject to taxation under this subtitle only to the extent provided in this section. A political organization shall be considered an organization exempt from income taxes for the purpose of any law which refers to organizations exempt from income taxes.

(b) Tax imposed.
(1) In general. A tax is hereby imposed for each taxable year on the political organization taxable income of every political organization. Such tax shall be computed by multiplying the political organization taxable income by the highest rate of tax specified in section 11(b).
(2) Alternative tax in case of capital gains. If for any taxable year any political organization has a net capital gain, then, in lieu of the tax imposed by paragraph (1), there is hereby imposed a tax (if such a tax is less than the tax imposed by paragraph (1)) which shall consist of the sum of—
(A) a partial tax, computed as provided by paragraph (1), on the political organization taxable income determined by reducing such income by the amount of such gain, and
(B) an amount determined as provided in section 1201(a) on such gain.
(c) Political organization taxable income defined.

(1) Taxable income defined. For purposes of this section, the political organization taxable income of any organization for any taxable year is an amount equal to the excess (if any) of—
(A) the gross income for the taxable year (excluding any exempt function income), over
(B) the deductions allowed by this chapter which are directly connected with the production of the gross income (excluding exempt function income), computed with the modifications provided in paragraph (2).
(2) Modifications. For purposes of this subsection—
(A) there shall be allowed a specific deduction of $100,
(B) no net operating loss deduction shall be allowed under section 172, and
(C) no deduction shall be allowed under part VIII of subchapter B (relating to special deductions for corporations).

(3) Exempt function income. For purposes of this subsection, the term "exempt function income" means any amount received as—

(A) a contribution of money or other property,

(B) membership dues, a membership fee or assessment from a member of the political organization,

(C) proceeds from a political fundraising or entertainment event, or proceeds from the sale of political campaign materials, which are not received in the ordinary course of any trade or business, or

(D) proceeds from the conducting of any bingo game (as defined in section 513(f)(2)).

to the extent such amount is segregated for use only for the exempt function of the political organization.

(d) Certain uses not treated as income to candidate.

For purposes of this title, if any political organization—

(1) contributes any amount to or for the use of any political organization which is treated as exempt from tax under subsection (a) of this section,

(2) contributes any amount to or for the use of any organization described in paragraph (1) or (2) of section 509(a) which is exempt from tax under section 501(a), or

(3) deposits any amount in the general fund of the Treasury or in the general fund of any State or local government,

such amount shall be treated as an amount not diverted for the personal use of the candidate or any other person. No deduction shall be allowed under this title for the contribution or deposit of any amount described in the preceding sentence.

(e) Other definitions.

For purposes of this section—

(1) Political organization. The term "political organization" means a party, committee, association, fund, or other organization (whether or not incorporated) organized and operated primarily for the purpose of directly or indirectly accepting contributions or making expenditures, or both, for an exempt function.

(2) Exempt function. The term "exempt function" means the function of influencing or attempting to influence the selection, nomination, election, or appointment of any individual to any Federal, State, or local public office or office in a political organization, or the election of

Presidential or Vice-Presidential electors, whether or not such individual or electors are selected, nominated, elected, or appointed. Such term includes the making of expenditures relating to an office described in the preceding sentence which, if incurred by the individual, would be allowable as a deduction under section 162(a).

(3) Contributions. The term "contributions" has the meaning given to such term by section 271(b)(2).

(4) Expenditures. The term "expenditures" has the meaning given to such term by section 271(b)(3).

(f) Exempt organization which is not political organization must include certain amounts in gross income.

(1) In general. If an organization described in section 501(c) which is exempt from tax under section 501(a) expends any amount during the taxable year directly (or through another organization) for an exempt function (within the meaning of subsection (e)(2)), then, notwithstanding any other provision of law, there shall be included in the gross income of such organization for the taxable year, and shall be subject to tax under subsection (b) as if it constituted political organization taxable income, an amount equal to the lesser of—

(A) the net investment income of such organization for the taxable year, or

(B) the aggregate amount so expended during the taxable year for such an exempt function.

(2) Net investment income. For purposes of this subsection, the term "net investment income" means the excess of—

(A) the gross amount of income from interest, dividends, rents, and royalties, plus the excess (if any) of gains from the sale or exchange of assets over the losses from the sale or exchange of assets, over

(B) the deductions allowed by this chapter which are directly connected with the production of the income referred to in subparagraph (A).

For purposes of the preceding sentence, there shall not be taken into account items taken into account for purposes of the tax imposed by section 511 (relating to tax on unrelated business income).

(3) Certain separate segregated funds. For purposes of this subsection and subsection (e)(1), a separate segregated fund (within the meaning of section 610 of title 18 or of any similar State statute, or within the meaning of any State statute which permits the segregation of dues moneys for exempt functions (within the meaning of subsection (e)(2))) which is maintained by an organization described in section 501(c) which is exempt from tax under section 501(a) shall be treated as a separate organization.

(g) Treatment of newsletter funds.

(1) In general. For purposes of this section, a fund established and maintained by an individual who holds, has been elected to, or is a candidate (within the meaning of paragraph (3)) for nomination or election to, any Federal, State, or local elective public office for use by such individual exclusively for the preparation and circulation of such individual's newsletter shall, except as provided in paragraph (2), be treated as if such fund constituted a political organization.

(2) Additional modifications. In the case of any fund described in paragraph (1)—

(A) the exempt function shall be only the preparation and circulation of the newsletter, and

(B) the specific deduction provided by subsection (c)(2)(A) shall not be allowed.

(3) Candidate. For purposes of paragraph (1), the term "candidate" means, with respect to any Federal, State, or local elective public office, an individual who—

(A) publicly announces that he is a candidate for nomination or election to such office, and

(B) meets the qualifications prescribed by law to hold such office.

(h) Special rule for principal campaign committees.

(1) In general. In the case of a political organization which is a principal campaign committee, paragraph (1) of subsection (b) shall be applied by substituting "the appropriate rates" for "the highest rate".

(2) Principal campaign committee defined.

(A) In general. For purposes of this subsection, the term "principal campaign committee" means the political committee designated by a candidate for Congress as his principal campaign committee for purposes of—

(i) section 302(e) of the Federal Election Campaign Act of 1971 (2 U.S.C. 432(e)), and

(ii) this subsection.

(B) Designation. A candidate may have only 1 designation in effect under subparagraph (A)(ii) at any time and such designation—

(i) shall be made at such time and in such manner as the Secretary may prescribe by regulations, and

(ii) once made, may be revoked only with the consent of the Secretary.

Nothing in this subsection shall be construed to require any designation where there is only one political committee with respect to a candidate.

Sec. 528. Certain homeowners associations.

(a) General rule.

A homeowners association (as defined in subsection (c)) shall be subject to taxation under this subtitle only to the extent provided in this section. A homeowners association shall be considered an organization exempt from income taxes for the purpose of any law which refers to organizations exempt from income taxes.

(b) Tax imposed.

A tax is hereby imposed for each taxable year on the homeowners association taxable income of every homeowners association. Such tax shall be equal to 30 percent of the homeowners association taxable income.

(c) Homeowners association defined.

For purposes of this section—

(1) Homeowners association. The term "homeowners association" means an organization which is a condominium management association or a residential real estate management association if—
(A) such organization is organized and operated to provide for the acquisition, construction, management, maintenance, and care of association property,
(B) 60 percent or more of the gross income of such organization for the taxable year consists solely of amounts received as membership dues, fees, or assessments from—
(i) owners of residential units in the case of a condominium management association, or

(ii) owners of residences or residential lots in the case of a residential real estate management association.
(C) 90 percent or more of the expenditures of the organization for the taxable year are expenditures for the acquisition, construction, management, maintenance, and care of association property,
(D) no part of the net earnings of such organization inures (other than by acquiring, constructing, or providing management, maintenance, and care of association property, and other than by a rebate of excess membership dues, fees, or assessments) to the benefit of any private shareholder or individual, and

(E) such organization elects (at such time and in such manner as the Secretary by regulations prescribes) to have this section apply for the taxable year.

(2) Condominium management association. The term "condominium management association" means any organization meeting the requirement of subparagraph (A) of paragraph (1) with respect to a condominium project substantially all of the units of which are used by individuals for residences.

(3) Residential real estate management association. The term "residential real estate management association" means any organization meeting the requirements of subparagraph (A) of paragraph (1) with respect to a subdivision, development, or similar area substantially all the lots or buildings of which may only be used by individuals for residences.

(4) Association property. The term "association property" means—

(A) property held by the organization,

(B) property commonly held by the members of the organization,

(C) property within the organization privately held by the members of the organization, and

(D) property owned by a governmental unit and used for the benefit of residents of such unit.

(d) Homeowners association taxable income defined.

(1) Taxable income defined. For purposes of this section, the homeowners association taxable income of any organization for any taxable year is an amount equal to the excess (if any) of—

(A) the gross income for the taxable year (excluding any exempt function income), over

(B) the deductions allowed by this chapter which are directly connected with the production of the gross income (excluding exempt function income), computed with the modifications provided in paragraph (2).

(2) Modifications. For purposes of this subsection—

(A) there shall be allowed a specific deduction of $100,

(B) no net operating loss deduction shall be allowed under section 172, and

(C) no deduction shall be allowed under part VIII of subchapter B (relating to special deductions for corporations).

(3) Exempt function income. For purposes of this subsection, the term "exempt function income" means any amount received as membership dues, fees, or assessments from—

(A) owners of condominium housing units in the case of a condominium management association, or

(B) owners of real property in the case of a residential real estate management association.

Index

Smithsonian magazine, 2, 18
Social welfare organizations, in IRS code, 222
Soliciting funds, 6-7
Special duties, exemption from, 8
Special meetings, 144
Special-purpose tax exemptions, 43-51
  annual financial reports, 50
  Form 990, 73-77
    instructions, 53-71
      schedule A, 87-91
      schedule A instructions, 79-86
  Form 990 EZ (short form), 105-6
    instructions, 93-104
  information to be reported, 50-51
  IRS standards for exemptions, 44-45
  organizations eligible for, 45-49
  other categories of section 501(c), 45
  unrelated business income, 49-50
State information, on corporate laws and forms, 215-19
Statement of purpose, 21, 115-18
Stock corporations, 26

T
Tax code, 2

Tax exemption, 5-6. *See also* Special-purpose tax exemptions
  application, 127, 153-201
    advance rulings, 154
    checklist for completing IRS form 1023, 156-59
    definitive rulings, 153-54
    forms and IRS publications, 155
    questions from IRS, 159
    where to send, 159
  types of organizations exempt, 221-38
Teachers' retirement funds, in IRS code, 223
Telephone company, mutual or cooperative, in IRS code, 223
Tort liability, immunity from, 8
Trustees. *See* Board of directors

U-V-W
Unemployment compensation, in IRS code, 224-25
Unrelated business, defined, 2, 49-50
Use agreement, 16
User fee determination letter request, 195-96
Voting, in bylaws, 144
Waiver of notice, 151